# The Growing Out-of-School Time Field: Past, Present, and Future

A Volume in:
Current Issues in Out-of-School Time

*Series Editor*

Helen Janc Malone

# Current Issues in Out-of-School Time

Series Editor

Helen Janc Malone
Institute for Educational Leadership

*The Growing Out-of-School Time Field: Past, Present, and Future (2017)*
*Helen Janc Malone and Tara Donahue*

# Current Issues in Out-of-School Time Book Series Boards

# The Growing Out-of-School Time Field: Past, Present, and Future

*Edited by*

**Helen Janc Malone**
**Tara Donahue**

**≡IAP**

**INFORMATION AGE PUBLISHING, INC.**
Charlotte, NC • www.infoagepub.com

*Dedicated to the*
*American Educational Research Association*
*Out-of-School Time Special Interest Group*

**Library of Congress Cataloging-in-Publication Data**

The CIP data for this book can be found on the Library of Congress website (loc.gov).

Paperback: 978-1-64113-028-8
Hardcover: 978-1-64113-029-5
eBook: 978-1-64113-030-1

Printed in the United States of America

# CONTENTS

SECTION III

## PROFESSIONAL DEVELOPMENT WITHIN OST

SECTION IV

## RESEARCH- AND EVALUATION-INFORMED FIELD

SECTION V

## OST ADVOCACY

SECTION VI

## FUTURE DIRECTIONS FOR THE OST FIELD

## CONCLUSION

# ENDORSEMENTS

It has been clear for some time that the so-called achievement gap is driven in part by gaps in educational opportunities. Providing access to high-quality out-of-school learning experiences is one of the most important measures that can be taken to reduce disparities and level the playing field. The authors in this important new book show us not only how to create such programs but why it matters to our collective future. Timely, relevant, and readable, this book is an invaluable resource for anyone seeking to close gaps in educational opportunities.

—Pedro A. Noguera, Ph.D.
*Distinguished Professor of Education*
*UCLA Graduate School of Education & Information Studies*

As the chair of the NAS/NRC committee that wrote the report *Community Programs to Promote Youth Development*, I am delighted by this book. When we wrote the report in 2002, there were few systematic attempts to organize and theorize the emerging field of positive youth development. As the editors and chapter authors in this book make very clear, a great deal has happened at all levels of scholarship in this field over the last 15 years. Both this volume and the new book series that it is initiating signal the maturing of this field from childhood, through adolescence, and now into emerging adulthood. The breadth of work discussed in this collection is exceptionally broad, ranging from psychological theorizing about the impact of youth serving programs in the out-of-school time period to

*The Growing Out-of-School Time Field: Past, Present, and Future,*
pages ix–xiv.
Copyright © 2018 by Information Age Publishing

social policy analyses of how to grow the profession of OST youth professionals and create steady funding streams to support OST programming. All topics are critically discussed and new directions are suggested. I consider this book to be required reading of all students, scholars, professional, and practitioners in the field of positive youth development and OST programming. I go even further by suggesting it be read broadly by anyone interested in the education and development of young people around the world. There is no better collection available for educators, parents, community activists, and social policy makers concerned with positive youth development. I believe this collection lays a very strong foundation for achieving the goal set forth by Karen Pittman for the field to move from "where and when to what and how."

—Jacquelynne S. Eccles
*Distinguished University Professor of Education*
*University of California, Irvine*

The impressive growth of OST programs represents one of the brightest spots on the American educational landscape. Importantly, as this book portrays, what began a series of programs and local initiatives has now grown into a maturing field, with standards, scholarship, organizations, policies, and funding at the national, state, and local levels. And more than a field, OST carries the urgency, energy, and passion of a movement for social justice.

*The Growing Out-of-School Time Field* offers a comprehensive review of earlier decades of work and points the way forward for the field's future development. It should be read not only by those involved in the OST field, but by all educators who seek to create inclusive and powerful learning environments. Policymakers, as well, would benefit from deeper knowledge of this movement. It holds a key to preparing today's youth for an uncertain future, where the nature of work is changing, norms of society are shifting, and multicultural, global perspectives are needed.

—Milton Chen, Ph.D.
*Senior Fellow & Executive Director Emeritus*
*George Lucas Educational Foundation (edutopia.org)*

Having watched the landscape develop and evolve over the past 20 years, I was pleased to read such a comprehensive account of the afterschool and expanded learning field. Helen Janc Malone and Tara Donahue, and everyone who contributed to this anthology, have much to offer those who care deeply about youth development and closing the opportunity gap. I was particularly struck by the call for research around the role of out-of-school time to support developmental transitions, as well as including students with disabilities in this research and bringing an international perspective to practice and policy. Given our long history of building systems and advocating for public support of quality learning time beyond the traditional school day, our organization welcomes this book to the canon of supporting literature in the field.

—Lucy N. Friedman
*President and Founder, ExpandED Schools*

This new book captures many important developments in providing more and better opportunities in afterschool and summers—key out-of-school time (OST) spaces. The volume indicates the growth and maturity of the field and strengthens the fields' ability to understand and deliver on its growing potential.

In the Introduction, Helen Janc Malone provides a taste of why this field is increasingly important, "(t)he hallmark of the OST field has been the ability to remain adaptable to change in a way that complements the field and supports young people in diverse ways."

The book describes an increasingly sophisticated set of learnings, especially over the past 15–20 years, about how to provide better OST opportunities in a variety of settings.

The continuing challenge, however, is how can local, state, and national governments provide more of these vital safe, engaging, and enriching opportunities in after school and summers and on weekends for working, low- and middle-income families...especially in and near schools and neighborhoods that need them the most. As Dale Blyth explains in the Foreword, this is a critical "time period that can contain both threats to and opportunities for learning and development."

—Terry Peterson, Ph.D.
*Senior Fellow, College of Charleston*
*2016 National Champion of Children Awardee from Foundations, Inc.*
*Executive Editor,* Expanding Minds and Opportunities *(4ᵗʰ printing, 2016)*

This edited volume by Helen Janc Malone and Tara Donahue is "must reading" for researchers, graduate students, practitioners, and policymakers with interests in the burgeoning out-of-school-time (OST) field. The 20 chapters are written by respected academic researchers, program evaluators, and organizational leaders. These authors have provided thoughtful analyses of the seminal work that grounds the OST field as well as nuanced descriptions of the issues facing contemporary programs, including the pressing needs of the diverse youth and staff in afterschool and summer programs. The specific roles of research, evaluation, and advocacy in contemporary OST programming also are examined in several chapters. This volume should have a place on your book shelf next to Peterson's (2013) *Expanding Minds and Opportunities: Leveraging the Power of Afterschool and Summer Learning* and Eccles' (2002) *Community Programs to Promote Youth Development.* Collectively, these three volumes make a strong case for the importance of out-of-school time as a developmental context for children and youth.

—Deborah Lowe Vandell
*Professor of Education*
*University of California, Irvine*

This volume provides an authoritative overview of important issues in the out-of-school time (OST) field. Leading researchers and practitioners summarize the field's recent advances regarding effective strategies for working with diverse populations and describe state-of the art professional development training for

OST providers. They also highlight future priorities for OST research, practice, and policy. The editors and authors provide critical readings for people who want the best current information about innovative approaches to enhance the positive development of young people.

—Roger P. Weissberg, Ph.D.
*UIC Distinguished Professor of Psychology and Education*
*University of Illinois at Chicago*
*Chief Knowledge Officer*
*Collaborative for Academic, Social, and Emotional Learning (CASEL)*

As the executive director of an afterschool program and an active advocate for quality out-of-school time practice for more than thirty years, I watched the field grow rapidly, begin to develop an academic and professional tradition, and finally receive the recognition it deserves for the critical impact it makes on the lives of children and families. Yet it remains a relatively young and widely diverse field. Malone and Donahue capture that diversity by gathering an impressive array of the strongest voices working today in OST, representing their individual roles and perspectives while creating a cohesive picture of the field. The outstanding contributors provide research and practice-based information on topics from creating programs to meet the developmental needs of youth, and closing the opportunity gap, to addressing the professional needs of a uniquely diverse workforce and developing leadership to ensure a commitment to quality going forward. The collective wisdom in this volume would provide value to a new practitioner striving for excellence, a seasoned professional seeking to reflect on their practice, or anyone whose work could benefit from a solid understanding of the OST field, past, present, and future.

—Denise Trasatti Sellers
*Retired Executive Director*
*Haddonfield Child Care*

*The Growing Out-of-School Time Field* represents an impressive commitment on the part of the publishing house, and if the launch is any indication, those who follow the series will be richly rewarded. As the book's subtitle indicates, the volume looks back at the emergence of OST as a (reasonably) coherent whole, looks around with a status report on many of the most pressing issues of the day, and looks ahead to help guide future directions. The emphasis is on OST as a vehicle for supporting positive youth development.

That indeed is how OST is thought of today, but my own entry into this space was narrowly focused on summer learning loss among Baltimore's poor children in the academic realm. My colleagues and I began in 1994 with research contributions. Since then, the practical import of our work, and that of others, began to garner attention, in large measure owing to vigorous outreach by what is now the National Summer Learning Association (NSLA).

While NSLA was working hard to get summer time on the practice and policy agendas much the same was happening along two other closely related strands—preschool and afterschool programming—as all three were addressing the same problem: strengthening out-of-school learning opportunities for children, our neediest children, in particular.

The emergence of OST as a unifying umbrella for me is one of the most exciting developments of the last decade, and one of the most promising. It is my expectation that this OST series will both catalyze and accelerate that process.

The present volume ably documents that my agenda from an earlier era is but a small piece of what has become a much larger whole. It is no longer just test scores, but also socio-emotional learning and college and career readiness; it is not just low income urban youth, but also youth with disabilities, rural youth, ELL youth, and LGBTQ youth; it is no longer just schools, but "any time; anywhere" learning opportunities spanning a whole host of venues and institutional settings; and, perhaps most importantly, we have moved beyond "documentation" to identify theoretically informed and research validated best practices for programming and policy.

—Karl Alexander
*Executive Director*
*Thurgood Marshall Alliance*
*John Dewey Professor Emeritus of Sociology*
*Johns Hopkins University*

It is so good to see a book full of thoughtful chapters on the various dimensions of out-of-school time (OST). Using OST to help struggling students – both those that are behind academically and those accelerated students who are bored – is a hugely promising practice, but one that is woefully under-researched and too rarely discussed among educators and policymakers. This book provides a solid theoretical foundation for effective OST practices and prompts the reader to understand what cultural responsiveness should look like to maximize the comfort levels and outcomes for young people. It provides excellent guidance for preparing adults to facilitate student learning and results and discusses some of the findings and challenges in the research that supports the field. There is practical advice for advocates, along with thought-provoking discussions of future directions. This book is clearly written and an important source of current information for OST practitioners, researchers, and policymakers alike.

—Shelley H. Billig, Ph.D.
*Vice President*
*RMC Research Corporation*

Millions of individuals in the U.S. and internationally participate actively in out-of-school-time (OST) programs during their adolescence. Integrating the empirical findings, professional experiences, and wisdom of the researchers and practitioners studying, enacting, and evaluating OST programs, this important and timely volume uniquely advances understanding about and application of the role of OST programs in the positive development of diverse youth. The book is an invaluable resource for researchers, youth-serving professionals, policymakers, and families interested in engaging young people in this key context of adolescent development.

—Richard M. Lerner, Ph.D.
*Bergstrom Chair in Applied Developmental Science and*
*Director, Institute for Applied Research in Youth Development,*
*Tufts University*

One of the most significant contributions to the establishment of out-of-school time as a critical setting for youth development is the rise of coordinated system-building efforts that began to emerge around twenty years ago. I commend Helen Janc Malone and Tara Donohue and all the esteemed authors who contributed to *The Growing Out-of-School Time Field Past, Present, and Future* for sharing their lessons and insights. Section 5 on Advocacy eloquently speaks to the rise of city and statewide systems and the continued need for local advocacy efforts to grow investments. We need these investments to ensure young people in the highest need communities have more opportunities to grow, learn, and develop through after-school and expanded-learning.

—Jessica Donner
*Executive Director*
*Every Hour Counts*

This is an invaluable book. It provides broad state-of-the-art coverage of the out-of-school field, with excellent chapters on young people's development in programs, issues of diversity and equal access, professional development, program evaluation, and advocacy. It is essential reading for up-to-date knowledge on how all the parts of this complex field function, including current debates, needs in the field, and powerful visions for the future.

—Reed Larson
*Professor*
*University of Illinois*
*Urbana-Champaign*

# FOREWORD

### Dale A. Blyth

In my 40-year career I have had the good fortune to see the growth and development of three areas of work that in many ways now come together in the field of out-of-school time (OST). In the 1970s and 1980s, as a graduate student member of a research team studying transitions and an emerging professional, I witnessed (and hopefully, came to contribute to) the rising importance of research on adolescent development. From the founding of the Society for Research on Adolescence to the increasing sophistication, quality, and volume of research on adolescents, the shift was dramatic and has been sustained. Critical in that shift was the creation and availability of both presenting and publishing opportunities—particularly professional meetings, new journals, and a series of edited and single-authored books. The work that had been scattered and episodic was becoming connected and forming a field of study with major multiyear research studies that attracted and retained bright and talented people.

In the 1980s and 1990s, while with the Search Institute, I became part of the shift from "just" studying adolescents' development to trying to contribute more directly to supporting the development of youth and the assets they needed to thrive. Over time, positive youth development grew as applied research and evaluation started connecting to program design and the professional development of practitioners and growing awareness of the larger role of community supports. Once again, the emergence of this area of work was significantly advanced by the

*The Growing Out-of-School Time Field: Past, Present, and Future*,
pages xv–xvii.
Copyright © 2018 by Information Age Publishing

growing number of professionals who came together to articulate and capture lessons learned and build the theoretical, empirical, and practical foundations for a field in special volumes, new journals, and opportunities to exchange ideas.

In the last 20 years, I have watched and contributed to the emerging field of OST. A field that has its roots primarily in over 100 years of practices in the U.S. and about which I learned a great deal in trying to steer the University of Minnesota Extension Center for Youth Development. Here I came to see the importance of bridging practice, policy, program, research, and public understanding of what happens during these important time slots that are active contexts for learning and development.

It is from these perspectives that I now look at the publication of this book, and especially the launching of this new Information Age Publishing (IAP) book series. This series represents a significant turning point for OST on the long journey of becoming a recognized and respected multidisciplinary field with multiple levels—from front-line practitioners to program managers to intermediary system builders to researchers and policymakers. As with most journeys, this turning point does not represent a final destination but rather a critical transition in the growth and unity of longstanding practices of child and youth care and youth work with research, policy, program design and delivery, and the professionalization of the workforce.

Although youth programs and services have been around for a long time and many national youth organizations are celebrating 100 plus years of operation, the journey of OST efforts has only in the last 20 years really started to take shape as a field in the U.S. Far too often it is still defined by *what it is not*—not school, not formal learning—and *when it occurs*—the time when outside of the classroom. In reality, the emerging field of OST is multidisciplinary and multileveled, and it has evolved to be much more.

OST is a significant time period when youth are not in school. More importantly, it has come to be recognized as a time period with significant promise for supporting and advancing the learning and development of children and young people. A time period that has multiple dimensions from before and after school to weekends and summers. A time period when youth build relationships, explore and expand their capacities, and learn social and emotional competencies critical to their success in school, work, and life. A time period that can contain both threats to and opportunities for learning and development.

Over the years, practitioners, researchers, and policymakers have come to recognize that OST is actually an *important context for development*—a context to be studied, shaped, and utilized to promote the healthy, positive development of children and youth—a context that has special characteristics, flexibility, and an almost infinite diversity of activities that take place within it. In the 1970s, when the Society for Research on Adolescence was founded, the only contexts being seriously studied were family, school, and peer relationships. We now see a growing

volume of work on the places, programs, and possibilities young people experience in the context of how they use their time beyond the classroom.

OST has become more than a context in how it is talked about and seen—it has
also become an approach to learning: an approach that is less formal and content-
centered and more informal or nonformal in nature and youth-centered. While
nonformal learning and social pedagogy has a rich history in many European
cultures, it has had trouble fully establishing itself as a distinct, valued, and viable
approach to learning in the U.S. While experiential learning, service learning, and
project-based learning have all established themselves as useful pedagogues, recognizing the youth-centric and informal and nonformal unifying nature of these
approaches has been less widely accepted, labeled, or understood. Part of the reasons for the long journey is the rich diversity of OST practices, places, and people
who shape, manage, and deliver OST activities. This diversity remains both a
great strength of the field and an ongoing challenge.

Why do the launching of this new book series and the solid foundations laid
by this initial volume represent a turning point in my view? For a field to become
viable and respected, it needs to have rich opportunities for presenting and publishing its principles and practices. It needs ways of circulating its basic ideas and
drawing lessons from its past as well as present to see where it can go—and opportunities to talk about where it might go.

This book, supported by key leaders in the practice, research, and policy cor-
ners of the field, represents a significant opportunity to both advance and system-
atize the field and an opportunity to do so every year through thoughtful topics
organized into complete volumes—volumes that not only establish a foundation
but also continue the building of the field. Many thanks go to IAP for providing
this ongoing opportunity for our field and to the Advisory Board and Editorial Review Board that have pulled it together. Special thanks to Helen Janc Malone, the
book series editor-in-chief, and Tara Donahue, who have brought this first volume
into reality along with the many authors who have contributed.

The opportunity, and dare I say responsibility, for contributing to our emerging
field now lies with you, the reader. I hope you use this volume to learn and challenge your thinking. Use it to stimulate new work—whether research or practice.
Use it to help craft your own contributions to the field—and because of this ongoing series, know that you will have a place to publish that work so others may
learn and build on the best work and thinking in the field.

—Dale A. Blyth, Ph.D.
*Profession Emeritus and former Howland Endowed Chair in Youth*
*Leadership Development University of Minnesota*

CHAPTER 1

# INTRODUCTION

Helen Janc Malone

The out-of-school time (OST) field has over the last two decades evolved and strengthened across both the human services and education fields (Malone, 2013). The OST field, associated with child-care and place- and time-based structured play, has evolved into a multidisciplinary field that attends to both the learning and development of young people. Through research, evaluation, high-quality practices, and advocacy, the OST field has become a vehicle for closing the opportunity gap. The field has also remained responsive to the needs of families, communities, and institutions. This has enabled the field to weave together diverse funding streams, broaden its scope, and strengthen delivery mechanisms, programmatic elements, and professional capital (Hargreaves & Fullan, 2012).

Today, the field sits on a foundation of burgeoning evidence, growing systems and networks, and ample practices that further its development. At the same time, the field has an opportunity to evolve further, by looking toward new development and learning frames emerging in the national discourse, by questioning how it positions itself relative to the education and workforce sectors, and by looking globally for points of intersection that could inform the current issues in OST. This book, *The Growing Out-of-School Time Field: Past, Present, and Future*, is a beginning of a conversation on the pressing matters facing the field and the paths that could chart the course for the field's future.

*The Growing Out-of-School Time Field: Past, Present, and Future,*
pages 1–9.

## DEFINING THE OST FIELD

OST is a multidisciplinary, cross-sectoral field whose flexible terminology has allowed for great adaptability of shared language within the field. Each terminology evolution signaled growing relevance, legitimacy, and maturity of the field both within human service and education sectors, from custodial care to enriching learning and positive developmental spaces (Malone, 2013). As Robert Halpern (2003) notes about OST programs:

> [Programs] have often stood—or found themselves—at the intersection of ideological crosscurrents in American society; between romantic and instrumental views of children, between play and work, between the traditions of local communities and those of the larger society, and between a view of low-income children as vulnerable and a view of them as threatening. (pp. 2–3)

The OST field has effectively supported the space and time between school and home, as Noam and Tillinger (2004) refer to it as the "intermediary space." In recent decades, OST has applied the following terms: school-age childcare, youth work, afterschool, out-of-school time, expanded learning opportunities—and it is in the midst of another evolution, responding to the emerging foci on social-emotional learning, deeper learning, and student-centered learning.

The field has traditionally not had a common set of uniform definitions, a reflection of the large, inclusive tent of diverse programs and experiences. Within this book, we refer to the OST field as encompassing of place (programs and activities that are school- or community-based, in libraries or museums, camps or parks and recreational programs, linked to businesses or universities, etc.), time (before and after school, on weekends, holidays, and in the summer), content (academic, 21$^{st}$ century skills, college/career readiness, sociocultural, STEM, kinetic, etc.), and approaches (formal, nonformal, informal), focused primarily on young people (children and youth in middle childhood, early to middle adolescence), roughly corresponding to K–12 education system (Blyth & LaCroix-Dalluhn, 2011; Halpern, 2003; Murphy & Knight, 2016; Nagaoka, Farrington, & Ehrlich, 2015; Rogoff, Callanan, Gutiérrez, & Erickson, 2016). We encourage future volumes in this book series to push the boundaries of this broad definition to reflect the field's evolution across dimensions of place, time, duration, intensity, age group, pedagogical approaches, purposes, and other foci.

## THE PURPOSE OF THIS ANTHOLOGY

The new Information Age Publishing book series, Current Issues in Out-of-School Time, is designed with a purpose to both promote and disseminate original theoretical and empirical research and promising practices that further the OST field. This first book sets the foundation on which the book series rests upon, by offering an analysis of the progress made since the 2000s, as well as by looking toward the future for areas of considerations. We hope the book inspires both reflections and conversations on how to further grow and strengthen the field, critically examining both assets and gaps, and to explore innovative ways forward. The book is not intended to be an all-encompassing compendium of the field, but rather to offer both retrospective analyses and future directions on ways to intentionally bridge research and practice and to explore new areas of inquiry within the following six sections:

1. OST as a Vehicle for Young People's Development
2. Social and Cultural Dimensions in OST
3. Professional Development Within OST
4. Research- and Evaluation-Informed Field
5. OST Advocacy
6. Future Directions for the OST Field

## AN OVERVIEW OF THE BOOK'S SIX SECTIONS

### Section 1: OST as a Vehicle for Young People's Development

The book opens with a focus on young people (children and adolescents) at the center. This first section, OST as a Vehicle for Young People's Development, explores what we have learned since the 2000s about child and youth development. The section opens with a retrospective chapter by Sandra Simpkins, Yangyang Liu, and Nickki Pearce Dawes, "15 Years After Community Programs to Promote Youth Development," an analysis of progress the field has made since the seminal 'blue book' emerged in 2002 by the National Research Council's Committee on Community-Level Programs for Youth (Eccles & Gootman, 2002). The chapter offers a pre/post analysis of the field's advancement in four areas—OST participation, program quality, setting, and positive youth development across demographic dimensions. The authors note that the NRC book has offered both a foundation and a validation to OST on which the field has made significant gains in addressing needs of young people and cultivating high-quality, engaging, and enriching spaces. Peter Scales' chapter, "High Quality OST Activities and Programs: Using the RISE Approach (Relationships, Interest and Sparks, Empowerment) to Promote Thriving in Youth and Their Settings," offers a literature review of developmental theories that the field has applied across OST settings. Scales proposes the relationships, interests, sparks, and empowerment (RISE) approach as a seminal framework for positive youth development. This section offers a foundation and a vision of the role the OST field plays in cultivating well-rounded learning and development.

In the first section, the authors emphasize the importance of maintaining the OST field's foundation in whole-child and positive youth, assets-driven development, the long-held tradition that has been embedded in practice across programs and activities. The emerging national discourse on 21st-century skills, character, grit, and social-emotional learning affords the OST field an opportunity to be at the forefront of these conversations on how to create and sustain supportive developmental and learning spaces for young people. Particularly because of the historical nature of OST programs, the field has extensive expertise in designing supportive, personalized spaces that promote learning and engagement with young people at the center. At the same time, the authors raise questions: What are the ways in which the field can continue to balance a developmental lens while also broadening a learning frame? How do we mitigate issues associated with disengagement?

## Section 2: Social and Cultural Dimensions in OST

Children and youth served by OST programs are increasingly demographically diverse. The OST field is at the forefront of establishing and maintaining engaging and enriching environments that pay attention to equity, poverty, race, and identity, and various social dimensions. As the OST field evolves, the contributors of this section, Social and Cultural Dimensions in OST, argue that it is necessary that the field builds sociocultural competencies to adequately support young people served. The section opens with Nickki Pearce Dawes' chapter "Access to Out-of-School Time Programs for Underserved Youth," which addresses issues of both access and engagement of two particular populations: low-income boys of color, and LGBTQ young people. Within the chapter, Dawes argues that youth are attracted to OST programs because of their positive social climate and inclusion, engagement, agency and efficacy, learning, and peer relationship. She calls on research and practice to explore strategies and environments that facilitate participant engagement. Judith Cruzado-Guerrero and Gilda Martinez-Alba expand on the issues of access and engagement for English language learners with an emphasis on immigrant youth and young people in rural areas, in "Responding to Shifting Demographic Contexts." Given the demographic shifts across our communities, they indicate that there are implications and responsibilities for the OST field to respond to in an increasingly culturally and linguistically diverse world in which it operates. Mavis Sanders, Karen Lewis-Watkins, and Keshara Cochrane's chapter, "The Role of Out-of-School Time Programs in Bridging the Diversity Gap and Improving Educational Opportunities for African American Students," round out the section. They call attention to the diversity gap among OST youth-serving professionals who work with young people of color, as well as the need for culturally responsive school-family-community aligned OST experiences for African American children and youth, more specifically. Their chapter offers a bridge to the next section, which focuses on building professional development and capacity within the OST field.

Section 2 expands upon the questions of development and learning, by challenging the field to maintain its focus on equity, particularly in creating accessible, inclusive, and culturally-responsive environments. With the changing demographics across the country, coupled with the empirical data on sociocultural awareness, the authors posit two field challenges: bridging the diversity gap and being responsive to multiple dimensions of demographic characteristics among OST participants—meaning, how do we build and sustain pre- and in-service professional development that is culturally responsive? What incentive structures and mechanisms should the field invest to attract more OST professionals of color? Furthermore, the OST field stands to benefit from additional investments in both research and practice that pays attention to multiple demographic dimensions of participants served. The OST research and practice to date have helped to advance quality practices by zeroing in on race, ethnicity, identity, geography, socioeconomic status; however, more work is needed to understand the interplay among these dimensions. Taken together, the authors' arguments lead to important inquiries that could expand field's knowledge.

### Section 3: Professional Development Within OST

The third book section, Professional Development Within OST, is dedicated to professional development, leadership, and capacity building of the field. The section opens with a retrospective chapter by Elizabeth Starr and Ellen S. Gannett, "The State of Professional Development: Past, Present, and Future," chronicling the ebbs and flows and future directions of professional development and capacity building of OST professionals, including the challenges of unifying a fragmented field (school-age, afterschool, and youth work), the development of core competences for the field, and the focus on strengthening workforce policies and ladders. Gina Hilton Warner, Heidi Ham, and Melissa S. Pearman Fenton build from this chapter in "Core Competencies for the OST Field," discussing the purpose, goals, and applications of the National AfterSchool Association Core Knowledge and Competencies for Afterschool and Youth Development Professionals as a vehicle toward field professionalization. They argue that the core competencies are the key to creating career ladders and promoting high-quality programs that support learning and development of the OST participants. Sara L. Hill, Joy Connolly, Thomas Akiva, and Anne McNamera, in "Taking It to a New Level: Inquiry-Based Professional Development as a Field-Building Enterprise," offer an in-depth analysis of one professional development program, the National After School Matters Practitioner Fellowship, and make the case for inquiry-based professional development as an ongoing vehicle to cultivate knowledge, skills, and competences among OST staff. The section concludes with an examination of leadership development within the field. Elizabeth M. Fowlkes and Tony McWhorter's chapter, "The Leadership Imperative," offers an in-depth literature review on the growing need for effective leadership on all levels in OST, highlighting the Boys & Girls Clubs of America as an illustrative case study on strategies to build leadership capacity within OST staff, as well as the barriers and strategies facing the field. They argue that leadership development must be a critical component of professional development within the OST field, as youth-serving professionals are among critical adults that help cultivate the next generation of leaders.

Over the last couple of decades, the field has expanded staff-oriented capacity building mechanisms and pathways to create robust options for OST professionals, ongoing support, and ladders to a sustainable, fulfilling career. Healthy debates continue pertaining to professionalization and appropriate vehicles for professional development. The section authors probe further on ways to make OST professional development even more robust by asking timely questions: What are the incentive structures for entry, advancement, and sustained participation of OST professionals in the field? How do we build career ladders and ongoing professional and leadership development to support high-quality OST staff?

## Section 4: Research- and Evaluation-Informed Field

The fourth section of the book, Research- and Evaluation-Informed Field, bridges practice and research across four issue-areas: evaluation, data systems, research–practice partnerships, and system-wide quality standards. The section opens with Christina A. Russell's chapter, "The Growth, Evolution, and State of OST Evaluation," which identifies key phases in OST evaluation, examines past and current trends, and looks at the shift in evaluation priorities and approaches. She acknowledges that evaluation has played a significant role in driving program-level improvement. She concludes that the future of evaluation will continue to be driven by a focus on quality improvement, by an exploration of clearly defined outcomes, and by policy influences that could drive the evolution of program approaches. Gil G. Noam, Patricia J. Allen, Ashima Mathur Shah, and Bailey Triggs, in "Innovative Use of Data as Game Changer for OST Programs: The Example of STEM," apply The PEAR Institute's model for OST STEM programs as an example of ways to strengthen school–community partnerships through a shared framework, common data collection tools, and rapid reporting strategies that enable programs to be responsive to students' needs and interests. Their chapter addresses the OST field's call for shared data systems, application of common tools as a responsive quality improvement mechanism for sharing best practices, supporting student-level learning and engagement, and informing policy and practice. Ken Anthony's chapter, "Exploring the Need for Research–Practice Partnerships," surfaces the present disconnect between research and practice, the role of community-based research design, and how to bridge the gap with intentional research–practice partnerships. Drawing attention to promising partnerships across the field, the author advocates for research–practice partnerships as a field-building tool that could have an impact on both local and statewide quality systems. The section concludes with a chapter, "Building Quality in Out-of-School Time," by Jaime Singer, Jessica Newman, and Deborah Moroney, in which the authors describe advances and approaches to quality, including development of national and statewide standards, tools, and systems that support the field. They conclude by proposing future directions for the OST quality movement.

The OST field is predominantly practice-driven. The accelerated investments over the past two decades in program-level evaluation and field research have deepened our understanding of the diversity of OST options, what constitute high-quality settings and engagement, what is appropriate duration and dosage, and how to link and align OST with the education sector, among many other areas of inquiry. The authors in Section 4 emphasize the importance of bridging research and practice and leave us with questions focused on feedback loops, mainly: Do OST programs have the necessary structures to deliver consistent high-quality programming? How do we build and align data systems that are responsive to the young people, their families, and practitioners involved? How do we create meaningful research–practice partnerships? How do we create closer collaboration between OST research and practice to more effective share knowledge?

## Section 5: OST Advocacy

The fifth section, OST Advocacy, features a pair of advocacy-oriented chapters, each addressing the interplay between OST and equity, making an argument for OST programs as a vehicle to narrow the opportunity gap during the school year and in the summer. The first advocacy chapter by Jen Rinehart and Nikki Yamashiro, "Meeting the Growing Demand for Afterschool and Summer Learning Programs: The Role of Federal Education Policy in Closing the Opportunity Gap," makes an equity-driven argument that OST is a vehicle to close the opportunity gap faced by many young people, and that the federal government and state policies have a role to play to support OST. The second advocacy chapter, "Closing the Summer Gap," by Sarah Pitcock, tackles the common myths about summer learning, emphasizes the importance of summer programs as an equity strategy to minimize the "summer slide," and offers an overview of macro policy trends that are supporting summer learning. Together, this section advocates for deeper investments in collaborative, system-wide partnerships that expand access to high-quality OST programs to meet the needs of young people year-round.

The authors in Section 5 remind us of the significant progress made in local, city, state, and federal investments in OST. Since 2000, we have seen a rise in city-wide and statewide OST networks, integrated systems across sectors, and agencies to promote program access and quality. Due in part to consistent advocacy on all levels, there are multiple streams and resources available to the field and the young people OST serves. At the same time, the authors warn that the advocacy must be sustained to both preserve and grow investments to further remove gaps in access and opportunities to OST.

## Section 6: Future Directions for the OST Field

The concluding, sixth section of the book, Future Directions for the OST Field, orients us toward the future, critically examining gaps in the existing body of knowledge and elevating areas of foci for further consideration. The issues raised are not intended to be an all-encompassing list of future directions, but rather, to elevate concerns and opportunities that garner our collective attention. The section's first contribution is by Elizabeth Devaney and Deborah Moroney, "Out-of-School Time Learning and 21st-Century Skills: Building on the Past to Shape the Future." The authors offer a history of definitions and approaches to building 21st-century skills within OST programs. The chapter then moves into a discussion of current forces that are expanding the 21st-century skills debate beyond the labor market argument and toward social-emotional learning, as one of the primary new directions in the field's thinking about what it means to prepare students for their postsecondary futures. Joseph L. Mahoney and Shannon Haley-Mize's chapter follows, "Knowing Better, Doing Better: Three Gaps to Fill in the Next Decade of Research in Out-of-School Time." They posit that although the field has made significant strides in understanding OST access, engagement, quality, and systems, there are three areas where further research and practice-based knowledge is needed: the role of OST in supporting critical developmental transitions, the inclusion of students with disabilities, and the expansion toward international perspectives on OST. The final chapter in this section comes from Karen Pittman, "Securing the Future: Pivoting OST From Where and When to What and How," in which she notes that the OST field stands to benefit by evolving focus toward what skills, behaviors, and capacities is OST developing, for whom, and how we are monitoring and measuring performance. She argues that the field has a choice to make, whether to see itself as a "second shift" delivery system or a "first shift" system responsive to learning environments.

The last section of the book pushes the field toward new frontiers, areas of practice and inquiry not sufficiently explored to date. With the rise of a more nuanced view of what it takes to prepare all young people for their postsecondary futures, the OST field, section authors posit, has an important role to play, as a creative, innovative partner to the school day; as an exploratory space to prepare students for college, career, and citizenship; and as a developmental area that builds social-emotional skills and competencies for success. But, doing so effectively, authors note, demands that the OST field agrees on a common language, strategies, and practices, be intentional, and to pay attention to staff and contexts, including global perspectives. Does OST want to remain as the where/when field or does it want to become the what/how field? What would this evolution of the field mean for its cohesion? How do we expand the knowledge base of collaborative approaches and partnerships? Ultimately, who do we want to become over the next decade on? Tara Donahue, the book's coeditor, concludes the anthology with a synthesis of key themes and a look to the future.

## CONCLUSION

The OST field has grown considerably since 2000s. Today, we have new frameworks, practice- and research-based knowledge and tools, and burgeoning venues (membership groups, conferences, networks, publications) to advance the field across multiple dimensions: demographic (e.g., race/ethnicity and identity), constituent groups (e.g., families, young people, youth-serving professionals), contexts (e.g., geographies, settings), systems and sectors (e.g., education, workforce), and disciplines (e.g., sociology, psychology, neuroscience, public policy). The hallmark of the OST field has been the ability to remain adaptable to change in a way that complements the field and supports young people in diverse ways. The authors of this anthology reflect on where our field has been and is at present, while also raising important questions for the field's future consideration. We encourage contributors to the Current Issues in Out-of-School Time book series to unpack these issues in greater depth.

## REFERENCES

Blyth, D. A., & LaCroix-Dalluhn, L. (2011). Expanded learning time and opportunities: Key principles, driving perspectives, and major challenges. *New Directions for Youth Development, 131,* 15–27. doi: 10.1002/yd.405

Eccles, J., & Gootman, J. A. (Eds.). (2002). *Community programs to promote youth development.* Washington, DC: National Research Council and Institute of Medicine, National Academy Press.

Halpern, R. (2003). *Making work play: The promise of after-school programs for low-income children.* New York, NY: Teachers College Press.

Hargreaves, A., & Fullan, M. (2012). *Professional capital: Transforming teaching in every school.* New York, NY: Teachers College Press.

Malone, H. J. (2013). *Building a broader learning agenda: The evolution of child and youth programs toward the education sector* (Unpublished doctoral dissertation). Harvard University, Cambridge, Massachusetts.

Murphy, P. K., & Knight, S. L. (2016). Exploring a century of advancements in the science of learning. *Review of Research in Education, 40,* 402–456. doi: 10.3102/0091732X16677020

Nagaoka, J., Farrington, C. A., & Ehrlich, S. B. (2015, June). *Foundations for young adult success: A developmental framework.* Chicago, IL: The University of Chicago Consortium on Chicago School Research.

Noam, G. G., & Tillinger, J. R. (2004, Spring). After-school as intermediary space: Theory and typology of partnerships. (pp. 75–114). *New Directions for Youth Development, 101,* 75–114.

Rogoff, B., Callanan, M., Gutiérrez, K. K., & Erickson, F. (2016). The organization of informal learning. *Review of Research in Education, 40,* 356–401. doi: 10.3102/0091732X16680994

# SECTION I

OST AS A VEHICLE FOR YOUNG PEOPLE'S
DEVELOPMENT

CHAPTER 2

# 15 YEARS AFTER COMMUNITY PROGRAMS TO PROMOTE YOUTH DEVELOPMENT

Sandra Simpkins, Yangyang Liu, and Nickki Pearce Dawes

In 2002, the National Research Council's (NRC) Committee on Community-Level Programs for Youth published a book entitled *Community Programs to Promote Youth Development* (Eccles & Gootman, 2002). When the NRC book was released, it was clear how important this report was to the field, partly because it provided a cogent case for why youth activities are important developmental contexts. It also explained how and why organized afterschool activities should be considered, alongside the home and school, as primary contexts for youth development. The report provided a framework regarding key features of youth activities that promote positive development. The authors acknowledged the limited research conducted on activities directly, which led to their reliance on research conducted on activity, family, and school settings. It called for greater focus on theory and research on activities, and that call was answered by many researchers.

If you begin to pen a list of what has changed over the last 15 years in terms of the activities youth attend or in terms of what the research evidence tells us about best practices, the list quickly becomes lengthy. In fact, the chapters in this book collectively serve as an indispensable resource on what has happened over the

*The Growing Out-of-School Time Field: Past, Present, and Future,*
pages 13–24.

past 15 years as well as where we are headed. In this chapter, we discuss four major advances that represent some of the most significant shifts in the afterschool field over the last 15 years: (a) participation in activities, (b) program quality, (c) activities as one setting in youth's lives, and (d) positive youth development for diverse youth.

## THINKING MORE DEEPLY ABOUT
## PARTICIPATION IN ACTIVITIES

One key development in the field is the specification of different dimensions of participation. The NRC book describes the diverse landscape of community programs. Consider, for example, youth in a dance program. Time in the dance program could be divided across a homework hour, strength training or drills, rehearsing choreographed dance sets, and socializing with friends before heading home. For youth in a service program, time could be devoted to working directly with community partners to do community service work, such as tutoring in the community. In both programs, there is a continuum of talent, motivation, and dedication. These examples highlight the reality that participation looks different across programs and for each participating youth. Fortunately, researchers and practitioners have gone beyond thinking about participation as merely whether or not youth attend a program. We now understand that participation has four core dimensions: (a) intensity, (b) duration, (c) engagement, and (d) breadth (Bohnert, Fredricks, & Randall, 2010).

*Participation intensity* refers to the amount of time youth spend in their activities. Time spent in activities is an important dimension of participation because time is related to increased opportunities for socialization. Time in the activity will influence youth learning, absorption, and practice of the skill or value/orientation (Bohnert et al., 2010). In other words, programs expose youth to knowledge and experiences. They are being socialized to think or act in ways that will advance their development as artists, young scholars, and community service agents. The amount of time spent in an activity will shape these learning and socialization processes. Empirical research suggests that more time in some activities (e.g., sports) is associated with more positive outcomes (e.g., Darling, 2005; Dotterer, McHale, & Crouter, 2007; Ripke, Huston, & Casey, 2006). Ripke and colleagues (2006), for instance, found that participation intensity predicted changes in self-concept and work habits. An important caveat in the field regarding the link between participation and outcomes is that the developmental outcomes that youth stand to gain are not the same across the landscape of programs.

*Participation duration* refers to the length of involvement in a particular activity over time (Bohnert et al., 2010). Human development is impacted not only by our exposure to different stimuli and various contexts, but also by the level and quality of the exposure. Examining duration in activity participation brings to the fore the idea that the acquisition of skills and beliefs takes time in supportive contexts that serve to introduce or reinforce principles and behavioral expectations. For example, it takes prolonged involvement to develop sports skills; the reinforcement from important people (i.e., coaches, families) can support this prolonged activity. A few researchers have empirically examined the connections between duration and outcomes. The findings to date suggest that longer duration is positively related to developmental outcomes (e.g., Gardener, Roth, & Brooks-Gunn, 2008; Mahoney, Cairns, & Farmer, 2003). However, more research is needed that builds on and extends the work of these early studies.

The prior two indicators, intensity and duration, focus on the amount of time. However, two youth can spend the same amount of time in an activity but garner differential benefits because one is engaged in the program and the other one is not. *Engagement* is a multidimensional construct that refers to the degree to which youth are cognitively, behaviorally, and emotionally invested in the activities of the program (Bohnert et al., 2010). Though progress has been made in terms of the development of measures to assess engagement, a limited number of research studies have focused on trying to understand what factors and processes shape activity engagement.

*Breadth* broadens the aforementioned indicators to capture participation across multiple activities. Specifically, breadth refers to the number of different activity contexts (e.g., community service, sports) in which youth are involved (Bohnert et al., 2010). Not only do research findings indicate that developmental benefits vary based on type of activity (Hansen, Larson, & Dworkin, 2003), focusing on breadth of participation highlights how interests and characteristics of youth may attract them to different types of programs at the same time.

Research suggests that involvement in more than one activity contexts may be particularly beneficial to youth development in the academic domain. The measurement of breadth is particularly intriguing in discussions about the dimensions of participation. There are different ways to measure breadth: total number of activities, total number of different activities contexts, activity dispersion (i.e., concentration of participation across types), and profiles. Profiles, for example, describe specific patterns or constellations of youth's participation across multiple activities. Zarrett, Fay, Li, Carrano, Phelps, and Lerner (2009) found that adolescents who participated exclusively or almost exclusively in sports did not fare as well compared to adolescents who participated in sports and other activities. Although studies such as these are small in number, they highlight the fact that knowing whether a youth participates or not in an activity is just the tip of the participation iceberg.

## PROGRAM QUALITY DIMENSIONS AND CONSEQUENCES

One of the central contributions of the NRC book was the point that, like schools, programs vary in quality and, therefore, their ability to promote positive development. Program quality was described in terms of eight features: (a) physical and psychological safety, (b) appropriate structure, (c) supportive relationships, (d) opportunities to belong, (e) positive social norms, (f) support for efficacy and mattering, (g) opportunities for skill building, and (h) integration of family, school, and community efforts (Eccles, & Gootman, 2002). Over the last 15 years, major advances have been made on program quality in terms of defining program quality and specifying how it is measured, as well as testing how program quality matters for youth's development.

*What Is Quality and How Is It Measured?*

Evidence from both research and practice have led to a growing consensus on what high-quality organized activities look like. Core attributes of high-quality activities include a safe environment, positive relationships between adults and youth, meaningful youth engagement, social/behavioral norms, skill building opportunities, and appropriate structure/routine (Yohalem, & Wilson-Ahlstrom, 2010). In addition, diversity, access, and equity are considered key indicators of program quality as most activities now serve an increasingly diverse youth population (California AfterSchool Network, 2014).

One new development in people's thinking about program quality is the distinction between point-of-service quality features, which was the focus of the NRC book, and programmatic quality features. Point-of-service quality features focus on the experiences youth and staff have during the activity, whereas programmatic quality features are those that are "behind the scenes," including staff recruitment, professional development, program management, and collaborative relationships among stakeholders (California AfterSchool Network, 2014; Smith, Akiva, McGovern, & Peck, 2014). Scholars argue that these program-level features are important because they can be regulated and provide the foundation for point-of-service quality features as well as youth's outcomes (Vandell, Larson, Mahoney, & Watts, 2015). However, programmatic features are new and have been studied less than point-of-service features, and thus need more attention in the future.

Many assessment tools have been created by national and state afterschool organizations and child development scholars to measure quality during the past 15 years. In 2009, the Forum for Youth Investment published a review of 10 quality assessment tools (Yohalem, Wilson-Ahlstrom, Fischer, & Shinn, 2009). In 2014, California AfterSchool Network (2014) reviewed seven quality assessment tools out of 14 they identified that they felt demonstrated effectiveness in the field and addressed several indicators of program quality. Both reviews highlight the variation among assessment tools in terms of the purpose and how quality is measured. For example, some tools were primarily designed to be used for an internal assessment that is completed by staff, whereas other tools were designed for formal evaluation executed by external observers. Also, the assessment tools differ in their target age group and require varying levels of training to be used effectively (California AfterSchool Network, 2014). It is unlikely that one assessment tool will work in all circumstances. Afterschool staff should select the tool that measures the features of interest and that fits their goals and resources.

*How Does Quality Matter for Youth Development?*

At the time of the NRC book, little systematic research existed testing whether aspects of program quality predicted youth development. Now, three meta-analyses, which statistically summarize data across multiple independent studies, have been published (Durlak, Weissberg, & Pachan, 2010; Lauer et al., 2006; Zief, Lauver, & Maynard, 2006). Much of the research to date has tested whether program quality predicts (a) youth's academic achievement and (b) youth's social and behavioral well-being. Though the effects are often small in size, research suggests participating in high-quality activities is beneficial. For example, Durlak et al. (2010) summarized findings from 75 studies on afterschool programs. Their results suggest that SAFE programs— programs that are sequenced, active, focused, and explicit—predicted more positive self-perceptions, higher school belonging, and fewer problem behaviors, whereas youth in the programs that did not meet the SAFE criteria did not experience such positive changes. Though more work is needed on all aspects of youth development, including physical development, the existing evidence suggests that program quality determines the extent to which an activity has the potential to impact positive youth development.

An important lingering question is how program features affect youth outcomes. Smith and colleagues (2014) describe the steps by which program quality translates into youth outcomes through their QuEST (quality, engagement, skills, transfer) model. They argue that high-quality activities should engage youth, which is necessary for youth to master skills and beliefs specific to the activity. These activity-specific skills and beliefs can then be transferred to other settings. For example, staff can help build youth's persistence and strategic thinking in a specific activity task (Larson, & Angus, 2011). Once youth develop these noncognitive skills, they can apply them to their work in school, which should positively influence their learning and grades. The QuEST model is helpful in that it requires individuals to explicitly delineate the processes that need to unfold for program quality to affect outcomes in another context, and by doing so, provides leaders and scholars with a list of proximal and distal outcomes they could assess.

In sum, the organized activity field has witnessed great advances since the NRC book on program quality. Emerging consensus on program quality and the application of available assessment tools deepened our understanding of youth development in activities. In future research and practice, more effort should be made to explore the mechanisms connecting different program features to all aspects of youth development and how these processes differ across program types and youth characteristics.

## AFTERSCHOOL ACTIVITIES AND
## YOUTH'S LIVES OUTSIDE OF ACTIVITIES

On any given day, youth move through multiple settings, including families, schools, friendship groups, neighborhoods, and afterschool activities. To fully understand the role of activities in youth's lives, one needs to understand how activities fit with other aspects of youth's lives. Indeed, one of the eight features of quality in the NRC book focused on how to integrate family, school, and community efforts within activities. Here, we focus on families and friendships because research in these contexts has experienced substantial growth over the last 15 years, and the research suggests that families and friends influence and are influenced by activities.

*Family and Afterschool Activities*

Families are important managers and supporters of youth's afterschool lives. Family provide necessary resources, search for and select activities, and become involved in youth's pursuits by being directly involved and supportive from home. Many of the early discussions on family influence focused on family socioeconomic status (SES), as researchers repeatedly found that youth from low SES families were less likely to participate in activities than their more affluent peers (for a review, see Vandell et al., 2015). Scholars attributed the lower participation to limited access, inadequate family resources (e.g., time, money, transportation), and under-resourced communities or neighborhoods with higher incidences of crime (Simpkins, Delgado, Price, Quach, & Starbuck, 2013). Though identifying such barriers to participation is critical, this created an implicit assumption that if the barriers were removed, youth would attend. It is more complex than that. Scholars have moved beyond a focus on barriers to describe families' beliefs about activities and how families and activities can work together to impact positive youth development (Mapp & Kuttner, 2014).

Youth's activity participation and family's support of that participation are not simply determined by external resources and barriers. Individuals' perceptions of the benefits and drawbacks of organized activities are critical (Simpkins, Fredricks, & Lin, in press). Some families believe activities provide beneficial opportunities, and in some cases the optimal opportunity, for their children to learn activity-related skills (e.g., playing the violin) and life skills, such as interpersonal skills, time management, and responsibility (Lin, Simpkins, Gaskin, & Menjívar, 2016). Other families believe their child would benefit equally from engaging in activities informally at home. Even when parents believe in the benefits of activities and have access to them, their child may not participate because the sacrifices are too costly, such as reducing family time spent together (Simpkins et al., 2013).

A second direction of recent work is to look at the positive ways families and activities influence one another. First, families can promote youth's participation through a variety of supportive behaviors, such as providing encouragement and coparticipating in activities (for a review, see Simpkins et al., in press). Although less studied, youth's activities affect families as well. Activities provide a pastime for family members to share and talk about, which is beneficial for family relationships (Lin et al., 2016). This work suggests that activities not only influence youth but also shape family relationships. One direction for the future is to understand how to maximize the mutually beneficial relationship between families and afterschool activities in an effort to support positive youth development (Mapp & Kuttner, 2014).

## Friends and Afterschool Activities

Not only do friends influence whether youth enroll and continue attending a particular activity (Fredricks & Simpkins, 2013), but they also partly explain how activities influence youth development. Youth's recurring and extended interactions with coparticipants in the same activity create a unique peer context, which has implications for youth development (Brown, 2013). Research and practitioners in the last 15 years have deepened our understandings of the role of friends in both aspects.

One of the main reasons youth go to an activity is to develop new friendships and to spend time with current friends (Fredricks & Simpkins, 2013). Having friends in an activity could greatly increase youth's likelihood of attending and becoming engaged (Hirsh, 2005; Simpkins, Vest, Delgado, & Price, 2012). Not only are friends a central reason to participate, but peer contexts within activities also help explain how activities are linked to youth development. First, activities often connect youth with well-adjusted peers who contribute to youth's overall wellbeing (Simpkins, Eccles, & Becnel, 2008). Second, peer interactions during activities help youth develop life skills, such as a sense of teamwork and responsibility (Wood, Larson, & Brown, 2009).

Though friends and peers at activities can have a positive impact, they can also push youth to drop out. Youth may stop going to an activity because they have unpleasant peer interactions at the activity or because the activity takes away time they could spend with their nonparticipating friends (Fredricks et al., 2002; Simpkins et al., 2013). These findings highlight how activities are connected to the other realms of youth's lives. The application of this more holistic perspective has increased our knowledge of youth development across contexts.

## POSITIVE YOUTH DEVELOPMENT FOR DIVERSE YOUTH

Youth in the U.S. are diverse in terms of race, ethnicity, social class, gender, sexual orientation, disabilities, cultural orientation, and immigration—to name a few. Much of what we knew up to the publishing of the NRC book focused on group differences based on gender, social class, race, and ethnicity. For example, boys participate more in sport activities and less in music activities compared to girls, and Caucasian youth are more likely to participate in a variety of activities compared to youth of color (Vandell et al., 2015). Understanding how one group fairs compared to another is helpful, but much of the work employed a selective definition of diversity. In the past 15 years, several advances had been made regarding diversity and activities.

One recent advance is that scholars have broadened the scope of diversity. Lareau's (2011) seminal work suggested that what many believed were racial differences in youth's participation in organized activities between Caucasians and African Americans were more strongly tied to differences in social class. This is one example of how scholars have moved away from a reductionist view to delve into the complexity of diversity. Some of our recent work has focused on the experiences of Latino families to understand the role of social class, ethnicity, culture, and immigration on youth's activities (e.g., Simpkins et al., 2013). The priority activities take in youth's lives depends not only on access and family financial resources, but also on families' history with activities in the U.S. and abroad, their culturally grounded beliefs about what experiences are critical to support their child's development, and the immigration laws that change how families parent, among other indicators. This work highlights the multitude of factors that determine the activities for diverse youth as well as the dangers of treating youth from the same demographic group, like Latino youth, as a monolithic group with uniform preferences, experiences, and needs.

An increasing number of activities depend on the success of diverse youth. The rapid increasing diversity among U.S. youth has altered whom activities serve. Moreover, the funding streams often require activities to demonstrate that their program fosters positive development among underachieving youth. Though historically scholars have studied the development of diverse youth through deficit-based perspectives, the focus has shifted to the strengths youth bring to activities and empowerment among diverse youth. Recent reviews suggest that activities promote positive development among youth who are diverse in terms of race/ethnicity (Fredricks & Simpkins, 2012), academic skills (Gardner, Roth, & Brooks-Gunn, 2009), and English language abilities (Maxwell-Jolly, 2011). High-quality activities can foster youth's ethnic identity and feelings that their ethnic group is respected, and even bridge intergroup differences (Deutsch & Jones, 2008; Ettekal, Gaskin, Lin, & Simpkins, 2015; Riggs, Bohnert, Guzman, & Davidson, 2010; Watkins, Larson, & Sullivan, 2007). All of which are important outcomes in their own right but also provide a solid foundation to promote other aspects of youth development.

The questions around promoting positive youth development for diverse youth also have shifted from whether youth from different groups experience similar outcomes to how we create activities that are responsive to youth. This shift is significant because it places diversity at the forefront and demands that diversity and cultural responsiveness are not "add on components" to an activity (Simpkins, Riggs, Ngo, Ettekal, & Okamoto, 2017; Williams & Deutsch, 2016). Rather, high-quality activities consider diversity, equity, and inclusion in every aspect of what they do. There are many examples of culturally responsive programs in the articles referenced earlier in this paragraph as well as in the work by Cole (2006) and Ginwright (2010). In these activities, youth voice, youth strengths and assets, celebrating diversity, and adaptation to the local cultural context are cornerstones.

The authors of the NRC book emphasized the importance of diversity; however, little work existed at the time for them to provide concrete advice. Over the years, the field has shifted from a largely singular focus on gender and racial/ethnic differences to a more complex and nuanced understanding of diversity and how multiple characteristics shape the lives of youth. That said, some groups and aspects of diversity continue to be underrepresented in the literature, including youth with disabilities; lesbian, gay, bisexual, and transgender youth; and Native Americans. This is a burgeoning area and will likely increase in productivity in the years to come.

## CONCLUSION

The NRC book continues to be a "must read" for out-of-school time leaders in the field and academic researchers alike. The authors assert that afterschool activities are not and should not be simply extensions of daycare or the school day. The characteristics that make OST activities unique also provide critical, unparalleled opportunities for positive youth development. The NRC book legitimized activities as a field of inquiry and set a research agenda in terms of program quality and the myriad of ways activities influence youth development. In this chapter, we described four of the major strides in the field since the book was published. Moving forward, two areas that are ripe for research are understanding the role of programmatic features in addition to point-of-service features of program quality and creating culturally responsive programs. We anticipate great discoveries and advancements over the next 15 years.

## REFERENCES

Bohnert, A., Fredricks, J., & Randall, E. (2010). Capturing unique dimensions of youth organized activity involvement: Theoretical and methodological considerations. *Review of Educational Research, 80*(4), 576–610. doi:10.3102/0034654310364533

Brown, B. B. (2013). Adolescents, organized activities, and peers: Knowledge gained and knowledge needed. *New Directions for Child and Adolescent Development, 140*, 77–96. doi:10.1002/cad.20038

California AfterSchool Network. (2014). *A crosswalk between the quality standards for expanded learning and program quality assessment tools.* Oakland, CA: Public Profit. Retrieved from http://www.afterschoolnetwork.org/post/quality-standards-expanded-learning-california

Cole, M., & The Distributed Literacy Consortium. (Eds.). (2006). *The fifth dimension: An after-school program built on diversity.* New York, NY: Russell Sage Foundation.

Darling, N. (2005). Participation in extracurricular activities and adolescent adjustment: Cross-sectional and longitudinal findings. *Journal of Youth and Adolescence, 34*(5), 493–505. doi:10.1007/s10964-005-7266-8

Deutsch, N. L., & Jones, J. N. (2008). "Show me an ounce of respect:" Respect and authority in adult–youth relationships in after-school programs. *Journal of Adolescent Research, 23*(6), 667–688. doi: 10.1177/0743558408322250

Dotterer, A. M., McHale, S. M., & Crouter, A. C. (2007). Implications of out-of-school activities for school engagement in African American adolescents. *Journal of Youth and Adolescence, 36*(4), 391–401. doi:10.1007/s10964-006-9161-3

Durlak, J. A., Weissberg, R. P., & Pachan, M. (2010). A meta-analysis of after-school programs that seek to promote personal and social skills in children and adolescents. *American Journal of Community Psychology, 45*(3–4), 294–309. doi:10.1007/s10464-010-9300-6

Eccles, J., & Gootman, J. A. (Eds.). (2002). *Community programs to promote youth development*. Washington, DC: National Research Council and Institute of Medicine, Board on Children, Youth, and Families, Division of Behavioral and Social Sciences and Education, National Academy Press.

Ettekal, A. E., Gaskin, E., Lin, A. R., & Simpkins, S. D. (2015). "You gotta respect" Mexican-origin adolescents' perspectives on respect in organized activities. *Journal of Youth Development, 10*(3), 74–87. doi: 10.5195/JYD.2015.9

Fredricks, J. A., Alfeld-Liro, C. J., Hruda, L. Z., Eccles, J. S., Patrick, H., & Ryan, A. M. (2002). A qualitative exploration of adolescents' commitment to athletics and the arts. *Journal of Adolescent Research, 17*(1), 68–97. doi:10.1177/0743558402171004

Fredricks, J. A., & Simpkins, S. D. (2013). Organized out-of-school activities and peer relationships: Theoretical perspectives and previous research. *New Directions for Child and Adolescent Development, 140,* 1–17. doi:10.1002/cad.20034

Fredricks, J. A., & Simpkins, S. D. (2012). Promoting positive youth development through organized after-school activities: Taking a closer look at participation of ethnic minority youth. *Child Development Perspectives, 6*(3), 280–287. doi:10.1111/j.1750-8606.2011.00206.x

Gardner, M., Roth, J., & Brooks-Gunn, J. (2008). Adolescents' participation in organized activities and developmental success 2 and 8 years after high school: Do sponsorship, duration, and intensity matter? *Developmental Psychology, 44*(3), 814–830. doi: 10.1037/0012-1649.44.3.814

Gardner, M., Roth, J. L., & Brooks-Gunn, J. (2009). *Can after-school programs help level the academic playing field for disadvantaged youth? Equity matters* (Research Review No. 4). New York, NY: Campaign for Educational Equity, Teachers College, Columbia University.

Ginwright S. A. (2010). *Black youth rising: Activism & radical healing in urban America.* New York, NY: Teachers College Press.

Hansen, D. M., Larson, R. W., & Dworkin, J. B. (2003). What adolescents learn in organized youth activities: A survey of self-reported developmental experiences. *Journal of Research on Adolescence, 13*(1), 25–55. doi:10.1111/1532-7795.1301006

Hirsch, B. J. (2005). *A place to call home: After-school programs for urban youth.* New York, NY: Teachers College Press.

Lareau, A. (2011). *Unequal childhoods: Class, ethnicity, and family life.* Berkeley, CA: University of California Press.

Larson, R. W., & Angus, R. M. (2011). Adolescents' development of skills for agency in youth programs: Learning to think strategically. *Child Development, 82*(1), 277–294. doi: 10.1111/j.1467-8624.2010.01555.x

Lauer, P. A., Akiba, M., Wilkerson, S. B., Apthorp, H. S., Snow, D., & Martin-Glenn, M. L. (2006). Out-of-school-time programs: A meta-analysis of effects for at-risk students. *Review of educational research, 76*(2), 275–313. doi:10.3102/00346543076002275

Lin, A. R., Simpkins, S. D., Gaskin, E. R., & Menjívar, C. (2016). Cultural values and other perceived benefits of organized activities: A qualitative analysis of Mexican-origin parents' perspectives in Arizona. *Applied Developmental Science, 76*(2),1–21. doi:1 0.1080/10888691.2016.1224669

Mahoney, J. L., Cairns, B. D., & Farmer, T. (2003). Promoting interpersonal competence and educational success through extracurricular activity participation. *Journal of Educational Psychology, 95*(2), 409–418. doi:10.1037/0022-0663.95.2.409

Mapp, K. L., & Kuttner, P. J. (2014). *Partners in education: A dual capacity building framework for school-family partnerships.* Austin, TX: Southwest Educational Development Lab.

Maxwell-Jolly, J. (2011). *English learners and out-of-school-time programs: The potential of OST programs to foster English learner success.* Davis, CA: University of California, Davis.

Riggs, N. R., Bohnert, A. M., Guzman, M. D., & Davidson, D. (2010). Examining the potential of community-based after-school programs for Latino youth. *American Journal of Community Psychology, 45*(3–4), 417–429. doi: 10.1007/s10464-010-9313-1

Ripke, M., Huston, A., & Casey, D. M. (2006). Low-income children's activity participation as a predictor of psychosocial and academic outcomes in middle childhood and adolescence. In A. Huston & M. Ripke (Eds.), *Developmental contexts in middle childhood: Bridges to adolescence and adulthood* (pp. 260–282). New York, NY: Cambridge University Press. doi: 10.1017/CBO9780511499760

Simpkins, S. D., Delgado, M. Y., Price, C. D., Quach, A., & Starbuck, E. (2013). Socioeconomic status, ethnicity, culture, and immigration: Examining the potential mechanisms underlying Mexican-origin adolescents' organized activity participation. *Developmental Psychology, 49*(4), 706–721. doi:10.1037/a0028399

Simpkins, S. D., Eccles, J. S., & Becnel, J. N. (2008). The mediational role of adolescents' friends in relations between activity breadth and adjustment. *Developmental Psychology, 44*(4), 1081–1094. doi:10.1037/0012-1649.44.4.1081

Simpkins, S. D., Fredricks, J. A., & Lin, A. R. (in press). Families and engagement in afterschool programs. In B. H. Fiese (Series Ed.), *APA Handbook of contemporary family psychology: Vol. 2. Applications of contemporary family psychology.* Washington, DC: APA Books.

Simpkins, S. D., Riggs, N. R., Ngo, B., Ettekal, A. E., & Okamoto, D. (2017). Designing culturally responsive organized after-school activities. *Journal of Adolescent Research, 32,* 11–36.

Simpkins, S. D., Vest, A. E., Delgado, M. Y., & Price, C. D. (2012). Do school friends participate in similar extracurricular activities?: Examining the moderating role of race/ethnicity and age. *Journal of Leisure Research, 44*(3), 332–352.

Smith, C., Akiva, T., McGovern, G., & Peck, S. C. (2014). Afterschool quality. *New Directions for Youth Development, 144,* 31–44. doi:10.1002/yd.20111

Vandell, D. L., Larson, R. W, Mahoney, J. L., & Watts, T. W. (2015). Children's organized activities. In M. H. Bornstein & T. Leventhal (Eds.), *Handbook of child psychology and developmental science, Vol. 4: Ecological settings and processes in developmental systems* (7th ed., pp. 305–344). Hoboken, NJ: Wiley. doi:10.1002/9781118963418

Watkins, N. D., Larson, R. W., & Sullivan, P. J. (2007). Bridging intergroup difference in a community youth program. *American Behavioral Scientist, 51*(3), 380–402. http://doi.org/10.1177/0002764207306066

Williams, J. L., & Deutsch, N. L. (2016). Beyond between-group differences: Considering race, ethnicity, and culture in research on positive youth development programs, *Applied Developmental Science, 20*(3), 203–213. doi:10.1080/10888691.2015.111 3880

Wood, D., Larson, R. W., & Brown, J. R. (2009). How adolescents come to see themselves as more responsible through participation in youth programs. *Child Development, 80*(1), 295–309. doi:10.1111/j.1467-8624.2008.01260.x

Yohalem, N., & Wilson-Ahlstrom, A. (2010). Inside the black box: Assessing and improving quality in youth programs. *American Journal of Community Psychology, 45*(3–4), 350–357. doi:10.1007/s10464-010-9311-3

Yohalem, N., Wilson-Ahlstrom, A., Fischer, S., & Shinn, M. (2009). *Measuring youth program quality: A guide to assessment tools* (2nd ed.). Takoma Park, MD: The Forum for Youth Investment. Retrieved from http://www.cypq.org/sites/cypq.org/files/publications/MeasuringYouthProgramQuality_2ndEd.pdf

Zarrett, N., Fay, K., Li, Y., Carrano, J., Phelps, E., & Lerner, R.M. (2009). More than child's play: Variable-and pattern-centered approaches for examining effects of sports participation on youth development. *Developmental Psychology, 45*(2), 368–382. doi:10.1037/a0014577

Zief, S., Lauver, S., & Maynard, R. (2006). *Impacts of after-school programs on student outcomes. Campbell Systematic Reviews.* Retrieved from https://www.campbellcollaboration.org/media/k2/attachments/1011_R.pdf

CHAPTER 3

# HIGH-QUALITY OST ACTIVITIES AND PROGRAMS

## Using the RISE Approach (Relationships, Interest and Sparks, Empowerment) to Promote Thriving in Youth and Their Settings

Peter C. Scales

Much has been written about the features that define high-quality in out-of-school time (OST) activities and programs, from structure, to staff qualifications and development, to content. Although the quality of the relationships youth have in those settings has certainly not been overlooked, not enough emphasis has been given to a sufficiently broad range of the specific features of the relationships youth need to experience. Nor has enough exploration been done in the way those relationships connect with other aspects of positive youth development to promote optimal youth development or thriving. And most measures of program quality do not emphasize enough the perceptions of youth themselves, as compared with staff perceptions, or the observations of outside raters. In contrast, in this chapter, I elaborate on how when youth experience what I call the RISE approach—the intersection and linkage of truly "developmental" Relationships, youths' deep personal Interests and Sparks, and their Empowerment in OST ac-

*The Growing Out-of-School Time Field: Past, Present, and Future,*
pages 25–43.

tivities—what is promoted is not just adequate development, but thriving in both youth and the settings they inhabit.

I emphasize OST "activities" and not just technically defined OST "programs" in this discussion. Gardner, Roth, and Brooks-Gunn (2009) made a useful distinction between the two, specifically underscoring that activities may have a single focus, such as dance classes or sports teams, whereas OST programs must offer more than one activity. Yet, as they noted, the majority of young people participate in some sort of OST activity. The U.S. Census Bureau (2014) estimates 57% of 6–17 year-olds do, but only a minority, about 18% (Afterschool Alliance, 2014a), participate in OST programs as so defined. Thus, to ensure that the greatest percentage of youth experience developmentally beneficial OST settings, those single-focus OST activities must be as much a part of the discussion about access and quality as are the multifocused programs that garner most of the public policy emphasis.

## CONNECTION OF OST QUALITY TO SELF-DETERMINATION THEORY

The essential features common across most OST quality frameworks are the three ABC elements of "self-determination theory" (SDT)—autonomy, belonging, and competence (Ryan & Deci, 2000), or in slightly different fashion, as experiences that help youth answer "yes" to three fundamental questions of adolescent development: Am I normal (in my body, growth, feelings, etc.)? Am I competent? Am I lovable and loving? (McCoy & Wibbelsman, 2016; Scales, 1991). The "self" part of self-determination theory is a bit of a misnomer because belonging and relatedness to others are such a key part of SDT; good OST activities and programs have always been about building such pillars of development, albeit not always using this SDT language so explicitly. For example, Gil Noam's "Clover Leaf" model of children's basic needs includes assertiveness (i.e., voice and choice), belonging, and active engagement and reflection (aspects of autonomy) (Malti & Noam, 2009; Noam, Malti, & Guhn, 2012).

Benson and colleagues (2006) and, more recently, R. M. Lerner, J. V., Lerner, and colleagues (2013) have, in slightly different language, summarized this literature in ways that echo both the three-part ABCs of self-determination theory, and the three-part Roth and Brooks-Gunn (2003) formulation of what makes a youth program truly developmental. But what Benson et al. and Lerner et al. (2013) also highlight is a premise rarely emphasized. Optimal development or thriving is not just about how youth are doing, but how their well-being and the well-being of the families, schools, communities, activities, and programs they are in are bidirectionally connected.

For Benson et al. (2006), the three "major points of intervention" to promote "intentional change" (the "purposeful effort to enhance the fusion of person and context in a healthy way"—p. 910) are enhancing how settings can support and constructively challenge youth, build their competencies, and empower them as change agents. They too note that in both practice and research, "this form of intentional change travels under such concepts as youth leadership, service learning, youth empowerment, and youth engagement" (p. 910).

According to Lerner, Lerner, and colleagues (2013), the three fundamental characteristics of effective Positive Youth Development [PYD] programs are: (1) positive and sustained adult–youth relationships; (2) skill-building opportunities that allow youth to select and progress toward valued goals; and (3) youth leadership in family, school, and community. Like Benson et al. (2006), Lerner, Lerner, et al. argued that program features need to be present in PYD for it to be effective.

Blyth (2014) has summarized such formulations of positive youth development in a useful analogy with diet and exercise. Weight management and overall health require both. In the same way, PYD occurs when developmental nutrients such as high-quality relationships are paired with youth voice and engagement. These features of quality and effectiveness are pertinent regardless of the content focus of OST experiences, and regardless of whether they are single-focus activities such as sports or creative arts, or programs that have multiple focuses.

### Youth Thriving and a Revised Definition of OST Quality

It is necessary to introduce one more element to this discussion, to better understand the special role that OST activities and programs can play in promoting thriving. Benson and Scales (2009) described thriving as having three interconnected parts: (a) the intersection of young people's deep interests and contexts that support the development of those interests, (b) the general movement over time toward optimal development (what Lerner, Alberts, Anderson, & Dowling [2006] have called "idealized personhood"), and (c) a combination of current well-being and being on a positive life path that enhances their life and makes "full use of their special gifts in ways that benefit themselves and others" (Benson & Scales, 2009, p. 90); that is, that enables and promotes the pursuit of what Damon and colleagues have called "noble purpose" (Damon, Menon, & Bronk, 2003).

Putting all of this together leads to a different way of describing what high-quality OST activities and programs are. High-quality OST experiences:

- Provide sustained relationships that are both caring and challenging (Scales, 1999)
- Offer freely chosen opportunities to identify and have the support to pursue intrinsically motivating personal interests—sparks (combining the experience of flow [Csikszentmihalyi, 1990] and the exercise of initiative [Larson, 2000])
- Provide acquisition and growth in cognitive, social-emotional, psychological, and behavioral skills that empower young people to use the pursuit of their sparks to develop noble purpose (Damon) and to contribute (the "6th C" of positive youth development—the result of competence, confidence, connection, character, and caring—as articulated by Lerner, Lerner, & col-

leagues, 2005) in life domains that are both personally and societally valued—that is, that enable both young people and their settings to flourish.

This description of quality OST experiences pertains to both single-focus activities like lessons or sports and multifocus programs and is applicable regardless of the specific content of activities or programs.

## EXTENT OF YOUTH EXPERIENCE OF OST QUALITY

Put in those terms, it is doubtful that many youth actually experience OST activities and programs that emphasize all three of those indicators of high quality. Overall, only about 20% of children ages 6–12 attend an afterschool program at their schools, and roughly another 10% do so at a community-based OST program (Hynes & Sanders, 2010). Even if every one of those children participated in a high-quality program, an assumption that is not likely to be true, that still would mean that the great majority of children overall do not attend high-quality OST programs.

Although there are a number of good program quality measurement instruments (see Simpkins et al., this volume), it is surprisingly difficult to pin down the percentage of young people who actually do participate in a high-quality program. The Afterschool Alliance (2014a) nominated 10 states as the best for afterschool programs, in part based on quality ratings, but those were only parents' perceptions of quality and satisfaction with their child's program. Although clearly important, and reassuring that positive parent ratings seem to be increasing, those are hardly comprehensive evaluations. One of the landmark studies of afterschool program quality (Vandell, Reisner, & Pierce, 2007) was based on 35 programs that were already deemed to be of promising quality.

Scores of studies testify to the positive outcomes from programs that are high quality (Afterschool Alliance, 2014b), but few sources give a glimpse of how common high quality is. In the national 4-H Study of Positive Youth Development, Balsano, Phelps, Theokas, Lerner, and Lerner (2009) estimated that just one-third of sixth graders were in afterschool programs that emphasized the 5C's of positive youth development (competence, confidence, connection, character, and caring). Similarly, in a national study of 15-year-olds, Scales, Benson, and Roehlkepartain (2011) concluded that although 68% of those youth nationwide participated in OST programs, only 35% were in high-quality programs that emphasized the quality indicators of relational opportunities; identifying and pursuing youths' sparks or deep personal interests; and empowerment, service, and leadership opportunities, according to the youths' reports. Counting those who said they did not participate in OST programs at all, Scales et al. concluded that just 23% of the nation's 15-year-olds participate in such high-quality programs. Neither the Balsano et al. nor Scales et al. studies distinguished between multifocus programs and single-focus activities the way Gardner et al. (2009) did—youth who did single-focus activities and multifocus programs were counted as being in

OST programs. Thus, both activities and programs already are represented in the low levels of program quality each study yielded, suggesting that these figures are likely the most positive findings in current research on the extent of high-quality program participation.

So, whether it is 33%, 23%, something in between, or something even lower, it would seem that in addition to there not being enough OST programs to meet the demand (Afterschool Alliance, 2014a), the majority of youth do not participate in OST activities and programs that meet what appear to be reasonable criteria for being called high-quality experiences. This is especially troubling given the clear association of OST activities and programs with positive youth development outcomes and the finding that youths' OST activities appear to more frequently promote both personal (e.g., identity exploration, emotional learning) and interpersonal development (e.g., collaboration, communication, and problem-solving) than do academic classes or socializing with friends (Hansen, Larson, & Dworkin, 2003).

## RISE: A THRIVING FOCUS FOR STRENGTHENING QUALITY IN OST ACTIVITIES AND PROGRAMS

I now examine each of these three features of quality—Relationships, youths' deep personal Interests and Sparks, and Empowerment—what I call the RISE approach, in a bit more depth, briefly reviewing the research that suggests their role in youth thriving, and how they can be promoted in OST activities and programs. When youth experience RISE, they and their settings thrive.

### Relationships

Positive relationships are consistently found to be at the heart of why programs work. Indeed, Li and Julian (2012) called relationships the "active ingredient" of successful programs, regardless of the content focus of the program. Lerner, Lerner, and colleagues (2013) also found that, although institutional resources and program content of OST activities and programs matter for promoting PYD outcomes, it is the individual teachers, coaches, mentors, and others in those programs, in their relationship with young people, who consistently are the most powerful sources of positive developmental influence.

Most often, the quality of these PYD-necessary relationships has been described as some variation on "positive, "supportive," or "caring." For example, the National Research Council gave these as descriptors for supportive relationships: warmth, closeness, connectedness, good communication, caring, support, guidance, secure attachment, and responsiveness (Eccles & Gootman, 2002). Less frequently, descriptors beyond caring or supportive are noted, such as in discussions of how both care and challenge are features of both successful schools (e.g., Scales, 1999) and mentoring relationships (e.g., Deutsch & Spencer, 2009), or that effective relationships aren't just about caring but also about helping youth navigate real-world systems (Gambone & Connell, 2004) and even help them become "change-makers" (Pittman, Irby, Tolman, Yohalem, & Ferber, 2003).

Since 1990, Benson and colleagues (2006) promulgated the framework of developmental assets—external relationships and opportunities, and internal, personal strengths—that were found to be strongly linked to youth well-being, in the U.S. (Benson, Scales, & Syvertsen, 2011) and around the world (Scales, Roehlkepartain, & Shramko, 2016). The assets framework described four broad categories of relationship assets—support, empowerment, boundaries and expectations, and constructive use of time—reflected in and measured by 20 more specific indicators (e.g., having meaningful relationships with three or more adults, experiencing high expectations from parents and teachers, and having opportunities to contribute and serve).

Li and Julian (2012) offered a more nuanced definition of the dynamics of developmental relationships as bi-directional interactions between people who have an ongoing emotional attachment, that evolve into more complex relationships over time, and in which power and influence gradually shift from the adult to the youth. Pekel, Roehlkepartain, Syvertsen, and Scales (2015; see also Scales, 2016) have built on that foundation, as well as on the developmental assets framework, to elaborate a still more comprehensive theoretical and measurement framework of developmental relationships that articulates five major actions youth need to experience—express care, provide challenge, provide support, share power, and expand possibility— reflected in 20 more specific interactions between youth and adults, and youth and their peers. For example, the ways adults can help challenge youth to grow include (as expressed from the youth's point of view) expect my best (expect me to live up to my potential), stretch me (push me to go further), hold me accountable (insist that I take responsibility for my actions), and reflect on failures (help me learn from mistakes and setbacks) (The Developmental Relationships Framework, 2016). This developmental relationships framework is similar to, but in both theory and measurement more comprehensive than, the description of what Spencer and Rhodes (2014) in their discussion of successful afterschool programs called "growth-promoting" relationships, which also feature warmth and emotional support, appropriate structure, cultivation of youth initiative, and youth skill development.

Research has not yet been completed using the developmental relationships framework in OST settings. However, research has been done on developmental relationships in families and between students and teachers. In a national study of nearly 1,100 families with children ages 3–13, the five major actions youth need to experience were significantly associated with higher levels of motivation to learn, personal responsibility, emotional competence, and prosocial behaviors such as being kind to others and effortful control. Generally, sharing power, challenging growth, and expanding possibility were the strongest predictors (Pekel et al., 2015). The effect sizes of the associations between developmental relationships and those character strengths were substantial, ranging from .47 for children's effortful control to .66 for their motivation to learn and .68 for their taking personal responsibility for their actions (Syvertsen, Wu, Roehlkepartain, & Scales, 2015). The size of these relations is thus well in excess of the .25 effect size the U.S. Department of Education's What Works Clearinghouse defines as being of "substantive importance" (What Works Clearinghouse, 2008).

Similarly, in a study of 600 high school students in a diverse first-ring suburban high school in the Minneapolis area, students who reported higher levels of developmental relationships with their teachers were significantly more likely to feel connected to school and have higher actual GPAs (i.e., from student records, not self-report) than students with lower levels of developmental relationships (Scales, Pekel, Syvertsen, & Roehlkepartain, 2016). In a different longitudinal analysis of 370 high school students, Scales, Benson, and Mannes (2006) focused on the role that relationships with adults outside the family play in young people's well-being. They reported that young people with higher levels of community involvement in sixth through eighth grades (through volunteering, afterschool programs, and connection to religious programs) had fewer risk behaviors and more evidence of thriving, including higher school achievement, than those in 10th–12th grades. This association was partly explained by students with more community involvement in sixth through eighth grades subsequently having had more developmental relationships with non-family adults in those settings, such that the youth had higher levels of perceived support, boundaries and expectations, and empowerment in the seventh through ninth grades. More specifically, young people with above-average time spent in those contexts of youth programs, religious community, and volunteering were substantially more likely than youth with less community connections to say that nonfamily adults were involved with them by (a) reporting both positive behavior and misbehavior to their parents, (b) guiding young people's decision-making, (c) providing them opportunities to serve or help others, (d) seeking young people's opinions, (e) giving them financial guidance, (f) passing down cultural traditions, (g) having meaningful conversations with them where both adult and youth feel they are getting to really know each other, (h) playing sports or doing art activities together with the young people, and (i) discussing religious beliefs or personal values with them (Scales, Benson, & Mannes, 2006).

Similarly, in a different analysis of the same longitudinal sample, the researchers found that if youth experienced in middle school a largely relationship-based cluster of developmental assets they called "connection to community," which included participation in afterschool programs, connection to a religious community, service to others, and engagement in creative activities, the students were more than 300% more likely to have B+ or higher GPAs three years later in high school than were students who did not have those connections to community in middle school (Scales, Benson, Roehlkepartain, Sesma, & van Dulmen, 2006). These effects were stronger even than the effects on grades of a cluster of assets reflecting "norms of responsibility," including positive peer influence, quality time spent at home, a value of restraint from sexual activity and alcohol use, use of peaceful conflict resolution, and high levels of school engagement.

### Interests and Sparks

Several national studies of adolescents have shown that about 66–80% of youth can name at least one deep personal interest or spark they have (depending on how "spark" is defined for them), but that less than half experience relational opportunities to develop that spark, whether the spark is the arts, sports, science, technology, helping others, and so on (Benson & Scales, 2009). In a national study of U.S. adults, it was found that less than 10% of adults have both a strongly favorable personal attitude toward engaging with adolescents outside their families and a perception of social permission or expectation from others to do so (Scales et al., 2003).

In day-to-day interactions, then, there is little normative support for anything but superficial connection between most adults and teenagers. Even in schools, youth organizations, and religious congregations, where adults are permitted and expected as part of their job descriptions to get to know youth more personally, only a minority of adolescents say someone knows their spark in those settings and helps support it, and less than 20% say their neighbors do (Scales, Roehlkepartain, & Benson, 2009).

Studies have shown (summarized in Scales, 2010) that youth who can identify their sparks and have the support to develop them tend to be, and to feel, healthier. They tend to be less depressed, less worried, and more satisfied overall. They place greater importance on being connected to school and making contributions to society, which are factors strongly related to school success indicators such as academic confidence and grades. Helping young people to identify their sparks and providing them the opportunity to develop those interests appears to be important additions to academic educational methods and help students achieve school success, in addition to positive development beyond the academic realm.

However, only about one-third of young people say that three or more adults at school know what their sparks are, and another one-third of young people say they get no help at all to develop their sparks (Scales, 2010). In addition, two of the most commonly identified sparks for students are sports and the arts, areas that frequently are targeted when schools must make budget cuts. OST programs have tremendous potential to help youth identify and pursue their sparks, but the available data suggest that most young people do not get that experience either in school or in their OST activities or programs.

### Empowerment

A voluminous literature has shown the benefits accruing to young people and society when youth have opportunities to serve and contribute in their schools and communities (Benefits of Service-Learning, 2016). Among the benefits are improved values, academic success, planning and goal-setting, social skills, problem-solving skills, self-efficacy, psychological well-being, and civic participation (Roehlkepartain, 2007). For example, a study of the Student Conservation Corps (Syvertsen, Sullivan, & Wu, 2016) found that participation in the environmental leadership and stewardship activities of SCA produced significant growth in corps members' goal setting, self-efficacy, purpose, teamwork, perspective taking, and social responsibility, among other PYD outcomes.

Importantly, higher quality of programming made a significant difference in pre-post changes. High quality included opportunities for decision making, learning how to solve problems, and learning how to cooperate with others, as well as high levels of developmental relationships characterized by feelings of mutual respect with program leaders and leaders showing interest in youth as individuals, helping them feel they mattered, setting high expectations for them, and helping them explore new ideas and possibilities for themselves. Youth who said they had such a high-quality program experience were two to three times more likely than youth with lower-quality experiences to have high postprogram levels of stretching, being able to set goals, feeling efficacious, and being able to communicate well with others, among other outcomes (Syvertsen et al., 2016). The Teen Voice national study of 15 year-olds also found that young people who had chances to express their opinions and be taken seriously were much more likely than those low on voice to want to master what they study at school, have a high GPA, have a sense of purpose and hope for the future, a positive ethnic identity, believe that it's important to be involved in community issues, and actually volunteer (Scales, Roehlkepartain, & Benson, 2010).

Unfortunately, despite the great value of service and service-learning, the growth of these activities in schools has slowed substantially, compared to the 1990s, or in the case of service-learning—which represents the highest quality type of community service—declined meaningfully, with just 24% of K–12 schools in the U.S. offering service-learning, versus 32% in 1999. Although gaps in access to these empowerment opportunities by race and socioeconomic status have narrowed since the 1990s, youth of color and youth from lower-income backgrounds still are less likely to have meaningful opportunities to serve and contribute (Spring, Grimm, & Dietz, 2008). OST activities and programs increasingly are a key source of young people's access to civic participation, contribution, and influence, particularly for youth of color and low-income youth.

The 4-H Study of Positive Youth Development followed more than 7,000 youth from 5th grade through 12th grade and included examination of pathways to contribution (Jelicic, Bobek, Phelps, Lerner, & Lerner, 2007; Lerner et al., 2013). Youth who exhibited the 5C's of positive youth development—competence, confidence, connection, character, and caring—as well as youth who participated more frequently in OST activities and programs (e.g., 4-H, YWCA, YMCA) were more likely to exhibit both an ideological commitment to contribution as well as engaging more often in actual contribution. Contribution was described as "active engagement with the world around oneself. These activities consist of being a leader in a group, helping friends and neighbors, helping in sports activities, participating in school government and religious youth groups, volunteering in the community, and mentoring and tutoring others" (Lerner et al., 2005, p. 54).

Both the SCA and 4-H studies reached similar conclusions about the key mechanisms through which youth thriving is promoted in those settings, mechanisms that are well aligned with the framework used in the national Teen Voice study, although each of the studies used somewhat different language. The 4-H study described them as the "big three" of positive youth development programs, and the SCA study called them "best practices," with the Teen Voice study naming them as "three strengths." But each approach clearly taps what I have named the "RISE" aspects of youth thriving in this chapter: Relationships, Interests and Sparks, and Empowerment (to these, the SCA researchers added a fourth necessary element that is at the center of successful service-learning: Reflection about the service experiences). Table 3.1 compares the three studies.

Note that both Benson et al. (2006) and Lerner et al. (2005) underscored the theoretical need for young people to experience all three of these dimensions of program quality in order for PYD and thriving to be promoted. This theoretical importance of the integration of relationships, sparks, and empowerment was reflected in results from the national Teen Voice study. Youth could do well on some PYD outcomes (academic, social-emotional, psychological, behavioral) if they had only one or two of those quality elements. But only when youth had all three elements of relationships, sparks, and empowerment did they score higher than other youth on the prosocial outcomes of leadership, prosocial values, and intentions to be civically engaged, and only if they had two or three of the dimen-

TABLE 3.1.  Differing Vocabularies of Core Elements in Positive Youth Development

| Study Title | Author | Characteristics |
| --- | --- | --- |
| Teen Voice Study | Scales et al. (2011) | Relational opportunities<br>Sparks<br>Voice |
| 4-H Study | Lerner et al. (2013) | Positive and sustained relationships between youth and adults<br>Activities that build important life skills<br>Opportunities for youth to use these life skills as both participants in and as leaders of valued community activities |
| SCA Study | Syvertsen et al. (2016) | Building strong relationships<br>Providing high-quality skill-development experiences, including people skills, problem-solving, learning what it is they value, and doing something they are really excited about<br>Creating a space where members feel like they matter and are contributing |

sions did they score in the highest group on volunteering (Scales et al., 2011). The researchers concluded that having relational opportunities, or sparks, or opportunities to exert voice and contribute, may help in the individual youth's well-being, but not in promoting the well-being of both youth and setting (society), which is both the highest measure of thriving and also a necessity in promoting civil society. Thus, OST activities and programs must strive to provide all three.

Unfortunately, as we have seen, the reality is that too few youth in the United States experience any one of the three RISE elements of relationships, interests and sparks, and empowerment. Not surprisingly, then, the majority of youth do not come close to experiencing *all three* of these quality dimensions in their OST activities and programs. For example, just 9% of 15-year-olds nationally experienced high levels of all three of relationships, sparks, and empowerment in the Teen Voice study, and although youth who were in OST programs fared better— still just 23% of all youth overall participated in high-quality OST programs featuring all three of those strengths (Scales et al., 2011). In the 8-year 4-H Study of Positive Youth Development, just 25% experienced high levels of PYD and just 12% contribution (Lerner et al., 2013).

The situation is no better worldwide. In a large dataset encompassing 30 countries and more than 32,000 youth and young adults ages 9–31 (the great majority 11–18 and in the developing, majority world), Scales and colleagues (2016) found that the frequency of developmental relationships experienced is below adequate, placing youth in a life position where their well-being is vulnerable. These inferences are based on the repeated correlation of scores on relational assets with youths' academic, social-emotional, psychological, and behavioral well-being (Benson et al., 2011; Scales et al., 2016).

Table 3.2 shows that only in the school setting do a majority of youth have adequate developmental relationships with nonfamily adults, and even there, it is only a bare majority of 52%; nearly half of youth in this large worldwide sample report less than adequate developmental relationships with the adults in their school or learning settings. Outside of school, in the community setting, a whopping 75% of youth worldwide have inadequate levels of these developmental relationships.

The numbers from all these studies are not in exact agreement, but they do not have to be. One can see clearly that only a minority of young people, in the U.S. and across the globe, currently get the kind of developmentally nourishing

TABLE 3.2. Percentage of Youth Worldwide Experiencing Levels of Developmental Relationships with Nonfamily Adults: Level of Developmental Relationships

| Context | Very Vulnerable | Vulnerable | Adequate | Good |
|---|---|---|---|---|
| School | 19 | 29 | 21 | 31 |
| Community | 40 | 35 | 18 | 7 |
| Social | 22 | 34 | 23 | 22 |

experiences in OST activities and programs (and even outside of those programs, in schools, families, and neighborhoods) that can promote both their individual thriving and the well-being of the communities in which they live.

The trajectory of these elements of PYD poses further challenges. In an analysis of eight years of longitudinal data, Lerner and colleagues (2013) found four different groups of trajectories, reflecting optimal levels of PYD and contribution, problematic levels, and trajectories somewhere in between. The four PYD trajectories were quite stable from 5th grade to 12th grade, although the two lowest paths reflected dips in experiencing PYD between 7th and 10th grades. Three of the four contribution paths reflected an increase in contribution, each showing a relatively rapid rise across the middle-school years, and then a relatively flatter, more slowly increasing slope. But for the lowest contributing youth, the trajectory stayed flat from fifth through 12th grades.

All these data show that none of the RISE components are as prominent as they should be for young people and their contexts to thrive. Moreover, the 4-H study shows two other implications for action: (a) it takes particularly impressive experiences for youths' levels of PYD to vary from their levels seen as early as fifth grade, and (b) although contribution for most youth does increase (but for 14%, it does not), almost all the gains occur in middle school, with very small increases or stasis in contribution throughout the high school years.

These data suggest that OST activities and programs must be quite intentional about the relationships, spark-developing activities, and opportunities for contribution they provide young people, and especially the opportunities for voice, sharing power, and making a difference available to high school youth.

## The Central Role of Intentionally Focusing on Relationships in OST Quality

The preceding discussion leads to the reasonable conclusion that being intentional about promoting truly developmental relationships in OST settings is at the core of quality as youth perceive it, at the core of promoting both the 5C's of PYD and the sixth C of contribution, and therefore, at the core of thriving for both young people and the settings they are in.

To this point, we have discussed the "big three" RISE features of OST quality—relationships, interests and sparks, and empowerment—as if they are independent. However, relationship-promoting actions support spark development and empowerment as well. Indeed, the Teen Voice study found that teens high on relational opportunities (which included being in OST activities and programs) were also 86% more likely to be high on having deep personal interests or sparks than youth low on relationships. Further, youth high on sparks were more likely to report having voice and feeling valued for the contributions they can make (Scales et al., 2010). Promoting any of these three strengths is likely to have a positive effect on the other two, but it is relationships that are the glue that cements and integrates all three—relationships, interests and sparks, empowerment—in the deepest promotion of thriving. Or, as Jones and Deutsch (2011) put it in their observational study of an afterschool program, it is a "relational pedagogy," wholly apart from the content of program activities, which is the primary mechanism leading to beneficial outcomes.

Being intentional need not be overly complicated. For example, adults asking just six essential questions of young people could well help youth identify their sparks and enable the adults to be a greater resource to them:

1. What is your spark?
2. When and where do you express it?
3. Who knows your spark?
4. Who nourishes your spark?
5. What gets in your way?
6. How can I help? (Scales et al., 2011).

The very act of intentionally having such conversations reflects all five major actions that reflect a truly "developmental" relationship (per Pekel et al., 2015). It expresses care for young people, provides support, challenges them to grow, shares power with them, and expands their possibilities. Clearly, having such a spark-focused conversation with a young person can promote all three of the features of high-quality OST activities I have discussed, namely, relationships, sparks, and empowerment.

## HOW COACHES CAN BUILD DEVELOPMENTAL ASSETS, RELATIONSHIPS, AND PYD

I have drawn on my experience as a tennis teaching pro and high school tennis coach to also write about how coaches can build developmental assets, relationships, and PYD with their players (Scales, 2011, 2013, 2016). All of these suggestions are readily adaptable to almost any OST setting.

We do not have a profound impact on every high school student in our tennis program, of course, but feedback from our students and parents attests to something amazing going on for many of them, and perhaps, for a majority. They talk about how it was not only fun at the moment and useful for growing as tennis players, but it also gave them guidance for dealing with what life throws at them outside of tennis, helping them grow as persons who always give their best effort, are eager to learn more, and strive to behave with honor and grace through both successes and adversities. All this was articulated beautifully this past girls' season, at our season-ending awards banquet, when one of our graduating seniors shared her thoughts on our program and what it has meant to her:

> You are the best coaches, the nicest people, the most wonderful mentors and role models, and best leaders we could ever have hoped for. You embody what a coach should be. I have dreaded going to practices of other sports but never this one. You are always there to support us and always there to encourage us no matter what.

Even if we are losing by a lot you say to keep working. Tennis isn't just a sport, especially with you. It makes us better people. I could always talk to you about anything. We just show up after school and share whatever, and you always listen. That makes us all feel really good. I wrote [on a college application] about how tennis has changed my life for the better, how healthy it is, and how it's like therapy in sport, and how wonderful that is. So I wanted to say thank you so much for the years you have given us and we are better people because of you.

All coaches, staff, and volunteers in OST activities and programs should be on the receiving end of such a heartfelt and moving thank-you. The more they intentionally try to do the things suggested in Table 3.3, the better their chance of having that satisfaction.

TABLE 3.3.   How Coaches Can Promote Developmental Relationships with Student-Athletes

| Essential action | How coaches can promote |
| --- | --- |
| Express care: Show that you like me and want the best for me. | Get to know students as people beyond the sport.<br>Strive to understand and show sensitivity to others' feelings.<br>Build a positive rapport with students: Listen to them, give encouraging feedback and recognition, and make sure they are having fun.<br>Be dependable: Do what you say you will do, and keep your promises. |
| Provide support: Help me complete tasks and achieve goals. | Be enthusiastic.<br>Emphasize rewarding what students do correctly.<br>Minimize punishment and controlling behaviors.<br>Provide constructive feedback about undesirable performances.<br>Provide advice about how to stay confident and perform under pressure. |
| Challenge growth: Insist that I try to continuously improve. | Focus on self-improvement goals more than competitive outcomes.<br>Teach students that mistakes are necessary to improve.<br>Reward effort as much as outcome.<br>Reward correct performance technique, not just the outcome of a skill.<br>Help students set short-term learning goals that are attainable but require some stretch. |
| Share power: Hear my voice and let me share in making decisions. | Give students choices within rules and safety limits.<br>Allow students to work independently and to take initiative.<br>Ask for students' input on team-related decisions.<br>Emphasize building community and serving one another as teammates and members of the school community. |
| Expand possibility: Expand my horizons and connect me to opportunities. | Create environments that reduce fear of failure, where trying new skills is emotionally safe and enjoyable.<br>Talk about how sport lessons are related to school and life.<br>Model good sportsmanship.<br>Connect students with other coaches, sport camps, and sources of learning. |

*Note:* Reprinted with permission, from Scales, P. C. (2016). The crucial coaching relationship. *Phi Delta Kappan, 97*(8), 19–23.

## CONCLUSION

The core elements of high-quality OST activities and programs are present when OST settings enable youth to RISE, experiencing relational opportunities, the identification and pursuit of their deep personal interests and sparks, and chances to experience empowerment by expressing their voice, power, and influence. These features have a theoretical alignment with the central tenets of self-determination theory—autonomy, belonging, and competence—and have been shown in both cross-sectional and longitudinal studies to predict the 6C's of positive youth development, in the form of competence, confidence, connection, character, and caring, and ultimately, youth contribution. That is, when youth perceive that they experience developmental relationships, pursuit of interests and sparks, and empowerment, both youth and wider society benefit and may be said to be in a recursive cascade in which both are thriving, or, put another way, RISE ↔ THRIVE.

Yet, when youth themselves are asked to describe their environments, only a minority of youth, both in the U.S. and dozens of other countries (e.g., Albania, Bangladesh, China, Kazahkstan, Japan, Jordan, Mexico, Rwanda) report having such developmentally high-quality experiences in their communities and OST activities and programs. The process of enhancing young people's experience of quality need not be onerous or costly; it is rooted in the day-to-day, ongoing relationships young people have with the adults (the focus of this chapter) and peers in those settings.

Relational opportunities, the pursuit of interests and sparks, and empowerment have been shown to be both associated with each other and additive in their developmental power. Therefore, a core focus on intentionally promoting developmental relationships in OST activities and programs—expressing care about and to youth, providing them support, challenging them to grow, sharing power and influence with them, and expanding their possibilities—can also promote their cultivation of deep personal interests or sparks and provide them opportunities to express voice and offer contribution, with the result that both youth and societal thriving are strengthened. Such high-quality relationships and experiences can make a profound difference in the trajectory of development and change a young person's life for the better; multiplied across the globe, they can change the world.

## REFERENCES

Afterschool Alliance. (2014a). *America after 3PM: Afterschool programs in demand.* Washington, DC: Author. Retrieved from http://afterschoolalliance.org/documents/AA3PM-2014/AA3PM_National_Report.pdf

Afterschool Alliance. (2014b). *Taking a deeper dive into afterschool: Positive outcomes and promising practices.* Washington, DC: Author. Retrieved from http://www.afterschoolalliance.org/documents/Deeper_Dive_into_Afterschool.pdf

Balsano, A. B., Phelps, E., Theokas, C., Lerner, J. V., & Lerner, R. M. (2009). Patterns of early adolescents' participation in youth development programs having positive youth development goals. *Journal of Research on Adolescence, 19,* 249–259.

Benson, P. L., & Scales, P. C. (2009). The definition and preliminary measurement of thriving in adolescence. *Journal of Positive Psychology, 4*, 85–104.

Benson, P. L., Scales, P. C., Hamilton, S. F., & Sesma, A. (2006). Positive youth development: Theory, research, and applications. In W. Damon & R. M. Lerner (Eds.), *Handbook of child psychology* (6th ed., pp. 894–941). New York, NY: John Wiley.

Benson, P. L., Scales, P. C., & Syvertsen, A. K. (2011). The contribution of the developmental assets framework to positive youth development theory and practice. In R. M. Lerner, J. V. Lerner, & J. B. Benson (Eds.), *Advances in child development and behavior: Positive youth development research and applications for promoting thriving in adolescence* (pp. 195–228). London, UK: Elsevier.

Blyth, D. A. (2014, October). Reflections, research, and realities of after school. Presentation to 4th Annual University of Virginia Youth-Nex Conference, "Let's Talk After School." Charlottesville, VA. Retrieved from https://www.youtube.com/watch?v=kOT0X0IJsl8

Csikszentmihalyi, M. (1990). *Flow: The psychology of optimal experience*. New York, NY: Harper/Collins.

Damon, W., Menon, J., & Bronk, K. C. (2003). The development of purpose during adolescence. *Applied Developmental Science, 7*, 119–128.

Deutsch, N. L., & Spencer, R. (2009). Capturing the magic: Assessing the quality of youth mentoring relationships. *New Directions for Youth Development, 121*, 47–70.

Eccles, J., & Gootman, J. A. (2002). *Community programs for youth development*. Washington, DC: National Research Council and Institute of Medicine, Board on Children, Youth, and Families, Division of Behavioral and Social Sciences and Education, National Academy Press..

Gambone, M. A., & Connell, J. P. (2004). The community action framework for youth development. *The Prevention Researcher, 11*(2), 17–20.

Gardner, M., Roth, J. L., & Brooks-Gunn, J. (2009). Can after-school programs help level the academic playing field for disadvantaged youth? *Equity Matters*, Research Review No. 4. New York, NY: Campaign for Educational Equity, Teachers College, Columbia University.

Hansen, D. M., Larson, R. W., & Dworkin, J. B. (2003). What adolescents learn in organized youth activities: A survey of self-reported developmental experiences. *Journal of Research on Adolescence, 13*, 25–55.

Hynes, K., & Sanders, F. (2010). The changing landscape of afterschool programs. *Afterschool Matters, 12*, 17–27.

Interagency Working Group on Youth Programs. (2016). *Benefits of service-learning*. Washington, DC: Youth.gov. Retrieved from www.youth.gov/youth-topics/service-learning/what-are-benefits-service-learning

Jelicic, H., Bobek, D. L., Phelps, E., Lerner, R. M., & Lerner, J. V. (2007). Using positive youth development to predict contribution and risk behaviors in early adolescence: Findings from the first two waves of the 4-H Study of Positive Youth Development. *International Journal of Behavioral Development, 31*, 263–273.

Jones, J. J., & Deutsch, N. L. (2011). Relational strategies in after-school settings: How staff–youth relationships support positive development. *Youth & Society, 43*, 1381–1406.

Larson, R. (2000). Toward a psychology of positive youth development. *American Psychologist, 55*, 170–183.

Lerner, R. M., Alberts, A. E., Anderson, P. M., & Dowling, E. M. (2006). On making humans human: Spirituality and the promotion of positive youth development. In E. C. Roehlkepartain, P. E. King, L. Wagener, & P. L. Benson (Eds.), *The handbook of spiritual development in childhood and adolescence* (pp. 60–72). Thousand Oaks, CA: SAGE.

Lerner, R. M., Lerner, J. V., & colleagues. (2013). *The positive development of youth: Comprehensive findings from the 4-H Study of Positive Youth Development*. Medford, MA: Tufts University, Institute for Applied Research in Youth Development.

Lerner, R. M., Lerner, J. V., Almerigi, J. B., Theokas, C., Phelps, E., Gestsdottirand, S., . . . von Eye, A. (2005). Positive youth development, participation in community youth development programs, and community contributions of fifth-grade adolescents: Findings from the first wave of the 4-H Study of Positive Youth Development. *Journal of Early Adolescence, 25,* 17–71.

Li, J., & Julian, M. M. (2012). Developmental relationships as the active ingredient: A unifying working hypothesis of "what works" across intervention settings. *American Journal of Orthopsychiatry, 82,* 157–166.

Malti, T., & Noam, G. G. (2009). A developmental approach to the prevention of adolescent's aggressive behavior and the promotion of resilience. *International Journal of Developmental Science, 3,* 235–246.

McCoy, K., & Wibbelsman, C. (2016). *The teenage body book.* Hobart, NY: Hatherleigh Press.

Noam, G., Malti, T., & Guhn, M. (2012). From clinical-developmental theory to assessment: Holistic student assessment tool. *International Journal of Conflict and Violence, 6,* 201–213.

Pekel, K., Roehlkepartain, E. C., Syvertsen, A. K., & Scales, P. C. (2015). *Don't forget the families: The missing piece in America's effort to help all children succeed.* Minneapolis, MN: Search Institute.

Pittman, K. J., Irby, M., Tolman, J., Yohalem, N., & Ferber, T. (2003). *Preventing problems, promoting development, encouraging engagement: Competing priorities or inseparable goals?* Washington, DC: The Forum for Youth Investment.

Roehlkepartain, E. C. (2007). *Benefits of community-based service-learning.* Minneapolis: Search Institute. Retrieved from http://www.search-institute.org/research/civic-development-service-learning

Roth, J., & Brooks-Gunn, J. (2003). What exactly is a youth development program? Answers from research and practice. *Applied Developmental Science, 7*(2), 94–111.

Ryan, R. M., & Deci, E. L. (2000). Self-determination theory and the facilitation of intrinsic motivation, social development, and well-being. *American Psychologist, 55,* 68–78.

Scales, P. C. (1991). *A portrait of young adolescents in the 1990s.* Minneapolis, MN: Search Institute.

Scales, P. C. (1999). Care and challenge: The sources of student success. *Middle Ground— The Magazine of Middle Level Education, 3,* 21–23.

Scales, P. C. (2010). Finding the student spark: Missed opportunities in school engagement. *Search Institute Insights & Evidence, 5*(1), 1–13.

Scales, P. C. (2011). Build your players' "Developmental Assets"–and chance for success. *ADDvantage Magazine, 35,* 9–11.

Scales, P. C. (2013). Mental toughness tips your players will remember. *ADDvantage Magazine, 36*(9), 17–18, 23.

Scales, P. C. (2016). The crucial coaching relationship. *Phi Delta Kappan, 97*(8), 19–23.

Scales, P. C., Benson, P. L., & Mannes, M. (2006). The contribution to adolescent well-being made by nonfamily adults: An examination of developmental assets as contexts and processes. *Journal of Community Psychology, 34*(4), 401–413.

Scales, P. C., with Benson, P. L., Mannes, M., Hintz, N. R., Roehlkepartain, E. C., & Sullivan, T. K. (2003). *Other people's kids: Social expectations and American adults' involvement with children and adolescents.* New York, NY: Kluwer Academic/Plenum.

Scales, P. C., Benson, P. L., & Roehlkepartain, E. C. (2011). Adolescent thriving: The role of sparks, relationships, and empowerment. *Journal of Youth and Adolescence, 40*(3), 263–77.

Scales, P. C., Benson, P. L., Roehlkepartain, E. C., Sesma, A., & van Dulmen, M. (2006). The role of developmental assets in predicting academic achievement: A longitudinal study. *Journal of Adolescence, 29*(5), 691–708

Scales, P. C., Pekel, K., Syvertsen, A. K., & Roehlkepartain, E. C. (2016). The association of the REACH model of motivation and perseverance with students' school success. Unpublished paper in preparation, Search Institute, Minneapolis, MN.

Scales, P. C., Roehlkepartain, E. C., & Benson, P. L. (2009). *Teen Voice 2009: Tapping the hidden strengths of 15 year olds.* Richfield and Minneapolis, MN: Best Buy Children's Foundation and Search Institute.

Scales, P. C., Roehlkepartain, E. C., & Benson, P. L. (2010). *Teen Voice 2010: Relationships that matter to America's 15-year-olds.* Richfield and Minneapolis, MN: Best Buy Children's Foundation and Search Institute.

Scales, P. C., Roehlkepartain, E. C., & Shramko, M. (2016). Aligning youth development theory, measurement, and practice across cultures and contexts: Lessons from use of the Developmental Assets Profile. *Child Indicators Research,* 1–34 doi: 10.1007/s12187-016-9395-x

Spencer, R., & Rhodes, J. E. (2014). Growth-promoting relationships with children and youth. *New Directions for Youth Development, 144,* 59–72.

Spring, K., Grimm, R., & Dietz, N. (2008). *Community service and service-learning in America's schools.* Washington, DC: Corporation for National and Community Service.

Syvertsen, A. K., Sullivan, T. S., & Wu, C. (2016). *SCA's human impact: Youth development through service to nature.* Minneapoli, MN: Search Institute.

Syvertsen, A. K., Wu, C. Y., Roehlkepartain, E. C., & Scales, P. C. (2015). *Don't forget the families—technical appendix.* Minneapolis, MN: Search Institute.

The Development Relationships Framework. (2016). Minneapolis, MN: Search Institute. Retrieved from www.search-institute.org/research/developmental-relationships

U.S. Census Bureau. (2014). Survey of income and program participation (SIPP), 2008 panel, wave 10 (Table D13. Extracurricular activities of school-age children). Retrieved from https://www.census.gov/programs-surveys/sipp/data/2008-panel/wave-10.html.

Vandell, D. L., Reisner, E. R., & Pierce, K. M. (2007). *Outcomes linked to high-quality afterschool programs: Longitudinal findings from the Study of Promising Afterschool Programs.* Report to the Charles Stewart Mott Foundation. Retrieved from https://

www.researchgate.net/publication/237263207_Outcomes_Linked_to_High-Quality_Afterschool_Programs_Longitudinal_Findings_from_the_Study_of_Promising_Afterschool_Programs.

What Works Clearinghouse. (2008). *What Works Clearinghouse evidence standards for reviewing studies, version 1.0.* Washington, DC: U.S. Department of Education.

# SECTION II

SOCIAL AND CULTURAL DIMENSIONS IN OST

CHAPTER 4

# ACCESS TO OUT-OF-SCHOOL TIME PROGRAMS FOR UNDERSERVED YOUTH

### Nickki Pearce Dawes

One of the early points made in the 2002 National Research Council (NRC) report on Community Programs to Promote Youth Development was that young people who are poor and live in high-risk neighborhoods spend a lot of their time out of school in unsafe and unsupervised settings. The authors also stated that the NRC committee was particularly interested in understanding community programs for young people "who had the greatest need coupled with the fewest resources" (Eccles & Gootman, 2002, p. 5). Growing research interest in community-based youth programs at that time seemed to underscore a belief that such programs could support and complement schools and families in the mission to prepare young people for success in the 21st century (see Chapter 2 for the NRC retrospective). Alas, the report also stated that the authors found "very little research specifically about the kinds of programs that would be particularly appropriate for these disadvantaged and underserved youth" (Eccles & Gootman, 2002, p. 5). Indeed, OST programs have had a place in many communities in the United States for decades. Many emerged in response to the needs of immigrants and families with low incomes who needed a safe space for youth to be when parents were at

*The Growing Out-of-School Time Field: Past, Present, and Future,*
pages 47–60.
Copyright © 2018 by Information Age Publishing

work during nonschool hours (Halpern, 2003). However, at the time of the NRC report, research on this context was just developing steam, particularly regarding the experience of underserved young people. In this chapter, underserved refers to when a group of people are not getting the type or amount of service and support they need. For example, generally speaking, a well-served community/group of youth would have access to appropriate medical health and dental care, good schools, and OST programs. This term would capture the problem of children and adolescents who do not have adequate access to enriching out-of-school time activities because the demand for programs that fits the needs of the youth is more than the available programs. Of course, there are many social, cultural, and economic forces that contribute to the problems of underserved youth in general, and their access to OST programs specifically. Indeed, the position and ideas are presented in full acknowledgment of the structural and institutional forces on adolescent lives and opportunities to thrive. Additionally, youth from diverse backgrounds (i.e., race/ethnicity, gender, urban/rural) are impacted by these forces. In this chapter, with the focus on the impact of family engagement on access, the experience of adolescent boys of color and LGBTQ youth, I highlight issues and two demographic groups that illustrate the value and potential impact of OST program since the NRC was published.

Today, OST programs still serve as important settings that complement the home and school contexts in fostering positive youth development. In 2014, Afterschool Alliance published its third report on the participation trends. It showed that more children have access to afterschool programs than they did in 2009 (8.4 to 10.2 million) but also that there remains a high unmet need for access to OST programs and that children from low-income households are still more likely to participate in available programs (see chapter 15 in this book). The demand for access is particularly high among children from low-income households. Thus, the good news is that since the NRC report was released, stakeholders' (i.e., families, schools) interest in OST programs has remained strong, and access has improved (Eccles & Gootman, 2002). However, there are still barriers limiting access by all the young people who could benefit. There needs to be a continued focus on understanding what promotes access.

## WHAT YOUNG PEOPLE GAIN FROM ACCESS

Before further discussion on factors that shape access, it is important to address the question: access to what? I join scholars Heath (2000), Halpern (2003), and Nocon and Cole (2006), who draw attention to OST programs as informal and flexible learning spaces that have the potential to support the diverse developmental needs of youth. In response to pressure to extend instruction time on academic subjects, like reading and math, some OST programs have become extensions of the regular school day (e.g., Lauer et al., 2006). While the need to support students who are underachieving in core subjects is crucial, the development of OST programs as just an extension of the school day is a lost opportunity for all kids, but particularly for underserved youth. Halpern (2002) put it this way:

> Low and moderate-income children deserve the same access to enriching organized activities as their more advantaged peers. Yet low-income children, as all children, need space—social as much as physical space—to develop their own thoughts, to daydream and reflect; to dabble and dawdle; to pretend, try on, and rehearse different roles and identities; to learn friendship and to learn how to handle interpersonal conflict; to rest and be quiet; and not least to have fun and take risks of their own design and choosing. (p. 206)

For underserved youth, OST programs can be powerful settings that indirectly and directly advance academic growth as well as character development. From an academic perspective, access to OST programs holds the promise for offering youth opportunities to try new skills and to learn from wins and losses in a low-stakes setting. By this I mean that projects and activities in OST are not graded, and there is an absence of punitive feedback. These opportunities are invaluable for helping youth develop self-efficacy and confidence in their ability to succeed in their academic and nonacademic pursuits.

Unfortunately, many schools respond to the challenge to meet dictated standards for their students' aggregate performance by investing significant time and resources on teaching styles and practices that may leave some students marginalized academically. In the end, if a student's style and history of learning varies from the style being used or validated in the classroom, the likelihood that the student will get adequate opportunities to feel competence and accomplished academically is diminished. Furthermore, in some cases, limited resources or policy decisions may limit opportunities to explore art, music, and other interests outside of the required academic subjects. Students with athletic talent from low-income families may not have the resources to participate in sports leagues that could support the development of their talent, which means that they have to navigate additional barriers to achieving confidence, competence, and a sense of accomplishment.

Another perspective involves youth's socioemotional development via participation in OST programs. For many youth, access to OST programs promises a refuge. That is, in some cases, time in OST may be only opportunities they get to hang out with their peers in informal ways. This opportunity may be especially consequential for boys because, during the school day, boys are expected to keep hands and feet to themselves, wait their turn, and generally stay quiet. In less structured settings, their natural urges to be competitive and physical with each other are likely to emerge. A good quality OST program can provide the right atmosphere for them to participate in those types of interaction in safe and constructive ways. Furthermore, these opportunities or developmentally supportive environments can be helpful for sustaining youths' perseverance in OST program activities and back in the classroom.

In sum, in discussions about access, it is critical to think about what types of experiences youth are getting access to in OST programs. If the focus of activities is primarily on student advancement in the primary academic subjects (e.g., math scores) with little focus on the climate and opportunity to participate in fun, nonacademic activities, then the full developmental impact youth could obtain may be lost.

## BARRIERS AND FACILITATORS OF ACCESS

Although many students will likely turn away from an OST context that is essentially an extension of the regular school day, another, perhaps bigger concern is persistent barriers that serve to restrict initial access to programs. Some of the barriers are well known, but others, such as family engagement, have received less attention. It is important to restate that the number of children with access to OST shows an upward trajectory (Afterschool Alliance, 2014). It will take intentional efforts by program staff and policymakers to continue this trend, particularly for underserved youth who often face unique obstacles to participation.

### Family Engagement

Family involvement in shaping youth access to and participation in OST programs has been getting increased attention from researchers in the field since the publication of the NRC report in 2002 (e.g., Kreider & Raghupathy, 2010; Larson, Pearce, Sullivan, & Jarrett, 2007; Simpkins, Vest, Dawes, & Neuman, 2008; Simpkins, Vest, & Price, 2011). There is general consensus in the literature that family engagement supports children's educational and developmental outcomes (Hoover-Dempsey & Sandler, 1997; Kreider & Raghupathy, 2010). In the case of OST programs, parents and caregivers who are connected to their child's school or program can leverage this relationship to support their attendance and reiterate program values and the benefits of adhering to them. Additionally, connected family members could experience more opportunities to see their children showcasing their talent or demonstrating character development via their contribution to projects. Given the importance of family engagement, there is a long history of interest in learning about what factors support it. An important contribution in the field came from Hoover-Dempsey and Sandler (1997), who developed a model conceptualizing the factors that shape caregiver's decisions about involvement in school contexts that is applicable to the OST contexts as well. Hoover-Dempsey and Sandler presented three major factors as integral to a parent's decision-making process about basic involvement.

First, their beliefs about their role in supporting their children's education can impact parents' involvement. There is a range in parents of understanding or familiarity with OST programs, which has an influence on their involvement. For a variety of reasons, many caregivers are not familiar with the OST landscape in their community and, subsequently if and how their involvement is needed to support their child's interest and participation. For many parents, OST programs exist to fill a need that caregivers cannot provide because of work or other factors. Thus, the idea that their involvement is important for the success of their child may not be at the forefront of their minds.

The second factor in the model involves parents' sense of efficacy for helping their children succeed in school. In the context of OST, many caregivers may believe that they do not have the requisite educational background or practical experience that they could transfer to supporting their children. However, some OST programs might be uniquely situated to benefit from the wide range of skills and interests many parents have (e.g., arts and crafts; event planning). The third factor Hoover-Dempsey and Sandler (1997) posited as central to caregivers' involvement is specific opportunities, requests, and demands for them to participate. OST programs may be well suited to take advantage of their flexible structure to engage caregivers, but the mechanisms for communicating to parents effectively needs to be established. For example, some OST programs schedule events to showcase children's talent, celebrate community traditions (e.g., public holidays), and so forth. Asking parents to attend and participate in programming is one strategy some programs use to foster family engagement (e.g., Kreider & Raghupathy, 2010).

While more research is needed in this area, there are some basic steps programs could take to foster family engagement based on our existing understanding of what shapes parent involvement. First, programs can schedule orientation sessions to educate caregivers about the program goals and ways that family members can be involved. Additionally, this orientation could also aim to give youth tools they can use to communicate about the overall mission of the program and their individual interests and goals for participating in the OST program. Importantly, programs can also work to develop and communicate a climate that is welcoming to all families. This might involve doing training or workshops to enhance cultural awareness and learn about perspectives and needs of families with varied ethnic and socioeconomic backgrounds. Of course, there are challenging barriers (e.g., language barriers or limited time) to implementing even the most innovative family engagement initiative. However, in the end, the work to foster and support positive developmental outcomes is worth it.

## Structural Forces

Some of the obstacles to access facing young people are structural or institutional (e.g., Beck, 1999), which, on the bright side, suggests that they could be adjusted via policy change. In this context, structural forces are practices, policies, and attitudes that permeate OST programs. One factor is the pay-to-play system that characterizes most OST programs, in that a fee is charged for access to programming. This fee can be prohibitive for many families, especially in cases where two or more children want to participate. The location of OST activities off school campuses is also a structural factor that can limit young people's access to a wider range of options that match their interest. This issue may be elevated in communities where there are limited OST programs offered on school campuses due to insufficient resources or infrastructure. For instance, in some schools, there are limited slots on sports teams for all youth who may be interested. This may be particularly relevant for older adolescents. In bigger schools, there is more competition, which means youth have to be highly skilled to earn a position on teams. This reality may be particularly challenging for low-income youth who are competing with youth who have had the resources to be involved in skill development activity since early childhood.

Transportation is a longstanding challenge that impacts access to community-based programs. For many students, the OST program that fits best with their interests and talent (e.g., performing arts) is based in the community (i.e. not on the school campus). Young people from families who do not have the resources to arrange for transportation to these programs are essentially shut out from the opportunity to participate in OST programs that may be positioned to support their unique developmental needs. Fortunately, some OST programs offer transportation, but this practice is also dependent on the investment of resources by agencies, private and public, that are committed to helping young people get access to safe and constructive ways to spend their time at the end of the school day. Overall, these are some of the longstanding barriers to access, but since the NRC report was written more attention has been focused on issue of improving access and participation. More research is needed that focuses on both individual and structural practices that shape participation.

From a practice perspective, and with the experience of underserved youth in mind, there are a few strategies that may enhance access. First, programs could develop or adopt a flexible programming structure. This would be particularly relevant to older adolescents whose participation pattern may not be seamless because of environmental factors outside of their control. For example, sometimes family demands, such as taking care of a younger sibling, make it hard for youth to attend a program consistently every day or week. Programs could be structured so that youth can start at different time points in a semester and also rejoin easily if they need to discontinue participation for a period of time. This open-door policy, or flexible programming, will open access for youth who need the flexibility in order to manage their busy and sometimes unpredictable lives (Fashola, 2003). These youths would benefit from having the latitude to rejoin when they are ready. In my research, youth have shared how meaningful it was to them that the program staff and youth welcomed them back when they returned after a break from the program due to a family crisis that prevented them from attending consistently. The typical youth can pick up on signs that suggest they are being judged for not attending consistently.

A flexible programming structure might set off alarm bells for those who believe that such a style would jeopardize developmental growth because youth are not able sustain participation on a task or project. To address this challenge, a diverse set of programs need to be implemented and highlighted. Some programs could be designed such that once-per-week attendance is sufficient for accomplishing the goals of the program. However, others could be designed or modified such that daily attendance is not required to complete all projects. Research suggests that youth are more likely to benefit the longer they stay involved in programs (Roth, Malone, & Brooks-Gunn, 2010), but to date nothing suggest that the length of time has to be exactly the same for all youth. Indeed, the dosage question that gets discussed in literature on OST programs needs appropriate contextualization. Questions about dosage and evaluation of impact should be tailored to specific programs. The amount of time youth need to attend a sports or arts program, for example, to achieve important outcomes like self-confidence or a sense of accomplishment will vary. Additionally, it should be acknowledged that not all youth will get the identical benefits from participation. Adopting a developmental perspective regarding assessment or evaluation of youth outcomes seems crucial. For instance, a model where youth outcomes are assessed on both short-term- and long-term-based metrics might be appropriate. Consequently, during the first-year, a youth's attendance might be spotty, and gains on a particular metric might not be significant. However, because the youth perceived the program as open and welcoming, they returned after their scheduled settled or the problem in their lives resolved (e.g., temporary homelessness).

Opportunities for diverse contributions are another feature of OST programs that may be particularly relevant for addressing access for underserved youth for marginalized groups. Youth will respond positively to a setting that legitimizes their contribution, whatever form it takes. This approach should not to be mistaken for a program culture where there are no rules or standards. Rather, the idea is that youth from diverse backgrounds will have different lenses through which to look at the world, interpret information, and engage with others. OST programs tend to be attractive to youth because they value and welcome the diverse ways they can contribute. This can be life-changing for some youth because in other learning contexts, what they bring to the table may not have been valued. Nolen, Horn, and Ward (2015) provided a rich example of how students' experience in their core classes, such as math, can either get "access to positions as mathematicians" or not based on the classroom norms and or teacher practices. Students had access to positions as "knowers" or "receivers." With some changes in practices, "new mathematical identities became available, allowing previously marginalized students (e.g., students who may not know the correct answer but have a good-sense making question) to participate productively in the classroom" (Nolen et al., 2015, p. 240). This example from the school context illustrates the idea that settings like OST programs can provide access to learning identities that many youth do not have in the traditional school day. One way that programs can be personally meaningful involved how they to work to consider the cultural and developmental needs of the youth children and youth participants.

As mentioned above, research on the unique experience of underserved youth in community-based OST programs was just emerging at the publication of the NRC report. Although programs serving this particular group of youth have a long history in many communities in the U.S., the research has definitely started to catch up in the last couple decades (e.g., Bohnert, Richards, Kolmodin, & Lakin, 2008; Dotterer, McHale, & Crouter, 2007) and no doubt will provide useful guides as programs continue to develop with underserved youth in mind. Some research groups (e.g., Larson et al., 2007) have taken the approach of focusing on programs with a history of attracting and engaging underserved youth, which has helped to fill the gap in research on this population. In the next section, I present illustrative examples that highlight how some existing OST programs can and do focus on the needs of underserved youth.

## ENHANCING ACCESS: ILLUSTRATIONS

There are programs that tailor their focus and activities with the goal of giving vulnerable youth access to positive developmental experiences. Examples include those that provide fine arts enrichment to underserved urban youth, those that utilize rites of passage programming to meet the needs of African American boys, and those programs that are tailored to the needs of LGBTQ youth.

### Urban Youth and African American Boys

Some programs are particularly in tune with challenges faced by youth living in urban underserved communities and subsequently develop their programming to fit their context. For instance, many youth attend schools where arts education is a small part of the curriculum or not offered at all (e.g., Kraehe, Acuff, & Travis, 2016). Therefore, for many poor youth, what could have been a passion or outlet for creativity and self-expression would be lost were it not for the access they had to arts-based OST programs. Indeed, OST programs that offer these opportunities are in effect proving enrichment in academic and socioemotional domains that students in higher income brackets are getting during the regular school day. To provide this access, one practice has been to identify assets in a major city that could be leveraged to support the needs of youth. For instance, OST programs in major cities like Chicago have partnered with art museums to offer internships and skills development classes to low-income urban youth. These partnerships facilitate youth's exploration of art in the context of their neighborhoods and lives as well as skill development (artistic and general) that can be parlayed into the market force. Aside from marketable skills and competences, access to OST programs can provide youth with an invaluable outlet for creativity and self-expression. They can learn about what it takes to develop ideas and bring them to reality via a work of art (e.g., Prettyman & Gargarella, 2012). They also learn to persevere in the face of setbacks, such as a when a project does not go as planned (e.g., Larson & Walker, 2006). Additionally, youth could get the opportunity to be among like-minded students interested in arts. Adolescents desire opportunities for experience a sense of belonging and outlets for self-expression (Ruck, Abromvitch, & Keating, 1998; Steinberg & Morris, 2001).

Another example comes from urban community activism programs in the city of Boston. In these programs, the focus of adult staff members is to scaffold youths' development of their skills and talents. Most youth enter the program with very little experience in the core activities of the program, but the program assigns newcomers with manageable tasks that serve to awaken their interest and develop skills. All contributions are welcome and youth are given constructive feedback on how to build on their current skill set. The goal of this approach is to let youth know that whatever skill, experience, and interest they bring to the table it is welcome. But, importantly, the growth mindset and climate that permeates the setting guarantees that participating youth will grow (Dawes, Pollack, & Gaza Sada, in press). Additionally, these programs focus heavily on creating opportunities for youth to earn money or work experience (e.g., paid summer internships). The adult staff understand that many youth who might be interested in accessing program also need to earn money in order to contribute to family finances.

African American boys are another group of youth who tend to be underserved and can benefit from the capacity of OST programs to tailor programming. Woodland (2008) discussed how OST programs can be well suited to "merge Black culture with the core elements...allowing programs to develop instructional strategies that resemble and capitalize on the cultural strengths of young Black males" (p. 552). Drawing on the work of Gloria Ladson-Billings (1995), he explains that to do this work, OST staff needs to have an "unconditional belief in the ability of children of color, specifically young Black males." He argues that a culturally relevant context must be created. Rites of passage (ROP) programming is one strategy used to help youth contextualize their experience within society. ROP programs are geared specifically for Black boys (Woodland, 2008) and thus are able to leverage the traditions and practices of boys' families and communities in ways that would be challenging in the typical classroom or school setting. These programs are intentional about teaching youth about African cultural practices that counter the pervasive focus and prioritizing of Eurocentric customs. The mission of ROP programs is to promote positive youth development by drawing attention to aspects of their cultural heritage that have served as protective forces for generations. Another goal is to help young people identify strengths in their cultural practices that are sometimes diminished in the mainstream academic curriculum of public schools. This strategy of empowerment and acceptance is heralded by scholars who have studied the experience of young men of color (e.g., Gilgoff & Ginwright, 2015).

In sum, time and resource limitations in many underserved, urban public schools serve to limit the capacity for them to scaffold youths' learning experiences by creating differentiated and empowering educational outlets. Some urban OST programs are able to tailor their programming to the needs of the underserved population they serve and have been successful at attracting youth's interest and sustaining their engagement. Youth will gravitate to settings where programming is personally meaningful or relevant to their current and aspirational, educational, social, and economic status (Dawes & Larson, 2011; Greene, Lee, Constance, & Hynes, 2013).

### LGBTQ Identified Youth

A recent policy report by SRCD states that young people are coming out in larger numbers and at younger ages (Russell, Kosciw, Horn, & Saewyc, 2010). In efforts to provide the necessary support for this population, legislation was proposed to address problems with discrimination and barriers to young people getting access to positive educational experience. The report acknowledged the need for more research about the risks and protective factors shaping the educational experience of LGBTQ youth. Some of this work might focus on the context of OST programs and their role in support LGBTQ youth. Community-based programs have long provided a support for the positive social and psychological development of LGBTQ youth (Allen, Hammack, & Himes, 2012).

According to Allen et al. (2012), the range of support provided to youth is unmatched in other settings. For instance, OST programs provide access to facilitated peer support groups run by supportive nonparental adults. Research shows that empathic peer support is essential for healthy self-esteem—hence the importance of OST programs where young people have access to accepting peers and nonparental adults who understand the types of supports they need to thrive. Additionally, programs offer educational sessions on topics like coming out, dealing with homophobia, and dating and romance. The authors stress that community-based OST programs may be well-suited to support the needs of LGBTQ youth because many are not as burdened by school policies that serve to restrict the range and depth of attention school faculty and staff can give to the needs of marginalized youth.

Some challenges facing community-based programs for LGBTQ young people include the reality that many programs are outside an adolescent's neighborhood (Allen et al., 2012), which means that lack of transportation and time restraints will limit their access. Additionally, because many are part of adult programs, an important concern is how well the programming meets the developmental needs of early and late adolescents. Each age group has its unique needs in terms of the support they require to thrive. In light of these challenges, there are some well-marked avenues for changes that could positively affect access.

First, staff and policymakers could engage in training and individual development to better understand the systemic context within which LGBTQ youth are living. Also, youth-serving organizations and practitioners can seek partnerships with community-based LGBTQ youth-serving organizations to identify and develop opportunities for LGBTQ youth that will advance their identity development. Partnering with LGBTQ programs could widen the capacity of programs without needing to revamp or invest/redirect limited resources. Partnerships also might support dialogue between practitioners and agencies that can provide an ongoing outlet/support infrastructure. Finally, practitioners should aim to develop their competence at articulating their knowledge and understanding of the micro- and macro-level forces affecting the lived experiences of youth, especially those with intersecting identities. For example, the family and school climate can impact youth experience of OST programs. Program practitioners should be open and ready to build relationships with family members as appropriate and be prepared to help build bridges to families, if appropriate (Ryan, Russell, Huebner, Diaz, & Sanchez, 2010).

## CONCLUSIONS AND FUTURE STEPS

This chapter focused on the topic of access to OST programs for underserved youth. In the approximately 20 years since the publication of the NRC report, access to OST programs has improved. This trend is encouraging and bodes well for the many youth who still need access to constructive OST programs in their communities. The chapter presented examples of current practices that seem to have a positive impact on youth's perceptions of the program and their access. The field stands on the shoulders of practitioners and program administrators who interface with our children and oversee the operation of programs. To support the continued upward trend in access by underserved youth, policymakers responsible for practitioner training should to look for ways to support the growth of youth workers by borrowing from existing practices in other disciples such as education. Nolen and colleagues (2015) writes about a process called "guided participation" (p. 238), which could help staff develop their identities as youth workers. Additionally, information sharing among programs that are successful should be supported. Agencies should try to support programs to connect with each other. Perhaps these exchanges are already occurring in the OST field. If so, more should be done to publicize and study the process.

Next steps for the research sector could include broadening the theoretical perspectives that we use to guide the development of research questions and analyses of relationships we observe in the various OST programs that serve underserved youth. For example, the concept of situating motivation that Nolen and colleagues (2015) have put forth seems well suited for conceptualizing how various personal and contextual factors work in unique and interrelated ways to determine diverse adolescents experience with OST programs. Another research implication involves the issue of how programs are using research to guide program planning and daily implementation of program elements. There has been an increase in the number of research studies that explore the outcomes for participants in OST programs. But are programs using these studies? Seeking answers to these questions would contribute to shaping the trajectory of research development and dissemination. Similarly, a continued focus on methods that facilitates learning more about the processes that support developmental outcomes is critical. Qualitative or mixed methods research holds the promise of helping us to understand the forces behind the relationships that we find among variables we study. For example, there are many sociocultural issues that need close study to get at deep meaning so that real, positive, sustainable change can be promoted in the context of OST programs.

In sum, the promise of OST programs to impact the developmental needs of youth with multiple intersecting identities makes it one of the most important, yet understudied contexts in which many young people spend significant amounts of their time. In this chapter, I highlighted how OST programs serve urban youth, adolescent boys of color, and LGBTQ youth. It is not a stretch of the imagination to think of a program that is uniquely situated to support the African American, LGBTQ male in a rural community. The field faces the twin challenge of addressing multiple interrelated factors that can influence access to OST programs and continuing to examine and capitalize on the opportunities for OST programs to be tailored to meet the developmental needs of the whole child.

## REFERENCES

Afterschool Alliance. (2014). *America after 3 PM: Afterschool programs in demand.* Washington, DC: Author. Retrieved from http://afterschoolalliance.org/documents/AA3PM-2014/AA3PM_National_Report.pdf

Allen, K. D., Hammack, P. L., & Himes, H. L. (2012). Analysis of LGBTQ youth community-based programs in the United States. *Journal of Homosexuality, 59*(9), 1289–1306. doi: http://dx.doi.org/10.1080/00918369.2012.720529

Beck, E. L. (1999). Prevention and intervention programming: Lessons from an afterschool program. *The Urban Review, 31*(1), 107–124.

Bohnert, A. M., Richards, M. H., Kolmodin, K. E., & Lakin, B. L. (2008). Young urban African American adolescents' experience of discretionary time activities. *Journal of Research on Adolescence, 18*(3), 517–539.

Dawes, N. P., & Larson, R. W. (2011). Engaging adolescents in organized youth programs: An analysis of individual and contextual factors. *Developmental Psychology, 47,* 259–269

Dawes, N. P., Pollack, S., & Gaza Sada, G. (in press). Key components of engaging afterschool programs for children and adolescents. *Advances in Child and Family Policy & Practice.*

Dotterer, A. M., McHale, S. M., & Crouter, A. C. (2007). Implications of out-of-school activities for school engagement in African American adolescents. *Journal of Youth and Adolescence, 36,* 391–401. doi: 10.1007/s10964-006-9161-3

Eccles, J., & Gootman, J. A. (2002). *Community programs to promote youth development.* Washington, DC: National Research Council and Institute of Medicine, Board on Children, Youth, and Families, Division of Behavioral and Social Sciences and Education, National Academy Press.

Fashola, O. S. (2003). Developing the talents of African American male students during the non-school hours. *Urban Education, 38,* 389–430.

Fredricks, J. A., & Eccles, J. S. (2006). Is extracurricular participation associated with beneficial outcomes? Concurrent and longitudinal relations. *Developmental Psychology*, *42*(4), 698.

Gilgoff, J., & Ginwright, S. (2015). Toward more equitable outcomes: A research synthesis on out-of-school time work with boys and young men of color. *Afterschool Matters*, *21*, 11– 19.

Greene, K. M., Lee, B., Constance, N., & Hynes, K. (2013). Examining youth and program predictors of engagement in out-of-school time programs. *Journal of Youth and Adolescence*, *42*(10), 1557–1572. doi: 10.1007/s10964-012-9814-3

Halpern, R. (2002). A different kind of child development institution: The history of afterschool programs for low-income children. *Teachers College Record*, *104*(2), 178–211.

Halpern, R. (2003). *Making play work: The promise of afterschool programs for low-income children.* New York, NY: Teachers College Press.

Heath, S. B. (2000). Making learning work. *Afterschool Matters*, *1*(1), 33-45.

Hoover-Dempsey, K. V., & Sandler, H. M. (1997). Why do parents become involved in their children's education? *Review of Educational Research*, *67*(1), 3–42.

Kraehe, A. M., Acuff, J. B., & Travis, S. (2016). Equity, the arts, and urban education: A review. *Urban Review*, *48*, 220–224. doi:10.1007/s11256-016-0352-2

Kreider, H., & Raghupathy, S. (2010). Engaging families in Boys & Girls Clubs: An evaluation of the Family PLUS pilot initiative. *School Community Journal*, *20*(2), 9.

Ladson-Billings, G. (1995). Toward a theory of culturally relevant pedagogy. *American Educational Research Journal*, *32*, 465–491.

Larson, R. W., Pearce, N., Sullivan, P. J., & Jarrett, R. L. (2007). Participation in youth programs as a catalyst for negotiation of family autonomy with connection. *Journal of Youth and Adolescence*, *36*(1), 31. doi: 10.1007/s10964-006-9133-7

Larson, R. W., & Walker, K. C. (2006). Learning about the "real world" in an urban arts youth program. *Journal of Adolescent Research*, *21*(3), 244–268.

Lauer, P. A., Akiba, M., Wilkerson, S. B., Apthorp, H. S., Snow, D., & Martin-Glenn, M. L. (2006). Out-of-school-time programs: A meta-analysis of effects for at-risk students. *Review of Educational Research*, *76*(2), 275–313.

Nocon, H., & Cole, M. (2006). School's invasion of "after-school": Colonization, rationalization, or expansion of access? *Counterpoints*, *249*, 99–121. Retrieved from http://www.jstor.org/stable/42979591

Nolen, S. B., Horn, I. S., & Ward, C. J. (2015). Situating motivation. *Educational Psychologist*, *50*(3), 234–247. doi:10.1080/00461520.2015.1075399

Prettyman, S. S., & Gargarella, E. (2012). The power of art to develop artists and activists. *International Journal of Education & the Arts*, *14*(SI 2.7). Retrieved from http://www.ijea.org/v14si2/

Roth, J. L., Malone, L. M., & Brooks-Gunn, J. (2010). Does the amount of participation in afterschool programs relate to developmental outcomes? A review of the literature. *American Journal of Community Psychology*, *45*(3–4), 310–324.

Ruck, M. D, Abromvitch, R., & Keating, D. O. (1998). Children's understanding of rights: Balancing nurturance and self-determination. *Child Development*, *64*, 404–417.

Russell, S. T., Kosciw, J., Horn, S., & Saewyc, E. (2010). Safe schools policy for LGBTQ students. *Society for Research in Child Development*, *24*(4), 1–25..

Ryan, C., Russell, S. T., Huebner, D., Diaz, R., & Sanchez, J. (2010). Family acceptance in adolescence and the health of LGBT young adults. *Journal of Child and Adolescent Psychiatric Nursing, 23*, 205–213.

Simpkins, S. D., Vest, A. E., Dawes, N. P., & Neuman, K. I. (2010). Dynamic relations between parents' behaviors and children's motivational beliefs in sports and music. *Parenting: Science and Practice, 10*(2), 97–118.

Simpkins, S. D., Vest, A. E., & Price, C. D. (2011). Intergenerational continuity and discontinuity in Mexican-origin youths' participation in organized activities: Insights from mixed-methods. *Journal of Family Psychology, 25*(6), 814.

Steinberg, L., & Morris, A. S. (2001). Adolescent development. *Annual Review of Psychology, 52*(1), 83–110.

Woodland, M. H. (2008). Whatcha doin' after school? A review of the literature on the influence of after-school programs on young Black males. *Urban Education, 43*(5), 537–560.

CHAPTER 5

# RESPONDING TO SHIFTING DEMOGRAPHIC CONTEXTS

Judith Cruzado-Guerrero and Gilda Martinez-Alba

The population of the United States is becoming more diverse each year. The demographic shifts that are occurring in the nation are evident. Just from 1980 to 2015, we saw the Caucasian population decrease from 80% to 63%, while the Latino population went up from 6% to 17%; the Asian population rose from 2% to 8%, and the African American population increased from 12% to 13%. As of 2015, there were four majority-minority states: California, Hawaii, New Mexico, and Texas (Teixeira, Frey, & Griffin, 2015). These changes have influenced the demographics in school communities, and therefore, opportunities and resources for students in out-of-school time (OST) (see chapters 2 and 4 in this book for examples of demographic impacts on OST pertaining to access, engagement, quality, and professional capacity building among youth-serving professionals). This chapter will discuss the impact of demographic shifts in student populations within OST contexts, with specific attention to English language learners (ELL).

*The Growing Out-of-School Time Field: Past, Present, and Future,*
pages 61–70.
Copyright © 2018 by Information Age Publishing
All rights of reproduction in any form reserved.

## THE SHIFTING DEMOGRAPHICS
## IN OST SETTINGS: BACKGROUND

ELLs are students who are learning English as their second language. These students are culturally and linguistically diverse and may be immigrants, refugees, or born in the United States. Due to the diverse characteristics of this population, we must understand the demographic shifts in schools across the United States. Over the past 20 years, there has been a significant increase in the number of ELL students in the United States. In 2015, there were approximately 4.8 million ELL students (Office of English Language Acquisition, 2017). A majority of the states with the highest ELL populations are in the Western part of the United States. Alaska, California, Colorado, Nevada, New Mexico, Texas, and Washington DC have 10% or more of ELL students out of their total student populations, with California having the highest percentage at 22.7%. There are 17 states with 6–10% of ELL students, followed by 13 states with 3–6%, and only 14 with less than 3%. The states with the second highest percentage (between 6 and 10%) are spread out throughout the United States (from West to East: Hawaii, Washington, Oregon, Arizona, Kansas, Oklahoma, Minnesota, Illinois, Arkansas, Florida, North Carolina, Virginia, Maryland, Delaware, New York, Rhode Island, and Massachusetts). Kansas, which might not have been considered to have a significantly rising ELL population, has had the largest increase with 4.6% (National Center for Education Statistics, 2016). These statistics demonstrate that working with ELL students and their families is a nationwide matter in most areas, and the numbers are on an upward rise.

The changes in ELL demographics directly impact OST enrollments and the nature of these programs (Bhattacharya & Quiroga, 2011). Per the Afterschool Alliance (2012), 14% of all afterschool participants are ELL students. However, the enrollment data for ELL students participating in OST programs is difficult to report due to the diversity of this population and the lack of information about their language proficiency. Bhattacharya and Quiroga (2011) suggest that OST programs must have access to students' English language assessment data to accurately identify ELLs, assess their language proficiency levels, and address their language needs. OST programs could also provide ELLs academic support while they are learning English. Often, ELL students show academic achievement gaps in mathematics and reading compared to non-ELL students at all socioeconomic levels (Fry, 2007; Garcia & Frede, 2010).

Aside from language and academic challenges, ELL students who have an immigrant or refugee status may face unique hurdles in their academic journey, such as exclusion from the mainstream population, poverty, separation from their family, unfamiliarity with the new language and culture, and the need to establish their identity in a new country (Harris, 2004). It is important to note that the number of ELL children of immigrant status is also changing. In 2012–2013, children of immigrant families represented 25% of the young population. Ninety four percent of these children were born in the United States and 52% of their parents were classified as ELLs (Park, McHugh, & Katsiaficas, 2016). These changes in demographics provide OST programs with opportunities to address the strengths and needs of this unique diverse population of ELLs. Bhattacharya and Quiroga (2011) remind us that OST programs must not just focus on providing English and academic support to ELL students, but also to address their cultural, emotional, and social needs and strengths. However, many OST programs are not equipped to serve ELLs due to their lack of resources, personnel, and professional development opportunities to learn more about how to support these students (Holstead & Doll, 2015).

ELL students may also encounter other challenges if they live in rural settings and do not have access to OST programs. The ELL families in rural communities may struggle with similar life circumstances as other families in rural contexts, such as high levels of poverty, lower wages, and lower educational levels (Afterschool Alliance, 2016; Budge, 2006). Despite these challenges, 1.2 million children in rural communities participate in afterschool programs, but there are still 39% who are unable to participate due to accessibility (Afterschool Alliance, 2016). The families in rural communities also face other barriers to OST access, such as not being able to afford the programs or not finding information about available programs (Afterschool Alliance, 2016). The percentage of ELL students is not often reported in surveys. Nonetheless, the Afterschool Alliance's rural survey accounts for an unmet demand for afterschool programs among 51% of rural Hispanic families who reported that they would enroll their children if there were programs accessible to them. Although we must not assume that all Hispanic students are ELLs or that this is the only ethnic group represented in rural communities, we do know that the top language spoken by ELL students is Spanish in at least 28 states across the United States (Migration Policy Institute, 2015). It is important to remember that other states with OST rural and/or urban programs may have ELL students who represent other cultural and linguistically diverse backgrounds. States with other top languages include Vermont (Nepali), Maine (Somali), and Montana (German) (Migration Policy Institute, 2015).

## OST AS A DEVELOPMENTAL SETTING FOR ELL POPULATIONS

Learning another language takes time, and there are factors that may impact the language development of ELL students. OST settings could provide the time and support needed to increase social and academic language. In addition, learning a new culture could be a difficult and stressful transition for ELLs (Bhattacharya & Quiroga, 2011; Gast, Okamoto, & Feldman, 2017). OST programs support this journey by taking a holistic and culturally responsive approach in their program design (Bhattacharya & Quiroga, 2011). A holistic approach integrates and validates the strengths of ELL students to meet their specific needs in a culturally responsive manner (see e.g., Quality English Learner Principles developed by California Tomorrow (2003) as cited in Bhattacharya & Quiroga, 2011) to improve programmatic practices). These principles focus on (a) knowing the strengths and needs of ELL students, (b) providing cultural support to families by sharing resources and information about the school and community, (c) building cross-cultural leadership skills among students by connecting them with other English speaking students, (d) supporting the language development of ELLs using best practices, (e) creating a safe space and affirming environment in which ELLs feel they could practice their language skills, (f) promoting the home culture and language for healthy identity development, and (g) customizing the program with the information learned about the ELLs to meet their specific needs (California Tomorrow, 2003 as cited in Bhattacharya & Quiroga, 2011).

Getting to know the linguistic and cultural backgrounds of ELLs is important to customize the language and provide academic, social, and emotional support OST students need to succeed in school. For ELL students to succeed in OST programs, they need language instruction, time to practice the language (reading, writing, listening, and speaking), and assistance with vocabulary they encounter in their school subjects (Afterschool Alliance, 2011). London, Gurantz, and Norman (2011) found that students who participate in OST programs are likely to improve their English proficiency, although the authors of this study found that students did not get fluent proficiency levels sooner than students who did not participate in OST programs. Therefore, OST programs could be more intentional in providing language instruction and activities to increase fluency in language proficiency.

Language and academic learning opportunities in OST settings are critical for ELL students. For ELL students to successfully take advantage of these types of activities, the activities must include a social interaction component (Peregoy, Boyle, & Cadiero-Kaplan, 2013; Téllez & Waxman, 2010) in a low-risk environment (Krashen & Terrell, 1983). ELL students could play games or participate in projects that require them to work on their speaking skills. They can also have individualized attention with teachers or mentors while working on their English proficiency in a relaxed environment (Afterschool Alliance, 2011). OST staff could use a variety of materials to support ELLs' comprehension during instruction and use activities such as multilingual resources, props, pictures, visuals, and manipulatives (Echevarria, Vogt, & Short, 2013).

Creating project-based learning opportunities and providing the ELL students with extended time to complete the projects can be also very helpful. These projects motivate students to learn because the activities deal with real-world problems (Tamim & Grant, 2013). In addition, these projects are student-centered, which increases students' interest levels and provides them with opportunities for social interaction in small groups using hands-on activities (Dole, Bloom, & Kowalske, 2016). Homework assistance is another strategy that promotes positive outcomes for ELL students (Holstead & Doll, 2015). ELL students who have been surveyed and interviewed shared how they appreciated having time in OST programs to have homework help one-on-one, which included help with preparing for tests (Pray, 2013).

Before- and afterschool programs are especially helpful for adolescent ELLs. It is important to note that having the programs available in the morning and afternoon increases the likelihood of adolescent ELLs being able to participate because they may have to work during one of those time slots. Programs could include authentic and meaningful activities that can help students learn about basic life skills that they might not have anyone to ask about or are too shy to ask due to the language barriers, such as where you get a bus pass or how you get a bank account. In addition, providing academic support and project-based learning opportunities can be beneficial. These students can not only use the assistance of a teacher, but they also might need the space to be able to do their homework since their homes might be shared by many other family members. They also might not have a computer in their home, so having access to that in the program would be very helpful for them to complete their homework (Cloud, Lakin, Leininger, & Maxwell, 2010). Another suggestion for OST programs is to include opportunities for community service, internships, and trips, which can provide support to adolescents and enhance their skills for the workforce and higher education (O'Donnell & Kirkner, 2016).

Students that attend OST programs consistently demonstrate better attendance in school, fewer behavior issues, improvement in their grades, and they are less likely to drop out of school (Pray, 2013). Students' English proficiency skills can improve through OST programs even if they are not focused on language development because students will have the extra time to use and practice their English, and it provides them with a stable and safe environment (Afterschool Alliance, 2011). In addition, students can create strong connections with students and teachers with similar backgrounds. For this reason, it is useful to hire teachers and staff from the community's area to gain a diverse and multilingual staff who will not only share the backgrounds of the families they serve but also will be committed to the area and can in time work in administrating the programs (Pray, 2013; see the Sanders et al. chapter in this volume).

OST settings using a more holistic approach in their program can also impact the social and emotional development of ELLs and their families. Research demonstrates that children are more likely to perform better in school if families are involved in the learning that occurs in OST settings and in social interaction activities with peers (Lopez & Caspe, 2014; Weiss, Little, Bouffard, Deschenes, & Malone, 2009). ELL families may not get involved in the education of their children due to cultural and language barriers or because they are unaware of the school expectations (Turney & Kao, 2009). OST programs can provide support to both children and families to promote healthy relationships, involvement in learning, and use of community resources. OST programs could provide support to families to help their children. For example, teaching parents how to use reading strategies with wordless books as well as books in English and/or in their native language can demonstrate to them how they can truly help build their child's academic skills even if they do not have English skills (Pray, 2013). Having materials in the native language of the families in the program also helps with engagement (Schuster, 2016). Another way to include families is by inviting them to music performances or plays (Afterschool Alliance, 2011) to get them interested in coming, and then at that time other potential home–school connections can be introduced. Moreover, to help with participation, having a parent liaison personally reach out to parents and providing child care, a translator, a meal, and varying the times of programs will ensure families are more likely to attend (Michigan Department of Education, 2011). Building a strong family–OST relationship helps with children's consistent attendance to OST programs. OST staff could reach out to families to explain the program and expectations, as well as to reassure them that the program will provide a safe environment.

Having ELL teachers and guidance counselors can help the programs' success rates because students enjoy coming if they see familiar faces (Cloud et al., 2010). O'Donnell and Kirkner (2016) found that one of the most important components of OST programs is having a supportive staff and strong role models to create a positive environment for youth. In this positive environment, ELL students' culture and language can be celebrated and valued, which will allow them to feel proud of their cultural backgrounds (Bhattacharya & Quiroga, 2011). In addition, the teachers and staff hired for the program should have professional development provided about teaching ELLs (Cloud et al., 2010).

## IMPLICATIONS FOR PRACTICE

The demographic shifts discussed in this chapter reinforce that the number of ELLs in public schools and OST settings has increased dramatically over the years. Teachers and OST staff are now likely to have to support ELL students regardless of their preparation in this area. Therefore, it is critical that teachers and OST staff have positive attitudes towards language diversity. Beliefs and attitudes are infused in the daily interactions between teachers and students. If teachers bring negative attitudes into the classroom, ELLs' well-being and academic progress can be jeopardized. These attitudes will impact teaching practices and consequently ELLs' academic achievement (Castro, Ayankoya, & Kasprzak, 2011; Pettit, 2011). Unfortunately, some teachers do not believe they are adequately prepared in preservice programs to teach ELLs (Rubinstein-Avila & Lee, 2014). Consequently, OST programs should respond to this need by providing professional development opportunities focusing on the knowledge and skills necessary to support ELLs via workshops, courses, or certification programs specifically for OST staff. ELL teachers could also provide support in OST programs to meet community demands. Since 2008, the United States Department of Education has provided $328 million toward professional development of teachers, administrators, and paraprofessionals working with ELLs. In 2016, they presented 53 awards between $350,000 and $550,000, which were intended to be contributed each year for up to five years to provide ELLs with quality programming to academically support ELLs (Schaffhauser, 2016). Ideally, OST programs could partner with schools who are receiving this professional development to also assist OST programs.

To obtain professional development, some OST centers have formed partnerships with colleges or online educational programmers. The participants might learn in hybrid classes, where part of their instruction is online and part is face-to-face. Through a blended class, students have more flexibility when they complete the course requirements, and the classes can meet the needs of a variety of learning styles (Roberts-Doctolero, 2016). In addition, in rural areas, where it might be more difficult to travel to a class, it makes the professional development experience easier to access.

Last, seeking funding to ensure that programs are sustainable is crucial. There are a variety of federal funding sources to help programs work with the changing demographics. For example, the 21st Century Community Learning Centers initiative provides support for programs that provide academic support to low socioeconomic area programs. Title III offers the possibility for programs to partner with schools to help develop English language and literacy skills. The Refugee School Impact Grants assist refugee students between the ages of 5 and 18 to work on English skills and provide academic support, and it includes families. Ongoing evaluation work has demonstrated student progress, particularly pertaining to access, dosage, and programming (Afterschool Alliance, 2011).

## CONCLUSION

OST programs will continue to reflect the growing diversity of the U.S. population, since OST programs are especially helpful for children in low socioeconomic areas and in rural areas and who are ELLs. Children can feel supported through mentoring, can possibly get a chance to eat a meal, will exercise their brains and/or their bodies, and can make friends with similar interests and backgrounds. The benefits outweigh any drawbacks that can be associated with OST programs. Funding is needed to create and sustain the programs to serve families and to meet their needs regardless of where they live, the language they speak, or their income. In this chapter, based on the research from the field and the authors' expertise, we recommend the OST field's attention to the following practices that have been shown to support ELL students: having a safe setting, an accessible location, flexible hours, free programming (for example, for academic support), stakeholder engagement, ongoing professional development, interactive programming, accessible information in the native language of the participants (in writing and orally), and linkages to additional support services, such as childcare, transportation, and meals. The strategies can benefit not only ELL students, but all learners. Students can use the additional support provided by OST programs to help with their academic success as well as their social and emotional wellbeing.

OST programs stand to gain by remaining responsive to the demographic shifts and by customizing programs with a holistic approach that meets the needs of culturally and linguistically diverse children and families. Resources and professional development opportunities are needed to adequately prepare OST staff to support ELL students and families. Demographic shifts reflect diversity in OST settings, which offers an opportunity to broaden the enrichment experiences for ELL students across contexts and geographies.

## REFERENCES

Afterschool Alliance. (2011, June). English language learners: Becoming fluent in after-school. Afterschool Alert Issue Brief, 49, 1–8. Retrieved from http://www.after-schoolalliance.org/issue_briefs/issue_ELLS_49.pdf

Afterschool Alliance. (2012). *Uncertain times: Afterschool programs still struggling in to-day's economy*. Washington, DC: Author. Retrieved from http://www.afterschoolal-liance.org/documents/Uncertain_Times/Uncertain-Times-2012.pdf

Afterschool Alliance. (2016, March). *America after 3 pm special report: The growing im-portance of afterschool in rural communities*. Washington, DC: Author. Retrieved from http://www.afterschoolalliance.org/AA3PM/Afterschool_in_Rural_Commu-nities.pdf

Bhattacharya, J., & Quiroga, J. (2011). Learning English and beyond: A holistic approach to supporting English learners in afterschool. *Afterschool Matters, 14*(14), 13–19. Retrieved from http://files.eric.ed.gov/fulltext/EJ980181.pdf

Budge, K. (2006). Rural leaders, rural places: Problem, privilege, and possibility. *Journal of Research in Rural Education, 21*(13), 1–10.

Castro, D. Ayankoya, B., & Kasprzak, C. (2011). *New voices, nuevas voces: Guide to cultural linguistic diversity in early childhood*. Baltimore, MD: Paul H. Brookes.

Cloud, N., Lakin, J., Leininger, E., & Maxwell, L. (2010). *Before and after-school support for adolescent ELLs. Colorin Colorado! A Bilingual Site for Educators and Fami-lies of English Language Learners*. Retrieved from http://www.colorincolorado.org/article/after-school-support-adolescent-ells

Dole, S., Bloom, L., & Kowalske, K. (2016). Transforming pedagogy: Changing perspec-tives from teacher-centered to learner-centered. *Interdisciplinary Journal of Prob-lem-Based Learning, 10*(1), 45–58.

Echevarría, J., Vogt, M., & Short, D. (2013). *Making content comprehensible for English learners: The SIOP® model*. Boston, MA: Pearson.

Fry, R. (2007). *How far behind in math and reading are English language learners?* Washington, DC: Pew Hispanic Center. Retrieved from http://www.pewhispanic.org/2007/06/06/how-far-behind-in-math-and-reading-are-english-language-learn-ers/

Garcia, E. E., & Frede, E. C. (2010). *Young English language learners: Current research and emerging directions for practice and policy*. New York, NY: Teachers College Press.

Gast, M. J., Okamoto, D. G., & Feldman, V. (2017). We only speak English here. English dominance in language diverse, immigrant afterschool programs. *Journal of Adoles-cent Research, 32*(1), 94–121.

Harris, E. (2004). Out of school time opportunities for immigrant youth. *The Evaluation Exchange, 10*(1), 12. Retrieved from http://www.hfrp.org/var/hfrp/storage/original/application/c2dda25c82b71415c1ea669ffbf55925.pdf

Holstead, J., & Doll, K. (2015). Serving English Language Learners Afterschool. *Mid-Western Educational Researcher, 27*(4), 383–389.

Krashen, S. D., & Terrell, T. D. (1983). *The natural approach: Language acquisition in the classroom.* Oxford: Pergamon.

London, R., Gurantz, O., & Norman, J. (2011). The effect of afterschool program participation on English language acquisition. *After School Matters Journal, 22*–29. Retrieved from http://niost.org/2011-Spring/the-effect-of-afterschool-program-participation-on-english-language-acquisition

Lopez, M., & Caspe, M. (2014). Family engagement in anywhere, anytime learning. *Family Involvement Network of Educators (FINE) Newsletter, 6*(3). Retrieved from http://www.hfrp.org/publications-resources/browse-our-publications/family-engagement in-anywhere-anytime-learning

Michigan Department of Education. (2011). Collaborating for success: Parent engagement toolkit. Retrieved from http://www.michigan.gov/documents/mde/4a._Final_Toolkit_without_bookmarks_3701 1_7.pdf

Migration Policy Institute. (2015). Top languages spoken by English language learners nationally and by state. *ELL Information Center Fact Sheet Series, 4.* Retrieved from http://www.migrationpolicy.org/research/top-languages-spoken-english-language learners-nationally-and-state

National Center for Education Statistics. (2016, May). *English language learners in public schools.* Retrieved from http://nces.ed.gov/programs/coe/indicator_cgf.asp

Office of English Language Acquisition. (2017). *Profiles of English learners.* Retrieved from http://www.ncela.us/files/fast_facts/05-19-2017/ProfilesOfELs_FastFacts.pdf

O'Donnell, J., & Kirkner, S. (2016). Helping low-income urban youth make the transition to early adulthood. *Afterschool Matters, 23,* 18–27. Retrieved from https://www.niost.org/Afterschool-Matters-Spring-2016/helping-low-income-urbanyouth-make-the-transition-to-early-adulthood-a-retrospective-study-of-the-ymca-youth institute

Park, M., McHugh, M., & Katsiaficas, C. (2016). *Serving immigrants through two-generation programs: Identifying family needs and responsive program approaches.* Washington DC: Migration Policy Institute.

Peregoy, S. F., Boyle, O., & Cadiero-Kaplan, K. (2013). *Reading, writing, and learning in ESL: A resource book for teaching K–12 English learners.* Boston: Pearson.

Pettit, S. K. (2011). Teachers' beliefs about English language learners in the mainstream classroom: A review of the literature. *International Multilingual Research Journal, 5,* 123–147.

Pray, L. (2013). Supporting English language learners: In-school, afterschool and summer. In T. K. Peterson (Ed.), *Expanding Minds and Opportunities: Leveraging the Power of Afterschool and Summer Learning for Student Success* (pp. 88–94). Washington, DC: Collaborative Communications Group, Inc.. Retrieved from http://www.expandinglearning.org/sites/default/files/em_articles/1_supportingenglish.pdf

Roberts-Doctolero, J. (2016, September/October). Blended learning for today's out-of-school time professionals. *School Age After School, 231,* 60–65. Retrieved from http://eds.a.ebscohost.com/eds/pdfviewer/pdfviewer?sid=300052b6-ae9f-490e-8148-d4cd65a6ff88%40sessionmgr4010&vid=36&hid=4111

Rubinstein-Avila, E., & Lee, E. H. (2014). Secondary teachers and English language learners (ELLs): Attitudes, preparation and implications. *Clearing House, 87*(5), 187–191.

Schaffhauser, D. (2016). ED opens competition for ELL professional development grants. *The Journal Transforming Education through Technology*. Retrieved from https://thejournal.com/articles/2016/01/07/ed-opens-competition-for-ell-professional-development.aspx

Schuster, E. (2016, July/August). Out of school time programs: Advice and lessons learned. *Dimensions, 52*–58.

Tamim, S. R., & Grant, M. M. (2013). Definitions and uses: Case study of teachers implementing project-based learning. *Interdisciplinary Journal of Problem-Based Learning, 7*(2), 71–101.

Teixeira, R., Frey, W. H., & Griffin, R. (2015, February). States of change. *Center for American Progress*. Retrieved from https://www.americanprogress.org/issues/democracy/reports/2015/02/24/107261/states-of-change/

Téllez, K., & Waxman, H. C. (2010). A review of research on effective community programs for English language learners. *School Community Journal, 20*(1), 103–119.

Turney, K., & Kao, G. (2009). Barriers to school involvement: Are immigrant parents disadvantages? *The Journal of Educational Research, 102*(4), 257–271.

Weiss, H. B., Little, P. M., Bouffard, S. M., Deschenes, S. N., & Malone, H. J. (2009). Strengthen what happens outside school to improve what happens inside. *Phi Delta Kappan, 90*(8), 592–596.

CHAPTER 6

# THE ROLE OF OUT-OF-SCHOOL TIME PROGRAMS IN BRIDGING THE DIVERSITY GAP AND IMPROVING EDUCATIONAL OPPORTUNITIES FOR AFRICAN AMERICAN STUDENTS

Mavis Sanders, Karen Lewis-Watkins, and Keshara Cochrane

Nearly half of the 50 million children and youth in U.S. public schools are of color—24% Hispanic/Latino, 15% African American/Black, 5% Asian American/ Pacific Islander, 1% American Indian/Alaskan Native, and 3% two or more races (National Center for Educational Statistics, 2016). In contrast, approximately 85% of teachers are Caucasian (Feistritzer, Griffin, & Linnajarvi, 2011). Despite teacher hiring efforts to reduce this diversity gap, it may be decades before the nation's teaching force reflects the diversity of its students unless there are dramatic improvements in the racial and ethnic composition of candidates enrolling in and graduating from teacher certification programs (Putman, Hansen, Walsh, & Quintero, 2016). While it is imperative that federal and state policymakers, school system officials, and institutions of higher education continue efforts to achieve

*The Growing Out-of-School Time Field: Past, Present, and Future,*
pages 71–83.

the goals of diversifying the nation's teaching force, more immediate strategies to expose students to diverse teachers and role models are also needed. This chapter describes out-of-school time (OST) programs as one viable approach, focusing specifically on African American students for whom the diversity gap is large and widening (Hrabowski & Sanders, 2015).

The chapter is organized into four sections. The first section describes the diversity gap and its implications for African American students. The second section delineates the features of OST programs that make them particularly suitable for addressing the diversity gap and enhancing the educational experiences of African American students. It also describes the role of community partnerships in assisting OST programs to achieve these overlapping goals. Drawing on the third author's experience as a servant leader intern,[1] existing research, and program documents, the third section presents the Children's Defense Fund (CDF) Freedom Schools program as an illustrative case, briefly describing its history, implementation, and participant outcomes. The concluding section describes areas for future research and practice in the OST field to enhance the educational experiences of racially and ethnically diverse students.

## THE DIVERSITY GAP IN PREK–12 SCHOOLS AND AFRICAN AMERICAN STUDENT SUCCESS

The diversity gap in U.S. public schools is present for all populations of color and in all 50 states and the District of Columbia; however, it is most pronounced in large states with heterogeneous populations such as Illinois, Nevada, and California (National Collaborative on Diversity in the Teaching Force, 2004). While the diversity gap has decreased slightly over the past 25 years due to increases in the percentages of Latino and Asian American teachers, teachers of color still account for only about 15% of the teaching force (Feistritzer et al., 2011). Nationally, African American teachers have remained at between 6% and 7% of public school teachers over the past three decades (Feistritzer et al., 2011). However, their numbers are declining in some states as a generation of teachers retires without sufficient African American graduates of teacher certification programs to replace them (see Hrabowski & Sanders, 2015). Thus, African American students have increasingly limited exposure to same-race teachers and role models despite research showing their importance for these students' academic success and socioemotional wellbeing.

### African American Students and Same-Race Teachers

Studies have shown the benefits of same-race teachers for African American students' achievement (Dee, 2004; Egalite, Kisida, & Winters, 2014), placement in gifted and talented programs (Grissom & Redding, 2016), mathematics course selection (Klopfenstein, 2005), behavior assessments (Downey & Pribesh, 2004; Mashburn, Hamre, Downer, & Pianta, 2006), and classroom experiences (Howard, 2001; Sanders, 1998; Wilder, 2000). For example, using student and teacher data from Tennessee's Project STAR class-size experiment, Dee (2004) found that Black and White students' one-year assignment to a same-race teacher significantly increased their math and reading achievement by roughly three to four percentile points. Analyzing data from Florida public school students in grades 3–10, Egalite and colleagues (2014) reported similar results and found that same-race effects on achievement were more pronounced for low-performing students than their higher-performing counterparts. In addition, using nationally representative longitudinal data, Grissom and Redding (2016) found that African American students were three times more likely to be referred to gifted programs when taught by same-race teachers, especially in reading. Focusing on mathematics course taking, Klopfenstein (2005) found a positive relationship between the percentage of Black math teachers in a school and the likelihood that Black geometry students will subsequently pursue higher-level math courses.

Same-race teachers have also been linked to nonacademic outcomes for African American students. For instance, in a quantitative study of kindergarten and eighth grade students using ECLS and NELS data,[2] Downey and Pribesh (2004) found that Black teachers were more likely than White teachers to favorably rate Black students' behavior. The authors found evidence of this pattern for both younger and older students. Mashburn and colleagues (2006) similarly found that African American boys in preK classrooms were reported to have fewer behavior problems when they were paired with a same-race teacher. Qualitative research suggests that these outcomes are partially explained by African American students' perceptions of same-race teachers as more accessible and caring and their classrooms as more engaging and culturally responsive (Howard, 2001; Sanders, 1998; Wilder, 2000).

### African American Students and Culturally Responsive Learning Environments

Houchen (2013) describes culturally responsive pedagogy (CRP) as a body of knowledge that theorizes frameworks, describes practices, and provides evaluations of culturally centered classroom strategies. Houchen cites the following components as key to CRP:

- "Use of instructional strategies that are culturally familiar, differentiated for student abilities, focused on student interests and goals, and that set mastery as a benchmark;
- Developing, supporting, and encouraging critical, sociopolitical consciousness, and cultural and historic rootedness in students by infusing background subject knowledge and cultural connections that reflect their everyday lives;
- Creating an atmosphere of care and mutual respect for students and teachers;

- High expectations of student engagement in the learning process; and
- Maintaining a learning environment that is nurturing, safe, authoritative, and achievement oriented." (pp. 96–98)

An emerging line of research illustrates how CRP diversifies learning environments in ways that bolster achievement among African American students (Brittian & Gray, 2014; Cholewa, Amatea, West-Olatunji, & Wright, 2012). For instance, teachers who successfully incorporate CRP into their classrooms engage in activities that promote sociocultural identity, enhance racial visibility, and embrace a variety of student dialects (e.g., formal, vernacular). The goal of these practices is to create safe learning spaces where students feel valued, welcomed, and unthreatened by stereotypes during the learning process (Levy, Heissel, Richeson, & Adam, 2016; Watkins-Lewis, 1998).

It is important to note that culturally responsive practices are not limited to pedagogy and are inclusive of broader actions that also ensure students' academic, social, and emotional wellbeing. Culturally responsive schools, for example, explore the lived experiences of their students through homes visits and neighborhood and community partnerships. These schools also provide academic support services (e.g., tutoring), financial assistance when available, and emotional support in the event of tragedy or loss (Howard & Terry, 2011). Favorable outcomes manifest through enhanced academic performance, higher student efficacy, and increased student interest in attending college (Gay, 2000; Nasir, McLaughlin, & Jones, 2009). Researchers argue that these outcomes are tied to the development of cultural integrity and that risk ensues when classrooms dismiss the social capital African-American students bring to the learning process (Boykin & Allen, 2004; Hubert, 2014; Ladson-Billings, 1995). Such findings underscore the sociocultural dimension of education, which is significant for students' learning in and out of school.

## OST PROGRAMS, THE DIVERSITY GAP, AND STUDENT OUTCOMES

OST programs provide supervised learning and extracurricular activities for children and adolescents during nonschool hours. In 2014, 10.2 million young people participated in OST programs. While most (71%) were European American, over one third of the participants were children and adolescents of color (15% African American, 11% Latino/Hispanic, 8% Asian American, and 2% Native American). By ethnicity, a larger percentage of children of color (29% Latino/Hispanic, 24% African American, 20% Asian American) than European American children (12%) participated in OST programs (Afterschool Alliance, 2014).

The racial and ethnic makeup of OST program participants and the growing demand for such programs in communities of color (see Afterschool Alliance, 2013) make them especially well-suited to help bridge the diversity gap in U.S. public schools. That is, because they are more flexible and less bureaucratic than traditional schools, OST programs can more immediately provide youth of color with high-quality teaching and mentoring staff who reflect their diversity. To achieve this promise they must meet critical standards in the field. The National Afterschool Association (NAA) (2011), for example, has developed a set of standards for quality school-age care that are organized into six categories: (a) human relationships; (b) indoor environment; (c) outdoor environment; (d) activities; (e) safety, health, and nutrition; and (f) administration. Each of these categories includes observable items that further define the elements of high-quality OST programs. The human relationships and administration categories include items that support culturally responsive programming. Specifically, the human relationships standard states that OST program staff should share the languages and cultures of the students and families they serve. Similarly, the administration standard states that OST program policies and procedures should encourage the engagement and respond to the needs of participants' families and communities (NAA, 2011). When children and youth participate in high-quality OST programs, academic and nonacademic benefits result.

## OST Programs and Student Outcomes

Several studies have reported the benefits of OST programs for students generally, and African American students specifically. Lauer and colleagues (2006), for example, analyzed 35 studies in a meta-analysis of the relationship between OST program participation and student outcomes. The researchers found that OST program participation positively influenced students' test scores in reading and mathematics. Larger effect sizes were associated with specific OST program features such as tutoring in reading. The authors further noted that these effects were reported for both after-school and summer OST programs. Similarly, in a longitudinal study of primarily African American (97%) students participating in Teach Baltimore, an 8-week academically intensive summer program, Borman and Dowling (2006) found a positive effect of participation on students' achievement in reading and mathematics. They found that treatment students who regularly attended the program outperformed students with similar backgrounds and prior achievement assigned to the nontreatment condition. The researchers concluded that students' participation in Teach Baltimore helped to prevent summer learning loss and had a cumulative effect on their school achievement.

Research further suggests that same-race teachers and role models are associated with positive student outcomes and OST program effectiveness. For example, in a longitudinal study of eighty 12- to 14-year-olds, Zirkel (2003) found that race- and gender-matched role models helped youth of color to develop a deeper sense of their place and value in the larger society than mentors who did not share these characteristics. Likewise, when examining the attributes of effective OST programs for African American male students, Martin and Jefferson (2011) found that they provided students with supportive learning environments, access to enriching and relevant educational and career experiences, continuity and consistency of goals and expectations over time, and interactions with highly competent race- and gender-matched role models. These findings confirm previous research suggesting that race- and gender-matched role models help African American adolescents and other youth of color understand the social resources they can draw on to achieve their personal, academic, and professional goals, as well as guide their positive racial identity development (see Nieto, 1998). OST programs can achieve standards and expectations for staff diversity by partnering with and drawing on the resources of community volunteers and organizations.

## Community Partnerships to Enhance Diversity in OST Programs

Noting the growing diversity of OST participants, Laurie Olsen with California Tomorrow observed that "many out-of-school time program staff members are now working with some youth with whom they do not share a background or identity" (Harvard Educational Research Project, 2003, p. 4). She contends that these programs must strive to build the cultural competence of their staff members to better serve their diverse participants. While such efforts are necessary, they are not sufficient. To effectively meet their students' needs and standards in the field, OST programs must also attract and retain high-quality volunteers and staff who reflect participants' diversity. One way to do so is through community partnerships.

OST programs can link with a variety of community partners including businesses, universities and educational institutions, government and military agencies, healthcare organizations, faith-based organizations, national service and volunteer organizations, senior citizen organizations, cultural and recreational institutions, media organizations, sports franchises and associations, and other groups such as fraternities and sororities to provide resources and social support for their participants (Sanders, 2006). Partnerships can be student-centered, family-centered, or community-centered. Student-centered activities include those that provide direct services to students, such as mentoring and tutoring (Sanders, 2006). Family-centered activities are those that have parents or entire families as their primary focus such as parenting workshops and GED and other adult education classes. Community-centered activities have as their primary focus the community and its citizens—for example, community development and service learning projects (Sanders, 2006). In general, community partnerships can increase the quality of OST programs and maximize the benefits derived for their participants.

For African American students, partnerships can tap into the legacy of educational engagement that has characterized African American communities for centuries. This engagement has taken a variety of forms over time from fundraising and school construction to advocacy and policy making (Sanders & Campbell, 2007). Using partnerships, OST programs can draw on this tradition to provide African American students' access to same-race teachers and role models who are in short supply during regular school hours. Recognizing that high-quality OST programs benefit from such partnerships, Kennedy, Bronte-Tinkew, and Matthews (2007) encouraged these programs to invite "speakers and visitors from the community and find volunteers or pay employees from various cultural ethnic, racial, sexual, linguistic and religious backgrounds or orientations" (p. 3). The following section presents CDF Freedom Schools as an example of OST programs that use partnerships to help bridge the diversity gap and advance participants' achievement and well-being.

## THE CHILDREN'S DEFENSE FUND
## FREEDOM SCHOOLS: AN ILLUSTRATIVE CASE

CDF Freedom Schools are grounded in an awareness of the need for African American and other historically underserved students to see highly competent teachers and mentors who look like them, and experience culturally responsive learning environments. Through partnerships with faith-based organizations, schools, nonprofits, universities, and other community organizations, CDF Freedom Schools establish sites around the country that are accessible, engaging, and empowering for all stakeholders. This section discusses the history, implementation, and outcomes of CDF Freedom Schools drawing on the first-hand experiences of the third author, who served as a summer servant leader intern in 2016.

### The History and Implementation of Freedom Schools

During the summer of 1964, two of the leading Civil Rights organizations, the Student Nonviolent Coordinating Committee and the Council of Federated Organizations, initiated the Mississippi Freedom Summer Project (Children's Defense Fund, 2016). The purpose of this program was to educate Mississippi citizens, primarily African Americans, of their basic rights as citizens of the United States, focusing mainly on the right to vote (Children's Defense Fund, 2016). One of the major aspects of the Freedom Summer project of 1964 was the implementation of Freedom Schools. Freedom Schools were significant because they provided African American children with an educational experience that was not offered in the traditional school setting (Children's Defense Fund, 2016). As an extension of the Freedom Summer of 1964, the Freedom Schools movement was reborn under the leadership of Marian Wright Edelman, founder of the Children's Defense Fund (2016). Under Edelman's leadership, the first two official CDF Freedom School sites opened in 1995. There are now 189 CDF Freedom School sites in 96 cities and 29 states, Washington DC, and the U.S Virgin Islands (Children's Defense Fund, 2016). Modern-day Freedom Schools are like those established during the Freedom Summer of 1964 in that there remains a focus on literacy and social action among African American children, and college-aged youth continue to serve as the schools' teachers and leaders (Children's Defense Fund, 2016).

CDF Freedom Schools serve students in grades 1–12. In 2010, of the 9,633 students participating in CDF Freedom Schools, the majority (90.6%) were African American. In 2015, the organization served 12,375 students[3] and employed

1,500 servant leader interns, of whom one-third were male, slightly over two-thirds were African American (68%), 14% were White, 7% were Latino, and 3% were Asian American, Native Hawaiian, or Pacific Islander (Children's Defense Fund, 2015).

The CDF Freedom School curriculum consists of four levels. Level 1 applies to students in grades 1–2, Level 2 to students in grades 3–5, Level 3 to middle school students, and Level 4 to high school students. The main instructional component of the Freedom Schools is the integrated reading curriculum (IRC). The IRC is different from the reading curricula offered in most traditional school settings because it consists of daily readings of books that reflect the heritage of participating students. These books introduce students to characters who look like them and have similar life experiences, thereby enhancing their passion for reading as well as improving their reading skills.

Jackson and Boutte (2009) explored the positive effects of the books included in the Freedom School curriculum in their article on liberation literature. Specifically, they discussed the positive messages conveyed in the book, *Grandpa, Is Everything Black Bad?* by Sandy Lynne Holman, the Level 2 curriculum book that the third author read to rising fourth grade students on their first day in the program. The lessons the protagonist of the book learns from his grandfather about African heritage and history validate Blackness and Black culture (Jackson & Boutte, 2009). Jackson and Boutte argued that liberation literature enhances students' love of reading. This is important because often, in traditional school settings, children of African descent and children who are members of other racial and ethnic minority groups in the United States are not exposed to books that contain characters and plots that positively reflect their reality.

Another major aspect of the Freedom School daily schedule is Harambee. Harambee is a Swahili word that means "let's pull together" (Children's Defense Fund, 2016). Each morning, Freedom School sites begin their programs with Harambee. These morning celebrations consist of cheers and chants, recognitions, read-aloud guests, announcements, and a moment of silence. Harambee is intended to celebrate and motivate the students as well as create a positive start to the day (CDF, 2016).

In addition to their literacy focus, Freedom Schools also enhance students' historical, social, and cultural awareness and provide opportunities for social activism and leadership (Jackson & Boutte, 2009). For example, the National Day of Social Action is a day in which Freedom Schools across the nation go into their communities to raise awareness of critical issues (Children's Defense Fund, 2016). The Freedom School where the third author served chose to explore the issue of lead in school pipes, which can result in lead poisoning if students drink water from the fountains and sinks. Freedom School staff and students investigated this topic and on the National Day of Social Action held a protest in the community surrounding the school. Students also wrote letters to members of the school board to express their concerns and request an immediate resolution of the problem.

Overall, CDF Freedom Schools have shown positive results for participating students. Per summer 2015 data, 84% of students enrolled in Freedom Schools maintained or improved their reading level, avoiding the negative effects of summer loss experienced by many low-income African American students (Children's Defense Fund, 2015; Taylor, Medina, & Lara-Cinisomo, 2010). In addition, the six-week program positively influenced participants' attitudes toward reading, school, and education as well as their racial and ethnic identities (Children's Defense Fund, 2015; Teaching Tolerance, 2013). CDF Freedom Schools are also associated with positive outcomes for servant leader interns and participants' families. For instance, servant leader interns reported developing more leadership skills and greater confidence in their future success, and 70% of students' families believed their parenting skills improved through program participation (Children's Defense Fund, 2015). Thus, CDF Freedom Schools demonstrate the potential of OST programs to bridge the diversity gap and provide African American students with unique learning experiences that validate their heritage, culture, and daily lives.

## DISCUSSION AND CONCLUSION

This chapter describes how OST programs can bridge the diversity gap in U.S. public schools and its implications for African American students. Specifically, it contends that high-quality OST programs are a viable means to ensure that African American and other students of color have the opportunity to benefit from same-race teachers and role models in culturally responsive learning environments. Additionally, it argues that through outreach to and partnerships with community organizations and volunteers, OST programs can broaden the diversity of their staff and benefit from the cultural resources embedded in their participants' communities. OST programs, therefore, should be part of national, state, and local efforts to address the educational needs of African American and other historically underserved students. As summarized by Toldson and Lemmons (2015) in a special issue of the Journal of Negro Education:

> The available statistics about Black students reveal pervasive challenges related to their progress in school. The potential consequences of Black students maintaining persistently high rates of suspension, grade retention, dropout, placement in special education, and underrepresentation in AP classes are far-reaching and threaten the long-term viability of our nation. Out-of-school time (OST) programs play a vital role in promoting academic success among Black students. (p. 207)

To bolster this role, OST program directors and researchers have equally important and mutually reinforcing parts to play. OST program directors must take decisive steps to ensure that their teaching and mentoring personnel reflect the diversity of the student populations they serve. CDF Freedom Schools illustrate how OST directors can achieve this goal through expansive community partnerships and intentional hiring practices.

Researchers can assist OST program directors in this critical work. Researchers can document the diversity of OST program personnel, including teaching and mentoring staff, locally and nationally, to identify trends, gaps, and areas for continued growth and improvement. Currently, there is no national data on the diversity of OST staff. However, some state data suggest that while OST staff generally reflect student diversity, program supervisors and managers are predominantly European American, a discrepancy that requires further attention if equity in OST programming is to be achieved (Dennehy & Noam, 2005).

Researchers can also identify effective strategies for recruiting and retaining racially and ethnically diverse personnel, factors facilitating and inhibiting staff diversity, and the effects of staff diversity on program participants' academic (e.g., literacy and numeracy skills, homework habits, research, and analytical skills) and nonacademic (e.g., leadership skills, racial identity development, and civic engagement) outcomes. Lastly, they can investigate the role of community partnerships in helping OST programs to achieve greater diversity among their personnel and provide culturally responsive learning opportunities for their participants. Deeper understanding of these issues will strengthen the capacity of OST programs to play an integral role in extending equal educational opportunities to African American students, and indeed, all the nation's children and youth.

## NOTES

1. CDF Freedom Schools servant leader interns serve as instructors in the classroom and as leaders of parent workshops and community outreach activities. Learn more at http://www.childrensdefense.org/programs/freedomschools/

2. Early Childhood Longitudinal (ECLS) Study—kindergarten class of 1998–99 and eighth graders from the National Education Longitudinal (NELS) study of 1988.

3. Demographic data for students enrolled in CDF Freedom Schools in 2015 were not reported.

## REFERENCES

Afterschool Alliance. (2013). *The importance of afterschool and summer learning programs in African-American and Latino communities*. Washington, DC: Author. Retrieved from http://afterschoolalliance.org//documents/issue_briefs/issue_African-American-Latino-Communities_59.pdf

Afterschool Alliance. (2014). *America after 3 p.m.: Afterschool programs in demand.* Washington, DC: Author. Retrieved from http://www.afterschoolalliance.org/documents/aa3pm-2014/aa3pm_national_report.pdf

Borman, G., & Dowling, N. (2006). Longitudinal achievement effects of multiyear summer school: Evidence from the Teach Baltimore randomized field trial. *Educational Evaluation and Policy Analysis, 28*(1), 25–48. doi: 10.3102/01623737028001025

Boykin, A. W., & Allen, B. A. (2004). Cultural integrity and schooling outcomes of African American children from low-income backgrounds. In P. B. Pufall & R. P. Unsworth (Eds.), *Rethinking childhood* (pp. 104–120). New Brunswick, NJ: Rutgers University Press.

Brittian, A. S., & Gray, D. L. (2014). African American students' perceptions of differential treatment in learning environments: Examining the moderating role of peer support, connection to heritage, and discrimination efficacy. *Journal of Education, 194*(1), 1–9.

Children's Defense Fund. (2015). *Children's Defense Fund Freedom Schools® program 2015 program description and fact sheet*. Washington, DC: Author.

Children's Defense Fund. (2016). *CDF Freedom Schools® program*. Washington, DC: Author. Retrieved from http://www.childrensdefense.org/programs/freedomschools/

Cholewa, B., Amatea, E., West-Olatunji, C., & Wright, A. (2012). Examining the relational processes of a highly successful teacher of African American children. *Urban Education, 47*, 250–279. doi: 10.1177/0042085911429581

Dee, T. S. (2004). Teachers, race, and student achievement in a randomized experiment. *Review of Economics and Statistics, 86*(1), 195–210. doi:10.1162/003465304323023750

Dennehy, J., & Noam, G. (2005). *Evidence for action: Strengthening after-school programs for all children and youth: The Massachusetts out-of-school time workforce*. Boston, MA: Achieve Boston.

Downey, D. B., & Pribesh, S. (2004). When race matters: Teachers' evaluations of students' classroom behavior. *Sociology of Education, 77*(4), 267–282. doi: 10.1177/003804070407700401

Egalite, A. J., Kisida, B., & Winters, M. A. (2014). *Representation in the classroom: The effect of own-race teacher assignment on student achievement*. Cambridge, MA: Program on Education Policy and Governance Working Papers Series.

Feistritzer, E., Griffin, S., & Linnajarvi, A. (2011). *Profile of teachers in the U.S., 2011*. Washington, DC: National Center for Education Information.

Gay, G. (2000). *Culturally responsive teaching*. New York, NY: Teachers College Press.

Grissom, J. A., & Redding, C. (2016). Discretion and Disproportionality. *AERA Open, 2*(1), 1–25. doi: https://doi.org/10.1177/2332858415622175

Holman, S. L. (1998).*Grandpa, is everything black bad?* Davis, CA: Culture C.O.-O.P.

Houchen, D. (2013). "Stakes is high": Culturally relevant practitioner inquiry with African American students struggling to pass secondary reading exit exams. *Urban Education, 48*(1), 92–115. doi: https://doi.org/10.1177/0042085912456845

Howard, T. C. (2001). Telling their side of the story: African-American students' perceptions of culturally relevant teaching. *The Urban Review, 33*(2), 131–149. doi: 10.1023/A:1010393224120

Howard, T., & Terry, C. L. (2011). Culturally responsive pedagogy for African American students: Promising programs and practices for enhanced academic performance. *Teaching Education, 22*(4), 345. doi: http://dx.doi.org/10.1080/10476210.2011.608424

Hrabowski III, F. A., & Sanders, M. G. (2015). Increasing racial diversity in the teacher workforce: One university's approach. *Thought & Action, 32*, 101–116.

Hubert, T. (2014). Learners of mathematics: High school students' perspectives of culturally relevant mathematics pedagogy. *Journal of African American Studies, 18*(3), 324–336. doi:10.1007/s12111-013-9273-2

Jackson, T. O., & Boutte, G. S. (2009). Liberation literature: Positive cultural messages in children's and young adult literature at freedom schools. *Language Arts, 87*(2), 108–116.

Kennedy, E., Bronte-Tinkew, J., & Matthews, G. (2007). Enhancing cultural competence in out-of-school time programs: What is it, and why is it important? *Research-to-Results.* Washington, DC: Child Trends.

Klopfenstein, K. (2005). Beyond test scores: The impact of black teacher role models on rigorous math taking. *Contemporary Economic Policy,* 23(3), 416–428. doi: 10.1093/cep/byi031

Ladson-Billings, G. (1995). Toward a theory of culturally relevant pedagogy. *American Educational Research Journal,* 32, 465–491. doi: https://doi.org/10.3102/00028312032003465

Lauer, P. A., Akiba, M., Wilkerson, S. B., Apthorp, H. S., Snow, D., & Martin-Glenn, M. L. (2006). Out-of-school-time programs: A meta-analysis of effects for at-risk students. *Review of Educational Research, 76*(2), 275–313. doi: 10.3102/00346543076002275

Levy, D. J., Heissel, J. A., Richeson, J. A., & Adam, E. K. (2016). Psychological and biological responses to race-based social stress as pathways to disparities in educational outcomes. *American Psychologist, 71*(6), 455–473. doi: 10.1037/a0040322

Martin, M., & Jefferson, N. (2011, April). *When black males aren't at school: A qualitative study of promising out-of-school-time (OST) programs serving black males.* Paper presented at the Annual Meeting of the American Educational Research Association, New Orleans, LA. Retrieved from http://www.inmotionmagazine.com/er11/mm_nj_ost.html

Mashburn, A. J., Hamre, B. K., Downer, J. T., & Pianta, R. C. (2006). Teacher and classroom characteristics associated with teachers' ratings of prekindergartners' relationships and behaviors. *Journal of Psychoeducational Assessment, 24*(4), 367–380. doi: https://doi.org/10.1177/0734282906290594

Nasir, N., McLaughlin, M., & Jones, A. (2009). What does it mean to be African American? Constructions of race and academic identity in an urban public high school. *American Educational Research Journal,* 46, 73–114. doi: 10.3102/0002831208323279

National Afterschool Association. (2011). *The NAA standards at a glance.* Oakton, VA: Author. Retrieved from http://www.statewideafterschoolnetworks.net/naa-standards-glance

National Center for Educational Statistics. (2016). *The condition of education.* Washington, DC: Author. Retrieved from http://nces.ed.gov/programs/coe/indicator_cge.asp

National Collaborative on Diversity in the Teaching Force. (2004). *Assessment of diversity in America's teaching force.* Washington, DC. Retrieved from: http://www.ate1.org/pubs/ uploads/diversityreport.pdf

Nieto, S. (1998). *Affirming diversity: The sociopolitical context of multicultural education* (3rd ed.). New York, NY: Longman.

Putman, H., Hansen, M., Walsh, K., & Quintero, D. (2016). *High hopes and harsh realities.* Washington, DC: The Brookings Institute.

Sanders, M. (1998). The effects of school, family and community support on the academic achievement of African-American adolescents. *Urban Education, 33*(3), 385–409. doi: 10.1177/0042085998033003005

Sanders, M. (2006). *Building school-community partnerships: Collaboration for student success*. Thousand Oaks, CA: Corwin Press.

Sanders, M., & Campbell, T. (2007). Securing the ties that bind: Community involvement and the educational success of African-American children and adolescents. In J. Jackson (Ed.), *Strengthening the educational pipeline for African Americans: Informing policy and practice* (pp. 141–164). Buffalo, NY: State University of New York (SUNY) Press.

Simpkins, S. (2003). Does youth participation in out-of-school time activities make a difference? *The Evaluation Exchange, 9*(1), 2–3, 21.

Taylor, D., Medina, A., & Lara-Cinisomo, S. (2010). *Freedom school partners Children's Defense Fund Freedom Schools® program evaluation report*. Charlotte, NC: The Center for Adolescent Literacies at UNC Charlotte. Retrieved from http://www.childrensdefense.org/library/data/charolette-fsp-evaluation-report.pdf

Teaching Tolerance. (2013). *No school like Freedom School*. Retrieved from http://www.tolerance.org/no-school-like-freedom-school

Toldson, I. A., & Lemmons, B. P. (2015). Out-of-school time and African American students: Linking concept to practice (editor's commentary). *The Journal of Negro Education, 84*(3), 207–210.

Watkins-Lewis, K. (1998). *The cultural bases for teachers' perceptions of their classroom practices: Implications for Black students who display differing cultural orientations* (Unpublished master's thesis). Howard University, Washington, DC.

Wilder, M. (2000). Increasing African American teachers' presence in American schools: Voices of students who care. *Urban Education, 35*(2), 205–220. doi: https://doi.org/10.1177/0042085900352005

Zirkel, S. (2003). Is there a place for me? Role models and academic identity among White students and students of color. *Teachers College Record, 104*(2), 357–376. doi: 10.1111/1467-9620.00166

# SECTION III

PROFESSIONAL DEVELOPMENT WITHIN OST

CHAPTER 7

# THE STATE OF PROFESSIONAL DEVELOPMENT

## Past, Present, and Future

### Elizabeth Starr and Ellen S. Gannett

A burgeoning body of research demonstrates what the out-of-school time (OST) field has known for many years: Not only does the quality of OST programming matter for achieving positive youth outcomes (Durlak &Weissberg, 2007; Lauer et al., 2006; Vandell, Reisner, & Pierce, 2007), but the quality of staff directly impacts program quality and child and youth outcomes (Costly, 1998; Guskey, 2000; Miller & Hall, 2007). Even before these findings, the OST field had been striving to build a strong and stable workforce that could provide high-quality programming. Though achievements have been made over the last several decades, progress has been slow, and initiatives often have not been sustained.

In this chapter, we examine some of the challenges slowing progress. Next, we summarize the history of OST professional development in the field's three major sectors: school-age care, afterschool, and youth work. Then we focus on today's landscape, in which the sectors seem to be coming together. Finally, we offer future directions that can lead to a unified, strong, and stable workforce.

*The Growing Out-of-School Time Field: Past, Present, and Future,*
pages 87–102.
Copyright © 2018 by Information Age Publishing
All rights of reproduction in any form reserved.

## WHAT IS PROFESSIONAL DEVELOPMENT
## AND WHY DOES IT MATTER?

Research has confirmed a connection between OST staff quality and positive youth outcomes (Costly, 1998; Eccles & Gootman, 2002; Grossman, Campbell, & Raley, 2007; Guskey, 2000; Miller & Hall, 2007). The increasing expectation that OST will achieve challenging academic and nonacademic outcomes, particularly for disadvantaged children and youth, makes improving staff quality more important than ever.

The field does not have one consistent definition of professional development. We adopt Nancy Peter's (2009) broad definition, "A spectrum of activities, resources, and supports that help practitioners work more effectively with or on behalf of children and youth" (p. 39). This definition includes a variety of professional development formats, such as workshops, conferences, technical assistance, peer mentoring, coaching, professional memberships, apprenticeships, certifications and credentials, college coursework and degrees, peer networking, and professional learning communities (Peter, 2009).

Additional supportive elements create a *system* of professional development, which is needed to support and sustain a strong workforce (National Center on Child Care Professional Development Systems and Workforce Initiatives, 2013; School's Out Washington, 2008; Starr & Gannett, 2014). These elements include (Starr & Gannett, 2015, p. 6):

- defined standards of quality for programs and individual staff (quality program standards and core competencies)
- academic pathways for continuing professional growth, including credentials and access to training and higher education
- registries, or central repositories where staff can record trainings attended and credentials or degrees earned
- career pathways that tie professional development to advances in position and salary
- compensation increases to keep salaries commensurate with education and experience
- incentive programs to reward credentials and other training
- funding, both public and private, to support and sustain a career development system
- links to larger system building efforts, such as quality improvement systems
- connections with other organizations and fields striving for the same goals

### CHALLENGES FOR OST PROFESSIONAL DEVELOPMENT

Challenges to sustainable professional development for OST staff include the fragmentation of the field and aspects of the state of the workforce.

*Fragmentation of the Field*

OST is made up of several sectors: primarily school-age care, afterschool, and youth work, but also summer learning programs, summer camps, and recreation programs. Understanding the differences in and overlap among these sectors can be confusing, for those within the field and outside of it. For the most part, these sectors operate separately; each has its own approach to workforce development.

*School-age care* grew out of the early childhood field, so it has a child development perspective. School-age care programs receive funding from the Child Care Development Fund (CCDF), a federal funding stream for early care and education. These childcare programs—daycare centers or family childcare homes—provide care for children ages 5–13 after school hours. *Afterschool*, by contrast, comes from an education perspective, funded primarily through the 21st Century Community Learning Centers (21st CCLC). Their primary goal is to close the achievement gap between impoverished and economically privileged students. Afterschool also includes school-run programs that occur after school hours—typically for elementary age children—as well as community-based programs for children and youth ages 5–18. *Youth work* programs—including Boys and Girls Clubs, YMCA, 4H, and many other community-based programs—have traditionally served older youth. Historically, youth work focused on character development. The programs are often privately funded. To these three sectors, add recreation programs, summer camps, summer learning programs, museum education, and more. All have their own histories, philosophies, and funding streams.

These differences can dramatically influence staff qualifications and training. For example, CCDF regulates inputs and comes with an extensive internal regulatory framework. 21st CCLC stresses outputs—specifically, academic success—and has no licensing requirements. CCDF sets minimum requirements for preservice training and ongoing professional development. 21st CCLC does not; it is assumed that most staff will be certified teachers (Cole, 2011).

Furthermore, each sector has differing philosophies about professionalization. School-age care, as part of the early childhood field, tends to look to standards and requirements as a path to professionalization. By contrast, many in the youth work sector have been wary of requirements that might impose unintended barriers to entry, such as the cost of certification. To preserve the "art" of youth work and the staff diversity made possible by freedom from regulations, some stress reflective practice and similar informal approaches to professional development (Cunnien, 2011; Walker & Walker, 2012).

Despite their differences, these sectors overlap. They all emphasize positive youth development, social-emotional learning, and enrichment activities (Halpern, 2006). They all work to achieve positive outcomes for children, youth, and families. Working in partnership as a unified field would help all sectors to strengthen the workforce.

*The State of the Workforce*

Two studies conducted in 2005, one by the National AfterSchool Association (NAA) and one by The Forum for Youth Investment (Yohalem & Pittman, 2006), came to similar conclusions about the OST workforce. These studies of more than 5,000 workers did surface some positive findings: high job satisfaction, with nearly 80% of workers reporting being satisfied or very satisfied; diversity in terms of age, backgrounds, and prior experiences; and high levels of education, with over half of workers reporting a four-year degree or higher. Study respondents cited as an advantage the flexibility that part-time work offers (Yohalem & Pittman, 2006).

Many of the survey results, however, were grim. The workforce faced low compensation and high turnover; pay was cited as the number one reason people left the field. The largely part-time workforce included many temporary workers who did not plan to stay in the field for long and who held other jobs. Career advancement was rare, while stress and burnout were high. The perceived low status of OST work was a public relations problem (Yohalem & Pittman, 2006).

These issues have translated into challenges for professional development. OST work is often seen as a stepping stone to other careers with better pay, making it difficult to argue for investment in workers who will just take their skills elsewhere. Furthermore, part-time employees who work other jobs tend not to have time for advanced training. Full-time employees can have the same problem—in the 2005 surveys, over half of part-time workers held another job, but so did 27% of full-time workers (Yohalem & Pittman, 2006). Even a positive finding, high satisfaction, may have worked against professionalization. A perception is that people are fueled by their passion to help children and youth and so, the argument goes, will continue to do the work without higher compensation and other workplace improvements even as they achieve higher levels of training.

The fragmentation of the field and its workforce issues have profoundly affected the history of OST professional development.

## A BRIEF HISTORY OF PROFESSIONAL DEVELOPMENT IN OST

Early OST programs were established in the last quarter of the 19th century, as settlement houses created programs for children and small "boys' clubs" were founded. Then as now, most programs relied on part-time workers and volunteers who considered the work a calling, as well as on people with specific skills who taught a few classes (Halpern, 2002).

Workforce issues—many of which will sound familiar—emerged, according to Halpern (2002), in the late 1920s, when criticisms about program quality were tied to staffing. One program report from that era noted that "club leaders who only came once a week for the meeting of their club failed to connect with or understand the larger program" (Halpern, 2002, p. 192). Other reports from the 1920s, 1930s, and 1940s describe ongoing struggles to find and retain club leaders and staff with specific vocational and artistic skills. Furthermore, some reports indicated about 50% year-to-year turnover among volunteers, as well as turnover during the year, which affected "the momentum of clubs as well as participants' morale and attendance" (Halpern, 2002, p. 192).

OST leaders felt a need to improve their status by professionalizing this work and articulating its methods (Halpern, 2002). Beginning to describe their work as a "profession," they debated what formal knowledge was central to it. These efforts were picked up again decades later.

Growth in employment of women in the 1970s and 1980s led to interest in programs that could provide childcare after school. A patchwork of programs run by schools, churches, YMCAs, parents, and other organizations fit the needs (Halpern, 2002). There were signs of emerging interest in professionalization, and the sectors of school-age care, afterschool, and youth work became more defined as separate funding streams were established.

In the 1990s, policymakers, the media, child development professionals, and parents focused increased attention on the afterschool hours, viewing them as a time of unusual "risk and opportunity" (Carnegie Council on Adolescent Development, 1994; Halpern, 2002). Many entities focused on creating a stronger workforce, though efforts were not necessarily coordinated. Through the 1990s and into the early 2000s, funders (including Lucille and David Packard, Annie E. Casey, Cornerstones for Kids, Barr, Atlantic Philanthropies, Robert Bowne, Wallace, and Mott) supported workforce projects. Their interest led to research, nascent professional development systems, and advocacy efforts that have brought the field to where it is today.

The rest of this section summarizes the history of school-age care, afterschool, and youth work separately, focusing on the 1970s, 1980s, and 1990s. Though there is overlap among the sectors, this division reveals how OST professional development came to be so fragmented.

*School-Age Care*

In the 1970s and 1980s, school-age care—center- and family-based programs caring for school-age children after school—looked to early childhood and the U.S. military for workforce initiatives. Though national efforts did not come to fruition, states began to develop local initiatives.

The professionalization of the early childhood workforce paved the way for the OST field. In the mid-1970s, the Child Development Associate (CDA) early childhood credential was developed with funding by the HHS Administration on Children, Youth, and Families (the credential is now administered by the Council for Professional Recognition, a nonprofit organization) (Council for Professional Recognition, n.d.). Based on core competencies, the credential requires demonstration of knowledge and skills. Today, the CDA is a key step along the early childhood career pathway; research shows that it has led to increases in staff and program quality (Dennehy, Gannett, & Robbins, 2006).

In 1978, the Child Care Employee Project was formed (later to be called the National Center for the Early Childhood Workforce). In 1989, this grassroots organization of childcare teachers in the San Francisco Bay Area conducted the National Child Care Staffing Study, the first study to document how staff and working conditions affected the quality of care in early childhood centers (Whitebook, Howes, & Phillips, 1989). This study brought national attention to poverty-level wages and high turnover among early childhood staff and to the subsequent negative consequences for children (American Federation of Teachers, n.d.).

The attention, in part, led to the establishment of the Child Care Development Fund in 1990—authorized under the Child Care Development Block Grant—to subsidize childcare for low-income families and improve the quality of care. Since the program funded subsidies for children up to age 13, it brought school-age care under an early child care umbrella, though the focus was largely on very young children.

Marking the beginning of system approaches to workforce issues, the Wheelock College Center for Career Development in Early Childhood and Education developed a framework for early childhood professional development systems. The Wheelock center staff provided technical assistance to states developing their own professional development systems. Also during this time, the National Center on Child Care Professional Development Systems and Workforce Initiatives was established under the U.S. Department of Health and Human Services (HHS) Office of Child Care to build states' capacity to prepare and sustain a qualified early childhood workforce.

The U.S. military took a leading role in professionalizing the early childhood and school-age workforce when the Military Child Care Act of 1989 promoted quality and stronger workforce practices (Campbell, Applebaum, Martinson, & Martin, 2000). The U.S. Department of Defense (DoD) required every military childcare program to be certified based on quality standards; the lead staff had to hold credentials developed by DoD, and wages increased with training. The military is still known for its strong early childhood and school-age care system (Campbell et al., 2000).

School-age care tried to replicate and adapt the credentialing and professional development system-building efforts of early childhood and the military (these existing efforts were focused on very young children or were for the military specifically). The National Institute on Out-of-School Time (NIOST) led the way in adapting and expanding the Wheelock model to school-age care. In the early 1990s, a committee of the NAA (at that time known as the National School Age Care Alliance) tried to establish a credential, but the response of the field was that with no requirements or incentives, there was no market.

In the absence of a national professional development system, states began independently to develop credentials and career pathways. Much of this work was done at the state level, and any national approach needs to build on that progress.

*Afterschool*

Since the 1970s and 1980s, programs for children after school, housed and run in and by either schools or community-based organizations, have flourished. As the field began to coalesce, some early efforts at professional development were initiated. For example, in the early 1980s, the Bowne Foundation brought together those discussing afterschool as a field and began to fund professional development initiatives, particularly those aimed at literacy skills (Afterschool Matters, 2015). City- and state-wide networks began to form to provide training and technical assistance to afterschool programs.

In 1994, Congress authorized the 21st Century Community Learning Centers (CCLC) program. The first grants were given in 1998 to support the creation of community learning centers that focus on improving academic outcomes and providing enrichment opportunities during non-school hours, particularly for students who attend high poverty and low-performing schools. 21st CCLC is the primary federal funding source for afterschool, expanding from $40 million in 1998 to $1.4 billion in 2014 (You for Youth, n.d.). Though the program has raised the visibility of afterschool and improved the accessibility of quality programming, it arguably has been detrimental to the progress of workforce initiatives. 21st CCLC programs tend to rely on certified teachers who come with credentials and degrees and who already earn full-time salaries for their school-day work. Furthermore, 21st CCLC, though aimed at community-based organizations as well as school-based programs, has been largely used for school-based programs. This reality reduced the perceived need to train and compensate the OST workforce. The 2000s saw accelerating efforts in afterschool professional development initiatives, which continue today.

*Youth Work*

Youth work began establishing itself as a field in the 1970s and 1980s. Initially, funding and policy supported specialized areas to reduce risky behaviors, such as drug abuse or teen pregnancy (Hahn, Lanspery, Aaron, Hostetler, & Peaslee, 2002). For example, the National Network for Youth, a public education and advocacy organization focused on youth homelessness, began in the mid-1970s. The National Collaboration for Youth, a coalition committed to advocating with and on behalf of youth also began during this time. In the late 1980s, positive youth development gained prominence, replacing a deficit view of youth (Roth & Brooks-Gunn, 2016).

In the early 1990s, researchers, practitioners, and policymakers began to use positive youth development framework to understand adolescent development and to improve youth programs (Roth & Brooks-Gunn, 2016; Roth, Brooks-Gunn, Murray, & Foster, 1998). The positive youth development awareness led to an increase in youth-focused community-based programming and research (Roth et al., 1998). Though the field has not agreed on the youth work characteristics

(Lerner et al., 2013), the youth development literature does consistently empha-size positive, supportive, and sustained adult–youth relationships as a "critical ingredient" in successful programs (Rhodes, 2004; Roth & Brooks-Gunn, 2016).

Professional development initiatives began to take shape in the 1990s, with new training models and youth worker alliances to promote professionalism. For example, the Dewitt Wallace Reader's Digest Fund supported a professional learning community created by the National Network for Youth, as well as many training events. The fund first provided organizations with resources to train their own staff, and later encouraged grantees to use a sector-wide approach. (Hahn et al., 2002).

The Advancing Youth Development curriculum, a youth worker training root-ed in the principles of positive youth development, was a significant contribution to the professional development of the field. The curriculum, produced in 1991 by the Academy for Educational Development (AED) Center for Youth Develop-ment and Policy Research in collaboration with the National Network for Youth, is the basis for the National BEST (Building Exemplary Systems of Training Youth Workers) Initiative, launched in 1996 with funding from the Wallace-Reader's Di-gest Funds. The BEST Initiative continues to build local infrastructure, tailored to local communities, to provide professional development systems for youth work-ers (Youth Work Central, n.d.).

## Coming Together

Accelerating workforce efforts in the early 2000s included a broad certifica-tion, workforce studies, the development of professional development systems, and new definitions for the field. Broader thinking is bringing the sectors together, recognizing the continuum on which young people develop from 5 to 18 years.

For example, the Association for Youth Care Practice helped to promote a uni-fied professional field by developing a certification process for youth workers. The certificate, developed between 2000 and 2007, defines a common body of skills, knowledge, and values that transcend settings, participant ages, and popu-lation demographics (Curry, Schneider-Munoz, Eckles, & Stuart, 2012). Ground-ed in the belief that a credible national professional development system requires rigor, the certification process involves a written exam, 250 training hours, and an electronic portfolio, as well as references and a supervisor assessment (Curry et al., 2012).

The first workforce studies were conducted in the early 2000s. Building a Skilled and Stable Workforce, a project conducted by NIOST and the AED Cen-ter for Youth Development and Policy Research (2003), with funding from the David and Lucille Packard Foundation, was a two-year process of investigations and conversations with a national advisory committee. The process culminated in a national strategic plan with recommendations that included determining a national set of standards and compensation benchmarks for OST workers, uniting stakeholders to advocate for resources, and replicating successful models like the

U.S. military's system. The 2005 Next Generation and NAA workforce surveys (Yohalem & Pittman, 2006) added substantially to the knowledge base.

Cities and states began to develop the first professional development systems. Boston, for example, received funding from the Barr Foundation to support a pilot called the Achieve Boston Initiative, focused on professionalizing the field and enhancing careers, in part through the development of a credential. The initiative developed the credit-bearing School Age and Youth Development (SAYD) credential, a collaborative effort with local colleges (Hall & Surr, 2005). What Achieve Boston lacked was financial support, without which the initiative was not able to sustain its efforts—the SAYD no longer exists.

Another substantial effort was the Next Generation Youth Work Coalition, funded by Cornerstones for Kids and Annie E. Casey to provide advocacy and research to prepare and support practitioners and to professionalize the field. In 2004, the Coalition's definition of youth workers helped unite the field across sectors and funding streams, defining youth workers as "individuals who work with or on behalf of youth to facilitate their personal, social and educational development and enable them to gain a voice, influence and place in society as they make the transition from dependence to independence" (Stone, Garza, & Borden, 2004, p. 9). Their broad definition invited the various sectors to see themselves as part of one field. The Coalition's Career Pathways Project established a learning community among networks in nine cities to build on efforts toward comprehensive workforce development systems (Starr, Gannet, & Garza, 2008). Out of this project grew a pilot using the popular T.E.A.C.H. early childhood scholarship model for school-age and afterschool professionals (Starr et al., 2008). Though funding for some of these workforce projects of the early 2000s ended, they laid a foundation for work on comprehensive systems of professional development across participant ages and funding streams.

## THE LANDSCAPE TODAY

Though large-scale workforce studies have not been conducted since the 2005 NAA and Next Generation studies, smaller studies seem to show some progress toward professionalization. In a 2013 survey of its members, the NAA (2015) again found high levels of education, with 34% holding a master's degree. It also found more longevity than in the 2005 survey: Almost half of respondents had been in the OST field for more than 10 years, and 39% had been with their current employer for that long. Furthermore, 70% of respondents were salaried employees (NAA, 2015).

However, workforce issues still plague the field. A study of the early childhood field 25 years after the National Child Care Staffing Study found little improvement in teacher wages, despite a dramatic increase in cost to families. Even more discouraging, the study found that increases in staff of education did not affect salaries (Whitebook, Phillips, & Howe, 2014).

The good news is that focus on these issues is increasing in all three sectors, with workforce initiatives being led primarily by early childhood and the NAA. In early childhood and school-age care, a 2015 report by the Institute of Medicine with the National Research Council sets out what is known about child development, the quality of early child care, and implications for professionals. The bottom line? Much is known about how to provide quality programming that improves outcomes for young children, but that knowledge is not necessarily reflected in practice, policy, and infrastructure. The report sets out a blueprint for action to achieve a stronger workforce, stressing unity among professionals who work with children from birth through age eight. It recommends actions aimed at improving higher education and professional learning, strengthening qualification requirements based on core competencies, and promoting evaluation that leads to continuous improvement in professional practice (Institute of Medicine & National Research Council, 2015).

The early childhood field already has many pieces of professional development systems in place, including the early childhood credential, core competencies, training registries, and career pathways. School-age care remains a significant part of early childhood, with about a third of subsidy dollars going to programs for children ages 5–13 years (Administration for Children and Families, 2015). In 2015, the Office of Child Care established several national centers to promote early childhood quality and access, including the National Center on Afterschool and Summer Enrichment, focusing much-needed attention on the role OST plays in early childhood (Administration for Children and Families, n.d.). Ideally, this emphasis would lead to the full inclusion of school-age care in the early childhood professional development system.

In the afterschool sector, the NAA has intentionally placed greater emphasis on professional development in recent years. The association has been promoting its Core Knowledge and Competencies for Afterschool and Youth Development Professionals (adopted in 2011) and accompanying self-assessment. NAA provides an annual convention and ongoing online professional development workshops, newsletters, and podcasts aimed at afterschool providers (NAA, n.d.).

Other workforce initiatives are underway in the U.S. Department of Education as well as private organizations. 21st CCLC developed You for Youth, an online professional learning community driven by interactive multimedia learning modules, in response to the need for high-quality, low-cost professional development. Recent changes in legislation have increased the 21st CCLC "quality set-aside" dollars that can be spent on activities to improve quality, such as professional development. Statewide afterschool networks, funded by the C. S. Mott Foundation, exist in most states, working to advocate for and strengthen the field. The networks initiated state standards of quality programming and offer professional development (often centering on STEM and literacy). While not focused on workforce issues specifically, the Afterschool Alliance—originally established as a public-private partnership between the C. S. Mott Foundation and the U.S. Department of Education to raise public awareness of the 21st CCLC program—has promoted public policy in the field since 2000 (Afterschool Alliance, n.d.). The Association for Youth Care Practice continues its work, providing research and training for professionals who work with children and youth across ages and settings.

In addition, the OST field now has quality assessment tools readily available. These tools help programs identify areas where specific staff training and support might be needed (Yohalem, Wilson-Ahlstrom, Fischer, & Shinn, 2009). Perhaps more importantly, many states have professional development systems that specify core competencies, offer credentials and degrees, and outline career pathways. The field also boasts countless examples of site-based training, coaching and mentoring, and communities of practice to support those who have chosen to make OST their profession.

Recent legislation has incorporated workforce issues. The 2015 reauthorization of the 21st CCLC in the Every Student Succeeds Act still includes funding for quality and professional development. The CCDF 2016 Final Rule, which updates regulations for the first time since 1998, addresses concerns about quality in part by increasing the proportion of funds states must use for quality and requiring states to tie training requirements to a professional development pathway (Administration for Children and Families, 2016).

Not only are the three sectors working independently on workforce initiatives, but their strands of influence are continuing to merge. In the past, the sectors were separated not only by history and funding, but also by the ages of children served. Though each age group has specific needs, the OST field now thinks about its work across the continuum of ages 5–18. Early childhood is working intentionally to attend to the older children it serves, as shown in the establishment of the National Center on Afterschool and Summer Enrichment. There are more efforts to align early childhood professional development systems with those in afterschool and youth work. For example, several states have core competencies that apply to multiple sectors, and many states have aligned academic and career pathways. Such efforts can reduce redundancies by, for instance, allowing common trainings for afterschool and early childhood providers or including multiple sectors in the same training registry. Taken together, these efforts will lead to a stronger, more unified field.

Further, federal initiatives are encouraging partnerships across systems. The Workforce Innovation and Opportunity Act (WIOA) of 2014 brings a unique opportunity to build the capacity of OST workers serving vulnerable youth in such a cross-system approach. The Departments of Education and Labor have jointly issued final rules to implement the legislation, designed to strengthen and improve the public workforce system.

## WHAT'S NEXT?

The way forward to a strong, stable OST workforce involves building on what has already been accomplished. Holistic efforts to build comprehensive systems, across sectors and funding streams, are key to success.

### Strengthen Workforce Policies by Focusing on the Whole, Not the Parts

Specific workforce efforts should continue while recognizing that professional development systems are part of larger quality improvement systems. Specific efforts, such as shaping community college courses around core competencies, increasing public and private partnerships to provide incentives and rewards for people who earn credentials, and improving workplace conditions, remain important. But there is no one silver bullet. The field and its component networks and advocates need to work simultaneously on all of the elements of a professional development system: common definitions of quality, academic and career pathways, training registries, and compensation strategies.

Leaders must also think systemically about sustainability. To sustain professional development initiatives into the future, they must focus now on building partnerships, diversifying funding, getting across the right messages, advocating for children, and embedding quality and professional development throughout programs and organizations.

### Bring Sectors Together

The sectors of OST—school-age care, afterschool, and youth work—are beginning to come together as one field with common characteristics and desired outcomes. Aligned efforts not only strengthen the workforce, but also maximize funding and resources. States, local communities, and organizations are already beginning to embrace common core competencies and quality practices. Career paths can cross settings; current career pathway systems can be expanded to include additional sectors—for example, early childhood career pathways can include school-age care and beyond. Training opportunities can be designed for multiple sectors. Professional development is a relatively easy place to begin aligning the sectors to strengthen the field.

### Create a Strong Academic Discipline of OST in Higher Education

The field needs training options that support both temporary workers who might not have much formal education and people who wish to remain in the field, regardless of their level of formal education. On-the-job professional development is part of a broad education strategy to address staff quality, but degrees and credit-bearing programs also play an important role. Furthermore, having a strong academic discipline, one with a coherent formal structure informed by a body of knowledge, will ensure that OST does not continue to sit at the periphery of academic departments, vulnerable to shifts in funding while struggling to maintain enrollment (Fusco, 2012).

## Advocate for Public Recognition of OST as a Profession

The 2005 NAA and Next Generation workforce surveys made clear that lack of public recognition was a challenge for the field. Leaders in the field at all levels need to advocate for changes in policy that acknowledge OST as a profession, such as more subsidies for school-age care to provide increases in teacher wages and more federal funds for professional development. When there is public recognition of and support for the field, funding will follow. Then initiatives to maintain a well-educated and highly skilled workforce can be sustained. Though beyond the scope of this chapter, recent interest in expanded learning time heightens the need to define and advocate for OST as a profession to maintain its unique strengths and their benefit to children and youth. (For further discussion on the expanded learning time context, field credentialing, and how a broad credential can bring the sectors together, see Starr & Gannett, 2016.)

The field has reached a critical moment in our history when we have amassed the skills and knowledge we need to create that highly skilled workforce. Public and private funders have invested in our field. Advocates have worked tirelessly for legislation and public support. The research community has conducted important studies documenting the effects of quality practice on youth outcomes. Thanks to those efforts, we are well positioned to achieve public recognition of our profession and sustain the strong, stable workforce our children and youth need and deserve.

## REFERENCES

Administration for Children and Families. (n.d.). National Centers. Retrieved from https://www.acf.hhs.gov/ecd/interagency-projects/ece-technical-assistance

Administration for Children and Families. (2015). *Characteristics of Families Served by Child Care and Development Fund (CCDF) Based on Preliminary FY 2014 Data.* Retrieved from https://www.acf.hhs.gov/occ/resource/characteristics-of-families-served-by-child-care-and-development-fund-ccdf

Administration for Children and Families. (2016). *Overview of 2016 Child Care and Development Fund Final Rule.* Retrieved from https://www.acf.hhs.gov/sites/default/files/occ/ccdf_final_rule_fact_sheet.pdf

Afterschool Alliance. (n.d.). *Our vision.* Retrieved from http://www.afterschoolalliance.org/aboutUsVision.cfm

Afterschool Matters. (2015). A deep passion for reading and writing: An Interview with Lena Townsend. *Afterschool Matters, 22,* 1–3.

American Federation of Teachers. (n.d.). *Center for the Childcare Workforce.* Retrieved from http://www.aft.org/node/10415

Campbell, N., Appelbaum, J. C., Martinson, K., & Martin, E. (2000). *Be all that we can be: Lessons learned from the military for improving our nation's child care system.* Washington, DC: National Women's Law Center.

Carnegie Council on Adolescent Development. (1994). *A matter of time: Risk and opportunity on the out-of school hours: Recommendations for strengthening community programs for youth.* New York, NY: Carnegie Corporation of New York.

Cole, P. (2011). Building an afterschool workforce: Regulations and beyond. *Afterschool Matters, 13,* 12–21.

Costly, J. (1998). *Building a professional development system that works for the field of out-of-school time.* Wellesley, MA: National Institute on Out-of-School Time.

Council for Professional Recognition. (n.d.). *About the Council for Recognition.* Retrieved from http://www.cdacouncil.org/about/the-council

Cunnien, K. (2011). *It's complicated: Crafting a system to support youth work.* St. Paul, MN: University of Minnesota. Retrieved from http://www1.extension.umn.edu/youth/Training- Events/docs/It's-Complicated.pdf

Curry, D., Schneider-Munoz, A., Eckles, F., & Stuart, C. (2012). Assessing youth worker competence: National child and youth worker certification. In D. Fusco (Ed.), *Advancing youth work: Current trends, critical questions* (pp. 27–38). New York, NY: Routledge.

Dennehy, J., Gannett, E., & Robbins, R. (2006). *Setting the stage for a youth development associate credential: A national review of professional credentials for the Out-of-School Time workforce.* Wellesley, MA: National Institute on Out-of-School Time, Wellesley Centers for Women.

Durlak, J. A., & Weissberg, R. P. (2007). *The impact of after-school programs that promote personal and social skills.* Chicago, IL: Collaborative for Academic, Social, and Emotional Learning.

Eccles, J. S., & Gootman, J. A. (Eds.). (2002). Features of positive developmental settings. In J. S. Eccles & J. A. Gootman (Eds.), *Community programs to promote youth development* (pp. 86–118). Washington, DC: National Research Council and Institute of Medicine, Board on Children, Youth, and Families, Division of Behavioral and Social Sciences and Education, National Academy Press.

Fusco, D. (2012). On becoming an academic profession. In D. Fusco (Ed.), *Advancing youth work: current trends: Critical questions* (pp. 111–126). New York, NY: Routledge.

Grossman, J., Campbell, M., & Raley, B. (2007). *Quality time afterschool: What instructors can do to enhance learning.* Philadelphia, PA: Public/Private Ventures.

Guskey, T. (2000). *Evaluation professional development.* Thousand Oaks, CA: Corwin Press.

Hahn, A., Lanspery, S., Aaron, P., Hostetler, B., & Peaslee, L. (2002). *Youth development policy: What American foundations can do to promote policy in support of the emerging field of youth development.* Kansas City, MO: Ewing Marion Kauffman Foundation.

Hall, G., & Surr, W. (2005). *Achieve Boston: The story of a planning process for building a professional development system for the Out-of-School Time workforce.* Wellesley, MA: National Institute on Out-of-School Time, Wellesley Centers for Women.

Halpern, R. (2002). A different kind of child development institution: The history of after-school programs for low-income children. *Teachers College Record 104*(2), 178–211.

Halpern, R. (2006). *Confronting the "big lie": The need to reframe expectations of after-school programs*. Chicago, IL: Erikson Institute.

Institute of Medicine and National Research Council of the National Academies. (2015). *Transforming the workforce for children birth through age 8: A unifying foundation*. Washington, DC: Author.

Lauer, P. A., Akiba, M., Wilkerson, S. B., Apthorp, H. S., Snow, D., & Martin-Glenn, M. L. (2006). Out-of-school time programs: A meta-analysis of effects for at-risk students. *Review of Educational Research, 76*(2), 275–313.

Lerner, J. V., Bowers, E. P., Minor, K., Lewin-Bizan, S., Boyd, M. J., Mueller, M. K., … Lerner, R. M. (2013). Positive youth development: Processes, philosophies, and programs. In R. M. Lerner, M. A. Easterbrooks, & J. Mistry (Eds.), *Handbook of Psychology, Volume 6: Developmental Psychology* (2nd ed., pp. 365–392). Hoboken, NJ: Wiley.

Miller, B., & Hall, G. (2007). What counts in afterschool? Findings from the Massachusetts Afterschool Research Study (MARS). *Journal of Youth Development, 55*(3), 98–114.

National AfterSchool Association. (n.d.). *About us*. Retrieved from http://naaweb.org/about-us

National AfterSchool Association. (2015). *The state of afterschool quality: Promoting professionalism*. Washington, DC: Author. Retrieved from http://naaweb.org/images/final_NAA_3_F.pdf

National Center on Child Care Professional Development Systems and Workforce Initiatives. (2013). *Aligned Professional Development Systems Planning and Implementation Guide*. Washington, DC: Author.

NIOST & the AED Center for Youth Development and Policy Research. (2003). *Strategic plan: Building a skilled and stable out-of-school time workforce*. Wellesley, MA: Authors.

Peter, N. (2009). Defining our terms: Professional development in out-of-school time. *Afterschool Matters*. Wellesley, MA: National Institute on Out-of-School Time.

Rhodes, J. E. (2004). The critical ingredient: Caring youth-staff relationships in afterschool settings. *New Directions for Youth Development, 101*, 145–161.

Roth, J., & Brooks-Gunn, J. (2016) Evaluating youth development programs: Progress and promise. *Applied Developmental Science, 20*(3), 188–202. doi: 10.1080/10888691.2015.1113879.

Roth, J., Brooks-Gunn, J., Murray, L., & Foster, W. (1998). Promoting health adolescents: Synthesis of youth development program evaluations. *Journal of Research on Adolescence, 8*(4), 423–459.

School's Out Washington. (2008). *A well-prepared workforce brings out the best in our kids: A framework for a professional development system for the afterschool and youth development workforce in Washington State*. Retrieved from http://www.schoolsoutwashington.org/documents/workforce%20study%20full%20report.pdf

Starr, E., & Gannett, E. (2014). *A proposed framework for a statewide career development system. Wyoming Afterschool Alliance*. Retrieved from http://wyafterschoolalliance.

org/wp-content/uploads/2013/08/Wyoming-Career-Development-System-Summa-ry-Final.pdf

Starr, E., & Gannett, E. (2015). *Exploring the promise of a continuum approach to career development systems: Aligning efforts across early childhood, afterschool and youth development.* Wellesley, MA: National Institute on Out-of-School Time, Wellesley Centers for Women. Retrieved from http://www.niost.org/pdf/ExploringContinuu-mApproach_May2015_v2.pdf

Starr, E., & Gannett, E. (2016). Credentialing for youth work: Expanding our thinking. In K. M. Pozzoboni & B. Kirshner (Eds.), *The changing landscape of youth work* (pp. 31–50). Charlotte, NC: Information Age.

Starr, E., Gannett, E. & Garza, P., with Goldstein, S., & Yohalem, N. (2008). *Clear policies for career pathways: Lessons learned.* The Next Generation Youthwork Coalition. Retrieved from http://forumfyi.org/files/Next%20Gen%20Lessons%20Learned%20Final.pdf

Stone, B., Garza, P., & Borden, L. (2004). Attracting, developing and retaining youth workers for the next generation. *Wingspread Conference Proceedings.* Washington, DC: National Collaboration for Youth/National Assembly.

Vandell, D. L., Reisner, E., & Pierce, K. (2007). *Outcomes linked to high-quality afterschool programs: Longitudinal findings from the study of promising practices.* Irvine, CA: University of California and Washington, DC: Policy Study Associates

Walker, J., & Walker, K. (2012). Establishing expertise in an emerging field. In D. Fusco (Ed.), *Advancing youth work: Current trends, critical questions* (pp. 39–51). New York, NY: Routledge.

Whitebook, M., Howes, C., & Phillips, D. (1989). *National child care staffing study: Who cares? Child care teachers and the quality of care in America.* Oakland, CA: Child Care Employee Project.

Whitebook, M., Phillips, D., & Howe, C. (2014). *Worthy work, STILL unlivable wages: The early childhood workforce 25 years after the National Child Care Staffing Study.* Berkeley, CA: Center for the Study of Child Care Employment.

Yohalem, N., & Pittman, K. (2006). *Putting youthwork on the map: Key findings and implications from two major workforce studies.* Washington, DC: Forum for Youth Investment for the Next Generation Workforce Coalition.

Yohalem, N., Wilson-Ahlstrom, A., Fischer, S., & Shinn, M. (2009). *Measuring youth program quality: A guide to assessment tools, Second Edition.* Washington, DC: The Forum for Youth Investment.

You for Youth. (n.d.). *About 21st Century Community Learning Centers.* Retrieved from https://y4y.ed.gov/about

Youth Work Central. (n.d.). *BEST Initiative* [website]. Retrieved from http://youthwork-central.org/best-initiative/

CHAPTER 8

# CORE COMPETENCIES FOR THE OST FIELD

Gina Hilton Warner, Heidi Ham, and Melissa S. Pearman Fenton

Researchers in the field support out-of-school time (OST) professionals as a key factor to quality OST programs that produce positive youth outcomes (Larson, Rickman, Gibbons, & Walker, 2009; Little, 2004). Mahoney and Warner (2014) identified staff knowledge and competence as one of four foundational ideas that contribute to program quality. Staff contributions in providing youth with "safe, supportive relationships and a positive emotional climate" (Palmer, Anderson, & Sabatelli, 2009, p. 8) were included in eight quality frameworks for OST. Strong staff–youth relationships were connected to academic engagement and future aspirations in Huang and colleagues' (2007) study of LA's BEST OST program. The research clearly supports that OST professionals are an important contributor to program quality and youth outcomes (Russell, Mielke, & Reisner, 2009).

OST professionals possess a variety of educational levels, backgrounds, and prior related experiences (Nee, Howe, Schmidt, & Cole, 2006). This variability in the workforce creates a need to identify the basic knowledge and competencies to be successful working with youth. Cole (2011) identified establishing competencies that address the basic level of knowledge frontline staff need to positively impact youth development as a key strategy for improving program quality. The National Institute on Out-of-School Time (NIOST) and AED Center for Youth

*The Growing Out-of-School Time Field: Past, Present, and Future,*
pages 103–114.
Copyright © 2018 by Information Age Publishing
**103**

Development and Policy Research (2003) called for standards for skills needed by OST workers to advance workforce development strategies. Borden and Perkins (2006) endorsed adopting a systematic theory to inform practice and a system-wide code of ethics, along with meeting the educational needs of youth development workers to professionalize the field. Several researchers have recommended the development of a consistent set of core competencies in youth development that spanned the diversity of the youth development field (Astroth, Garza, & Taylor, 2004; Stone, Garza, & Borden, 2004). Professional core competencies are the key to addressing staff qualifications by defining standards for staff, guiding assessment, and supporting training (Afterschool Investments Project, 2009).

The National AfterSchool Association (NAA) Core Knowledge and Competencies (CKCs) for Afterschool and Youth Development Professionals addressed the needs identified in the literature. The NAA CKCs present the knowledge, skills, and dispositions needed by OST professionals to provide high-quality youth development programming to support the learning and development of children and youth (National AfterSchool Association, 2011). "Core knowledge refers to the expertise needed by professionals to work effectively with school-age children and youth and competencies refer to concrete, observable, and achievable behaviors that establish standards of practice" (National AfterSchool Association, 2011, p. 3). Core knowledge and competencies also bring related youth development fields such as school-age care, OST, recreation, and summer learning together, something the field of OST and youth development has struggled to accomplish (Starr, Yohalem, & Gannett, 2009; Stone et al., 2004).

The NAA CKCs[1] were developed by NAA and NIOST, in cooperation with the Florida Afterschool Network and Pennsylvania Key (National AfterSchool Association, 2011). The project began with a comparison of competencies and indicators included in a sample of existing frameworks. Next, project leaders selected a subset of the numerous state and organizational competency frameworks, focusing on those that target professionals working with a broad range of children and youth ages 5 to 18, and started the framework building process using the Kansas/Missouri model (National AfterSchool Association, 2011). The Kansas/Missouri model was selected as the foundational competency framework due to the linkage to professional development, descriptions of knowledge and skills, and use of indicators divided into levels to establish skills needed by OST professionals entering the field and those advancing in the workforce (Starr et al., 2009). After the collection of competency frameworks, NAA engaged in a pilot and review process (National AfterSchool Association, 2011). Six sites from across the nation participated in pilot projects, testing the competencies in a variety of ways, including cross walking them with their own existing state competencies and quality rating and improvement systems (QRIS), examinations by staff earning credentials in the field, sharing the draft with providers, and as a tool for hiring and evaluating staff (National AfterSchool Association, 2011). The draft was widely disseminated throughout the field for review, and close to 100 reviewers from across the country provided feedback using an online survey. Thus, the NAA CKCs are a composite of what has already been tested through practice.

Reflective practice is a key component in learning theories (Kolb, 1984), and experts recommend that staff identify their weaknesses and create plans for improvement (Astroth et al., 2004); thus, a set of leveled CKC Self-Assessment Tools was designed to empower individuals to assess their knowledge and skills based on the competencies outlined in the NAA CKCs. The CKC Self-Assessment Tools are organized by level and allow group leaders, youth workers, or other youth development professionals to assess the level of knowledge and skills in each one of the ten content areas, identify specific areas for future professional development, and plan specific actions that will lead to improvement. Administrators and supervisors, alongside OST professionals, can use the CKC Self-Assessment Tools to guide staff evaluation, assessment of skills, and needs-based professional development discussions. The CKC Self-Assessment Tools do not attempt to define specific indicators or examples of each of the competency statements. This national document leaves room for states and local organizations/programs to customize indicators that meet specific state and program needs (National AfterSchool Association, 2011).

The NAA CKCs answered the call for a unifying set of knowledge and competencies; however, the NAA CKCs will not impact the OST field without quality professional development systems for OST professionals. Mahoney, Levine, and Hinga (2010) found that OST educators benefited from foundational courses on OST learning, child and adolescent development, educational approaches for diverse youth, and content knowledge in areas relevant for OST programming, in their case studies of two university–community partnerships. Preservice training and ongoing professional development efforts are needed to ensure that OST professionals have foundational knowledge in OST learning and youth development, can demonstrate competencies in their important work with youth, and remain in their positions to gain experience and practice these competencies. Huang and Dietel (2011) discovered that high-quality programs tended to have low staff turnover rates and recommended educational opportunities and other incentives to build staff retention. Weiss and colleagues (2006) asserted that professional development and organizational capacity to support staff improved the practices of the workforce and professionalized the field, leading to quality experiences for children and youth, and ultimately improved outcomes for children and youth. Investing in professional development will improve staff, the programs they work in, and in turn, the OST field (Peter, 2009). This chapter provides promising practices for integrating the NAA CKCs into professional development systems and a call to action for the field to support developing OST professionals to support program quality.

## METHODS

The purpose of this chapter is to describe the ways in which national professional development providers, higher education entities, states, counties, and cities used the NAA CKCs in their professional development systems. A request for participation and 15 written, open-ended questions were sent to 15 OST professional development system administrators, who implemented the NAA CKCs as part of their system. Representatives from nine organizations agreed to submit written responses to be featured practices. The authors contacted the system administrators to ask clarifying questions, as needed. Responses were used to find common themes and build practice descriptions. Quantitative data were included to illustrate the reach and use of the professional development experiences that integrated the NAA CKCs. Promising practices and concrete examples are featured to help advocates; policymakers; OST program directors/administrators; and federal, state, and local agencies implement the NAA CKCs in similar ways to unify their respective professional development systems.

## PROMISING PRACTICES

Five different types of systems were identified in the review of the interview responses. Each system voluntarily integrated the NAA CKCs into their respective professional development systems following their release and distribution to OST professionals in 2011 (National AfterSchool Association, 2011). The descriptions are identified by the organization that submitted the interview responses, any participant and quantitative data are reported in aggregate form, and individual quotes and responses have been kept confidential. A description of each system and discussion of common themes follows.

### National Professional Development System

Penn State Extension's Better Kid Care provides affordable, online, and "evidence-informed professional development to early care and education and youth development professionals to improve the quality of their care and educational practices" (n.d., para. 1). The NAA CKCs were selected to link and align the professional development system with a nationally recognized, research-based, and established core body of knowledge and competencies (National AfterSchool Association, 2011). The NAA CKCs frame and inform the content of the three major school-age youth projects within the organization's On Demand Professional Development system. Learners earn a certificate of completion after completing the training modules, which can be submitted to state child care licensing and/or QRIS for professional development credit. Out-of-school time professionals can also earn CEUs through Penn State University by completing the training modules offered by this system. Penn State University administers this online system and their portfolio of funding includes state and national agency funding, grants, foundation support, and user-generated fees. Over 6,000 participants have completed the school-age, youth development web lessons. For all modules, two questions are asked of learners to determine knowledge gained and intent to apply that knowledge to their settings. A four-point Likert-type scale (1=nothing at all to 4=a great deal) was used and the means for all modules for both questions is above 3.3. Qualitative data are also collected at the end of the module, ensuring that learners are gaining knowledge and plan to apply this knowledge to their program responsibilities.

## Higher Education Professional Development System

Clemson University, a tier-one research and land grant university, offers two online degree programs in youth development. The Master of Science (MS) online degree in youth development leadership prepares professionals to lead, grow, and create youth-serving environments and collaborate with community partners. The Bachelor of Science (BS) online degree completion program in youth development studies prepares graduates to be qualified to serve in the youth development profession in a variety of youth-serving organizations, institutions, and agencies. The NAA CKCS were used to guide the youth development program curriculum. Student tuition, state of South Carolina funding, and research awards and activity from state and federal agencies, and foundations fund the degree programs. Clemson developed the MS program in 2006, with 157 graduates of the program and 35 students receiving a certificate in youth development leadership. The BS program was developed two years ago. The following results attest to the success of the youth development degree programs. Since 2006, 61 MS youth development leadership graduates reported an increase of skill enhancement on multiple benchmarks between the inception of their enrollment and current work responsibilities. The benchmarks included child and youth assessment, connecting with communities, theories of youth development, cross-cultural competence, grant writing, staff and volunteer development, organizational effectiveness, youth empowerment, incorporating best practices, and building leadership and advocacy. When respondents were asked how obtaining a MS youth development leadership degree helped them professionally, 40% reported that they were assigned greater responsibility in their current work environment, 30% received a pay increase, 15% were promoted to a higher positon, 17% left their previous employer for a higher-level position, and 7% received a higher pay at their new position (Garst, Bowers, Quinn, & Gagnon, 2016).

## State Professional Development Systems

Utah, Michigan, New Hampshire, and Wisconsin use a professional development system that offers credentials to OST professionals. These credentials have varying requirements, and different administrators and agencies supporting the credentials and professional development; however, they all aligned the professional development experiences required for the credential to the NAA CKCs.

The Utah Afterschool Network (UAN) recently revamped their credentialing system and the supportive coursework is built upon the NAA CKCs. The new credentialing system was rolled out this year and includes the CKC Self-Assessment Tools, as part of the credential requirements, to help OST professionals determine areas they need specific training in to provide higher-quality care.

The Michigan School-age Youth Development (SAYD) certificate and credential included a professional development plan based on the first two levels of the NAA CKCs and categorized all professional development opportunities into the ten content areas of the NAA CKCs. The credential provides recognition to the committed OST professionals for training and experience. Individuals pay a fee for the certificate or credential and the initial development of the credential system was supported by funds generated by the statewide collaborative conference. The NAA CKCs and SAYD certificate and credential were included in the school age QRIS design and state sponsored professional development system. To date, 230 individuals have established accounts in the SAYD system.

New Hampshire requires OST professionals to document coursework or ongoing professional development trainings in the NAA CKCs content areas. The state Department of Health and Human Services (DHHS), Department of Children and Families (DCYF), and Child Development Bureau's (CDB) Afterschool Support Services require that all professional development opportunities offered in the state tie back to the content areas in the NAA CKCs. New Hampshire DHHS, DCYF, and CDB administer the professional development system and provide financial support through the Afterschool Provider Support Services contract. Out-of-school time professionals also pay a credentialing fee to support the system. As of September 2016, 9,544 individuals participated in workshops and trainings, 365 individuals received technical assistance for the credential, 855 program sites received technical assistance, and 279 OST professionals received their afterschool credential.

Wisconsin provides an Afterschool and Youth Development (ASYD) credential and threaded the NAA CKCs throughout the credential's four required courses. The four-course sequence (total of 12 credit hours) is taught by a professional educator through a state institution of higher education with the NAA CKCs embedded into learning activities in the courses. Out-of-school time professionals are required to submit a portfolio with specific work samples from the credential courses and a completed CKC self-assessment to earn the ASYD credential. These work samples document the credential candidate's proficiency in the NAA CKCs. This credential was implemented in 2014 and 60 ASYD Credentials have been awarded to date. The professional development system is supported by the Wisconsin Early Childhood Association, Supporting Families Together Association, Department of Public Instruction, University of Wisconsin, Wisconsin Technical College System, Wisconsin Afterschool Network, Wisconsin Department of Children and Families, and the Waisman Center. The credentialing system is supported by tuition costs and commission fees paid for by participants. Scholarships are available in the state to support a significant portion of the cost of a credential.

## County Professional Development Systems

The Kalamazoo Youth Development Network (YD Network) serves as an intermediary organization for a county section of OST programs in Michigan. The YD Network provided training, coaching, and technical assistance based on the NAA CKCs, supporting the Michigan SAYD certificate and credential. The YD Network provides training aligned to the NAA CKCs for 30 organizations with 400 OST professionals that serve over 6,000 youth in their county and tracks the types and amount of training each organization receives. Using this intervention data and organizations' program evaluation scores, the YD Network will be able to understand the relationship between the training in the NAA CKCs and program quality. Funded by three local foundations and another private funder, the YD Network is partnering with a local university to create a Bachelor of Science degree in youth development with courses based on the NAA CKCs.

The professional development system in Cuyahoga County, Ohio, supports the growth and development of OST professionals in the child and youth development workforce. The County Youth Work Institute (CYWI) provides workshops and other support to individuals working with youth ages 5–18. This work is funded by Ohio Child Care Resources and Referral, and participants pay minimal fees for workshops. All workshops offered by the CYWI are aligned to the NAA CKCs. The CYWI is using results from the CKC Self-Assessment Tools to tailor training and technical assistance for the 400 youth development professionals served by this system. From 2012 to the present, 1,143 OST professionals have participated in professional development trainings aligned to the NAA CKCs through CYWI.

## City Professional Development System

The Philadelphia OST professional development system provides OST professionals with content knowledge, mindset, and skills to provide quality programming that can lead to positive youth outcomes, particularly for high-risk and Department of Human Services (DHS)-involved youth. The city's DHS funds the citywide professional development system that coordinates professional development opportunities, a trainer approval and evaluation system, and aligns all professional development opportunities to the NAA CKCs. The CKC Self-Assessment Tools were integrated to gather data and other information to determine progress in achieving overall objectives and informing target areas for additional support and resources. The system also collects and analyzes data from the 1,275 individuals who have participated in the professional development opportunities. The online and in-person workshops, small-group coaching, technical assistance, and credentialing are delivered by partners including the library, a council on health, a foundation, and a community college.

*Discussion of Themes*

Each system reported integrating the NAA CKCs into their respective professional development programs because they are a nationally recognized, research-based framework that identified standards of practice and knowledge OST professionals need to be effective youth development professionals and leaders. These systems emphasized that grounding their professional development programs in a national framework gave credibility to the professional development experiences. The NAA CKCs provided an opportunity for the professional development experiences to support a common language and competencies that OST professionals need to be successful working with youth. A director of youth and community programs noted that they aligned professional development offerings to the NAA CKCs to "ensure they were high-quality and that the skills and competencies taught were relevant to youth-work professionals and nationally recognized." A network director commented, "We believe that without the NAA CKCs our field would not have a common framework for understanding what it means to be a youth development professional."

A common vision for each professional development system also emerged as a theme. The noted professional development systems were designed to ensure that OST professionals have the skills and competencies they need to provide high-quality programming for youth and to strengthen the field of professionals who work in OST. The systems' common goal was to professionalize the OST and youth development field and create a stable, skilled workforce. Systems also recognized the link between staff skill and competence to higher-quality programs and positive youth outcomes. Preservice and ongoing professional development are key to building and developing these skills in OST professionals. A 21st Century Community Learning Center (CCLC) coordinator shared that "the NAA CKCs were included in this system because of a strong belief and research review that shows that staff who have credentials and training appropriate to the work of youth development and school-age programming will more likely provide higher quality programs for children and youth."

Each of these systems also reported similar challenges to implementing professional development experiences aligned to the NAA CKCs. Existing professional development offerings were compared to the NAA CKCs and adapted to reflect the content areas not reflected in existing training. The initial work of aligning existing training, workshops, and courses to the NAA CKCs was reported as challenging due to the financial costs and lengthy review process. Many systems reported that the lack of OST professionals pursuing professional development experiences and credentials was a barrier that the systems are working to overcome. "The biggest challenge that we have is for many OST/youth development professionals, there is no incentive for continuing professional development" a system administrator shared. The profession is still in its infancy, relative to other career fields, and there is a lack of clear career pathways for OST professionals, contributing to this barrier. An afterschool network lead noted that "it has been a challenge having OST staff view themselves as professionals."

## RECOMMENDATIONS

These recommendations draw from the analysis of progress in building a shared basis of knowledge and competencies for the OST workforce through adoption and implementation of the NAA CKCs. The recommendations consider current limitations of both human and financial resources inherent in many OST programs but also advance aspirational goals to grow, diversify, and enhance the development of the individuals who comprise the OST workforce. Taken together, the recommendations below present a blueprint for action to support and promote the professionalism of the field of OST.

### Recommendation 1: Generate Stronger Evidence to Strengthen the OST Workforce

As this chapter demonstrates, systems are developing models to provide OST professionals with the knowledge and competencies to provide high-quality programs to children and youth. However, the current body of academic research in the field does not adequately reflect that. These practices provide researchers with models to test, bridging the gap between research and practice.

### Recommendation 2: Increase Political Will and Financing for Professionalizing the Workforce

While much progress has been made in recent years to build financial support for greater access to programs for youth, there is still much to be done to support longer-term sustainability for building knowledge and competencies of the OST workforce. Increased evidence of the positive effects of trained professionals on youth outcomes will enable stronger advocacy for funding resources for this work at the local, state and federal level. More research on the broader impacts of such investments will also be useful in attracting new resources to this work. Engaging the private sector as partners, who will benefit from greater support for the education and childcare needs of their current employees and are the future beneficiaries of a more educated and prepared workforce, will build the financial resources needed to help accomplish this goal of knowledgeable and skilled OST professionals.

### Recommendation 3: Provide Equitable Access to High-Quality Professional Development and Learning

OST professionals need access to appropriate, high-quality professional development. Promising practices in this chapter have highlighted successful efforts that can serve as models for replication. Higher education partners, educational and training institutions, and organizations need to connect data about the current workforce to identify education and training gaps and to create programs and trainings to meet those needs. Further documentation of effective ways to accredit and recognize training is needed, and additional questions about how incentives influence participation in professional development opportunities need to be answered. However, unless there is an intentional focus on equitable access to high-quality professional development and learning, we will create gaps in opportunity for those working in underserved communities. This will result in diminished outcomes for the children they serve. Intentional focus on equitable access should include use of the NAA CKCs as a no-cost framework, widely accepted in the field. The CKC Self-Assessment Tools are available to programs at no cost to identify the education and training gaps and assess OST professionals' skills and abilities in positive youth development.

### Recommendation 4: Create Systems to Recruit, Retain, and Advance the Leadership of the Profession

Strong leaders are central to strong organizations. While other sectors and professions have been successful in identifying strategies that are effective in preparing and supporting leaders, the field of OST has struggled to create a coherent strategy to form a pipeline from staff to leader, resulting in frequent staff turnover that has negative financial and programmatic impacts on organizations. The NAA CKCs are intended to set a foundation for such career advancement, allowing for the identification of—and investment in—those individuals who demonstrate the capacity for leadership early in their careers, allowing them to advance in the field of OST (National AfterSchool Association, 2011).

### Recommendation 5: Promote the Vision of a Cohesive and Comprehensive Workforce That Includes Individuals Working in Diverse OST Settings

Children and youth are engaged in out-of-school experiences in several diverse school and community settings that include recreation facilities, libraries, museums, science centers, and others. Despite a shared objective of youth success, those individuals working directly with youth in these varied settings are not often viewed as part of what is commonly thought of as the OST workforce. With a nationally recognized framework grounded in research based practices, the NAA CKCs can serve as a unifying tool that brings these related fields together to ensure high-quality experiences for children across a variety of settings. Broad adoption of the CKCs by more cities, states, and youth-serving organizations would improve efforts to move the field forward in a way that embraces the strength of its diversity while elevating the profession.

## CONCLUSION

This chapter highlighted the research base that supports the contributions OST professionals make to high-quality programs that positively impact the youth they serve. Promising practices were shared to provide models of national professional development providers; higher education entities; and state, county, and city systems that are utilizing the NAA CKCs as a framework in their quality professional development offerings for OST professionals. Recommendations were shared as to call to action for the professionalization of the OST field. Through investments in the professional development systems that promote the building of knowledge and competencies in the OST professionals influencing our nation's youth, OST professionals will begin to see themselves in the terms they are described, as true professionals.

## NOTE

1.   This paragraph is adapted from the National AfterSchool Association. (2011, September). *Core knowledge and competences for afterschool and youth development professionals* (2nd ed.). McLean, VA: National AfterSchool Association. Retrieved from http://naaweb.org/resources/core-compentencies.

## REFERENCES

Afterschool Investments Project. (2009, September). Using the child care and development fund to support a system of quality improvement for school-age programs. Washington, DC: US. Department of Health and Human Services. Retrieved from http://www.researchconnections.org/childcare/resources/17370/pdf

Astroth, K. A., Garza, P., & Taylor, B. (2004). Getting down to business: Defining competencies for entry-level youth workers. *New Directions for Youth Development, 104,* 25–37.

Borden, L. M., & Perkins, D. F. (2006). Community youth development professionals: Providing the necessary supports in the United States. *Child & Youth Care Forum, 35*(2), 101–158. doi:10.1007/s10566-005-9005-4

Cole, P. (2011). Building an afterschool workforce: Regulations and beyond. *Afterschool Matters, 13,* 12–21.

Garst, B., Bowers, E., Quinn, W., & Gagnon, R. J. (2016). Building pathways from research to practice: Preparing youth development professionals through an online master's degree program. In K. M. Pozzoboni & B. Kirshner (Eds.), *The changing landscape of youth work: Theory and practice for an evolving field* (pp. 91–108). Charlotte, NC: Information Age Publishing.

Huang, D., Coordt, A., La Torre, D., Leon, S., Miyoshi, J., Perez, P., & Peterson, C. (2007). *The afterschool hours: Examining the relationship between afterschool staff-based social capital and student engagement in LA's BEST.* (CSE Technical Report No. 712). Los Angeles, CA: University of California.

Huang, D., & Dietel, R. (2011). *Making afterschool programs better* (CRESST Policy Brief). Los Angeles, CA: University of California.

Kolb, D. A. (1984). *Experiential learning: Experience as the source of learning and development.* Englewood Cliffs, NJ: Prentice-Hall.

Larson, R. W., Rickman, A. N., Gibbons, C. M., & Walker, K. C. (2009). Practitioner expertise: Creating quality within the daily tumble of events in youth settings. *New Directions for Youth Development, 121,* 71–88. doi: 10.1002/yd.297

Little, P. M. (2004). A recipe for quality out-of-school time programs. *The Evaluation Exchange, 10*(1), 18–19.

Mahoney, J. L., Levine, M. D., & Hinga, B. (2010). The development of after-school program educators through university–community partnerships. *Applied Developmental Science, 14*(2), 89–105. doi: 10.1080/10888691003704717

Mahoney, J. L., & Warner, G. (2014). Issue editors' notes. *New Directions for Youth Development, 144,* 1–10. doi: 10.1002.yd.20108

National AfterSchool Association. (2011). *Core knowledge and competencies for afterschool and youth development professionals.* Oakton, VA: Author.

National Institute on Out-of-School Time, AED Center for Youth Development and Policy Research. (2003). *Strategic plan: Building a skilled and stable out-of-school time workforce.* Retrieved from http://www.niost.org/pdf/building_workforce_niost.pdf.

Nee, J., Howe, P., Schmidt, C., & Cole, P. (2006). *Understanding the afterschool workforce: Opportunities and challenges for an emerging profession.* Houston, TX: National Afterschool Association for Cornerstones for Kids.

Palmer, K. L., Anderson, S. A., & Sabatelli, R. N. (2009). How is the afterschool field defining program quality? A review of effective program practices and definitions of program quality. *Afterschool Matters, 9,* 1–12.

Penn State Extension's Better Kid Care. (n.d.). About us. Retrieved from http://extension.psu.edu/youth/betterkidcare/about

Peter, N. (2009). Defining our terms: Professional development in out-of-school time. *Afterschool Matters, 9,* 34–41.

Russell, C. A., Mielke, M. B., & Reisner, E. R. (2009). *Evidence of program quality in the DYCD out-of-school time initiative: Report on the initiative's first three years.* Washington, DC: Policy Studies Associates.

Starr, E., Yohalem, N., & Gannett, E. (2009). *Youth worker core competencies: A review of existing frameworks and purposes.* Washington, DC: Next Generation Youth Work Coalition.

Stone, B., Garza, P., & Borden, L. (2004). *Wingspread conference proceedings: Attracting, developing, and retaining youth workers for the next generation.* Retrieved from https://cyfar.org/sites/default/files/Stone%202004.pdf.

Weiss, H., Klein, L., Little, P., Lopez, M. E., Rothert, C., Kreider, H., & Bouffard, S. (2006). Pathways from workforce development to child outcomes. *The Evaluation Exchange, 11*(4), 2–4.

CHAPTER 9

# TAKING IT TO A NEW LEVEL

## Inquiry-Based Professional Development as a Field-Building Enterprise

### Sara L. Hill, Joy Connolly, Thomas Akiva, and Anne McNamara

National and regional membership organizations representing out-of-school time (OST) and youth development professionals have established a consensus regarding the basic competencies needed for OST staff to do their jobs well (National Afterschool Association, 2011; Starr, Yohalem, & Gannett, 2009; see Warner, Ham, and Fenton's chapter, this volume). Competencies, however, are just a starting point; professional development (PD) is needed to effectively deal with the complexities of youth work (Larson, Walker, Rusk, & Diaz, 2015; Walker & Walker, 2012). As Larson et al. summarized, "running a program and facilitating youth development is more challenging and multidimensional than is generally appreciated" (2015, p. 74). We need PD that not only teaches competencies but enables and helps staff to grow as professionals and thought leaders.

In studies of OST programs, well-trained and knowledgeable staff members are a central feature (Bouffard, 2004; Hall & Gruber, 2007; Metz, Bandy, & Burkhauser, 2009). Indeed, decades of research on effective practices in OST programs point to the importance of staff (Hirsch, Deutsch, & DuBois, 2011; McLaughlin, Irby, & Langman, 2001). Staff–child relationships have been called

*The Growing Out-of-School Time Field: Past, Present, and Future,*
pages 115–132.

the "active ingredient" for settings that involve children and youth (Li & Julian, 2012). This is a case where research supports what most practitioners know: Staff members' skills and actions are crucial factors in determining the quality and outcomes of OST programs.

Staff preparation for today's OST youth programs often consists of either limited preservice training focusing on program procedures and regulations, state-mandated child care training on a narrow range of topics, or in-house, inservice PD.[1] In addition, PD developed outside of organizations is available for many program providers. Such PD programs are designed and delivered by national organizations, local intermediary organizations, and funders. Although OST PD is increasingly available, the types of PD, or the design, has often been limited.

OST PD trainings often take the form of single conference workshops or short-term opportunities, sometimes jokingly called "spray and pray," whose effect can be short-lived (Akiva, Martin, Galletta, & McNamara, 2016). Little attention has been paid to the format of inservice PD—that is, *how* it is designed and delivered to staff. Nor have there been many studies of OST PD programs designed with intentional pedagogical and andrological theories that engage participants in constructivist learning, leadership development, and inquiry (for one counterexample, see Akiva et al., 2016).

Research on PD in the education field has identified practices and factors that can increase its effectiveness. In a literature review, Hill (2014) identified studies of PD for in-school teachers that link professional development to improved teaching practice (Guskey, 2002). The findings demonstrate that time span and contact hours have a substantial positive influence on fidelity of implementation (Garet, Porter, Desimone, Birman, & Yoon, 2001, p. 933). PD that encourages collective participation and professional communication among practitioners, in other words, builds learning communities, tends to produce better outcomes (Cochran-Smith & Lytle, 1999; Finley, Marble, Copeland, Ferguson, & Alderete, 2000; Garet et al.; Wei, Darling-Hammond, & Adamson, 2010). Studies also suggest that "coherence" is important in PD—that is, opportunities for participants to make connections to practice through reflection and active learning. Akiva et al. (2016) describe strengths-based approaches to PD that build from program and adult strengths rather than target weaknesses to fix. In these strengths-based approaches to PD, "adults' experiences are the foundation for learning" (Akiva et al, 2016, p. 5).

Although practitioners in the OST field are charged with creating supportive communities for young people, they, themselves, often do not belong to a sustained community of practitioners who can guide them in reflective activities, provide opportunities to step into a leadership role, improve upon their practice, and contribute to knowledge in the field. Even if practitioners are fortunate enough to work at an organization that supports PD, the opportunities available to them are seldom, if ever, inquiry-based or those that encourage reflective practice.[2] Nor are there many opportunities for practitioners to participate over an extended period with the same group or cohort across sites within an organization or across OST program contexts. This may be because of a lack of understanding on the part of organizations regarding the benefits of inquiry-based PD or a lack of commitment to this long-term approach to PD. However, such opportunities foster the development of professional relationships and opportunities to share resources and successful strategies—generating and documenting knowledge that can move the needle on program quality.

This chapter will describe a research study and in-depth analysis of a PD program for OST staff that exhibits many effective practices of quality professional development: The National Afterschool Matters Practitioner Fellowship (the Fellowship). The Fellowship, which engages participants in an extensive, inquiry-based learning process over the span of several months, was founded in 2003 and has engaged nearly 200 youth work practitioners in several cities across the U.S. In addition, the chapter will describe two other inquiry-based PD programs available in the OST field, the boOST Your Expertise program and the Leading with Emotional Intelligence Fellowship. Finally, the chapter will end with a set of recommendations for how to offer high-quality, inquiry-based PD for youth staff, along with policy recommendations that can help to implement this type of PD.

## THE NATIONAL AFTERSCHOOL MATTERS PRACTITIONER FELLOWSHIP

The Fellowship has operated for 13 years, in six cities, serving approximately 197 youth work practitioners and teachers. Although slightly modified from the format in which it started 13 years ago, the Fellowship is still in existence.[3] Distinguished by the following features, the Fellowship is intentionally designed to:

- provide long-term and sustained (18 + months) PD
- engage a cohort of youth practitioners from across youth agencies (and sometimes schools)
- focus on building community and creating a safe learning environment
- build on participants' existing expertise and strengths
- engage practitioners in reflection, action research, and practitioner inquiry
- encourage participants to share their work with the larger community via published articles, conference presentations, and other venues

The Fellowship was originally funded and implemented by the Robert Bowne Foundation in New York beginning in 2003. Between 2007 and 2012, the Robert Bowne Foundation provided a grant to the National Institute on Out-of-School Time (NIOST) at Wellesley College, Wellesley Centers for Women, and the National Writing Project (NWP) to work in partnership to manage the Fellowship. After the program was assumed by NIOST and NWP, Fellowship sites received funding for two years, after which they had to find funding to continue the Fellowship. Six cities have hosted the Fellowship: Minneapolis, New York, Philadelphia, Pittsburgh, San Francisco, and Seattle. Some cities hosted the Fellowship for multiple years. One exception, the New Jersey Fellowship, was state-wide. The prototypical Fellowship allows fellows to generate their own topics of inquiry. In a couple of cases, the Fellowship has focused on specific topics, such as STEM or working with older youth. This has occurred because of interest on the part of local funders. In addition, two Fellowship sites have brought together in-school personnel and OST practitioners.

A Fellowship cohort consists of 10–15 practitioners who are working in OST youth development programs (except for Fellowships that included in-school personnel whose school may or may not have an afterschool program). The target audience for the Fellowship is mid-career or "seasoned" youth work professionals—that is, those with advanced degrees and/or those with two or more years of experience. Fellows are selected by application and are drawn from a range of nonprofit agencies. These include community-based nonprofits, parks and recreation, and government agencies, as well as school-based afterschool, weekend, and summer programs. The participants provide a range of OST services to children and youth: community and civic involvement, arts and media, social work, academic support, and sports.

Once selected, fellows meet twice a month for four months and then monthly to reflect upon their practice, identify their own critical issues and questions, read professional articles, engage in inquiry and action research, and hone their skills towards the goal of program improvement and dissemination of their work emerging from the Fellowship. Two facilitators lead each site. One is a local teacher consultant trained by the NWP. The other is a facilitator with experience in the OST field, and, optimally, one with experience in inquiry or research. Fellows from earlier years have served as facilitators. The Fellowship site is selected if (a) there is a strong local writing project and (b) if there is a community-based host or partner. In Minneapolis and San Francisco, participants were eligible for college credit at a reduced rate through the local writing project.

During the Fellowship sessions, participants read and discuss assigned readings on topics of action research, inquiry methods, data analysis, or general articles about the OST field. There is a strong reflective emphasis; fellows engage in activities in which they are guided to think and write about their practice. There is structured time during the sessions to read each other's writing and provide feedback. Fellows learn and then practice basic inquiry methods, such as observation and interviewing techniques. They practice the methods at the Fellowship session and then again at their own programs. There is an intentional focus on community building, and every session begins with an icebreaker/community-building activity.

## THREE ANALYTIC LENSES

We considered and analyzed the Fellowship using three theoretical frameworks: action research, community of practice, and social capital. These frameworks provide lenses for understanding an inquiry-based approach to PD who's goal is a field-building enterprise, and not that of just teaching basic competencies.

## Action Research

Action research can be traced back to the work of Kurt Lewin (1948, 1951). It is known by many similar but not completely interchangeable terms: teacher research, action research, community-based action research, teacher inquiry, and practice-centered inquiry, to name a few. The approach has also led to specific variations such as youth participatory action research and shares important characteristics with iterative improvement approaches such as design-based implementation research (Russell, Jackson, Krumm, & Frank, 2013).

Action research has been described as a "form of inquiry that enables practitioners everywhere to investigate and evaluate their work" (McNiff & Whitehead, 2006, p. 7). In this approach, the practitioner *is* the researcher, and the researcher-practitioner integrates social scientific knowledge with organizational and professional knowledge to solve real-world problems of practice (Coghlan & Brannick, 2005). Action research is highly pragmatic, and "sets out to explicitly study something in order to change and improve it" (Wadsworth, 1998, p. 4). A key goal of action research is to bridge the gap between "academic research and day-to-day applications" (Nolen & Vander Putten, 2007, p. 401).

Teacher inquiry or teacher research, a strand of action research, is an over 20-year movement that profiles teacher knowledge and emphasizes the importance of teachers in improving practice. Teacher research engages teachers in identifying questions and problems in their own practice and then examining these problems systematically and reflectively in order to make "coherent instructional decisions" (Finley et al., 2000, p. 1). As part of this movement, teacher-training models have moved from a focus on discrete skills to those of teachers learning in "professional communities" (Finley, et al., p.1). Teacher research is a way to investigate teachers' own teaching as well as "students' learning in and outside the classroom," (Nolan & Vander Putten, 2007, p. 401). Teacher research can affect program quality and inform "what is known about teaching, learning, and content and curriculum design" (Nolan & Vander Putten, 2007, p. 401).

## Community of Practice

The theory of Community of Practice (CoP) was first developed by Lave (1991) and Lave and Wenger's (1991) work on situated learning, which built on Leont'ev's (1978) activity theory. In this framework, learning is grounded in a sociocultural, historical context—defined by the interrelated processes of mind, culture, history, and the social world (Lave, 1991). According to Lave, "learning is defined as the process of becoming a member of a sustained community of practice" (p. 65). Identity development as a member of a community as well as gaining the skills and knowledge associated with membership are part of the process (Lave, 1991). Developing the knowledge and skills needed for community membership serves to motivate, shape, and provide meaning to participants' identity making during a transformational process.

Often used interchangeably with the term *professional communities*, CoPs are "groups of people informally bound together by shared expertise and passion for a joint enterprise" (Wenger & Synder, 2000, p. 139). Engagement in the practices and relationships within the CoP help to create identity and meaning for individuals and groups. More specifically, for individuals learning is "engaging in and contributing to the practices of their communities and for communities, learning is a process of refining their practice and ensuring new generations of members" (Wenger, 1998, p. 7).

## Social Capital

Social capital is a term that grew from theories of power and class system reproduction, particularly the work of Bourdieu (1986), who, rather than referring to material wealth, refers to the resources of social relationships and "networks of relationships" used to achieve economic and social success (Camras, 2004). Putnam (2000) defined social capital as "connections among individuals—social networks and the norms of reciprocity" (p. 19).

Yosso (2005), however, challenged the assumption that one type of social capital is better than other—for example, those that privilege White, upper-middle-class values. She identified specific types of social capital that spring from communities of color and challenge the deficit view that these communities are lacking in resources. Some of this type of social capital includes aspirational capital, which "refers to the ability to maintain hopes and dreams for the future, even in the face of real and perceived barriers" (Yosso, 2005, p. 10); linguistic capital, the "intellectual and social skills attained through communication experiences in more than one language and/or style" (p. 11); and familial capital, "which refers to those cultural knowledges nurtured among familia (kin) that carry a sense of community history, memory and cultural intuition" (p. 11).

Social capital has also been categorized in other ways: notably, "binding" or "bridging." Some types of social capital are within-group (binding) and some involve reaching across groups (bridging). Binding social capital tends to "reinforce group identities and...build solidarity" (Camras, 2004, p. 22). Immigrant communities, for example, are rich in binding social capital. Bridging social capital "incorporates people across a range of social dimensions...it generates broader social identities and long-term social relations" (Camras, 2004, p. 22). Bridging social capital allows access to resources outside one's immediate family and community.

## RESEARCH STUDY OVERVIEW

Our research study addressed three main components of the National Afterschool Matters Fellowship design: engaging participants in action research, seeking to build a community of practice, and facilitating the growth of participants' professional social capital. Specifically, we investigated the following research questions (RQs):

RQ1. How does engaging participants in inquiry-based action research affect their professional outlook and practices, professional identity, and views of research?

RQ2. To what extent and how did Fellowship participants experience a community of practice during and after the Fellowship?

RQ3. To what extent and how did participating in the Fellowship expand or enhance participants' professional social capital?

We hypothesized that the Fellowship provides effective PD for participants in all three of these areas. That is, we expected participants to (RQ1) report improvements in their professional self-beliefs and their views of research as integral to continuous improvement in OST (RQ1). We expected them to feel that they became part of a dynamic and professionally productive community of practice via participation in the Fellowship (RQ2). We expected that participants built social capital that continued to help them progress in their careers (RQ3). However, it is possible that our hypotheses were overly optimistic; we intentionally aimed to maintain a critical, balanced analytic perspective.

In addition, it is important to note our positionality: Some of the authors of this chapter were involved in leading and/or bringing the Fellowship to cities. We do not claim objectivity about this PD program; indeed, we advocate for the Fellowship and believe it provides a form of strengths-based, non-entry-level PD that fills an important niche in the OST field. However, as researchers, we wished to subject our beliefs about the Fellowship to data-based inquiry and were intentionally aware of and took steps to limit the potential for bias during design and analysis for this study.

The research team gathered data from multiple sources and perspectives. These included program documents, such as application forms and Fellowship websites.[4] In addition, the team conducted 20 telephone interviews from a randomized list of 176 past fellows. The interview protocol was designed using the three theoretical lenses: action research, communities of practice, and social capital. Other criteria for selecting participants were that they completed the Fellowship and were at least one year out of the program. Since the Fellowship took place in several cities, we made efforts to interview fellows from each of the cities.

Analysis consisted of two main parts. First, we analyzed a list of fellows' inquiry topics from the years 2003–2010, grouping them into categories through an iterative process. Next, we analyzed interview responses, with each team member reviewing data independently, and then grouping text using the three lenses for analysis. Through this process, we were collectively able to identify themes in each area. In addition, we collected and analyzed archived materials and products generated by Fellowship sites over the years. We present a combined analyses below but address our three research questions primarily with analysis of interview data.

## FINDINGS

### Action Research

To address RQ1, we first conducted a review of fellows' inquiry project topics from 2003–2010 to provide a descriptive picture of the types of projects participants conducted. As shown in Table 9.1, projects fell into four main categories: improving programs, building connections, helping youth develop and learn, and developing quality OST staff.

During interviews, fellows discussed reasons they chose their inquiry topic. The majority chose topics based on where they saw a need in their current experiences in their OST program. Some asked youth or other stakeholders (e.g., teachers, principals) about what would be useful. Others found inspiration through Fellowship activities such as reading research articles or engaging in personal reflection. Notably, several fellows reported that choosing a topic for inquiry was both an important and difficult task.

In interviews, participants discussed many additional aspects of their Fellowship experience, beyond the choice of topics. Perhaps because the Fellowship was intentionally designed to engage fellows in reflection, many of the respondents mentioned that the Fellowship provided them with the time and space to step back from intense, day-to-day practice and think, reflect, read, write, and inte-

TABLE 9.1.  Categorization of Inquiry Project Topics From 74 Participants in 2003–2010

| Category | Percent |
| --- | --- |
| Improving programs | 29% |
| Implementing specific curriculum (8%); supporting enrichment content (6%); developing a positive program culture (5%); improving academic content (3%); building time for free play (3%) | |
| Connections with schools, parents, and others | 29% |
| OST program and schools (8%); OST program and parents (5%); Across community partners (4%); OST program and community (3%); Other (5%) | |
| Helping youth develop and learn | 21% |
| Youth development (11%); academic learning (5%); youth engagement (3%) | |
| Developing quality OST staff | 21% |
| Professional development (7%); reflective practice (4%); staff retention (3%); leadership skills (3%), hiring practices (3%) | |

grate learning. That is, they described the importance of being able to step back from what Larson, Rickman, Gibbons, and Walker (2009) referred to as the "daily tumble of events" in youth program settings (p. 71). As one fellow mentioned, "It was one of my first opportunities with a group of people to reflect and think about what we were doing and take it to a different level." Several of the respondents mentioned that they found their "voice" and the Fellowship "validated their personal experience." Indeed, legitimizing the voice of teachers and lived experience is a central tenet of practitioner research.

Several respondents also noted that their views of research and practice shifted. They learned that they could be both a practitioner and a researcher and said that the Fellowship gave them "permission" and confidence to do so. Participants mentioned that they had learned a "new paradigm" that opened research in a way that they hadn't previously imagined. They realized that their own program could be a "laboratory," and that they were "sitting" on valuable information. They felt that what they learned through their inquiry helped them to revision their programs and to make changes in the way they supported staff or in their program design, another principle of action research; that is, research is used to provide solutions to a real-world problem.

Finally, fellows articulated an increased appreciation for the value of research; they became less "intimidated" by research, and in some cases, this shift in identity redirected their professional and intellectual trajectories. Several of them went on to participate in other research fellowships and academic ventures as well as publishing their work and presenting at professional conferences.

### Community of Practice

The design of the Fellowship and its group structure fostered CoP, and interviewees roundly found this to be a key aspect of their experience. Each Fellowship group was coordinated by two outside organizations and involved substantial and intentional facilitation by the leaders; interviewees noted that the facilitation of group activities and conversations was a key component in how they remembered this PD experience.

Additionally, participants reported that they gained a notable sense of belonging to a CoP from the diversity of the Fellowship members. When asked to tell about the group and how they interacted, most fellows described diversity and like-mindedness. For example, one said, "There were people in the group that were like-minded, it was a diverse group—age, race, [and] there were many different voices." This community-building across OST sectors, staff positions, race/ethnicity, gender, age was a unique and valued component of the Fellowship. Fellows articulated that they became resources for each other outside of the assigned group, acknowledged the rarity of this kind of opportunity to engage in cross-cultural dialogues, and identified the need/desire to continue to build upon these relationships.

Participants generally endorsed the notion that participants shared values, and the data illuminated some of these values: specifically, (a) a shared vision for children/youth, (b) an approach to participation within the group (i.e., openness, willingness to be reflective, and mutual support), and (c) a broad commitment to the OST field. Fellows were invested in gaining a deeper understanding of each other's roles within and outside of the Fellowship. This commitment was both guided by formal protocols and heightened by the shared values of fellows; as one mentioned, "We want it to be meaningful personally and for others."

Integral components of a CoP include identity development as a member of a community and gaining the skills and knowledge associated with membership. Lave and Wenger (1991) refer to groups as having a "center" and a "periphery." This identification is not intended to suggest a linear movement given the complex, differentiated nature of communities. Full participation encompasses the diversity of relations involved in varied forms of community membership. Fellows varied in whether they reported participating in peripheral or central ways, and the degree to which they saw themselves as insiders vs. outsiders in a community of practitioner-researchers varied. However, several described moving from periphery to center and moving from outsider to insider as a practitioner-researcher. It is important to note that some fellows mentioned that after the Fellowship ended, they had difficulty maintaining reflective practice, and, as one recalled, "I feel like I have insider knowledge but [I am] not practicing regularly."

## Social Capital

Fellows described the social capital they were exposed to in the Fellowship as important for professional progression in their careers. Fellows stated they felt more equipped to do the job they had during the Fellowship and to seek new job opportunities after participating in the Fellowship. For many, the Fellowship was a key to opening doors. They reported learning new skills (e.g., conducting research), honing existing skills (e.g., critical thinking, intentional questioning), and being able to add experiences to their resume (e.g., publishing, presenting). In fact, several interviewees shared that their experience led to professional improvement. Some fellows were promoted "from front line worker to a leadership position," and others started new organizations. One interviewee stated that the Fellowship "sent my career in a new direction."

Through participation in the Fellowship, individuals also reported that they acquired linguistic capital, allowing them to bridge across groups (Camras, 2004; Yosso, 2005). Several interviewees said they were able to more effectively communicate about their work through writing, presenting, and publishing. For example, one participant said she began to use writing to "express...and talk to others about what I was doing, share with professionals in field." In addition, learning the language of research allowed participants to gain power and influence in their local settings. One fellow commented, "I shifted into being engaged not just as a practitioner, to share my thoughts, but now I was being engaged to share my thoughts as a thought leader."

Finally, through their participation Fellows developed connections to new people and networks. Interviewees talked about the benefits of building relationships with other fellows, facilitators, and community members. For example, one participant said that, "Later down the line when I was looking to collaborate I could reach out to them. Or, if I had a question or was struggling I had colleagues to reach out to." Fellows also appreciated opportunities to "connect to the larger field" including local OST intermediaries, national associations, and funding opportunities. These "networks of relationship" (Camras, 2004, p. 41) provided social capital for fellows going forward in their careers.

## CHALLENGES/LIMITS OF THE FELLOWSHIP AND OF THIS RESEARCH

Interviewees responded quite positively about the Fellowship. However, our sample, although randomized, may have been biased by those who chose to respond. The respondents may indeed be those who had particularly good Fellowship experiences. It is also possible that the interview questions we asked led to particularly positive descriptions from interviewees. We did have a small number of respondents who articulated problems they experienced in the Fellowship, which helped to balance the mostly positive responses.

Although our respondents consistently described their overall experience of the Fellowship as extremely positive, they also noted some challenges and limitations. Some fellows did not feel that there was enough writing support and found the transition from reflective writing (e.g., journaling) to academic writing to be difficult. It's important to note, however, that later iterations of the Fellowship were designed to address this challenge by including a second year with a writing retreat followed by monthly writing support groups via Google Hangouts. The current iteration of the Fellowship is a two-year program, with intensive writing support in the second year. In addition, the end product changed over the years to include, in addition to longer academic pieces, lower-stakes writing, such as short pieces that are published on the *Youth Today* OST Hub and online opinion pieces and commentary.

A few other challenges were only mentioned by 15% of the total sample. One was that, in some cases, the co-facilitators had trouble working together or communicating. Another identified challenge was that fellows could not find another ongoing professional learning community once the Fellowship was over and expressed a need for a similar experience later in their careers. Finally, and not surprisingly, funding was a challenge. Fellowship sites found it extremely difficult to fund the Fellowship beyond the two years of the initial grant. They reported that funders believed that because the Fellowship was limited to 10–15 fellows, the impact on programs and youth would not be worth the investment.

## OTHER PROGRAMS THAT ENGAGE
## PRACTITIONERS IN INQUIRY

Although the National Afterschool Matters Fellowship was the first of its kind in the OST field, other inquiry-based PD programs have emerged since that time: the ExpandED Schools Pathways Fellows in New York and the Northstar Youth Worker Fellowship, a collaboration between the Minnesota Department of Education, the Sabo Center for Democracy and Citizenship at Augsburg College, University of Minnesota Extension Center for Youth Development, and Youthprise. The following are descriptions of two such models, the Alleghany Partnership in Out-of-School's boOST program and the National AfterSchool Association's Leading with Emotional Intelligence Fellowship. They were selected because they are aligned with many of the structures and principles of long-term, inquiry-based PD.

### BoOST Your Expertise

The boOST Your Expertise program (boOST) is a collaboration between a local intermediary organization, Allegheny Partners for Out-of-School time (APOST), and researchers at the University of Pittsburgh. It was created to bring together youth work practitioners (i.e. OST and informal learning educators) and university students. The goal of the program is to provide participants the opportunity to engage in practice-based action research by investigating a relevant topic of their choice.

Across the 10-month program, participants create and implement an action research project related to the field of youth work. University students and youth practitioners begin the program with a weekend-long retreat and then meet once per month for three hours. Topics for each session are related to each step of the action research process, such as interviewing techniques, survey development, and data analysis. Two facilitators coordinate the program, facilitate meetings, and provide feedback to boOST participants. Participants also work collaboratively to strengthen each other's projects through feedback and review. In addition, fellows can connect with local experts for coaching in specific areas. The program culminates in a presentation of data analysis at a local conference with the goal of establishing expertise personally and publicly within a specific area of the youth work field. Additionally, university students receive course credit and can use the experience as their master's capstone project.

The boOST program is different from the Fellowship in that it is shorter (10 months vs. 18 months) and does not focus as heavily on writing, but rather, conducting a PD presentation/workshop at a local OST conference is the culminating product. Another important difference is that boOST brings together practitioners and university students in each cohort. In the 2015–2016 year, there were 16 participants (seven practitioners and nine university students). Practitioners were from a variety of youth work settings such as museums, environmental education, and afterschool programs. Students, both undergraduate seniors and individuals in their second year of a master's program, were engaged in placements at local school and nonprofit organizations. Practitioners and students acted as two distinct groups though group meetings were held together. For example, students and practitioners tended to sit together during monthly meetings. A benefit of this grouping is that it allowed for new relationships to form, and in some cases, practitioners took on a mentorship role for the university students.

## Leading with Emotional Intelligence

The 2015–2016 National AfterSchool Association's (NAA) Leading with Emotional Intelligence Fellowship was funded by the Robert Bowne Foundation. NAA worked with the organization, Development Without Limits, which led the Fellowship through a mostly online model, with one face-to-face meeting, designed to develop the emotional intelligence (EI) of afterschool leaders. The model includes strategies to improve program leadership, staff development, and relationships. The goal of the program was to provide an opportunity for participants to become more connected to their personal emotional intelligence and strengthen their ability to strengthen their ability to utilize and model strong social emotional skills on the job.

During this six-month fellowship, participants join a virtual professional learning community (PLC) comprised of two 10-week modules; six weeks of reflective application; a monthly synchronous webinar; interactions with experts in social emotional learning; a virtual 'book club;' an opportunity for participants to present their learning to a new audience; an in-person meeting at NAA's annual meeting; and individualized goal setting, journaling, and coaching. The PLC modules focus on an emotional competence framework, building key skills (self-awareness, self-management, social awareness, and relationship management), and providing space to design strategies to grow individual leadership abilities. During the reflective cycle, participants deepen relationships with targeted members of the group (their peer coach) and meet virtually with the PLC facilitator. This continuous individual attention functions to support relevance and rigor for the participants. PLC members are charged with introducing local and national audiences to how emotional intelligence influences interpersonal connections and workplace leadership.

As with boOST, the NAA Fellowship is substantially shorter (six months) than the National Afterschool Matters Fellowship (18+ months). Another important difference is the engagement with online content and a virtual professional learning community. Leaders of the NAA Fellowship utilize a variety of tools to facilitate the PLC including existing NAA platforms, Zoom for webinars, a blog page for assignments and discussion, Skype, podcasts, and video. This configuration allows participants to build a broad-based community of learners with colleagues from around the country.

## CONCLUSION

Inquiry-based professional development can help bridge the practice–research gap and provide an opportunity for seasoned staff to assume leadership roles in the OST field. Through the research study presented in this chapter, we found that past participants in the National Afterschool Matters Fellowship described it as providing a structured opportunity for staff to reflect, read, and write about their practice. In some cases, they described it as "transformational." In addition, it is an opportunity for youth practitioners to share work with the broader field and to become influencers and change makers.

Within our sample of interviewees, the overwhelming response to the Fellowship was positive. That is not to say that respondents were not realistic or critical; many found the aspects of finding time and the writing demands of the Fellowship to be great. We learned through this study that for several participants the lengthy, in-depth, substantial PD of the Fellowship was meaningful and useful to them in their OST careers. An 18-month inquiry-based PD experience may not be for everyone, especially given the high staff turnover in the OST field. But our research suggests that there exist, across multiple cities and states, seasoned professional OST providers who can benefit from an in-depth, multimonth, inquiry-based PD program in ways that other types of PD offerings do not address. Some of our recommendations for how to do so follow.

### Funding

Inquiry-based PD is expensive, and funding for it is a challenge. In the past, funders have balked at the small group size PD and questioned whether it is having an impact on programs and on youth outcomes. While tracking youth outcomes for any kind of PD is problematic, whether for in-school or OST PD (Hill, 2014), this type of PD can indeed have an impact on both practitioners and program quality. In fact, with the advent of new technologies, inquiry-based PD can take place across geographies and with larger cohorts (e.g., the NASM Fellowship and the NAA Leading with Emotional Intelligence Fellowship).

### Allocate PD Funds Strategically

Large national youth organizations and statewide networks spend a great deal of money on training and developing staff. They might want to consider an overall portfolio of technical assistance and training that includes inquiry-based approaches for practitioners who have moved beyond entry-level PD needs. Such PD may take practitioners to new professional levels and increase retention and job satisfaction.

*Use In-House Resources*

Many organizations have in-house educational specialists who are responsible for training frontline staff as well as providing materials and ensuring program quality. If these staff were to participate in one of the growing number of inquiry-based PD opportunities, they might then be able to take this PD back to their frontline staff. Indeed, several of the NASM Fellows who we interviewed did so with their own staff and were able to engage youth in inquiry in their organizations.

*Create Organizational Cultures of Inquiry*

It is important that leaders recognize that their organizational culture can instill and support inquiry. Instances of asset-based and inquiry-based approaches for organizational change have become popular in various sectors outside of OST and have been documented to effect positive change and higher-quality programs (Cooperrider & Whitney, 2005). If leaders can be introduced to such approaches, it can be used as a springboard and rationale for implementing inquiry with staff.

In conclusion, as the OST field matures, it is critical to diversify and deepen the PD available beyond compliance training and entry, pre- and basic inservice training. We need ongoing PD that supports practitioners as they mature and gain expertise across their OST careers. We need this type of PD to help practitioners as they move into new roles and to provide opportunities for engaging in reflection, research, writing, and sharing their work with the field. As the findings of this study suggest, inquiry-based PD is a wise investment that may produce long-term positive impact in OST practitioners and in turn improve the activities and programs they provide for children and youth.

### NOTES

1. Although still rare, there are a few cases where programs are able to connect staff to either credit-bearing coursework leading to a degree or credentialing programs in youth work or school-age care through a university or community college.
2. Barman (2002) defines inquiry learning as an active process, allowing learners to develop higher-order thinking skills that help foster the development of investigative skills.
3. The Fellowship, still operated by the National Institute on Out-of-School Time and the National Writing Project, began a 2015–2017 cohort of fellows drawn from OST programs throughout the United States. Fellows meet in person at two retreats over the course of the two years, and then virtually on a monthly basis in Google Hangouts with a facilitator.
4. Each Fellowship had its own Google site. There is also a national Google site that contains archived materials from all sites.

## REFERENCES

Akiva, T., Li, J. Martin, K. M., Galletta, C., & McNamara, A. (2016). *Simple interactions: Piloting a strengths-based and interaction-based professional development intervention for out-of-school time programs.* New York, NY: Springer Science+Business Media.

Barman, C. (2002). How do you define inquiry? *Science and Children, 40*(2), 8–9.

Bouffard, S. (2004). Promoting quality out-of-school time programs through professional development. *Evaluation Exchange, 10*(1), 1-12.

Bourdieu, P. (1986). The forms of capital. In John G. Richardson (ed.), *Handbook of theory and research for the sociology of education* (pp. 46–58). New York, NY: Greenwood.

Camras, M. (2004). Investing in social capital. Afterschool activities and social affiliation in immigrant youth. *Afterschool Matters Occasional Paper Series, No. 4.*

Cochran-Smith, M., & Lytle, S. L. (1993). *Inside outside: Teacher research as knowledge.* New York, NY: Teachers College Press.

Cochran-Smith, M., & Lytle, S. L. (1999). Relationships of knowledge and practice: Teacher learning in community. *Review of Research in Education, 24,* 249–305.

Coghlin, D., & Brannick, T. (2005). *Doing action research in your own organization* (2nd ed.). Thousand Oaks, CA: SAGE.

Cooperrider, D. L., & Whitney, D. (2005). Appreciative inquiry: A positive revolution in change. In P. Holman & T. Devane (Eds.), *The change handbook: The definitive resource on today's best methods for engaging whole systems* (pp. 245–263). Oakland, CA: Berrett-Koehler.

Finley, S., Marble, S., Copeland, G., Ferguson, C., & Alderete, K. (2000). Professional development and teachers' construction of coherent instructional practices: A synthesis of experiences at five sites. *Promoting Instructional Coherence, 19*(2), 74–86.

Garet, M. S., Porter, A. C., Desimone, L., Birman, B. F., & Yoon, K. S. (2001). What makes professional development effective? Results from a national sample of teachers. *American Educational Research Journal, 38*(4), 915–945.

Guskey, T. R. (2002). Professional development and teacher change. *Teachers and Teaching: Theory and Practice, 8*(3/4), 381–391. doi: 10.1080/13540600210000051 2

Hall, G., & Gruber, D. (2007). *Making the case: Quality afterschool programs matter.* Boston, MA: The Massachusetts Special Commission on After School and Out of School Time.

Hill, S. (2014). *Leap of faith. A literature review on the effects of professional development on program quality and youth outcomes.* Wellesley, MA: Robert Bowne Foundation/National Institute on Out-of-School Time.

Hirsch, B. J., Deutsch, N. L., & DuBois, D. L. (2011). *After-school centers and youth development. Case studies of success and failure.* New York, NY: Cambridge University Press.

Larson, R. W., Rickman, A. N., Gibbons, C. M., & Walker, K. C. (2009). Practitioner expertise: creating quality within the daily tumble of events in youth settings. *New Directions for Youth Development, 121,* 71–88.

Larson, R., Walker, K. C., Rusk, N. & Diaz, L. B. (2015). Understanding youth from the practitioner's point of view: A call for research on effective practice [Special issue].

*Developmental Science.* Retrieved from http://youthdev.illinois.edu/wp-content/up-loads/2015/10/LarsonWalkerRuskDias-From-the-Practitioners-Point-of-View.pdf

Lave, J. (1991). Situating learning in communities of practice. In L. Resnick, J. Levine, and S. Teasley (Eds.), *Perspectives on socially shared cognition* (pp. 63–82). Washington, DC: American Psychological Association.

Lave, J., & Wenger, E. (1991). *Situated learning: Legitimate peripheral participation.* Cambridge, UK: Cambridge University Press.

Leont'ev, A. N. (1978). *Activity, consciousness, and personality.* Upper Saddle River, NJ: Prentice-Hall.

Lewin, K. (1948). *Resolving social conflicts: Selected papers on group dynamics.* New York, NY: Harper & Row.

Lewin, K. (1951). *Field theory in social science: Selected theoretical papers.* New York: Harper & Row.

Li, J., & Julian, M. M. (2012). Developmental relationships as the active ingredient: A unifying working hypothesis of "what Works" across intervention settings. *American Journal of Orthopsychiatry, 82*(2), 157–166.

McLaughlin, M. W., Irby, M. A., & Langman, J. (2001). *Urban sanctuaries: Neighborhood organizations in the lives and futures of inner city youth.* San Francisco, CA: Jossey-Bass.

McNiff, J., & Whitehead, J. (2006). *All you need to know about action research.* Thousand Oaks, CA: SAGE.

Metz, A., Bandy, T., & Burkhauser, M. (2009). *Staff selection: What's important for out-of-school time programs?* Washington, DC: Child Trends.

National AfterSchool Association. (2011). *Core knowledge and competencies for afterschool and youth development professionals* (2nd ed.). Retrieved from http://naaweb.org/resources/core-compentencies

Nolen, A., & Vander Putten, J. (2007). Action research in education: Addressing gaps in ethical principles and practices. *Educational Researcher, 36*(07), 401–407.

Putnam, R. D. (2000). *Bowling alone: The collapse and revival of American community.* New York, NY: Simon & Schuster.

Russell, J. L., Jackson, K., Krumm, A., & Frank, K. (2013). Theories and methodologies for design-based implementation research: Examples from four cases. In B. J. Fishman, W. R. Penuel, A. R. Allen, & B. H. Cheng (Eds.), *Design based implementation research. National Society for the Study of Education Yearbook* (pp. 157–191). New York, NY: Teachers College Press.

Starr, B., Yohalem, N., & Gannett, E. (2009). *Youth work core competencies. A review of existing frameworks and purposes.* Seattle, WA: School's Out Washington.

Wadsworth, Y. (1998). What is participatory action research? *Action Research International,* Paper #2. Retrieved from http://www.scu.edu.au/schools/gcm/ar/ari/p-ywadsworth98.html

Walker, J., & Walker, K. C. (2012). Establishing expertise in an emerging field. In D. Fusco (Ed.), *On becoming an academic profession* (pp. 39–51). New York, NY: Routledge.

Wei, R. C., Darling-Hammond, L., & Adamson, F. (2010). *Professional development in the United States: Trends and challenges.* Dallas, TX: National Staff Development Council. Retrieved from https://edpolicy.stanford.edu/sites/default/files/publications/professional-development-united-states-trends-and-challenges.pdf

Wenger, E. (1998). *Communities of practice: Learning, meaning and identity.* Cambridge, UK: Cambridge University Press.

Wenger, E., & Synder, W. (2000). Communities of Practice: The Organizational Frontier. *Harvard Business Review, 78*(1), 139–145.

Yosso, T. J. (2005). Whose culture has capital? A critical race theory discussion of community cultural wealth. *Race Ethnicity and Education, 8*(1), 69–91. http://dx.doi.org/10.1080/1361332052000341006

CHAPTER 10

# THE LEADERSHIP IMPERATIVE

Elizabeth M. Fowlkes and Tony McWhorter

Focusing on human capital helps organizations stay on the leading edge by providing a platform for sustainable growth in intellectual and financial capital. What keeps nonprofit leaders up at night is whether they have the right people in place and if those people have the skills to help the organization thrive (AchieveMission, 2012).

In the out-of-school-time (OST) sector, human capital is particularly important because positive youth development relies on effective staff practice led by competent adults who make authentic connections with young people. But effective staff practice will not happen consistently over time—across different workers, in different programs, or at different sites—unless it is supported by both management and leadership practices. Good managers support staff practice by implementing effective systems for hiring, onboarding, training, communicating, and managing performance. These management practices lay a solid foundation for high-quality youth development practice.

While management and youth development competencies are critical elements in building the capabilities of human capital in the OST space, the hiring for and development of core leadership competencies are often under supported and underappreciated in this sector. This chapter focuses on *leadership* as a foundational component in maximizing human capital potential and addresses its relevance to effective program implementation, delivery of high-quality youth development practice, and ability of the OST sector to extend its reach and impact the lives of youth.

*The Growing Out-of-School Time Field: Past, Present, and Future,*
pages 133–144.
Copyright © 2018 by Information Age Publishing
**133**

## LEADERSHIP IN A NONPROFIT YOUTH
## DEVELOPMENT ORGANIZATION

In nonprofit OST organizations, volunteer boards are responsible for providing needed governance and leadership. They provide financial oversight, strategic direction, and lead the obtainment of resources needed to achieve mission, both capital and human. The board hires and oversees the work of a professional leader, typically a CEO or executive director, to execute on the strategy and lead day-to-day operations. Depending on the size and complexity of the organization, a senior management team may support the executive. For OST organizations that manage multiple sites, each site is typically led by full- or part-time leaders who oversee frontline staff who work directly with youth. Site leaders may have a variety of additional duties such as developing community partnerships, managing a local advisory board, organizing special events, or even running programs for youth. There may be additional site-level managers, such as directors of specific programs or program areas.

This structure has some parallels to K–12 education, in which superintendents and district leadership teams (organization leaders), principals (site leaders), and teachers (frontline staff) support students. However, in the K–12 education setting, four-year college degrees and certifications are standard for those professionals, whereas only about half of the OST workforce have a degree from a four-year institution (Yohalem, Pittman, & Edwards, 2010). While there is certainly a movement toward professionalizing the OST workforce, research into education leadership suggests this will not reduce the need for effective leadership. A report on education leadership commissioned by the Wallace Foundation found that "leadership not only matters: it is second only to teaching among school-related factors in its impact on student learning…[and] the impact of leadership tends to be greatest in schools where the learning needs of students are most acute" (Leithwood, Louis, Anderson, & Wahlstrom, 2004, p. 3).

For site-level leaders, basic functional competencies may include knowledge of developmental milestones for youth, safety practices, program delivery, or human resource management. For executive leaders or senior management teams, functional competencies include fundraising capability, ability to recruit and work effectively with board members, program development, or business acumen. While these are essential skills, managers who possess these types of functional competencies but lack core leadership capabilities will not be successful in leading a thriving OST program.

Strong leaders in OST increase youth engagement and reduce staff turnover by creating a culture in which staff feel supported, empowered, and connected to the work they do. Effective leaders communicate a compelling vision and build meaningful partnerships that enable them to sustain and grow their impact, even in the face of accelerating change. These leaders model the behaviors we aim to develop in youth because they are committed to learning, they are resilient in the face of setbacks, and they care deeply about making a positive impact on people and their communities.

## KEY LEARNINGS: THE EXPERIENCE OF
## BOYS & GIRLS CLUBS OF AMERICA (BGCA)

What follows is a case study of Boys & Girls Clubs, providing an illustrative example of the importance of leadership and leadership development in youth development organizations.

With over 150 years of experience in the field of youth development and a federated footprint of over 1,000 independent organizations, operating 4,300 Clubhouses across the country, Boys & Girls Clubs reflect the diversity of the OST sector. Clubs are in schools, public housing, and standalone facilities. Clubs exist in markets from major cities to rural communities and in areas with unique resource and situational challenges like Native lands and military installations. While the scope of the Boys & Girls Clubs network is large, 60% of club organizations have budgets under $1 million. Boys & Girls Clubs of America (BGCA) was founded by local clubs to support member organizations in deepening their impact, enhancing organizational development and expanding services to their community. Additionally, BGCA has worked with clubs to build a network-wide measurement system, the National Youth Outcomes Initiative (NYOI), which provides us with data to continuously improve clubs and inform the OST sector.

For nonprofit organizations in the OST space to have true and lasting impact, developing leaders at all levels must be a strategic priority. This has proven to be especially true for Boys & Girls Clubs for several reasons. In 2004, Boys & Girls Clubs had experienced a 10-year period of unprecedented growth, in which we saw the number of Clubhouses double from 2,000 to 4,000. During this time, there were also significant changes in the nonprofit landscape. The need for greater transparency, especially with finances, and an increase in investor expectations for proven results, elevated the need for a higher level of business acumen. At the same time, approximately 25% of club CEOs were poised to retire in the next 10 years. For these reasons, in 2006, BGCA made building a pipeline of capable, dynamic leaders a priority and began to completely revamp our leadership development programs starting.

Like most OST providers, when the Great Recession hit in 2008, we experienced significant challenges. However, a McKinsey & Company study found that, on average, leaders who had participated in our leadership programs from 2007 to 2009 outperformed their peers on every performance outcome measured, including youth participation and revenue (Cermak & McGurk, 2010). The study also identified leadership practices that differentiated performance among participants, which enabled us to refine new programs to include a stronger focus on leadership practices employed by top performers.

"Daring to Lead," a series of reports from CompassPoint, suggest that Boys & Girls Clubs are not unique in the challenges we face (Cornelius, Moyers, & Bell,

2011). Increased expectations for leaders and impending leadership deficits are common among nonprofit organizations.

## GROWING NEED FOR EFFECTIVE LEADERSHIP IN OST

Leadership is especially critical at this point in the history of OST due to the increased demand for OST services, increasing complexity of the work, and better understanding of how implementation impacts program outcomes.

There is increasing demand for OST services today due to the rise in the number of dual-income families, the increase in single-parent households, and the decline of extended family supports (Finn-Stevenson, 2014). The number of youth involved in OST programs increased by 3.7 million from 2004 to 2014. While 10.2 million youth were enrolled in OST programs in 2014, another 19.4 million were not enrolled but would have been if one had been available to parents. More than half of parents (52%) cited cost and nearly half cited hours of operation (44%) and availability (42%) as reasons for not enrolling their children in after-school programs. Today's OST leaders have to lead growth to meet increased demand while keeping costs low and navigating increasingly complex ecosystems.

The OST sector faces increased complexity for several reasons. One key driver is the need for OST providers to partner more closely with schools, families, and other social service providers. This is due to greater understanding of the benefits of a child-centered approach that connects these ecosystems in which youth engage and the growing appreciation of the importance of *all* domains of youth development (including increased awareness of the role that social, emotional, and physical development play in supporting cognitive development) (Finn-Stevenson, 2014). It is no longer sufficient for OST leaders to run strong programs within their sites. Management of OST is also growing in complexity due to increased regulation of OST and subsequent expectations for management and reporting.

Other reasons for increased complexity relate to youth served in OST and the world for which OST providers are preparing them. Increasing racial and ethnic diversity means that OST providers may experience population shifts and will need to develop new or improved cultural competence (Simpkins & Riggs, 2014). OST providers are also grappling with the need to prepare youth for success in a world that is rapidly changing. To stay relevant to the youth they serve, OST leaders must develop, adapt, and adopt new strategies quickly and ensure that these strategies are culturally relevant to the youth they serve.

Finally, OST providers face increased complexity due to the emerging infrastructures that aim to support the work. These "formal and informal intermediaries" include statewide afterschool networks, city and county systems, and other networks established by foundations or community-based organizations (Peterson, Fowler, & Ferinde Dunham, 2013). These support systems provide tremendous opportunity to support the OST field and deepen impact on youth. However, they also create complexity, particularly for OST providers whose scope intersects many different support networks, such as across geographic areas or different areas of focus.

In addition to managing increased demand for OST services and the increasing complexity of the industry, OST leaders have an important role to play in the effective implementation of programs. Programs are the critical intellectual capital for OST leaders, and "effective program implementation starts with strong, knowledgeable leaders who can create a positive organizational climate" (Huang, 2013, p. 392). Leadership is a key factor to overcoming barriers to effective implementation, including awareness of effective programs, motivation to adopt effective programs, implementation of the program, and sustaining the intervention. Implementation requires effective leadership, and program champions can make a difference (Durlak & DuPre, 2008).

## LEADERSHIP AT ALL LEVELS

In The Leadership Engine, Noel Tichy explains that winning companies succeed because they have capable leaders at all levels and make developing leaders a priority (Tichy, 2007). Organizations that embrace this are better prepared to respond to and take advantage of future uncertainties by building internal talent with both the skills and institutional knowledge needed to solve complex changes in the sector and specific organizational challenges. For OST providers, building leadership at all levels includes boards, executives, senior managers, site managers, and frontline staff. These roles require different knowledge or skills based on their function within the organization, but core leadership competencies form the foundation for human capital across all roles, even if the scope of leadership is different for different roles.

There are many different models for leadership, but two primary roles are common: leaders establish a vision and influence others to achieve it (Leithwood et al., 2004). In this chapter, we share four attributes critical to a leader's ability to effectively do these two things. These attributes are informed by the current landscape for OST providers and what we have learned through our work to support the development of professional leadership in the nonprofit OST sector. The strong OST leader cares and connects deeply with people, connects passion with mission, continuously drives change, and confidently rebounds from setbacks. Each of these is described in more detail below.

### Leaders Care and Connect Deeply With People to Create a Culture of Engagement and Empowerment

Highly successful mission-based organizations need leaders who garner the absolute best from everyone they lead, thus delivering on a high-impact agenda. Leaders who build strong, trust-based relationships in which they recognize each person's knowledge and experience foster creative, positive environments. More importantly, they understand that to be successful they must appreciate and tap into the collective wisdom of their team. As a result, they involve and solicit input from others to make decisions as appropriate. In these conversations, great leaders create a *virtuous teaching cycle*, an interactive cycle in which knowledge is shared and people become more aligned (Tichy, 2007).

These leaders also understand that personally investing in people's development shows their deep desire to see the people they lead be successful. This creates a highly engaged and empowered workforce that delivers results, even in tough times. This is particularly important in the out-of-school time sector, where leaders face several workforce challenges. The typical youth worker is young, works part-time, receives low compensation, and has relatively short tenure in his or her role (Vandell & Lao, 2016). Staff turnover results in additional costs to the program in the form of expenses related to recruiting, hiring, training, and potentially paying overtime to staff who must fill in during gaps. Turnover may also impact employee morale and, critically, the relationships between staff and youth. This is particularly important because the strength of the relationship between youth workers and youth is dependent on the quality and duration of the relationship (Vandell & Lao, 2016). When leaders connect with and invest in their staff, they create a deeper level of engagement with the organization and mission.

Connection to the mission can help reduce staff turnover (Kim & Lee, 2007). "Stability created from the retention of well-trained and educated youth workers is always critical, but is especially pressing when youth themselves experience uncertainty, as the present climate of economic instability affects domains such as housing, employment and higher education" (Thompson & Shockley, 2013, p. 447).

Leaders who build a culture of engagement and empowerment build more effective teams, which is important because collective staff efficacy impacts youth experience in programs. In 2016, BGCA collected data from approximately 10,000 youth development professionals and more than 170,000 youth and teens through our NYOI member and staff surveys. The data indicate that when staff are more satisfied with their work and teams, youth are more likely to feel engaged in their clubs. They are more likely to feel safe and supported, experience high expectations and recognition, and develop a sense of belonging to the program. Greater youth engagement in afterschool programs increases the likelihood of experiencing positive outcomes (Fredricks, Bohner, & Burdette, 2014). Thus, the ability of a leader to develop effective teams has a direct impact on the program and likelihood that it will achieve desired outcomes.

*Leaders Connect Passion With Mission to Create a Culture of Commitment and Advocacy*

Effective leaders understand and influence the contexts (i.e., people and systems) that affect their work. They create a compelling vision for how the organization impacts people and community and passionately communicate this vision to inspire others to higher levels of investment, involvement, and performance.

Great leaders tell stories. They use data to demonstrate a strong return on investment by articulating the difference the organization is making, but the message is humanized to tie emotional back to the mission. Research shows that organizations that connect passion with purpose see stronger results in all aspects of their work (Dions, Feldman, & Lash, 2016).

Leaders who connect passion with mission build lasting partnerships that support the mission with both internal and external stakeholders. Internally, OST leaders galvanize staff, board, and others to do the work that matters most for youth. One of the key barriers to the adoption of effective programs is motivation. Effective leaders motivate staff and other internal stakeholders to implement effective practice not because they are told to but because they believe it is the right work. Related to the first leadership competency, to do this well, leaders must also empower their staff.

External partnerships are increasingly important due to the rise of collective impact and growing understanding that youth are better served when there are connections among school, out-of-school, and home. As a result, the ability to understand and influence people and systems is a particularly important leadership competency in the OST sector. Many OST leaders, particularly those who serve multiple sites across geographic boundaries, must forge partnerships across multiple, sometimes overlapping, ecosystems including schools, school districts, cities, counties, and states. They may also collaborate with networks of providers working on a specific issue, supported by a common funder or using a shared intervention.

Nonprofit organizations also rely on the community for much-needed financial support to achieve their missions (Grace, 2005). Strong leaders cultivate a donor-centric approach to their fund raising. They look for those individuals, foundations, and corporations that share the mission's values and passion. Leaders view the funder as an investor and long-term partner in making meaningful and lasting change in the community. When leaders take a partner-centric approach and connect passion with mission, they build the commitment of the partner or funder to the mission of the organization, not to a specific individual, building sustainability through long-term partners and advocates.

While youth development and OST are better recognized today than in the past, significant gaps remain in access to programs and variability in the quality and efficacy of programs. Leaders who connect passion with mission are better able to advocate for the role of high-quality afterschool and summer programs and develop partnerships that amplify that message in local communities and across state and federal landscapes.

### Leaders Continuously Drive Change to Create a Culture of Risk-Taking and Innovation

Creating an organization that endures over time and leaves a legacy on the community requires a leader who continually embraces and drives change. Our data show that organizational performance begins to plateau after the leader has been in their role seven years. To continue to grow and meet the increasing need for quality OST programs, leaders cannot become complacent. They must create dissatisfaction with the status quo and develop a compelling vision for the future to gain buy in and reduce resistance to change.

Leaders must innovate to respond to external changes. Businesses have to learn and adapt quickly, so the ability to lead innovation is critical. Great leaders push for innovation and think creatively to bring new or additional value to the community. They also have a growth mentality, demonstrating a curiosity and thirst for continued personal and professional growth, understanding that an investment in talent development is one of the best investments they can make for the people they serve (Beer, 1998).

This ability to innovate is particularly important in the OST sector because research on program fidelity suggests that program adaptation is inevitable, and can even be beneficial, particularly if the adaptations are intended to work better within a specific local context (Durlak & DuPre, 2008). Today's OST leaders should drive an agile approach to assessing services, synthesizing information on effective practices (from within and from the broader sector), and continually making changes based on those findings. These leaders insist on the integration of evaluative thinking and use of data into day-to-day operations. This continuous improvement approach requires a change in the role of OST staff and significant investment by the organization in data systems, training, and staff development. While many of the competencies required to implement continuous improvement are functional in nature (e.g. data savvy), innovation and authentic change cannot take place without a leader who is proficient in this area.

## *Leaders Confidently Rebound From Setbacks to Create a Culture of Learning and Adaptability*

During the late 2000s, many nonprofit organizations either closed or greatly reduced the services they were providing, while many others actually grew and deepened impact. While this was a historic downturn in our economy, the reality is that challenges are and always will be a part of life. Resilient leaders not only survive these tough times but thrive because they see challenges as opportunities. They are not paralyzed by fear or uncertainty; rather, they find ways to get things done despite setbacks. They accept the realities of the situation, create a sense of urgency, and demonstrate confidence in the organization's ability to overcome adversity. They show a personal desire and willingness to learn from the experience, which helps them maintain an optimistic view in the midst of setbacks.

Based on our beliefs about the importance of leadership to our mission, BGCA created a leadership development program in conjunction with the University of Michigan, Ross School of Business. The Advanced Leadership Program (ALP) is designed to increase personal leadership skills and strategies; help leaders develop and articulate leadership point of view; gain advanced leadership, coaching, and feedback techniques; strengthen team alignment and effectiveness; and address key management challenges. During the six-month program, leadership teams execute projects that demonstrate team and individual leadership progress while addressing real-life challenges facing the organization. In 2010, the McKinsey & Company study conducted on the program found that participants had stronger performance than nonparticipants. They also found some commonality among top-performing participants, including these participants who were intentional about teaching what they had learned through the program to the rest of their staff.

Learning and resilience are at the heart of leadership and youth development. Leaders who create a culture of learning model key competencies that OST works to cultivate in youth (Huang, 2013). As OST providers, we support youth as they reach their full potential. To do this, they must learn to navigate relationships, cope with change, and overcome challenges. These are all aspects of successful leaders. When leaders create a culture in which these competencies are modeled and expected, staff are better able to support youth as they develop these skills. As organization-level leaders create a culture that empowers leadership at the site level, site-level leaders learn to create a culture that empowers frontline staff, who, in turn, empower youth to lead. This culture starts with the most senior leader and is reinforced by leaders at every level.

## BARRIERS AND OPPORTUNITIES FOR THE OST SECTOR

Real and perceived barriers influence hiring and limit participation in leadership development activities. Resource constraints are frequently cited as a barrier to effective leadership. Resource constraints come in two typical forms: money and time. In an industry that is underresourced, in which the majority of staff are compensated only slightly above the minimum wage, there is understandably pressure to direct any available resource to the core programmatic work of serving youth (Vandell & Lao, 2016). This comes in the form of internal, moral pressure for OST professional and volunteer leaders based on their personal commitment to their mission. It also comes in the form of external pressure from financial supporters who want to see their funds directly support specific, youth-facing programs. Similarly, OST providers feel compelled to focus their time on supporting their staff or working with youth and may feel self-indulgent to take time away to focus on their own development.

If you are a professional OST leader, consider your own development to be a mission-based imperative. Participating in leadership development is in and of itself a leadership practice. It is an opportunity to model learning and development as a lifelong process. One key to modeling this effectively is sharing your learning with others on a regular basis.

It is also helpful to consider leadership development as essential investment for sustainability, from both the financial and human capital perspectives. Effective leaders are better able to garner sustainable support by connecting supporters to the core mission. In addition, they are better able to respond and change course when external factors threaten organizational health. From the human capital perspective, leadership development is also essential for sustainability through succession planning.

Another barrier is related to resource constraints and staff turnover. OST leaders may be reticent to invest in leadership development for their staff if they are concerned that they will not stay with the organization. This is an understandable concern given the high turnover in the sector. However, staff are more likely to stay if they feel they are being invested in, and the organization could fare worse if the staff is not developed and they do stay.

Finally, the need or desire to hire for certain functional competencies may prevent selecting a leader who has the leadership competencies needed for long-term success. Sometimes this is due to a myopic focus on specific, urgent need for a specific skill set to fill a critical gap—such as the ability to fundraise, develop strong administrative controls, or exhibit strong financial management acumen—to the exclusion of leadership capabilities. In other cases, particularly in small communities, it may be due to practical constraints. In some OST organizations, the leader manages fundraising, finance, human resources, and the program. In these communities, it may be difficult to identify a leader who has the leadership and functional competencies necessary to carry out the requirements of the job.

## CONCLUSION

Supporting and developing strong leaders in OST is an important role for intermediaries that support networks of OST providers. As an example, BGCA supports a continuum of leadership development in local Clubs at all levels through leadership programs designed for leaders new to the role, advanced development for leaders and teams in programs like ALP, and mastery level development programs offered in conjunction with world-class partners like Harvard Business School, Stanford Graduate School of Business, and Linkage's Global Institute of Leadership Development. Participating organizations are experiencing higher levels of performance and reduced turnover. National networks, state networks, and other intermediaries can support the OST field by providing access to these kinds of supports and resources independent providers would find difficult to develop on their own.

Leadership is important in every sector, but it is particularly important in the youth development sector as we focus on preparing youth to become the next generation of leaders. For most OST providers, our biggest financial investment is in the people who carry out our mission. The stakes are too high not to insist on maximizing that investment by recruiting, supporting, and developing the very best leaders who can inspire and empower their teams, respond to change, stay relevant to youth, and build significant and sustained investment in the important work of youth programs.

We believe that leadership is not an inherited trait, but a skill that can be developed in everyone regardless of position in the organization. When OST providers make leadership an imperative, those leaders will build a more skilled, engaged workforce; forge deeper, more meaningful partnerships; elevate critical issues for youth in their communities; and garner more resources for their work—all of which ultimately lead to making a bigger difference for youth.

## REFERENCES

AchieveMission. (2012, November). The social impact of ROI of leadership development and talent management best practices. Retrieved from http://www.achievemission.org/resources/resourcecenter/view/the-social-impact-roi-of-leadership-development-and-talent-management-best-practices

Beer, M. (1998). Leading change. *Harvard Business School Background Note, 488–537.*

Cermak, J., & McGurk, M. (2010). *Putting a value on training.* Atlanta, GA: McKinsey & Company.

Cornelius, M., Moyers, R., & Bell, J. (2011). *Daring to lead 2011: A national study of executive director leadership.* San Francisco, CA: CompassPoint Nonprofit Services and the Meyer Foundation.

Dions, E., Feldman, J., & Lash, R. (2016, December 20). *Purpose powered success.* Washington, DC: Korn Ferry Institute. Retrieved from http://www.kornferry.com/institute/purpose-powered-success

Durlak, J. A., & DuPre, E. P. (2008). Implementation matters: A review of research on the influence of implementation on program outcomes and the factors affecting implementation. *American Journal of Community Psychology, 41,* 327–350. doi: 10.1007/s10464-008-9165-0

Finn-Stevenson, M. (2014). Family, school, and community partnerships: Practical strategies for afterschool programs. *New Directions for Student Leadership, 144,* 89–103. doi: 10.1002/yd.20115

Fredricks, J. A., Bohner, A. M., & Burdette, K. (2014). Moving beyond attendance: Lessons learned from assessing engagement in afterschool contexts. *New Directions for Student Leadership, 144,* 45–58. doi: 10.1002/yd.20112

Grace, K. S. (2005). *Beyond fundraising: New strategies for nonprofit innovation and investment.* Hoboken, NJ: Wiley.

Huang, D. (2013). Using research to continuously improve afterschool programs: Helping students to become 21st century lifelong learners. In T. K. Peterson (Ed.), *Expanding minds and opportunities: Leveraging the power of afterschool and summer learning for student success* (pp. 390–397). Washington, DC: Collaborative Communications Group.

Kim, S., & Lee, J. (2007). Is mission attachment an effective management tool for employee retention? *Review of Public Personnel Administration, 27,* 227–248. doi: 10.1177/0734371X06295791

Leithwood, K., Louis, K. S., Anderson, S., & Wahlstrom, K. (2004). *How leadership influences student learning.* New York, NY: The Wallace Foundation.

Peterson, T. K., Fowler, S., & Ferinde Dunham, T. (2013). Creating the recent force field: A growing infrastructure for quality afterschool and summer learning opportunities. In T. K. Peterson (Ed.), *Expanding minds and opportunities: Leveraging the power of afterschool and summer learning for student success* (pp. 357–363). Washington, DC: Collaborative Communications Group.

Simpkins, S. D., & Riggs, N. R. (2014). Cultural competence in afterschool programs. *New Directions for Youth Development, 144,* 105–117.

Thompson, A., & Shockley, C. (2013). Developing youth workers: Career ladders for sector stability. *Children and Youth Services Review, 35,* 447–452. doi: http://dx.doi.org/10.1016/j.childyouth.2012.12.019

Tichy, N. M. (2007). *The leadership engine.* New York, NY: HarperCollins.

Vandell, D. L., & Lao, J. (2016). Building and retaining high quality professional staff for extended education programs. *International Journal for Research on Extended Education, 4*(1), 52–64. doi: https://doi.org/10.3224/ijree.v4i1.24775

Yohalem, N., Pittman, K., & Edwards, S. L. (2010). *Strengthening the youth development/after-school workforce.* Washington, DC: The Forum for Youth Investment.

# SECTION IV

## RESEARCH- AND EVALUATION-INFORMED FIELD

CHAPTER 11

# THE GROWTH, EVOLUTION, AND STATE OF OST EVALUATION

Christina A. Russell

The evolution of out-of-school time (OST) evaluation has been closely inter-twined with the programmatic maturation of the field over the last two decades. The questions explored in OST evaluations reflect shifts in OST goals and policies over that time period, broadly moving from an emphasis on demonstrating the need for OST programs and generating evidence of their impact on the educational and social development of youth to examining the quality of OST implementation and the capacity of programs to contribute to successful learning and life outcomes for youth.

Evaluation has not been a passive bystander in this evolution; rather, evaluation findings have sometimes illuminated critical tensions about the expected role of OST programs and the anticipated pathways between OST program services and desired outcomes. OST evaluations have also evolved to reflect shifts in the priorities in the goals and expectations for OST programs within the educational landscape and new developments in evaluation methodologies and tools.

Policy Studies Associates (PSA) has evaluated the implementation and impact of OST program models, technical assistance interventions, and system-building

*The Growing Out-of-School Time Field: Past, Present, and Future,*
pages 147–160.

efforts since the late 1990s. Based on the author's experience conducting evaluations at PSA over that time period, as well as a broad reflection on the work of OST program partners, advocates, and researchers, this chapter presents an overview of the evolution and current state of OST evaluation. This chapter is not intended to be a comprehensive review of all OST evaluations, but rather to provide insight into key phases in the evolution of OST evaluation and a framing of the current state of evaluation. The discussion identifies the primary questions and purposes of evaluation, the standards of program practice and the expectations of OST program outcomes framing OST evaluation, and the precipitating factors that led to a shift in evaluation priorities or approaches.

## EVOLUTION IN THE FOCUS OF OST EVALUATION

Over time, the pendulum guiding the core measures used in OST evaluations has swung between indicators of academic outcomes, of youth development outcomes, and of implementation quality, driven by priority questions of funders, developments in education policy and context, and emerging findings.

### Demonstrating a Need for OST Programs

In the late 1990s and early 2000s, seeking to garner increased and sustained investments from public and private funders, OST program sponsors commissioned evaluations that addressed the broad question: Are OST programs meeting the needs of youth, their families, and the communities? Evaluations examined questions of increased access to OST opportunities as results of emerging program initiatives, questions of levels of participation and engagement, and questions of satisfaction with services to assess perceived quality and relevance of the programming offered.

These early evaluations of OST program initiatives typically examined the scope and scale of services offered and their effectiveness in engaging youth and in providing supports for students, families, and communities (e.g., Fiester, White, Reisner & Castle, 2000; Huang et al., 2004). By and large, leaders of OST initiatives sought to understand and provide evidence for the need for scaling systems of OST programs and services: What was the market for programs? Would youth attend? Were OST programs fulfilling the promise to families and communities of keeping youth safe and productively engaged during the critical afterschool hours?

Early OST evaluation was also rooted in youth development theory. The eight features of positive developmental settings identified by the National Research Council's Committee on Community-Level Programs for Youth (Eccles & Gootman, 2002; see Simpkins, Liu, and Dawes' chapter, this volume) guided the measurement of program implementation and success, focusing evaluation on indicators of physical and psychological safety; appropriate structure; supportive relationships; opportunities to belong; positive social norms; support for efficacy and making a difference; opportunities for skill-building; and integration of family, school, and community efforts. As OST programs proliferated, studies explored program practices that exposed youth to positive opportunities and were associated with youth development outcomes, such as improved relationships and increased sense of belonging (American Youth Policy Forum, 1997; Beckett, Hawken, & Jacknowitz, 2001; Catalano, Berglund, Ryan, Lonczak, & Hawkins, 1998; Eccles & Gootman, 2002; MacDonald & Valdivieso, 2000; McLaughlin, 2000; Pierce, Hamm, & Vandell, 1999; Pittman, Irby, & Ferber, 2001; Scales & Leffert, 1999; Vandell & Pierce, 2001).

## Demonstrating the Educational Impact of OST Programs

The emergence of large OST systems coincided with greater test-based educational accountability for schools, leading to expectations that OST programs would contribute not just to positive youth development but to improvements in school performance. Most notably, federal funding for the 21st Century Community Learning Centers (21st CCLC) program, a significant source of support for OST programming nationally, grew between 1997 and 2001, when the No Child Left Behind (NCLB) Act increased accountability requirements and expectations for federally funded programs to demonstrate measurable results (Weiss, 2013). This led to a shift in emphasis for OST programs from providing safe, developmentally appropriate spaces for youth to also demonstrating the effectiveness of program time in supporting measurable learning outcomes. As a result, evaluations also began to explore the question: To what extent do OST programs impact student performance?

Consequently, by the mid-2000s evaluations of OST programs strived to assess the educational outcomes of participating youth. Longitudinal evaluations of OST programs, particularly in their later years, reflected the increasing expectation of program funders that OST participation would contribute to improvements in educational performance. For example, evaluation of programs supported by The After-School Corporation (TASC), which provided funding and technical assistance for programming intended to enhance the availability and quality of OST opportunities in New York City, analyzed both the educational characteristics and changes of participants in grades K–12, using school district academic performance data (Reisner, White, Russell, & Birmingham, 2004). Similarly, a longitudinal evaluation of the Citizen Schools program for middle school students analyzed Boston Public Schools' performance data, focusing on state test results in literacy and math, report card grades, school attendance, grade promotion, and high school selection for participating students compared to a matched comparison group of Boston students (e.g., Arcaira, Vile, & Reisner, 2010).

However, tensions lingered about the extent to which OST programs could be expected to achieve academic outcomes. While some quasi-experimental program evaluations, including those referenced above, showed small positive impact on certain measures of academic success for regularly attending participants, including school attendance, promotion rates, and standardized test scores, an evaluation of the federal 21$^{st}$ CCLC Program using a random assignment design showed little impact of program participation on test scores (James-Burdumy et al., 2005). This raised concerns about the effectiveness of OST programs, leading to a recommendation by the U.S. Department of Education to significantly reduce program funding and pushback from advocates on this decision. This also sparked a discussion in the OST community on a range of issues related to the design of OST evaluations, including the significance of accounting for program quality and program dosage as mediators of program impact (Weiss & Little, 2003) and on appropriate outcome measures. Experts such as Halpern (2006) argued that an exclusive focus on performance detracted attention from other important developmental outcomes that OST programming could support. Although evaluations have continued to explore the effect of OST participation on educational gains (Pierce, Auger & Vandell, 2013), new directions for evaluation also began to emerge.

## Assessing the Quality of Implementation That Leads to Participant Outcomes

As debate over the use of measures of performance associated with OST participation continued, OST evaluations began to emphasize questions of program quality and of system building. Evaluations explored the questions: Do OST systems have the necessary structures in place to ensure the quality and sustainability of programs? And are OST programs implemented with a high level of quality and attended at high dosage?

Evaluations assessed the processes and extent to which OST programs developed the foundational systems and structures in place to ensure quality, which would ultimately contribute to the desired outcomes, including, for instance, a study of building a citywide system in Providence, RI (Kotloff & Korom-Djakovic, 2010) and studies of system building across multiple urban systems (e.g., Bodilly et al., 2010).

These OST system building evaluations have examined not just the extent to which OST programs are implementing promising practice and building towards structural sustainability, but also the ways in which OST system-building efforts increase the capacity of affiliated OST provider organizations (e.g., Fiscal Management Associates, 2008; Kotloff & Burd, 2012). Evaluations have also explored the capacity of OST program leaders and staff, the effectiveness of initiatives geared towards professionalizing the field of OST, and providing technical assistance to build the core competencies OST staff (e.g., Baker et al., 2012; Dennehy & Noam, 2005). Evaluations have also assessed the ways in which the partnerships have deepened to strengthen programs to more cohesively and collectively meet the needs of youth based on a shared vision for the needs of students and how OST programming can expand school-day learning (Henig, Riehl, Houston,

Rebell, & Wolff, 2016; Russell, Hildreth, & Stevens, 2016; see Noam et al. and Hill et al. chapters, this volume).

*Exploring the Social and Emotional Learning Contribution of OST Programs*

The role of OST programming in contributing to social and emotional learning has increasingly become a thread in program policy and practice as well as in evaluation. Making the case for social and emotional learning as an important focus for OST has been an incremental process. Recent research has highlighted the importance of positive academic mindsets in supporting the performance of youth (Farrington et al., 2012) and pointed to the educational value of self-efficacy skills and emotional regulation (Durlak, Weissberg, & Pachan, 2010), providing evidence that social and emotional development can be complementary to educational growth (see Devaney and Moroney chapter, this volume).

OST program developers can design activities to help youth develop these social and emotional skills through experiential and inquiry-based learning experiences that offer real-world connections to learning, and evaluations have examined implementation of these types of learning opportunities as a precursor to educational performance through the lens of academic mindsets (e.g., Russell, Sinclair, McCann, & Hildreth, 2014). However, social and emotional learning and related youth development outcomes are increasingly being considered OST outcomes in and of themselves, capitalizing on the positive youth development background of many program providers.

## EVALUATION USE: INFLUENCE OF OST
## EVALUATION FINDINGS ON THE FIELD

Significant investments in OST system building and evaluation were made by both public agencies—including through the U.S. Department of Education's 21st CCLC Program and the New York City Department of Youth and Community Development's Out-of-School Time Initiative, launched in 2005—and private ones, including The Wallace Foundation, the C.S. Mott Foundation, and The Ford Foundation. The ongoing support for both program initiatives and evaluations (including the majority of the studies referenced in this chapter) by this core group of funders championed learning and led to evolution of the field over time. These investments led to a widespread visibility for emerging OST program models and provided vehicles and audiences for disseminating the lessons learned for evaluation beyond the specific initiatives studied. The lessons learned through large-scale evaluations influenced expectations for future grant solicitations, shaped technical assistance offerings and professional development resources, and influenced the program offerings of individual programs.

This process was facilitated by rapidly growing OST networks and intermediaries seeking to support, strengthen, and professionalize the system, including the statewide afterschool networks (supported by the C.S. Mott Foundation), citywide intermediary organizations (many of which are part of the coalition now known as Every Hour Counts), and organizations such as the National Afterschool Association, the National Summer Learning Association, and the Afterschool Alliance. Foundations and advocacy organizations have compiled evaluation findings and field-based lessons on promising practices, as part of system-building efforts (e.g., Peterson, 2013). This section offers select examples of some ways in which OST evaluations have shaped the development of programs, from both a content and a process perspective.

### Identifying Areas for Improvement

OST evaluations have generally found that the programs with the greatest impact on youth were implemented with (a) high levels of exposure to program services, (b) high-quality activities in which youth apply learning to projects that interest them and are connected to real-world challenges, and (c) intentional activity design that promotes skill-building. Evaluations have consistently found that youth who participate in OST programming for a longer duration and with greater frequency display the strongest benefits on school attendance (e.g., Reisner et al., 2004) and on academic performance (Herrera, Grossman, & Linden, 2013). Research also indicates that OST programming is also most effective when activities intentionally target learning goals, focus on skill mastery, and build on youth strengths (Durlak & Weissberg, 2007; Eccles & Gootman, 2002; McLaughlin, 2000; Noam, 2008). This has led to efforts among OST program providers to promote and require regular program participation and to be more intentional in program planning and design.

Findings from OST evaluation have also helped to shape the conversation around important nuances in OST program approaches. One distinction that emerged from OST evaluation, for instance, was the need to offer unique models of programming to middle and high school students. Although program evaluations offered evidence that participation in OST programming in middle school could have an impact on student engagement in learning and long-term success, including thorough analyses of the high school trajectories of students who had participated in OST programs sponsored by Higher Achievement, Citizen Schools, and TASC during their middle grades years (Arcaira et al., 2010; Herrera et al., 2013; Russell, Mielke, Miller, & Johnson, 2007), there was also clear evidence that it was necessary to engage older youth in different ways to appeal to their unique interests and developmental needs (e.g., Deschenes et al., 2010; Russell et al., 2008). This led to the emergence of more club-based models of programming focused on leadership opportunities, career readiness opportunities, or specific content interests for older youth, rather than the comprehensive models of daily afterschool programming traditionally offered to elementary-grades students, including, for example, the expansion of the citywide system of OST programming for middle-grades students in New York City, branded School's Out

NYC (SONYC), which aims to help youth develop skills through experiential, leadership, and inquiry-based learning experiences that offer real-world connections to learning and contribute to their motivation to learn.

## Evaluation Use: Intersections between Research, Program Evaluation, and Self-Assessment

Although the term "OST evaluation" is frequently used as a catch-all phrase to encompass the body of knowledge that has been generated about and in support of the improvement of OST programs and systems, distinct approaches to (a) research, (b) program evaluation, and (c) self-assessment have all intersected to inform and advance the field. Foundational research on the ways that youth learn and on instructional design and program practices associated with growth and development, has provided a theoretical basis for the development of OST activities, curricula, and staff development approaches. The National Research Council's Committee on Community-Level Programs for Youth's eight features of positive developmental settings (Eccles & Gootman, 2002) guided the development of models of OST program initiatives, and meta-analytic research by Durlak and Weissberg (2007) informed ideas about the OST instructional approaches that could be expected to lead to positive outcomes. More recently, research on growth mindset (Dweck, Walton, & Cohen, 2014) and grit (Duckworth & Yeager, 2015) has influenced shifts in conversation about the ways in which OST programming can help youth develop skills and attitudes critical to success.

Program evaluation of OST initiatives has drawn on this research and further elucidated areas in which additional foundational research could inform and guide the OST field by deepening understanding of the connections and patterns identified in evaluation. Evaluations have examined the constructs surfaced in research as theoretically important for OST programs and helped to bridge research and practice by operationalizing these constructs in evaluation frameworks, tools, and reports designed to both assess and strengthen the quality and effectiveness of programs.

A number of these frameworks have been disseminated in both the practice and evaluation communities, reinforcing the connections between research-based constructs and measurement for evaluation, including the importance of examining the effectiveness of program structures and underlying systems that support the capacity and sustainability of OST programs, the quality of implementation of program practices, and the achievement of youth-level outcomes. These frameworks have often been constructed with interconnected levels of indicators and outcomes to facilitate the understanding of the connections and pathways between each of those levels. For instance, Every Hour Counts, formerly the Collaborative for Building After-School Systems, championed this comprehensive perspective through measurement frameworks that it commissioned in 2008 and in a 2014 update (Moroney, Newman, Smith, McGovern, & Yohalem, 2014); the Partnership for After School Education (2010) created an Afterschool Youth Outcomes Inventory; and the Forum for Youth Investment has compiled a collection of measures (Wilson-Ahlstron, Yohalem, Dubois, & Ji, 2011).

The transparency of OST evaluation frameworks is consistent with a third component of the evolution of OST measurement and evaluation. Encouraged by funder demands to demonstrate attentiveness to quality and responsiveness to the concerns in early evaluations that misalignment between the program implementation and expectation for outcomes contributed to lackluster impact findings, self-assessment as a method of program management and improvement has increasingly become the norm in OST programs. Often, self-assessment works in conjunction with external program evaluation: by remaining internally attuned to program quality and delivery through ongoing self-assessment, OST program providers expect to achieve a level of quality that will result in evaluations demonstrating successful program implementation and positive effects on participants.

As the field has matured, the capacity of programs to conduct self-assessment and to be attentive to the connections between the strength of system-level supports, of program quality, and of youth outcomes has been facilitated by the development of measurement tools. For example, the Weikart Center's Youth Program Quality Assessment (YPQA) and New York State Network for Youth Success observational tools were commonly adopted to measure and promote increased staff capacity and implementation of promising program practices.

A variety of management information systems have also been developed and marketed to help OST programs track program participation and outcomes, including, for instance, systems created by Efforts to Outcomes, CitySpan, and KidTrax. While the use of these data systems may have originated in a compliance goal for capturing key metrics to funders, the sophistication of OST provider organizations is increasing such that programs are reporting using these systems to run reports to assess their own trends and data patterns.

## NEXT STEPS FOR OST EVALUATION

As the field continues to evolve, OST evaluation can continue to play an important role in driving the improvement of OST program quality and, consequently, impact. To do so, OST evaluations must remain adaptive to and reflective of the role that OST plays within the education sector and home in on the specific programmatic elements and foci of programs to examine the pathways between participation, program delivery (including staff capacity and program design), and program outcomes. This means that there is unlikely to be a single coherent field of "OST evaluation"; as it has naturally evolved to-date, OST evaluation should and will likely continue to be driven by specific questions related to quality improvement and to the exploration of clearly defined outcomes and to the policy influences that drive the evolution of program approaches.

*Methodological Developments*

Shifts can be expected in the methodologies of OST evaluation that will strengthen designs and interpretation of findings. One challenge that OST evaluations have faced is the limited ability to attribute observed changes in participant outcomes to the OST programs: OST programs are typically attended by choice, and programs operate within a dynamic context of school improvements and reforms that influence student outcomes. Although quasi-experimental designs have matched participants to similar nonparticipating students on demographic and baseline educational characteristics using propensity matching techniques and used the level of OST participation as a control variable, it has generally not been possible to measure and control for other characteristics that might affect youth outcomes or engagement in OST programming, such as level of motivation, family supports, or participation in other enriching opportunities. Two multidistrict randomized control trial (RCT) evaluations have recently randomly assigned students who applied to be in summer OST programs to participate (the treatment group) or not (the control group) in summer programming, in order to better control for self-selection bias when analyzing the program impact (Augustine et al., 2016; Somers, Welbeck, Grossman, & Goodman, 2015). Although methodologically rigorous, RCTs require intensive time on the part of researchers and programs to recruit and retain study participants. Acknowledging these challenges, evaluators are also using additional quasi-experimental approaches to instead address the underlying motivational factors that may influence program outcomes. For example, youth survey measures about level of program engagement and self-reported reasons for joining programs can be linked to other outcome measures in statistical analyses (Berry & LaVelle, 2012).

The maturation of the OST field provides an opportunity for OST evaluation to deepen the evidence base and to clarify areas in which the connection between practice and impact is established and where evidence remains descriptive or exploratory. Although the dissemination of measurement tools and compendia of findings, discussed earlier, has helped to launch initiatives for OST program improvement and capacity building, there have also been some unintended consequences. In particular, the lines have sometimes been blurred between research, evaluation, and self-assessment of practice. The field has generated important research evidence about the competencies that matter for youth success and field-based lessons about successful strategies for implementation, along with evaluation evidence assessing the success of programs in implementing strategies and in productively engaging youth. But the connection between those elements remains weak. For example, there is widespread appreciation for "grit" as a competency and a belief that the project-based approaches common in OST programming can help to support youth in developing grit, but little evaluation evidence of OST programs effectively implementing strategies that lead to increased grit.

Next stages in OST evaluation can tie those elements together by homing in on the pathways through which promising field strategies support crucial research-based competencies. This will require the careful consideration of evaluation methodologies. Most importantly, it will require OST evaluators and program leaders to work closely together to clearly define and identify hypothesized pathways and connections between the implementation of specific OST approaches with targeted outcome goals, so that program intentionality is explicitly articulated and reflected in evaluation design. The field is at a stage where it is ready to draw on lessons learned from the past two decades to take that step to deepen learning.

## Changing Policy Context of OST Evaluation

The nature of collaboration between the OST field and traditional education system is also changing, so that the two sectors are becoming increasingly and strategically interconnected and sharing responsibility for youth outcomes. As OST becomes more of an integrated part of the school system and OST providers coordinate with, share data with, and strive towards common goals for student growth and learning with school partners, measuring the distinct outcomes of OST programming is no longer the core question: OST evaluation must evolve to account for this collaboration. Although OST programs still face pressure to contribute to learning outcomes for participants, they do so as collaborators with the school day. Therefore, future evaluations may further explore the strength of the alignment between OST programming and the school day and the quality of complementary activities. The evaluation field also faces decisions related to measuring outcomes in light of this policy context: If OST strategically partners with a school to serve all or most students, analyzing OST youth-level outcomes independent of the school day outcomes does not make sense. This requires appropriate methodologies for demonstrating the effectiveness and contribution of the OST field; if all students participate in OST services, what is the appropriate unit of analysis? Should measurement be at the student level? Or school level?

Finally, in the coming years, we can expect to see evaluation increasingly focused on ways in which the OST sector can support schools in achieving the goals of the federal Every Student Succeeds Act (ESSA). ESSA requires state accountability plans to include four academic indicators and an additional "fifth indicator" of school climate or student success, which will take effect beginning in the 2017–2018 school year. This has sparked momentum in the OST community to articulate the ways in which OST programs contribute to the educational and social development of youth and can support schools in achieving desired benchmarks and growth on this fifth indicator. Work is underway to guide State Education Agencies to identify and implement valid measures of success (Batel, Sargrad, & Jimenez, 2016; Darling-Hammond et al., 2016), and policy developments related to ESSA can be expected to influence the priorities and measurement approaches for OST evaluation as the law is implemented.

## NOTE

1.   The author expresses her thanks to Katie Brohawn, Jennifer Siaca Curry, Monica Ingkavet, and Saskia Traill from ExpandED Schools for contributing their policy, practice, and research reflections on the state of OST evaluation in preparation for this chapter.

## REFERENCES

American Youth Policy Forum. (1997). *Some things do make a difference for youth: A compendium of evaluations of youth programs and practices.* Washington, DC: Author.

Arcaira, E., Vile, J. D., & Reisner, E. R. (2010). *Citizen schools: Achieving high school graduation.* Washington, DC: Policy Studies Associates.

Augustine, C. H., Sloan McCombs, J., Pane, J. F., Schwartz, H., Schweig, J., McEachin, A., & Siler-Evans, K. (2016). *Learning from summer: Effects of voluntary summer learning programs on low-income urban youth.* Santa Monica, CA: RAND Corporation.

Baker, S., Johnson, L., Turski, K., Lockaby, T., Daley, K., & Klumpner, S. (2012). *Moving from afterschool training to the workplace: The second year of the Palm Beach County Afterschool Educator Certificate Program.* Chicago, IL: Chapin Hall at the University of Chicago.

Batel, S., Sargrad, S., & Jimenez, L. (2016). *Innovation in accountability: Designing systems to support school quality and student success.* Center for American Progress. Retrieved from https://www.americanprogress.org/issues/education/reports/2016/12/08/294325/innovation-in-accountability/

Beckett, M. K., Hawken, A., & Jacknowitz, A. (2001). *Accountability for after-school care: Devising standards and measuring adherence to them.* Santa Monica, CA: RAND Corporation.

Berry, T., & LaVelle, K. B. (2012). Comparing socioemotional outcomes for early adolescents who join after school for internal or external reasons. *The Journal for Early Adolescence, 33*(1), 77–103.

Bodily, S. J., McCombs, J. S., Orr, N., Scherer, E., Constant, L., & Gershwin, D. (2010). *Hours of opportunity, Volume 1: Lessons from five cities on building systems to improve after-school, summer school, and other out-of-school-time programs.* Santa Monica, CA: RAND Corporation.

Catalano, R. F., Berglund, M. L., Ryan, J. A. M., Lonczak, H. S., & Hawkins, J. D. (1998). *Positive youth development in the United States: Research findings on evaluation of positive youth development programs.* Seattle, WA: University of Washington, Social Development Research Group.

Darling-Hammond, L., Bae, S., Cook-Harvey, C., Lam, L., Mercer, C., Podolsky, A., & Stosich, E. L. (2016). *Pathways to new accountability through the Every Student Succeeds Act.* Stanford, CA: Learning Policy Institute and Stanford Center for Opportunity Policy in Education.

Dennehy, J., & Noam, G. (2005). *Evidence for action: Strengthening after-school programs for all children and youth: The Massachusetts Out-of-School Time Workforce.* Boston, MA: Achieve Boston, an Initiative of Boston After School & Beyond.

Deschenes, S. N., Arbreton, A., Little, P. M., Herrera, C., Grossman, J. B., Weiss, H. B., & Lee, D. (2010). *Engaging older youth: Program and city-level strategies to support sustained participation in out-of-school time.* Cambridge, MA: Harvard Family Research Project.

Duckworth, A. L., & Yeager, D. S. (2015). Measurement matters: Assessing personal qualities other than cognitive ability for educational purposes. *Educational Researcher, 44*(4), 237–251.

Durlak, J. A., & Weissberg, R. P. (2007). *The impact of after-school programs that promote personal and social skills.* Chicago, IL: Collaborative for Academic, Social, and Emotional Learning.

Durlak, J. A., Weissberg, R. P., & Pachan, M. (2010). A meta-analysis of after-school programs that seek to promote personal and social skills in children and adolescents. *American Journal of Community Psychology, 45,* 294–309.

Dweck, C., Walton, G., & Cohen, G. (2014). *Academic tenacity: Mindsets and skills that promote long-term learning.* Seattle, WA: Bill & Melinda Gates Foundation.

Eccles, J., & Gootman, J. A. (Eds.). (2002). *Community programs to promote youth development.* Washington, DC: National Academy Press.

Farrington, C. A., Roderick, M., Allensworth, E., Nagaoka, J., Keyes, T. S., Johnson, D. W., & Beechum, N. O. (2012). *Teaching adolescents to become learners: The role of noncognitive factors in shaping school performance: A critical literature review.* Chicago, IL: University of Chicago Consortium on Chicago School Research.

Fiester, L., White, R. N., Reisner, E. R., & Castle, A. M. (2000). *Increasing and improving after-school opportunities: Evaluation results from the TASC after-school program's first year.* Washington, DC: Policy Studies Associates.

Fiscal Management Associates, L.L.C. (2008). *Administrative management capacity in out-of-school time organizations: An exploratory study.* New York, NY: The Wallace Foundation.

Halpern, R. (2006). Confronting the big lie: The need to reframe expectations of after-school programs. In R. Halpern (Ed.), *Critical issues in after-school programming* (pp. 111–137). Chicago, IL: Erikson Institute.

Henig, J. R., Riehl, C. J., Houston, D. M., Rebell, M. A., & Wolff, J. R. (2016). *Collective impact and the new generation of cross-sector collaborations for education: A nationwide scan.* New York, NY: Teachers College, Columbia University, Department of Education Policy and Social Analysis.

Herrera, C., Grossman, J. B., & Linden, L. L. (2013). *Staying on track: Testing Higher Achievement's long-term impact on academic outcomes and high school choice.* New York, NY: A Public/Private Ventures project distributed by MDRC.

Huang, D., Choi, K., Henderson, T., Howie, J., Kim, K., Vogel, M., Yoo, S., & Waite, P. (2004). *Evaluating the impact of LA's BEST on students' social and academic development: Study of 100 LA's BEST Sites 2002–2003.* Los Angeles, CA: National Center for Research on Evaluation, Standards, and Student Testing (CRESST), University of California–Los Angeles.

James-Burdumy, S., Dynarski, M., Moore, M., Deke, J., Mansfield, W., & Pistorino, C. (2005). *When schools stay open late: The national evaluation of the 21st Century Community Learning Centers Program: Final report* (NCEE-2005–3002). Washington, DC: U.S. Department of Education, Institute of Education Sciences, National Center for Education Evaluation and Regional Assistance.

Kotloff, L. J., & Burd, N. (2012). *Building stronger nonprofits through better financial management: Early efforts in 26 youth-serving organizations.* New York, NY: The Wallace Foundation and Public/Private Ventures.

Kotloff, L. J., & Korom-Djakovic, D. (2010). *Afterzones: Creating a citywide system to support and sustain high-quality after-school programs.* Philadelphia, PA: Public/ Private Ventures.

MacDonald, G. B., & Valdivieso, R. (2000). Measuring deficits and assets: How we track youth development now, and how we should track it. In N. Jaffe (Ed.), *Youth development: Issues, challenges and directions* (pp. 149–184). Philadelphia, PA: Public/ Private Ventures.

McLaughlin, M. W. (2000). *Community counts: How youth organizations matter for youth development.* Washington, DC: Public Education Network.

Moroney, D., Newman, J., Smith, C., McGovern, G., & Yohalem, N. (2014). *Understanding key elements, processes, and outcomes of expanded learning systems: A review of the literature.* New York, NY: Every Hour Counts.

Noam, G. G. (2008). *A new day for youth: Creating sustainability quality in out-of-school time* [White paper]. New York, NY: The Wallace Foundation.

Partnership for After School Education. (2010). *Afterschool youth outcomes inventory.* New York, NY: Author.

Peterson, T. K. (Ed.). (2013). *Expanding minds and opportunities: Leveraging the power of afterschool and summer learning for student success.* Washington, DC: Collaborative Communications Group.

Pierce, K. M., Auger, A., & Vandell, D. L. (2013, April). *Narrowing the achievement gap: Consistency and intensity of structured activities during elementary school.* Unpublished paper presented at the Society for Research in Child Development Biennial Meeting, Seattle, WA.

Pierce, K. M., Hamm, J. V., & Vandell, D. L. (1999). Experience in after-school programs and children's adjustment in first-grade classrooms. *Child Development, 70*(3), 756–767.

Pittman, K., Irby, M., & Ferber, T. (2001). Unfinished business: Further reflections on a decade of promoting youth development. In N. Jaffe (Ed.), *Youth development: Issues, challenges, and directions* (pp. 17–64). Philadelphia, PA: Public/Private Ventures.

Reisner, E. R., White, R. N., Russell, C. A., & Birmingham, J. (2004). *Building quality, scale, and effectiveness in after-school programs: Summary evaluation of TASC.* Washington, DC: Policy Studies Associates.

Russell, C. A., Hildreth, J. L., & Stevens, P. (2016). *ExpandED Schools national demonstration: Lessons for scale and sustainability.* Washington, DC: Policy Studies Associates.

Russell, C. A., Mielke, M. B., Miller, T. D., & Johnson, J. C. (2007). *After-school programs and high school success: Analysis of post-program educational patterns of former middle-grades TASC participants.* Washington, DC: Policy Studies Associates.

Russell, C. A., Sinclair, B., McCann, C., & Hildreth, J. (2014). *ExpandED Schools: Developing mindsets to support academic success.* Washington, DC: Policy Studies Associates.

Russell, C. A., Vile, J. D., Reisner, E. R., Simko, C. E., Mielke, M. B., & Pechman, E. (2008). *Evaluation of the New York City Department of Youth and Community De-*

*velopment Out-of-School Time Programs for Youth Initiative: Implementation of programs for high school youth.* Washington, DC: Policy Studies Associates.

Scales, P. C., & Leffert, N. (1999). *Developmental assets: A synthesis of the scientific research on adolescent development.* Minneapolis, MN: Search Institute.

Somers, M.-A., Welbeck, R., Grossman, J. B., & Gooden, S. (2015). *An analysis of the effects of an academic summer program for middle school students.* New York, NY: MDRC.

Vandell, D. L., & Pierce, K. M. (2001, April). *Experiences in after-school programs and child well-being.* Symposium conducted at the biennial meeting of the Society for Research in Child Development, Minneapolis, MN.

Weiss, H. (2013). Fifteen years of evaluation of 21st century community learning centers: A driver for program quality and capacity in the field. In T. K. Peterson (Ed.), *Expanding minds and opportunities: Leveraging the power of afterschool and summer learning for student success* (pp. 187–193). Washington, DC: Collaborative Communications Group.

Weiss, H., & Little, P. (2003). *Why, when, and how to use evaluation: Experts speak out* (Issues and Opportunities in Out-of-School Time Evaluation, No. 5). Cambridge, MA: Harvard Family Research Project.

Wilson-Ahlstron, A., Yohalem, N., Dubois, D., & Ji, P. (2011). *From soft skills to hard data: Measuring youth program outcomes.* Washington, DC: The Forum for Youth Investment.

CHAPTER 12

# INNOVATIVE USE OF DATA AS GAME CHANGER FOR OST PROGRAMS

## The Example of STEM

**Gil G. Noam, Patricia J. Allen,
Ashima Mathur Shah, and Bailey Triggs**

In the past few years, there have been many advances in how out-of-school time (OST) programs collect and report data to foster continual program improvement and positive youth development. Driving these advances is an increased demand from OST program leaders, program staff, and funders for data to inform decision making. The science, technology, engineering, and math (STEM) field, in particular, has experienced improvements in data collection, reporting, and evaluation that make it an exemplar for OST programs in general. In the United States, policy decisions around STEM education have led to a growth in both STEM offerings and interest around improving program quality (Afterschool Alliance, 2015). In response, more funders are requiring quantitative data from programs as evidence of program improvement. While this can be a pain point for programs without an established data collection system, it is also an opportunity for programs to demonstrate their impact and improve their sustainability over time. Data can

*The Growing Out-of-School Time Field: Past, Present, and Future,*
pages 161–175.
Copyright © 2018 by Information Age Publishing
All rights of reproduction in any form reserved.

be used both to garner support from funders and to drive program improvement and student satisfaction and learning outcomes. Greater success can be achieved through continuous data-informed improvements, which can lead to additional support from stakeholders (e.g., funders, businesses, and families) to expand and increase opportunities for children and youth.

There are several factors that make STEM-focused OST programs well suited for creating rich innovation, including increased expectations and funding that drive afterschool to meet specific performance gaps; the hands-on, exploratory format of OST programming; established partnerships and collaborations OST programs have formed that pool resources; and increased stakeholder interest in making data-informed decisions about programming. This chapter will address what makes today's STEM-focused OST programs well positioned to lead the way, the growing call for a shared data system that will lead to program improvement and innovation, and a discussion of how that shared data system could be implemented across OST and incorporated into a program's evaluation and quality improvement efforts. To demonstrate how this data system could work, this chapter will discuss The PEAR Institute: Partnerships in Education and Resilience's model for OST STEM programs that includes the development of a shared framework, the use of a common tool for data collection, and the triangulation of multiple points of data into rapid reporting that allows programs to tailor offerings to student needs and interests.

## THE CURRENT STATE OF STEM AND OST

OST is increasingly conceptualized as a place to complement and supplement learning from the school day. OST STEM experiences include afterschool programming; visits to science museums, zoos, and nature centers; summer camps; and other community activities. If capitalized on, these experiences provide a valuable block of time that can greatly support youth development, social competence, and academic achievement (Shernoff, 2010). OST offers an important alternative setting to fill gaps created by limited in-school time devoted to STEM education, and it can create opportunities for students currently underrepresented in science (e.g., racial/ethnic minorities, children from low socioeconomic neighborhoods, and females) (Cunningham, Hoyer, & Sparks, 2015). The National Research Council (2015) finds that "there is growing evidence that opportunities to learn STEM outside of school directly affect what is possible inside classrooms, just as what happens in classrooms affects out-of-school learning" (p. 1).

STEM education was made a national priority by the U.S. government in 2009 because of declining scientific achievement and increased workforce demand (United States Department of Education, 2010). U.S. students are performing well below the average for all developed countries in science and mathematics (National Science Board, 2016; OECD, 2014). In addition, U.S. employment in STEM fields has grown rapidly from 2000 to 2010, increasing by 7.9%, a small but impressive increase when compared with non-STEM job growth of 2.6% during that same time period (Langdon, McKittrick, Beede, & Doms, 2011).

Millions of dollars have been invested in accountability systems that assess the effectiveness of STEM education for the entire U.S. student population. Through the National Assessment of Educational Progress (NAEP), it is possible to compare the annual improvement or decline in science and math performance across different age groups, states, and major cities; through the Programme for International Student Assessment (OECD, 2014), it is possible to compare the achievement of U.S. students in reading, science, and mathematics to those in other countries. At the local level, school leaders have systems and validated assessment tools to track the outcomes of their efforts and measure student achievement. Unfortunately, schools faced with accountability measures in reading and math have had a hard time allocating time into the school day to address the need for a STEM-trained workforce. Instead of focusing on science, instructional time for science in the elementary grades has dropped to an average of 2.3 hours per week, the lowest level since 1988. This reduced time for elementary science is correlated with lower NAEP science scores (Blank, 2012).

Recently, significant effort and resources have been invested by several foundations and state afterschool networks to support informal STEM learning by building capacity, providing tools and trainings, creating communities of practice, and sharing system-building strategies and advice (Allen et al., 2017). However, it is unclear what level of impact this tremendous effort is having on program quality or student outcomes. Such a major investment involving large numbers of state afterschool networks and organizations that reach many committed staff and students deserves an evaluation aimed to answer the question of whether OST STEM providers are learning how to advance the cause of STEM learning for children and youth in significant areas like STEM interest, engagement, skills, and motivation. We believe that OST experiences will bolster STEM learning and achievement, but to our knowledge there are no systematic, nationally representative studies of the impact of OST experiences on STEM outcomes. To test this hypothesis, The PEAR Institute (with support from the Mott and Noyce Foundations and assistance from state afterschool networks) led a systematic nationwide study of program quality and student outcomes in OST STEM programs using evidence-based tools described later in this chapter.

## THE FOUR "GAME-CHANGERS" OF OST STEM PROGRAMS

There is growing evidence that OST STEM programs provide more than subject-matter education, but also support positive youth development (i.e., positive feelings, social behaviors, and attitudes) and encourage positive relationships among youth and between adults and youth (Durlak & Weissberg, 2007; Noam & Shah, 2014). Recognizing the value of offering informal science experiences in OST, more funders are supporting these efforts (Afterschool Alliance, 2008). There have been multiple influential collaborations in both the public and private sectors to ensure that young people are motivated and inspired to excel in science and math. As a result, the role of OST is now shifting rapidly to incorporate access to science learning opportunities. OST settings are considered ideally situated to foster student interest and engagement in STEM, in part because they can offer more hands-on and exciting activities than those typically provided in regular school settings.

While there are many new developments in the educational and STEM space, in this chapter we chose to focus on four game-changers that we think have the potential to shift and shape the future of STEM in OST. Understanding these changes is critical to forming a unified framework for data creation and program improvement in OST.

## OST Takes on New Expectations

Science is sometimes short-changed as school districts face pressures to meet performance targets for subjects such as English and mathematics. The after-school environment will be increasingly tasked with filling in the gaps. These changes have placed added pressure on afterschool programs to provide quality science experiences, whether they are prepared to or not. A unified system of data collection and sharing across programs would help OST professionals address these new expectations, share with the field the differentiators that make their programs successful, help facilitators understand where improvements can be made, and demonstrate program impact.

## Science Teaching and Learning Look Different

School science is no longer about step-by-step lab experiments and passive learning. New educational standards are pushing for an integrated focus on content and practices in which students "learn by doing" and teachers support this hands-on exploration (NGSS Lead States, 2013). Additionally, these standards push for teaching, learning, and assessing students not only on what they know but also on whether they can demonstrate their knowledge. This emphasis on active performance can really build engagement, motivation, and interest—areas that are very important to the afterschool world (Krajcik, 2012). OST is an excellent place to change the structure and thinking around assessment because OST programs have goals beyond academic performance. These programs provide the opportunity for students to gain knowledge about real-life situations and promote youth development. By collecting and sharing data using innovative measures developed specifically for OST STEM, we can learn more about trends that cut across education, in and out of OST.

## Organizations Collaborate to Pool Resources and Expertise

OST programs are often at the nexus of different organizations and learning resources. Additionally, afterschool programs are increasingly finding themselves the beneficiaries of a trend toward collaboration, such as groups of funders or sponsors coming together as networks to improve afterschool programming on a larger scale. Partners can further leverage their collaborations by establishing a shared framework and goals across partnerships that will inform data creation and program implementation. Aggregation of data helps inform on local and national trends and, more importantly, helps to identify leading programs that can share best practices with other programs.

## Stakeholders Demand Academic Performance Improvement

The culture of assessment is here to stay and, similar to schools, the OST field feels increasing pressure to demonstrate outcomes. While the term "assessment" has negative connotations with many educators, families, and students due to concerns of over-testing and punitive accountability measures, we propose a re-framing of how evaluation is conducted in OST from an "assessment" tool to a "data-creation" tool. There is an opportunity in OST to change the common attitude about what evaluation and assessment mean to programs. Time limits, structural constraints, and differing goals inherent in OST make it a particularly fertile ground for reframing how we think about and use data in programs. For example, there are many goals an OST program is interested in measuring, including positive youth development and improved relationships with adults and peers.

In an educational climate shaped by these game-changers, the OST STEM field must build on existing evaluation work, consider the development of common tools that assess particular outcomes across sites, and capture evidence about science quality at different levels. In order to effectively leverage these diverse learning environments, stakeholders must come to some consensus about the best ways to engage youth in STEM during these additional hours. If the OST field does not take the lead in establishing relevant indicators and assessment tools, it will be forced to measure itself by state and national standards used in schools, which are often misaligned with the philosophy and goals of OST learning.

### DESIGNING DATA-CREATING TOOLS, SHAPING THE FIELD

The PEAR Institute has been involved with STEM activities and program improvement for many years. Our interest in promoting socio-emotional well-being in children, with a focus on informal learning, as well as our experience in developing assessment tools, led naturally to involvement with the movement to ensure that children have positive, high-quality experiences when they participate in OST STEM activities. To better understand the impact of OST STEM programs on students, staff, and organizations, The PEAR Institute developed a STEM toolkit comprised of a student self-report survey (the Common Instrument Suite), a STEM program quality observation tool (Dimensions of Success), and a practitioners' survey (Facilitators' Survey). OST programs across the U.S. are using these tools to better understand the impact of their efforts to improve STEM learning.

To get a full picture of program performance, there needs to be a triangulation of multiple methods of data collection. This multimethod approach provides insight into different perspectives: Families, teachers, evaluators, and students are able to all contribute insights that help tell a larger story.

### The Common Instrument and Common Instrument Suite

The student self-report survey, the Common Instrument (CI), a reliable and valid tool for OST (Noam, Allen, Sonnert, & Sadler, 2017), is necessary for understanding the impact of the OST field on STEM education. The CI measures student science interest/engagement in OST settings and was created in response to the informal science field's need for a brief, reliable, and valid self-report survey that can be used to measure the development of individual science interest/engagement following repeated engagement with STEM activities over time (Martinez, Linkow, & Velez, 2014; Noam et al., 2017). Our underlying assumption is that individual science interest and engagement during childhood and adolescence undergirds future school performance and STEM career pathways (Noam et al., 2017). Measuring students' science interest/engagement is the foundation to understanding mechanisms that foster STEM learning. A better understanding of the factors and processes that support positive STEM outcomes is crucial to improving OST programs in science content and youth development outcomes.

Aside from performance testing, there exist few systematic or longitudinal studies of student science attitudes, especially among students engaging in OST programs and other informal science learning opportunities. Few, if any, evidence-based tools have been developed and validated for use outside of the classroom. Many existing self-report surveys in science were developed for school settings and are highly structured and formatted like academic tests. The surveys are often localized, vary from evaluator to evaluator, and are frequently lacking established psychometric properties (Boiselle, Hussar, Noam, & Schwartz, 2008). In recent years, there has been a growing focus on the development of more rigorous assessment tools including those capable of measuring indicators of program quality (Noam & Shah, 2013). Evidence-based tools, like self-report surveys, are necessary to define the threshold of student engagement that will predict success, such as higher grades in STEM or increased enrollment in STEM courses.

The PEAR Institute has expanded the CI into the Common Instrument-Suite (CIS) to integrate other important science learning and youth development-related dimensions that can aid in the creation of more effective OST science programming, including STEM career orientation and intrinsic motivation (adapted from OECD, 2010), STEM self-identity (adapted from Aschbacher, Ing, & Tsai, 2014; Cribbs, Hazari, Sonnert, & Sadler, 2015), and 21st-century/socio-emotional skills such as critical thinking, perseverance, and relationships with peers and adults (adapted from the Holistic Student Assessment; Noam, Malti, & Guhn, 2012) (see Table 12.1).

TABLE 12.1. Outcome Measures for the Common Instrument Suite (CIS)

| Scales | Subscales | Items |
|---|---|---|
| STEM-Related Attitudes | STEM Interest/ Engagement | How interested and enthusiastic a student is about STEM and STEM-related activities |
| | STEM Identity | How much a student sees themselves as a STEM person |
| | STEM Career Interest | How motivated a student is to get a career in STEM |
| | STEM Career Knowledge | How knowledgeable a student is about obtaining a career in STEM |
| | STEM Enjoyment | How much a student enjoys participating in STEM-related activities |
| | STEM Activities | How often a student seeks out STEM activities |
| 21$^{st}$ Century Skills / Socio-emotional Learning (SEL) | Relationships with Adults | Positive connections and attitudes toward interactions with adults |
| | Relationships with Peers | Positive and supportive social connections with friends and classmates |
| | Perseverance | Persistence in work and problem-solving despite obstacles |
| | Critical Thinking | Examination of information, exploration of ideas, and independent thought |

The CI and CIS are examples of an attempt by researchers and practitioners to come together to address the need in OST for a common assessment tool. It's a movement toward a common framework and away from the homegrown surveys, observation tools, and written assessments that many OST programs use to internally monitor their progress that limit the opportunity for cross-program comparisons or aggregation of data to report trends across the field (Dahlgren, Larson, & Noam, 2008).

It is important to recognize that there are about a dozen instruments that have been used to measure student attitudes toward science and interest in science; however, the rationale behind developing the CI was due to the limitations in the development or application of these instruments (see review in Romine, Sadler, Presley, & Klosterman, 2014). For instance, more than half of published instruments have been tested in secondary and postsecondary school, limiting the generalizability of the tools for younger populations (and a large majority of students participating in OST programs are in elementary and middle school). Many of the tools lack a theoretical foundation, meaning that the outcomes do not fit with an established model that is predictive of achievement. Few tools exist that can report on psychometric properties or demonstrate validity for measuring change over time. Moreover, of those tools that do report on psychometric properties, most do not demonstrate item differentiation by gender or race/ethnicity. It is important to know whether the instrument is equally valid across all populations of students. Lastly, the primary audience in the development of these tools is students in day school, not those attending OST programs.

## Dimensions of Success Observation Tool

An example of how the OST STEM field can leverage multiple data sources in evaluation is the use of the Dimensions of Success (DoS) observation tool in combination with the CI or CIS. DoS is a program quality observation tool for STEM learning in OST programs (Papazian, Noam, & Rufo-McCormick, 2013; Shah, Wylie, Gitomer, & Noam, 2014). DoS was developed to support a cycle of observation, feedback, and support internally among afterschool professionals that teach STEM. With its roots in program quality improvement, versus high-stakes evaluation, DoS is able to become a core part of the language that practitioners use when designing and reflecting on their programming. Youth development is one of the core domains in DoS, which considers the importance of relationships in the learning environment, relevance to students' lives, and encouragement of youth voice. DoS is used for large-scale assessment of programs and day-to-day self-assessment by administrators and staff. External evaluators or funders can also use it to track program quality at the school district, state, or larger organization level. The tool goes beyond evaluating the proposed activity plan in a lesson plan, and instead captures real-time interactions during teaching and learning. The observation protocol leads to the collection of rich observation evidence that captures 12 dimensions of STEM program quality in OST along 4 organizing domains (see Table 12.2).

To perform DoS observations, observers must complete rigorous training in STEM program best practices and observation methodology, as well as complete a calibration and certification process that involves practice both with video cases and live activities. Observers record evidence of STEM learning during STEM activities for a minimum of 30 minutes (a maximum of 120 minutes, depending on activity length). Qualitative data from field notes are quantified using a standard rubric on a 4-point Likert scale from low (evidence absent) to high (compelling evidence). Field notes and ratings for each program are submitted electronically to The PEAR Institute, and feedback on program strengths and challenges is given to programs directly by DoS observers.

TABLE 12.2.  Dimensions of Success (DoS) Program Quality Tool—Domains

| Organization | Participation | STEM Content Learning | Relationships |
|---|---|---|---|
| Materials | Purposeful Activities | Inquiry | Relevance |
| Space Utilization | Engagement w/ STEM | Reflection | Youth Voice |

*Facilitator Survey*

To get a complete picture of the strengths and challenges of the participating OST program, a facilitator survey can be administered to OST leaders and staff to triangulate with the student self-report (CIS) and external program observations (DoS). The facilitator survey was developed to capture the unique qualities of STEM programs and the perspectives of those who teach the STEM activities. In the survey, facilitators are asked to rate the changes that both they and their students have experienced through the duration of their program. At the student-level, facilitators are asked to rate their perception of change in the students on math skills, math confidence, science skills, science confidence, and social skills. Additionally, facilitators were asked to rate their perceived confidence of the STEM-facilitation, ability to facilitate STEM, interest in STEM-facilitation, professional development for STEM-facilitation, frequency of attendance to professional development, and the priority placed on professional development (Allen et al., 2017).

## THE FIELD'S CALL FOR COMMON TOOLS, SHARED DATA SYSTEM

In 2016, The PEAR Institute conducted a survey of leaders from OST programs, STEM expert institutions, the private sector, and community-based organizations in 37 cities across the U.S. to better understand their experience, needs, and interest in using and collecting data in order to improve STEM learning. Respondents indicated that their top goals in using data were to demonstrate value of programming to stakeholders and potential partners and to guide the process of implementing system- and program-level changes (Allen & Noam, 2017).

When asked specifically what they hoped to learn using data collection tools, OST STEM leaders identified four common learning goals: (a) to learn how to use data collection tools to better understand how to generate value within their program's network, so that there is an equitable distribution of opportunity and support for all youth; (b) to gain a stronger sense of how efficiently and effectively their programs are currently able to achieve their goals; (c) to identify underperforming programs so that collaborations can share support, resources, and the best strategies to improve program performance; and (d) to help learn about the long-term impact of their partners' efforts to increase STEM learning and workforce preparation and to keep students in the STEM pipeline (Allen & Noam, 2016).

Along with a clear desire to incorporate data collection and management systems into their work, OST leaders in the STEM field also identified several challenges that they faced while trying to advance the evaluation and assessment of STEM learning in OST: (a) lack of a common, centralized database that automates analysis and reporting via an easily accessible portal to reduce the burden of data management and analysis on OST programs; (b) few assessment tools available with shared and commonly defined metrics that are effective for longitudinal tracking; (c) limited staff time and resources to implement rollout of new tools and data managements systems; and (d) a negative perception of assessment tools by families and staff resulting from the pressure put on programs to demonstrate student academic performance, and a general feeling of suspicion around current state-sponsored standardized tests (Allen & Noam, 2016). Despite these challenges, OST leaders in STEM who responded to the survey still expressed that they are "somewhat willing" or "very willing" (89% combined) to use common data collection tools across OST programs. There is also opportunity for OST programs to share and learn, not only with other OST programs, but also on the school and district level. Data collected by schools and OST programs on student engagement in areas like attendance and student behavior could be valuable data to share, provided a robust data privacy agreement is in place between OST and the school or district.

## RECOMMENDATIONS FOR EVALUATING AFTERSCHOOL PROGRAMS

Although OST STEM programs serve millions of children and youth annually, there is no generally accepted formal evaluation process in the informal and OST sector (Afterschool Alliance, 2015). Programs and even evaluators typically use homemade surveys or observation checklists, making comparison with other programs impossible. There are many assessments developed for evaluating student and teacher performance in schools, but there are not as many tools for measuring learning in OST. Recently, many OST leaders and programs have begun to align their goals and data collection methods within a common framework. These programs understand that by working with a common set of goals and tools, they can leverage those data for benchmarking, learning from leaders in the field, and increasing effective communication among programs.

The nation needs a system that can provide local leaders with validated tools and technical assistance to improve their programs, while also collecting and aggregating data to track trends and compare the effectiveness of different programs. Such a system needs to focus on program improvement and avoid any punitive use. In order to be effective, program staff need to take ownership of the data system and build its use into their professional and curriculum development. By shifting the focus from accountability to internal improvement and advancement, the data system can be used to demonstrate program impact and success, improving sustainability through increased enrollment and funding. The PEAR Institute has created a data and technical support hub for the OST field that provides local OST leaders and evaluators for validated, easy-to-administer assessment of interest, engagement, motivation, and career knowledge, as well as social-emotional skills that affect STEM learning, such as perseverance, cooperation, problem-solving, and critical thinking. This system analyses data collected by program staff and evaluators and provides actional reports for student and program improvement to the practitioners involved. It aggregates data from thousands of individual programs to allow comparisons across geographic regions, program types, dosages, quality, and other variations in STEM program characteristics.

In this chapter, we present recent advances in OST STEM as just one example of a greater movement in the field toward evaluation that not only informs on past success and challenges, but serves as an integral part of a program from its very beginning. In this way, an OST program can be poised to go beyond reflecting on past work; it can provide rapid, responsive quality improvement in real time based on the needs of its students currently in its program. To achieve this future, we would like to make the following recommendations to the OST field:

1.  Decide on common framework, goals, and tools within OST programs: OST leaders report a great deal of interest in having a common assessment across programs; however, they also have shown that there needs to be more cohesion among programs in terms of their current evaluation plans and data collection tools. This is not surprising because there are many ideas about values and practices for learning across diverse OST programs. However, identifying a unifying framework, or a common language to communicate learning goals, across programs and networks will sharpen the focus on which data collection tools to use to measure the progress of each program as a whole. A standard set of reliable and valid data collection tools is necessary to establish benchmarks that measure success. Though it is critical to identify a common metric across partners, we also strongly encourage flexibility if there are partners who want to continue to collect data quantitatively and qualitatively using their own methods. However, if there continue to be separate measurements for each context (i.e., one measure for museums, one measure for company mentoring programs, etc.), there will not be a way to communicate between partners.

2.  Shift the paradigm for data collection and use: We need a shift in thinking around the usage of data to increase programs' value and to better serve youth. Data collection often is accompanied by a sense of quid pro quo. For instance, practitioners often feel compelled to assist with data collection for important reasons like grant funding, but this can easily lead to an estranged and abstract relationship with assessment tools and data. We need to change thinking from "we're doing this because we have to" to "we're doing this because it will help us understand and educate our students." Rapid analysis and reporting of data at the start of programming would provide educators with information about students from the start that could lead to changes in activity planning or execution while the student is still participating in the program of programming/curriculum.

3.  Link multiple forms of data collection to gain a fuller picture of the learning environment: Connecting multiple pieces of evidence, such as attitu-

dinal and behavioral measures, program quality observations, and facilitator surveys, will better tell the story of learning than any one measure alone. Importantly, it will not be sufficient to use one tool in isolation, such as self-reported outcomes, to convince policymakers and funders about changes that would better support learning in OST programs. By looking at multiple data sources collected from various participants in the learning experience, from students, to trained observers, to facilitators, OST programs will be able to better understand their program quality and impact and make necessary improvements their specific program requires for continued success.

4. Establish a national data management system to track programs' progress and advocate for change: From surveying OST STEM leaders, it is clear that a large majority are willing to create a shared vision around evaluation and assessment across programs. However, OST programs can be very different (e.g., regionally, culturally, economically, and politically), and there are different motives for data collection (i.e., field building, development of best practices, and policy support), which can make this task especially challenging. However, there are at least three reasons for OST programs to unite on evaluation and assessment: (a) to learn from the strengths and needs of other programs, (b) to be motivated by the progress made by others, and (c) to use big data to advocate for policy changes. If all OST programs work together on evaluation and data creation, there would be significant power to inform on national trends of learning.

## DISCUSSION

Fully realizing these recommendations will take a shift in the culture of programs, funders, and networks around the use of data. It is a big shift, but one the OST STEM field has already begun. Much of the initial network-building work has been driven by funders like the C. S. Mott and Noyce Foundations through the establishment of STEM learning ecosystems and the funding of state afterschool networks and national working groups. The groups are working together to decide on a common framework and common goals. Funders, OST programs, business leaders, and communities of practice are collaborating to establish a system of support, increase funding for programs, and build networks that can inform policy.

With the adoption of a common framework and tools within OST, the next step is the adoption of a shared data system. The PEAR Institute, with support from the Noyce Foundation (now STEM Next), has developed a data system that provides organizations with access to a variety of survey tools, as well as fully analyzed data reports and program improvement recommendations. Programs are able to collect and analyze data on their students during the first week of programming to know every child at the beginning of the year, build stronger relationships, and increase student engagement in the program from the start. This data system serves as a translator of student information and provide organizations with a common vocabulary to communicate strengths and challenges within and between organizations, including comparisons based on a large de-identified database of youth participating in OST STEM across the U.S. While barriers remain, including the difficulty of agreeing on tools, concerns around privacy, negative thinking around assessment, and feelings of competition among organizations, there is a great opportunity for these ecosystems of OST STEM providers and supporters to come together and use this data system to share best practices, reduce staff time with efficient data collection tools, inform on national policy, and serve as the model for using data to drive quality improvement in the OST field. While this chapter shows the connection to STEM OST, the data system described is applicable to all elements of OST programming. As education ecologies are forming that link various groups in and out of school, the flow of data provides a greater opportunity and necessity to track progress and improve learning in these environments. Future publications will share our experiences with these expanded communities and assessments that go beyond STEM.

## REFERENCES

Afterschool Alliance. (2008). 21st century learning centers providing support to communities nationwide. Retrieved from http://www.afterschoolalliance.org/documents/factsResearch/21stCCLC_Factsheet.pdf

Afterschool Alliance. (2015). *Full STEM ahead: Afterschool programs step up as key partners in STEM education.* Washington, DC: Afterschool Alliance. Retrieved from http://www.afterschoolalliance.org/AA3PM/STEM.pdf

Allen, P. J., & Noam, G. G. (2016). *STEM learning ecosystems: Evaluation and assessment findings.* Belmont, MA: The PEAR Institute: Partnerships in Education and Resilience. Retrieved from http://stemecosystems.org/wp-content/uploads/2017/01/STEMEcosystems_Final_120616.pdf

Allen, P. J., Noam, G. G., Little, T. D., Fukuda, E., Gorrall, B. K., & Waggenspack, B. A. (2017). *Afterschool & STEM system building evaluation 2016.* Belmont, MA: The PEAR Institute: Partnerships in Education and Resilience.

Aschbacher, P. R., Ing, M., & Tsai, S. M. (2014). Is science me? Exploring middle school students' STE-M career aspirations. *Journal of Science Education and Technology, 23*(6), 735–743. https://doi.org/10.1007/s10956-014-9504-x

Blank, R. K. (2012). *What is the impact of decline in science instructional time in elementary school?* Retrieved from http://www.csss-science.org/downloads/NAEPElem-ScienceData.pdf

Boiselle, E., Hussar, K., Noam, G. G., & Schwartz, S. (2008). *Toward a systemic evidence-base for science in out-of-school time: The role of assessment.* Belmont, MA: Program in Education, Afterschool & Resiliency, Harvard University and McLean Hospital. Retrieved from https://www.mysciencework.com/publication/show/581f3c996e0780db3c0fa6a4987cb844

Cribbs, J. D., Hazari, Z., Sonnert, G., & Sadler, P. M. (2015). Establishing an explanatory model for mathematics identity. *Child Development, 86*(4), 1048–1062. https://doi.org/10.1111/cdev.12363

Cunningham, B. C., Hoyer, K. M., & Sparks, D. (2015). *Gender differences in science, technology, engineering, and mathematics (STEM) interest, credits earned and NAEP performance in the 12th grade* (NCES 2015-075). Washington, DC: Institute of Education Sciences, National Center for Education Statistics, U.S. Department of Education. Retrieved from https://nces.ed.gov/pubs2015/2015075.pdf

Dahlgren, C. T., Larson, J. D., & Noam, G. G. (2008). *Innovations in out-of-school time science assessment: Peer evaluation and feedback network in metropolitan Kansas City Summer METS Initiative.* Belmont, MA: Harvard University and McLean Hospital.

Durlak, J. A., & Weissberg, R. P. (2007). *The impact of afterschool programs that promote personal and social skills.* Chicago, IL: Collaborative for Academic, Social and Emotional Learning. Retrieved from http://www.uwex.edu/ces/4h/afterschool/partnerships/documents/ASP-Full.pdf

Krajcik, J. S. (2012). *Using the NRC framework to engage students in learning science in informal environments.* East Lansing, MI: CREATE for STEM, Michigan State University. Retrieved from http://sites.nationalacademies.org/cs/groups/dbassesite/documents/webpage/dbasse_072560.pdf

Langdon, D., McKittrick, G., Beede, D., & Doms, M. (2011). *STEM: Good jobs now and for the future.* Washington, DC: U.S. Department of Commerce Economics and Statistics Administration. Retrieved from http://www.esa.doc.gov/sites/default/files/stemfinalyjuly14_1.pdf

Martinez, A., Linkow, T., & Velez, M. (2014). *Evaluation study of Summer of Innovation stand-alone program model FY2013: Outcomes report.* Cambridge, MA: Abt Associates. Retrieved from http://www.nasa.gov/sites/default/files/soi_stand-alone_program_model_fy2013_outcome_report.pdf

National Research Council. (2015). *Identifying and supporting productive STEM programs in out-of-school settings.* Washington, DC: National Academies Press. Retrieved from http://www.nap.edu/catalog/21740

National Science Board. (2016). *Science and engineering indicators 2016.* Arlington, VA: National Science Foundation. Retrieved from https://www.nsf.gov/statistics/2016/nsb20161/#/

NGSS Lead States. (2013). *Next generation science standards: For states, by states.* Washington, DC: The National Academies Press. Retrieved from https://www.nap.edu/catalog/18290/next-generation-science-standards-for-states-by-states

Noam, G.G., Allen, P. J., Sonnert, G., & Sadler, P. M. (2017). *Validation of the common instrument: A brief measure for assessing science interest in children and youth.* Belmont, MA: The PEAR Institute: Partnerships in Education and Resilience.

Noam, G., Malti, T., & Guhn, M. (2012). From clinical-developmental theory to assessment: The Holistic Student Assessment tool. *International Journal of Conflict and Violence, 6*(2), 201–213.

Noam, G., & Shah, A. M. (2013). *Game-changers and the assessment predicament in afterschool science.* Belmont, MA: The PEAR Institute: Partnerships in Education and Resilience. Retrieved from http://www.pearweb.org/research/pdfs/Noam%26Shah_Science_Assessment_Report.pdf

Noam, G., & Shah, A. (2014). Informal science and youth development: Creating convergence in out-of-school time. *Teachers College Record, 116*(13), 199–218. Retrieved from http://www.tcrecord.org/content.asp?contentid=18331

OECD. (2010). *PISA 2009 results: What students know and can do - Student performance in reading, mathematics and science* (Vol. 1). Paris, France: Author. Retrieved from http://www.oecd-ilibrary.org/education/pisa-2009-results-what-students-know-and-can-do_9789264091450-en

OECD. (2014). *PISA 2012 results: What students know and can do* (Revised edition, Vol. 1). Paris, France: Author. Retrieved from http://www.oecd-ilibrary.org/education/pisa-2012-results-what-students-know-and-can-do-volume-i-revised-edition-february-2014_9789264208780-en

Papazian, A. E., Noam, G. G., & Rufo-McCormick, C. (2013). The quest for quality in afterschool science: The development and application of a new tool. *Afterschool Matters, 18*, 17–24. Retrieved from http://files.eric.ed.gov/fulltext/EJ1016826.pdf

Romine, W., Sadler, T. D., Presley, M., & Klosterman, M. L. (2014). Student interest in technology and science (SITS) survey: Development, validation, and use of a new instrument. *International Journal of Science and Mathematics Education, 12*(2), 261–283. https://doi.org/10.1007/s10763-013-9410-3

Shah, A. M., Wylie, C. E., Gitomer, D., & Noam, G. G. (2014). *Development of the Dimensions of Success (DoS) observation tool for the out of school time STEM field: Refinement, field-testing and establishment of psychometric properties.* Retrieved from http://www.pearweb.org/research/pdfs/DoSTechReport_092314_final.pdf

Shernoff, D. J. (2010). Engagement in after-school programs as a predictor of social competence and academic performance. *American Journal of Community Psychology, 45*(3–4), 325–337. https://doi.org/10.1007/s10464-010-9314-0

United States Department of Education. (2010). *A blueprint for reform: The reauthorization of the Elementary and Secondary Education Act.* Retrieved from http://www2.ed.gov/policy/elsec/leg/blueprint/

CHAPTER 13

# EXPLORING THE NEED FOR RESEARCH–PRACTITIONER PARTNERSHIPS

Ken Anthony

How do we build professional capacity in the field, establish a feedback loop, and bridge the gap between research and practice? Research–practitioner partnerships (RPPs) show promise not only from the bridging standpoint, but also from a field-building perspective. Over the past decade, research studies have validated the importance of the work of out-of-school (OST) practitioners. However, there is a disconnect between researchers and practitioners and a need for bridging this research to practice. Increasingly, scholars such as Hamilton (2015) and Coburn, Peneul, and Geil (2013) are examining this bridging phenomenon to include practitioners' voices in a relevant research agenda. Too often, research is conducted, findings are presented at conferences, and information is translated to line staff by someone from the afterschool program who attended. They see big ideas that may not be reflective of their programs. Connections are lost-in-translation from the researcher to the practitioner, causing a gap.

The voice of the staff working on the front lines often goes unheard regarding the impacts and challenges associated with the implementation of an evidence-based curriculum or initiative. Research has demonstrated the impact and positive

*The Growing Out-of-School Time Field: Past, Present, and Future,*
pages 177–194.
**177**

outcomes increased collaboration, deeper inquiry, and quality improvement and data collection have on program delivery and student outcomes (Bennett, 2015; Bevan et al., 2010; Harvard Family Research Project, 2010; Vandell, Reisner, & Pierce, 2007). These elements are increasingly required for public and private funding streams. There may also be internal pressures as these elements become embedded in organizational strategic planning efforts to align quality and increase capacity at the community level. This presents an opportunity for the field to connect multiple stakeholders in bridging the research-to-practice gap. It is possible that once problems of practice are defined, solutions that are relevant for research and practical application on the ground are created. In this context, RPPs are an equal relationship in which both researcher and practitioner bring knowledge and experience with the common goal of program inquiry to explore best practices, identify needs and strengths of the program through joint inquiry, and develop skills of both parties. Examples of such RPPs within the OST field are just beginning to take shape. Organizational and systemic buy-in and trust have to be developed and nurtured by state and local partnerships with a holistic focus with the voice of the practitioner becoming more prominent in informing research and policy agendas.

## SELECTED LITERATURE ON
## RESEARCH–PRACTITIONER PARTNERSHIPS

Partnerships are initially defined by the perspectives of various stakeholders. In turn, some will have a deeper investment in the process and outcomes, while others may stay on the fringe and either observe or not participate. The Bridging Intensity Typology provided by Noam, Biancarosa, and Dechausay (2003) is helpful in defining the various stages of development of partnerships. This framework is used in the context of school–afterschool partnerships. For the purpose of RPPs, the framework is used to represent the RPP with the concept of school being the researcher (higher education, intermediary, organization).

The bridging levels include self-contained (little association between school and afterschool), associated (afterschool program reserves a space for school input, but no solid connections outside of attendance/behavior), coordinated (school and afterschool program are aware of activities and special events, some degree of coordination), integrated (school and afterschool programs support one another through ongoing communication and meetings), and unified (seamless transition between school and afterschool program).

From an RPP lens, the current state of meaningful RPPs could be considered self-contained or associated, with some outliers that would fall in the coordinated or integrated realm. Programs that are aware of the state of their existing RPPs could help start the conversation about meaningful changes. If the degree of partnership is lower than desired, programs need to consider possible collaborators to make changes to current practice. Fullan (2016) writes that educational change "has meaning because it pursues moral purpose...bringing best knowledge to bear on critical issues of the day" (p. xiii). The potential of RPPs is based in this principle.

Collaboration is an essential element that, according to Coburn et al. (2013), leads to effective partnership that requires "long-term, mutualistic collaborations between practitioners and researchers, intentionally organized to investigate problems of practice and solutions" (p. 2). For sustainability, the partnership needs a long-term commitment by the district, researcher, and afterschool program. Coburn et al. highlight two areas to consider in developing effective RPPs:

- Focused on problems of practice: What are staff experiencing on the ground and practitioners want to find more information, answers, or strategies; likewise, what are researchers exploring that can be connected with practice and involve the voice of the practitioner in such research? What is important to the program, the district, and the community?
- Commitment to mutualism: Sharing of expertise between researcher and practitioner. Defined roles in the codesign process and sharing in the analysis and dissemination of findings. Additionally, there is a commitment of sharing and openness with equal voice.

## THE ROLE OF RESEARCH DESIGN: TRADITIONAL RESEARCH VS. COMMUNITY-BASED RESEARCH

Traditionally, research looks like an outside observer coming into a program, collecting data, analyzing it, and developing recommendations for practice based on the results, with the broader goal of advancing knowledge in the body of work. This methodology is what has helped the field of afterschool quantify its work. With the academic (Bennett, 2015; Vandell et al., 2007) and social-emotional (Durlak, Weissberg, & Pachan, 2010) gains established in the research, the field has been able to receive much-needed recognition for its contribution to the education and enrichment of children and youth.

RPPs build on this contribution and incorporate the community into the research planning, implementation, and design. Community-based research (CBR) emphasizes this principle in examining social change within a community. According to Strand, Marullo, Cutforth, Stoecker, and Donohue (2003), there are three components to CBR: (a) a collaborative enterprise between academic researchers (professors and students) and community members done with and for the community to address an identified need, (b) multiple sources of knowledge allowing for multiple methods of discovery and dissemination of the knowledge produced, and (c) social action and social change at the core of the effort.

Similarly, action research uses the frame of changing the view from strictly practitioner to "one of professional as creative investigator and problem solver" (Stringer, 1999, p. 3). This frame looks at the context of the situation in developing practice in place of standardized practices that are research based but may not be applicable. This lens allows for those who previously were the observed to become the observers and actively participate in the research process.

With a community-based action research agenda, a collaborative approach between researcher and practitioner could be established. These partnerships are developed to help practitioners deepen understanding and build the researcher's understanding of issues raised by the practitioner and centered on problems of practice.

Our field is not alone in examining the potential and impact of RPPs. The field of social work began looking at practitioners' understanding of research in the mid-1970s with the works of Kirk and Fischer (1976), who assert that research and practice are critical. One of the key questions raised by Kirk and Fischer was the use of research by the practitioner. Dissemination of findings may not be enough to influence practice on the ground. Scott (1990) explored the value of RPPs in social work on practice informing research agendas. Adaptations from other fields have already begun in the field of youth development. Hamilton (2015) put forth the model of translational research that was adopted from the medical community. The model supports the notion of practice leading to research. Through ongoing communication, practitioners can develop programs and practices, which are then validated by research. Hamilton also asserts potential research-to-research connections that would (a) be between applied research and "basic" research, (b) have intersections with models and applications, and (c) all be connected through practice (at the center).

There is also a role for intermediaries to distill knowledge and make research accessible to the practitioner. These could include practitioner-friendly research synthesis, distilling knowledge from various research sectors into white papers, reports, or tools for the field, and fostering collaboration and coordination between researchers and practitioners within a community or state.

With the recent passage of the Every Student Succeeds Act (ESSA), there are increased opportunities for RPPs that could include research-based practice, but reciprocally, for practice-based research. According to the American Youth Policy Forum (AYPF), "ESSA is the first federal law to define the term 'evidence-based' and distinguishes four separate tiers of evidence based on the rigor of the research and strength of evidence" (Deeds, 2016, p. 1). The systems ESSA requires are evidence-based, which means using evidence and data holistically for the purpose of continuous improvement. Deeds asserts that this creates a "deliberate and ongoing coalition between researchers and practitioners within a state or locality… partnerships are by no means a silver bullet, but they can certainly facilitate the communication, coordination, and even the social networks necessary to ensure research priorities are informed by the needs of a particular community" (2016, p. 2).

## Connecting Researchers and Practitioners

Afterschool professionals and advocates from around the country indicated RPPs in afterschool are not clear cut. While there is no formula for creating RPPs, there are promising clusters of work happening. These include fellowships in which practitioners do research, coauthored papers supported by grant funding, or statewide afterschool networks (SAN) based in higher education institutions (see Chapter 14 in this volume).

The North Star Youth Worker and Afterschool Matters Fellowships enable practitioners to research and write a paper about the experience, topic, or knowledge gained. Practitioners can be immersed in research methods and inquiry that lead to a deeper understanding and connection to research.

The Edmund A. Stanley Jr. research grants that were provided by the Robert Bowne Foundation highlighted RPPs in their 2013 and 2014 request for proposals and awarded additional points for such a collaboration (Youth Today OST Hub, 2016). Dr. Tom Akiva received one of these grants in 2014. In his study, the researcher took the role of "participant observer" and provided feedback on recruitment and professional development to the program director. This led to the director creating a two-hour professional development opportunity based on the findings. According to Akiva (2014), "Staff reported liking the way the program coordinator did trainings because they felt closer to how the staff would do activities with the kids, and was more experimental" (p. 11).

In another example funded by the Edmund A. Stanley Jr. grants, a 2014 study was conducted that included both the researcher and practitioner conducting research together and being published in the *Afterschool Matters* journal. The team included an associate professor from Brooklyn College, City University of New York, the director of youth learning and research and assistant director of youth initiatives at the American Museum of Natural History (Adams, Gupta, & Cotumaccio, 2013). The director of youth learning also held a doctoral degree and therefore had prior professional training in research methodology.

In addition to the Robert Bowne Foundation, philanthropy has a deeply rooted history in OST. As Gannett and Starr address in Chapter 7 of this book, the interest of funders in the early 2000s helped develop and establish field-building research such as the Massachusetts Afterschool Research Study (MARS). One could argue that without funding support, RPPs simply would not happen. However, as a result of the significant investment by the Charles Stewart Mott Foundation in SANs, there is now a network in every state. There is potential for RPPs to be nurtured within the SAN infrastructure connecting with existing cross-sector partnerships that are regularly convened.

## Creating a Space for Researcher–Practitioner Interactions

A small number of SANs are based in higher education institutions and are positioned to foster greater connections between researchers and practitioners.

Presently some have researchers on contract, or those that present to practitioners at conferences. However, formal RPPs are limited.

Similar to the model Hamilton (2015) described, SANs can provide intermediary support that can create a space to have meaningful interactions, dialogue, and ongoing professional development. Those SANs outside of institutions of higher education can also take a lead role in building RPPs, bridging communication barriers, and facilitating strong and successful relationships between researchers and practitioners. SANs connect with both grassroots and grass-top stakeholders and can convene meetings or work groups as part of their current charge focused on quality, supporting sustainable partnerships, and building internal and external capacity through networks that link stakeholders. Many SANs are actively forging partnerships that often transcend sectors. Building on this, it is possible that SANs could identify opportunities for action research, professional development, and visioning that involve researchers and practitioners (school and afterschool staff).

Deeper relationships can also be formed between school and afterschool staff, which will yield benefits by building the capacity of practitioners to conduct research. Projects such as the Akiva (2014) study help develop research and inquiry skills at the field level. This creates a cost benefit to the community partner and the school district in streamlining professional development and maximizing resources as both parties are trained in the same pedagogy and developmental principles of inquiry-based program delivery.

One example of this inquiry-based approach to program improvement is the CORAL initiative in California. According to the Afterschool Alliance (2014), programs that participated in the initiative saw improvements in program quality and gains in students' reading comprehension. One of the core findings described by the Afterschool Alliance was creating training and staff development based on data from their own findings using a continuous improvement cycle that included data collection, program monitoring, staff coaching, and data analysis. Additionally, the use of ongoing program assessment serves to advance the RPP to a more closely aligned level in the bridging intensity typology as discussed in "Selected Research on Researcher–Practitioner Partnerships" above.

## How Do Practitioners Connect with Research and Researchers?

As mentioned earlier, the common perception of research in the program is someone coming in to do an outside program evaluation where research is "imposed" on the program. Program staff need to see themselves reflected in the research design. Findings and recommendations have to be meaningful on a programmatic level, where they can observe change happening as a result of examining practice. With barriers such as chronic staff turnover, a lack of knowing how to use and interpret data and create buy-in from site staff to shift the culture related to quality improvement efforts to become data driven, and limited professional development funds, creating the space for implementation of research findings or even reflection on best practices is a challenge. The culture of each organization largely dictates the severity of at least two of these three barriers. Processes are needed that orient staff to best practice and a continuing commitment that allow for a practitioner voice.

Dr. Tracy Carmichael, former director of research and evaluation at THINK Together in Santa Ana, CA, and Dr. Deborah Moroney (a former practitioner), principal researcher and practice area director at the American Institutes for Research (AIR), provided their perspective on the topic of RPP. Serving 130,000 students last year, THINK Together is the largest service provider in California, operating over 400 sites across 38 districts, spanning six counties. As a trained program evaluator (outreach programs), Carmichael realized the benefit to being able to effectively communicate lessons from data to the field through action research. She was able to apply the community context in the research design. In her opinion, RPPs are created when programs provide more intentional programming (T. Carmichael, personal communication, September 27, 2016). However, she acknowledged a divide between research and practice as being multilayered. Through collaborative and intentional processes, this gap can be bridged.

Carmichael (personal communication, September 27, 2016) highlighted the disconnection between research and practice in three specific areas: (a) access, (b) capacity, and (c) interpretation. Community-based organizations running after-school programs may have difficulty *accessing* research or may not know where to search. Additionally, is there organizational *capacity* to read and interpret the research without a dedicated staff person for these purposes? Finally, how are the findings from the research being *interpreted* in practice, and is there someone who is able to translate this for practitioners to make this connection?

With limited budgets and resources, Carmichael acknowledged that creating RPPs requires a high level of commitment. There needs to be investment in this vital component of field-building. "It can build a sustainable culture of data reflection and application, so that research…is naturally embedded in the work we do" (T. Carmichael, personal communication, September 27, 2016). Through RPPs, according to Carmichael, practitioners can have exposure to relevant research that can impact outcomes, while researchers gain "firsthand exposure to the nuances of program administration." Research and practice must not exist in silos and should instead have a symbiotic interplay.

Dr. Deborah Moroney at AIR provided a national perspective on the state of RPPs in the OST field. She indicated that RPPs thus far have two definitive formats: formal and informal. Moroney (personal communication, October 10, 2016) asserts that formal RPPs tend to be funded through research-driven initiatives (government or foundation funding). These acknowledge the partnership but are primarily driven by a research agenda or funding focus. With this said, she explained that there may be examples of authentic partnerships that honor both the researcher and practitioner voices, but these have yet to be identified and scaled (D. Moroney, personal communication, October 10, 2016). Less formal RPPs may also arise from a shared mission or vision for a community or initiative.

When discussing the disconnection between research and practice, Moroney (personal communication, October 10, 2016) talked about the perspectives of each. The role of research is to build a knowledge base, while the role of practice is to fulfill a mission. She discussed the need for researchers and practitioners to come together on a shared vision to find a common goal. It is at this point that, in Moroney's opinion, we can authentically connect and shake the common perception that the researcher is the authoritative voice in the field. According to Moroney, "That power dynamic needs to be demystified in order to come together to build and share knowledge. Practice should have a voice informing research questions and focus, and have a hand in research, where interested and appropriate" (D. Moroney, personal communication, October 10, 2016).

Several opportunities have been created to foster RPPs. Public and private foundations such as the Institute for Educational Sciences (2016), the Spencer Foundation (2016), and William T. Grant Foundation (2016) have sought proposals that create RPPs that address problems of practice. These efforts are creating examples of successful RPPs that can demonstrate the value of a strong, carefully conceived RPP to communities and the field. According to Moroney (personal communication, October 10, 2016), as the field matures, RPPs can foster communication, ensure research is aligned, be respectful of practice, and ensure practitioners have access to relevant research.

## Hawaii RPP Case Study

The Hawaii State Department of Education (DOE) Community Engagement Office has worked to increase the capacity of researchers and practitioners to create, sustain, and grow engagement, partnerships, and relationships for student success. A confluence of several activities in the past year including the passage of ESSA, a revision of the Hawaii DOE strategic plan, and the Governor's Blueprint for Education task force have led to a more critical examination of practice and outreach efforts. These DOE partnerships with community stakeholders provide an ideal place to look at RPPs as a long-term collaboration.

Marlene Zeug is the director of the newly formed community engagement office for the Hawaii State Department of Education. According to Zeug, there have been efforts to identify bright spots throughout the district, and in examining these bright spots, conversations increasingly turn towards thinking about new and different relationships between practitioners and research. She admits that with her own academic training, the focus on partnering between research and practitioners is likely more acute. Her office also oversees the statewide implementation of afterschool programs and engages in their work through both researcher and practitioner perspectives. Zeug asserts that "not only can we work to inform the delivery of the program, and use the research to help inform policy and legislation, but it's important and healthy for my staff to engage in reflective inquiry and use the researcher mindset to reflect on their own mental models and constructs" (personal communication, October 30, 2016).

In the Hawaii DOE example, the program coordinator role, which traditionally functioned in a compliance and oversight capacity, has been shifted to embrace a research practitioner's inquiry-based skillset. In this role, the coordinator serves as researcher for the purpose of improving practice and strengthening the overall program. According to Zeug (personal communication, October 23, 2016), this integrates a regular practice of research and inquiry into program implementation.

Organizational and systemic barriers often impede deeper, more meaningful collaboration. Zeug believes there are three barriers to developing research–practitioner partnerships (RPP). These include (a) a lack of clarity on the part of both researchers and practitioners around defining problems of practice, (b) the time and effort involved in conducting research and practice together, and (c) long-term investment needed in formulating the trust inherent in the partnership itself, before embarking on the work together (M. Zeug, personal communication, October 23, 2016).

Some of the issue may be the "misperception about who is qualified to do research" (M. Zeug, personal communication, October 23, 2016). For example, the practitioner may not think they have the skills needed to conduct "research." Additionally, OST providers rarely have an organizational commitment to allow for the time to conduct more in-depth inquiry that might be considered "legitimate" by a formal researcher. As evidenced by the Afterschool Matters (National Institute on Out-of-School Time [NIOST], 2016) and Northstar Fellowship (Augsburg College, 2016) programs, practitioners who engage in research are already on board with the idea of improving their own practice. Some participants describe having a more inquiry-based approach to practice that drew them to the fellowship (Augsburg College, 2016). Zeug agreed with this notion:

> Research should help us explore issues and problems of practice and to inform policy and legislation. But research should also serve as a means of inquiry to improve one's own practice as an educator, in exploring the deep mental models and theoretical frameworks inherent in teaching and learning. (personal communication, October 23, 2016)

The intersection of research and practice follows this assertion, yet like many other layers of partnerships between the OST field and stakeholder groups, it will not happen overnight. One of the fundamental assumptions about these types of partnerships is that there is an underpinning mutual trust and strong relationship (M. Zeug, personal communication, October 23, 2016).

Typical research–practitioner connections exist largely through program evaluations. Practitioners see observers assessing the program or conducting focus groups, and they may complete surveys to gauge their perspectives, but largely the information is collected and disseminated by the researcher. Opportunities for relationship building and common understanding between researchers and practitioners are needed *prior* to the start of the research project. This includes developing shared goals that will help the practitioner gain the skills for inquiry, reflection, and continuous improvement. Additionally, problems of practice should be identified at the outset of the partnership and should help inform a research agenda that will be both meaningful and relevant for the practitioner at the close of the project.

Zeug affirms that the research–practice divide is something she often comes across in her work. Being positioned between the school and community, community engagement offices at the local or state level could be a place to bridge this gap. She asserts that there is immeasurable value to having a dedicated office and staff whose role is slightly removed from the "direct impact" of educating a child and instead is focused on engaging communities, families, and parents (personal communication, October 30, 2016). Sufficient resources are rarely dedicated to this work since the impact on students is perceived as indirect, and direct, research-based evidence into the benefit of OST community engagement is lacking. This is an excellent example of a situation where the needs and challenges faced by practitioners in the OST field could inform the research agenda, leading to an opportunity for a RPP project.

The main strategy of the community engagement office will be in developing professional learning networks that support the active investigation of problems of practice (and solutions for improving outcomes) through a community of practice framework in the next few years. In this strategy, the office will intentionally bring together practitioners (teachers, administrators, state education leaders), partners (whether internal to the Hawaii DOE or external), and researchers, not only to address problems of practice but also to lead to innovative approaches in education.

The professional learning networks developed thus far have included the topics of OST and parent, family, and community engagement. The OST group started as a legislative working group and has evolved into a community of practice. The group wanted to continue convening to evaluate and explore out of school time for all grades and its link to educational outcomes; the process here has been to focus on the problems of practice and introduce data. The second community of practice, focused on parent, family, and community engagement will be targeted at complex area superintendents (similar to district superintendents—Hawaii is one district) and their staff who focus on partnering with stakeholders. The intent is to deepen their practice and capacity in engaging with parents, families, and communities (M. Zeug, personal communication, January 7, 2017).

Partnerships such as the Hawaii example between research and practitioners could inform the education and OST field as research improves. This helps to inform better policy and legislation, as the broader field of education increasingly understands the importance of OST. RPPs also have the potential to shift the perception of public school educators and place a higher value on the professionalism and skill set provided by OST practitioners in a child's holistic development. The deepening of OST staff's understanding of their own practice could help define the educative role for practitioners. Perhaps, in time, such an approach could even lead to a shift away from the prevailing perception of OST as "nonschool" or literally, "out of school" and towards a more inclusive, collaborative, and collective role for OST in learning for our students (M. Zeug, personal communication, October 23, 2016).

## THE RESEARCH TO PRACTICE DISCONNECT

As discussed in previous chapters, over the past 20 years, the OST field has undergone a call for professionalization and standardization, and it has undergone extensive field building efforts. Throughout this time, practitioners' increased appreciation for and application of research has developed.

Rebecca Kelley, director of development for the National 4-H Council, has spent over 20 years working at the local, statewide, and national level. She acknowledged the interest in RPPs by practitioner experts, however, addressed the tension between service delivery and continuous improvement and field building efforts. Kelley (personal communication, October 30, 2016) asserts that over the past two decades, "more thought has been given to the infusion of research from program concept to continuous quality improvement." The Strive Effort Kelley was part of in Cincinnati adapted the Six Sigma model from General Electric in which a common language was established between the higher education, K–12 educators, early childhood educators, workforce development leaders, and more. In creating a shared set of benchmarks, Kelley (personal communication, October 30, 2016) noted that data was used more as a "flashlight" and less as a "hammer." The RPP allowed a space to discuss research findings and help rebuild trust among partners. While she has seen a few cases of practice informed research, Kelley asserts that it is usually researchers who approach practitioners eager to demonstrate the efficacy of an existing theory. From her national perspective, she sees this decreasing over time and morphing into more meaningful RPPs as funders look to wed practitioner expertise to evidence.

In conversations about RPPs with small community providers, the disconnection was more evident. As Carmichael (personal communication, September 27, 2016) indicated, providing staff with the requisite skill set needed to connect the research and practice worlds was not at the forefront of needs. Daily programming and program concerns were the primary drivers of professional development and administrative support that used synthesized research to develop program specific curriculum kits.

The William T. Grant Foundation funds research grants that seek to understand how research evidence is acquired, understood, and used in practice and decision-making. Funding streams such as this one that examine research use on the ground could allow for practice-based research and, in turn, inform larger funding opportunities and agendas.

## OPPORTUNITIES FOR DEEPER RPP

OST is a maturing field. Ellen Gannett has long addressed the need to unify the fragmented OST workforce and regularly advocates for professional development, informed practice, and continuous improvement that has a place for the researcher at the planning and implementation table (Hill, 2016). Continuous improvement cycles are embedded into models such as the National Institute on Out-of-School Time's A Program Assessment System (APAS) system and Weikart Center for Youth Program Quality (YPQA) tool. Through the practitioner-based inquiry required in this process, a feedback loop between research and practice can be created.

There is a need to bridge the researcher–practitioner gap in order for research to be effectively disseminated and adopted into practice. Findings and materials need to be easily translated into actionable steps practitioners can take. According to Diego Arancibia, director of ASAP Connect in San Jose, CA, there is a need for translators (Noguera & Arancibia, 2014) or, as Dr. Dale Blyth (see foreword of this book) calls them, "bridgers" that have both research and practice experience. As the field has matured, we are seeing more emerging researchers who have a practice background. Their insight into the needs and barriers of afterschool programs and understanding of research processes provide perspective in developing RPPs that are uniquely responsive and relevant to both. As a result, these researchers with this experience are uniquely positioned to provide input into distilling and disseminating research into meaningful shifts in practice for programs.

The role of reflection on the strengths and flaws of each unique RPP is one possible entry point to achieving stronger alignment between research and practice. It is an iterative process, much like the continuous improvement cycle, and helps build, grow, and sustain quality in programs. While programs often aspire to integrate or deepen a cycle of improvement, these efforts can be impacted by shifts in funding or administration. Reflective practice that develops inquiry skills should be embedded into the culture of OST programs and equip staff to be able to critically look at practice, be coached in the application, and be willing to self-assess the overall daily flow of the program.

Likewise, in translating research to practice, researchers need to begin the reflection process with whether the research questions and methodology are practical for informing program practice. This speaks to the need for RPPs, and specifically for dialogue in which the practitioner is actively involved in the research and intervention design and providing feedback on the practicality of the application to practice.

Bridging this gap will take work. There is a need for additional funding streams similar to the Bowne Foundation's Edmund A. Stanley research grants. This has proven difficult in a time of declining resources. Consideration should be given to the perceptual and cultural differences between the OST practitioner and the educational researcher, which are in some ways similar to the power dynamics and misalignment between school and afterschool staff. Are there structural barriers that prevent effective collaboration between researchers and practitioners? Is there time to create meaningful dialogue between researchers and practitioners based on program needs and scheduling? What is the sense of partnership between each?

The development of well thought-out partnerships that lead to scalable practice and professionalization is the next logical step in the growth of this area of the field. In the coming years, opportunities for OST will increase as the field is more formally recognized and compensated. This positive direction could lead to more and better research, identification of overlaps and increased connections between sectors, innovative practice not bound by walls or artificial barriers such as time or space, and increased funding supporting holistic systems.

In Connecticut, the Hartford Foundation for Public Giving (2016) has funded seven low-performing communities (alliance districts) to create an Office for Community and Family Engagement (similar to Hawaii) in their district. Meaningful, deeper partnerships focused on problems of practice are at the core of the investment. Each district team (which includes in- and out-of-school professionals) takes part in training and technical assistance provided by the Children's Aid Society and Connecticut Center for School Change. These learning communities are able to more rapidly adopt ideas and identify factors for evidence-based practice due to the localized nature of the design. This foundation could also be useful in developing and disseminating RPP findings to the funder or community. School–community partnerships are not a new idea but one that has demonstrated benefits to all parties involved over time.

In New Britain, Connecticut, the school district and the community have formed a strong partnership to implement a three-week summer program call the Summer Enrichment Experience (SEE) (Whipple, 2014). From the close of the program in September until the first day the following August, district- and community-based staff meet and plan the program. In its third year, the program incorporated the local state university (Central Connecticut State University) and codeveloped a school engagement scale to measure whether the SEE program had an impact after the close of the summer program. It is hopeful that the university, now in the program design meetings and actively involved in the assessment aspects of the program, will develop a deeper research–practitioner partnership.

The need for continuous improvement is an ongoing effort, even once the system is built. According to Dr. Vivian Tseng of the William T. Grant Foundation, "Partnerships like these can sharpen the field's understanding of how to build stronger connections between research and practice" (Tseng, 2012, p. 2). Sharing and highlighting examples of RPP development, progress, and lessons learned will be critical for sustainability.

## Models

While many of the models identified appear to focus on the link to schools and districts, all sought to promote diverse RPP goals. With multiple entry points for communities, how these inform our view of the value and importance of RPPs varies. An RPP that involves limited opportunities for communication between the researcher and practitioner may not be where one community is compared to another community that could be holding regular meetings that assess progress checks and impact and have a well-developed RPP. The diversity of approaches, partnerships, and goals in the OST field provide a myriad of opportunities for RPP development.

In the OST space, RPP models have been created in the area of science, technology, engineering, and math (STEM) programming. Bevan and colleagues (2016) discuss the development of an RPP through the California Afterschool Tinkering Network. The project involved four community providers (Fresno, Watsonville, Techbridge Discovery Cube, and Exploratorium's Afterschool Tinkering Program) and a research institution (Exploratorium). RPP teams collected video and field notes and jointly reviewed and evaluated the program and practices. Over time, the session depth developed as researchers and practitioners began offering deeper reflection and inquiry beyond a surface impact, but about "how STEM-rich Making could provide a context for expansive and equitable learning" (Bevan et al., 2016, p. 4). Intentionally designed RPPs require an ongoing cycle of learning (Deeds, 2016) such as this example.

Coburn et al. (2013) see research alliances as "a long-term partnership between the district and an independent research organization focused on investigating questions of policy and practice that are central to the district" (p. 4). Alliances are able to work with the district and community-based organizations to conduct the research and present findings back to the district. Coburn et al. further explain that there are two types of research alliances, one that works cross-sector and the other that works solely with the district. Each is place-based, focuses on local policy and practice first, develops and maintains data archives, has explicit roles for researchers and practitioners, and collaborates primarily at the beginning and end of the research process.

There is also the model of design research. This method aims to build and study solutions at the same time in real-world contexts such as instructional activities and taking curricula to scale (Coburn et al., 2013). This process creates partnerships and enables district leaders to design and test strategies for implementing findings and practices.

Finally, the Carnegie Foundation's Networked Improvement Communities (NIC) model looks through the lens of improvement science. Improvement science, according to the Carnegie Foundation (2016), accelerates how a field learns to improve. This initiative aims to hasten improvement in problems of practice through a series of tests that help guide development and redefining the research process. Models are tested and ideas modified in cycles of research and action. NICs operate through four tenets described by the Carnegie Foundation (2016): (a) focused on a well-specified common aim; (b) guided by a deep understanding of the problem, the system that produces it, and a shared working theory to improve it; (c) disciplined by the methods of improvement research to develop, test, and refine interventions; and (d) organized to accelerate interventions into the field and to effectively integrate them into varied educational contexts (such as OST). According to Lingenfelter (2016), these communities are needed in an effort to provide the education system with the policies and practical knowledge for navigating partnerships to support student success.

Partnership development and meaningful collaboration are the next phase of growth for the OST field. SANs have the potential for creating space for this dialogue. These efforts could be as simple as hosting a speakers' forum with leading researchers and practitioners. Afterschool networks and organizations such as the National Afterschool Association (NAA) can help not only disseminate research findings to the field, but also identify communities and research organizations that are trying to improve practice at the systemic level. In Connecticut, the Afterschool Network adapted a Vermont model (ISS-AP) into what is known as CLASP (Coaching and Learning for Afterschool Professionals) (Anthony, 2016). Previously, cohorts have been program coordinators, district staff, and community-based educators. In its third year, there is a cohort that focuses on social-emotional learning. With this, a research–practitioner cohort could be developed in the future.

## CONCLUSIONS

Future directions in RPPs show promise not only from the bridging standpoint, but also from field-building perspective. Research has demonstrated the impact and positive outcomes increased collaboration, deeper inquiry, and quality improvement and data collection have on program delivery and student outcomes (Bennett, 2015; Bevan et al., 2010; Harvard Family Research Project, 2010; Vandell et al., 2007). The growing attention to RPPs has been the catalyst for the development of learning communities that involve deeper communication and self-reflection between the researcher and practitioner.

With the passage of ESSA, there is a renewed discussion on community engagement. According to Ujifusa and Tully (2016), with responsibility over accountability shifting back to states and districts, there is an expectation that communities will have a larger voice at the education table. How districts and schools are connecting with communities could also be one indicator of school quality placed on assessments (Ujifusa & Tully, 2016). The shift provided by ESSA could also be an opportunity for SANs and SEAs to work alongside higher education to help build on this momentum. These foundational partnerships can support RPP development and inform both policy and practice. RPPs create the potential space to deepen partnerships while at the same time increase local capacity to institute broad based OST programming that impacts all facets of a child's life.

In sum, through continuous improvement efforts and improving upon developing models such as those mentioned earlier, RPPs can become a part of the culture of the OST field. Lessons learned can be translated in refining the model to integrate community voice and develop an appreciation of the multiple perspectives stakeholders contribute in the discussion. The local contexts of RPPs have the potential to have a profound impact on local and statewide quality systems that look at the whole child and the communities in which they live. Building on the research and practice base of the past 20 years will help to further advance the state of the recognition for the work we are doing in OST; illuminate the impacts effective high-quality programming and partnerships have on children, youth, families, and communities; and help inform the research through RPPs.

## REFERENCES

Adams, J., Gupta, P., & Cotumaccio, A. (2013). Long-term participants: A museum program enhances girls' STEM interest, motivation, and persistence. *Afterschool Matters, 20*, 13–20.

Afterschool Alliance. (2014). *Taking a deeper dive into afterschool: Positive outcomes and promising practices.* Washington, DC: Afterschool Alliance.

Akiva, T. (2014). *Bringing in the tech: The remake learning digital corps.* Pittsburgh, PA: University of Pittsburgh. Retrieved from http://youthtoday.org/hub/bowne-foundation/programs/edmund-a-stanley-jr-research-grants/edmund-a-stanley-jr-research-grants-archive/

Anthony, K. (2016). Providing a space to connect research to practice. *Afterschool Today, 7*(1). 12–13.

Augsburg College. (2016). North star youth worker fellowship. Retrieved from http://www.augsburg.edu/sabo/what-we-do/northstar-youth-worker-fellowship/

Bennett, T. L. (2015). Examining levels of alignment between school and afterschool and associations on student academic achievement. *Journal of Expanded Learning Opportunities, 1*(2), 4–22.

Bevan, B., Michalchik, V., Bhanot, R., Rauch, N., Remold, J., Semper, R., & Shields, P. (2010). *Out-of-school time STEM: Building experience, building bridges Trends.* San Francisco, CA: Learning and Youth Research and Evaluation Center (LYREC) Exploratorium, and SRI, International, Menlo Park.

Bevan, B., Ryoo, J., Shea, M., Kekelis, L., Pooler, P., Green, E., ... & Hernandez, M. (2016). *Making a strategy for afterschool STEM learning: Report from the California tinkering afterschool network research practice partnership.* San Francisco, CA: The Exploratorium. Retrieved from http://researchandpractice.org/wp-content/uploads/2016/04/Final_CTAN_Report_Jan2016_for_Bechtel.pdf

Carnegie Foundation. (2016). *Using improvement science to accelerate learning and address problems of practice.* Stanford, CA: Carnegie Foundation for the Advancement of Teaching. Retrieved from https://www.carnegiefoundation.org/our-ideas/

Coburn, C., Peneul, W., & Geil, K. (2013). *Research-practice partnerships: A strategy for leveraging research for educational improvement in school districts.* New York, NY: William T. Grant Foundation.

Deeds, C. (2016, October 3). Make evidence great again: Using evidence to inform decision-making [Blog post]. Retrieved from http://www.aypf.org/using-evidence-effectively/make-evidence-great-again-using-evidence-to-inform-decision-making/

Durlak, J. A., Weissberg, R. P., & Pachan, M. (2010). A meta-analysis of afterschool programs that seek to promote personal and social skills in children and adolescents. *American Journal of Community Psychology, 45*, 294–309.

Fullan, M. (2016). *The new meaning of educational change*. New York, NY: Teachers College, Columbia University.

Hamilton, S. (2015). Translational research and youth development. *Applied Developmental Science, 19*(2), 60–73.

Hartford Foundation for Public Giving. (2016). *Supporting the region's most challenged school districts through family, school and community partnerships*. Retrieved from http://www.hfpg.org/our-approach/learning/family-school-community-partnerships/

Harvard Family Research Project. (2010). *Partnerships for learning: Promising practices in integrating school and out-of-school time program supports*. Retrieved from http://hfrp.org/publications-resources/browse-our-publications/partnerships-for-learning-promising-practices-in-integrating-school-and-out-of-school-time-program-supports

Hill, S. (2016). *Conversation about the OST workforce: Unify a fragmented profession*. Kennesaw, GA: Youth Today. Retrieved from http://www.youthtoday.org/2016/06/conversation-about-the-ost-workforce-unify-a-fragmented-profession/

Institute for Educational Sciences. (2016). *Program announcement: Researcher-practitioner partnerships in education research CFDA 84.305H*. Retrieved from https://ies.ed.gov/funding/ncer_rfas/partnerships.asp

Kirk, S., & Fischer, J. (1976). Do social workers understand research? *Journal of Education for Social Work, 12*(1), 63–70.

Lingenfelter, P. (2016). *A partnership between evidence-based policy and practice-based evidence*. [Blog post]. Retrieved from https://www.carnegiefoundation.org/blog/a-partnership-between-evidence-based-policy-and-practice-based-evidence/

National Institute on Out-of-School Time (NIOST). (2016). What is the National Afterschool Matters Fellowship? Retrieved from http://www.niost.org/Practitioner-Fellowship/more-about-the-national-afterschool-matters-fellowship

Noam, G., Biancarosa, G., & Dechausay, N. (2003). *Afterschool education: Approaches to an emerging field*. Cambridge, MA: Harvard Education Press.

Noguera, P., & Arancibia, D. (2014). Researcher and practitioner dialogue with Pedro Noguera, PhD (New York University) and Diego Arancibia (ASAPconnect). *Journal of Expanded Learning Opportunities, 1*(1), 6–7.

Scott, D. (1990). Practice wisdom: The neglected source of practice research. *Social Work, 35*(6), 564–568.

Spencer Foundation. (2016). *Lyle Spencer research awards program statement*. Retrieved from http://www.spencer.org/lyle-spencer-research-awards-program-statement

Strand, K., Marullo, S. Cutforth, N., Stoecker, R., & Donohue, P. (2003). *Community-based research and higher education*. San Francisco, CA: Jossey-Bass.

Stringer, E. (1999). *Action research* (2nd ed.). Thousand Oaks, CA: SAGE.

Tseng, V. (2012). *Partnerships: Shifting the dynamics between research and practice*. William T. Grant Foundation. New York, NY.

Ujifusa, A., & Tully, S. (2016, March 22). ESSA may offer megaphone for parent, community voices. *Education Week*. Retrieved from http://www.edweek.org/ew/articles/2016/03/23/essa-may-offer-megaphone-for-parent-community.html

Vandell, D., Reisner, E., & Pierce, K. (2007). *Outcomes linked to high-quality afterschool programs: Longitudinal findings from the study of promising afterschool programs.* Washington, DC: Policy Studies Associates. Retrieved from http://www.eric.ed.gov/PDFS/ED499113.pdf

Whipple, S. (2014, August 7). United Way's summer enrichment program sees high attendance numbers. *New Britain Herald*. Retrieved from http://www.centralct-communications.com/newbritainherald/news/article_9a5aad5a-c7fa-54ae-a6c6-85003ba7348c.html

William T. Grant Foundation. (2016). *Improving the use of research evidence.* Retrieved from http://wtgrantfoundation.org/improving-use-research-evidence

Youth Today OST Hub. (2016). *History of the Edmund A. Stanley Jr. research grants.* Kennesaw, GA: Youth Today. Retrieved from http://youthtoday.org/hub/bowne-foundation/programs/edmund-a-stanley-jr-research-grants/history-of-the-edmund-a-stanley-jr-research-grants/

CHAPTER 14

# BUILDING QUALITY IN OUT-OF-SCHOOL TIME

Jaime Singer, Jessica Newman, and Deborah Moroney

The last two decades have seen a significant development of infrastructure—standards, systems, networks, professional pathways, and resources—to support and promote out-of-school time (OST) program quality. These developments have benefitted programs in a variety of ways, as programs (and systems of programs) have coalesced around a shared understanding of what quality programming is and how quality programs benefit youth.

Prior to the 1980s, OST was largely informal and existed primarily as a combination of extracurricular activities, including school-based clubs, student council, and athletic teams; community drop-in centers; prevention programming; and summer camps (Halpern, 2002). In the late 1990s, research suggested that engaging youth in strengths-based programs in partnership with schools and communities yielded positive youth outcomes (Catalano, Berglund, Ryan, Lonczak, & Hawkins, 2002). Additional studies on 7th–12th grade students, from a longitudinal sample, suggest that quality[1] extracurricular activities promoted a variety of positive outcomes, including increased academic success and reduction of risk-taking behaviors (Mahoney & Cairns, 1997). In the early 2000s, funders and OST intermediaries rallied in response to the growing research and understanding that structured, strengths-based OST programs that were coordinated with schools and

*The Growing Out-of-School Time Field: Past, Present, and Future,*
pages 195–210.
Copyright © 2018 by Information Age Publishing
All rights of reproduction in any form reserved.

communities were ideal to promoting positive experiences and outcomes. The W.T. Grant Foundation, under the leadership of Robert Granger, led the way in championing a body of research that defines what we know about program quality today. We present some important lessons learned from that body of work.

First, quality is a part of an interconnected system that includes the contribution of participants and their families and reflects the community (Durlak, Mahoney, Bohnert, & Parente, 2010). Second, program quality does not function in isolation. It is supported through systemic supports and strong organizational processes (Every Hour Counts, 2014; McElvain, Moroney, Devaney, Singer, & Newman, 2014). Third, program quality is hierarchical. The predominant thinking and practice frameworks suggest that participants should experience a safe and supportive environment, so that ultimately they can engage in positive relationships and skill building. Fourth, staff are the critical actors in implementing program quality (Smith et al., 2012). Finally, high-quality OST programs do in fact support positive youth outcomes (Vandell, Reisner, & Pierce, 2007).

We know quality matters and that it doesn't happen in a vacuum. We also know that quality efforts work best when they are coordinated. As such, systems and programs have evolved to implement new knowledge and the OST field increased efforts to promote coordination at the national, regional, city, and program levels. These system-wide efforts have provided OST professionals increased access to resources that allow them to offer high-quality programs. The OST field has moved forward with an emphasis on coordinated quality, in an effort that has been defined by the development of national and statewide standards, creation of quality assessment tools and systems, and growth of structures to support staff in the field. We describe these advances and approaches to quality in the sections that follow.

## APPROACHES TO QUALITY

Because OST programming is multilayered and multifaceted, approaches to support quality exist at the system and program level, each with their unique contributions and mechanisms for support. We focus, in particular, on the systems level in this chapter, as program-level quality is covered in greater detail in Sections 3 and 4 of this book.

### System-Wide Supports for Quality

The field has many champions of system-wide quality, as well as leaders and innovators in the quality movement. In this chapter, we highlight select national and citywide initiatives that have developed a coordinated system of supports for OST program quality. These supports may include standards, frameworks, and quality rating and improvement systems (QRIS), which may include credentialing systems, technical assistance, and professional development.[2] System-wide monitoring and evaluation are also important parts of quality supports but are not covered in this chapter.

### *National Systems*

The Charles Stewart Mott Foundation (Mott Foundation) has invested in OST for more than two decades by focusing on building "policies and practices to sustain and expand quality afterschool and summer learning opportunities" (Statewide Afterschool Networks, n.d.). To build a nationwide infrastructure, the Mott Foundation's support consists of strengthening a number of organizations that provide technical assistance, thought leadership, convenings, and professional development. The organizations range, for example, from the Afterschool Alliance to the National League of Cities. Together with other entities, they are helping to create an infrastructure for quality afterschool and summer learning opportunities across America (Peterson, Fowler, & Dunham, 2013).

Another important aspect of this work also includes the support of the Mott Foundation for the formation and sustainability of statewide afterschool networks, which support practice, partnerships, and policy for OST programs in their state. The goal was and is to bring together the varied organizations to work together to promote unified policies and practices while leveraging diverse funding opportunities (Chung, Hughes, & Dunham, 2013). At the time of this writing, the Mott Foundation supports statewide afterschool networks in all 50 states. They do this through funding, ongoing professional development, and a supportive community of practice that not only creates a network within the state but also brings together network leaders and key stakeholders from across the country. A statewide afterschool network may be made up of OST leaders, educational, community, business and other service provider leadership, and policymakers. Statewide afterschool networks champion a variety of initiatives to promote OST program quality including the adoption of standards, technical assistance systems, expanding partnerships, and professional pathways for staff. These networks uniquely engage a wide range of providers and support organizations across a state. Networks reach providers and support organizations in rural areas, small towns, and urban areas. Providers range from small community providers and faith-based groups to larger local and statewide initiatives, as well as 21st Century Community Learning Center grantees.

To better understand the spread of the quality movement, the Mott Foundation commissioned a scan of statewide afterschool network efforts around program quality. A team at American Institutes for Research first conducted the scan in 2013 and has updated the "Landscape of Quality" document twice since then, with the most recent iteration completed in 2016 (American Institutes for Research, 2016). The Landscape of Quality includes information on quality standards and guidelines, assessment tools, core knowledge and competencies, credential systems, and quality rating and improvement systems, and it accounts for efforts on the part of the statewide afterschool network or the product of a partnership with the state education agency or other government departments (e.g., health and human services, child and family services) or another organization or intermediary. Findings from the Landscape of Quality suggest that all statewide afterschool networks are working to support OST program quality. The statewide afterschool networks efforts are constantly evolving and moving forward, revising their standards as new research becomes available, for example, or developing new resources such as a standards-aligned assessment tool to continue the spread of quality in their state. Key to each network's efforts is an intentional alignment to the current context for OST in their state. That is to say, most states began by focusing on an element of quality—quite often, standards and indicators that define what quality programming looks like—but worked to ensure that those standards then aligned with other coordinated efforts, both in terms of the resources they developed next (e.g., aligned assessment tools and/or professional development) and the other key stakeholders in the state with whom they partnered to promote widespread uptake. Findings from the Landscape of Quality also suggest that there is no "one size fits all" approach to quality work across the statewide networks. Rather, the impetus for quality work varies and is context-dependent. In one state, standards may be developed to fill a gap and promote a shared language. In another state, the network has focused on emerging as the leader of all efforts uniformly whereas a network in a different state has partnered with another system in the development of a QRIS because that was a statewide priority.

In addition to the national network of statewide afterschool networks, there are national system builders that have a specific focus. For example, founded in 1988 as the National School Age Childcare Association, the National AfterSchool Association (NAA) is a membership organization for OST professionals. NAA works to "foster development, provide education, and encourage advocacy for the out-of-school-time community" (National AfterSchool Association, n.d.a). NAA hosts a widely attended annual convention for afterschool professionals with an evolving menu of sessions. NAA hosts online communities and meetings, an expert hub, and professional learning events and exchanges. Importantly, NAA drafted the pivotal set of national afterschool quality standards that have been widely adopted and adapted (discussed in more detail in the next section) and professional competencies for afterschool and youth development professionals (discussed in greater detail in Chapter 8). At the time of this writing, NAA has 30 state affiliates that strive to "promote quality afterschool programs and professional development in their states" (National AfterSchool Association, n.d.a). Both of these national initiatives have provided a valuable blueprint for system-wide program quality and have worked in conjunction with local efforts. In a number of states, the NAA affiliate and statewide afterschool network are closely aligned.

### Citywide Systems

In 2003, the Wallace Foundation invested significantly in citywide efforts to provide children and youth access to high-quality OST programs across five cities.

Findings from this initiative suggest that organizations involved in OST program-ming within each city *can* work together to coordinate programming services for youth and that, when they do, that coordination can improve access to programs and program quality (Bodilly et al., 2010). Other key findings focused on key in-frastructure to support not only citywide supports for OST but, more importantly, an approach to continuous improvement. Bodilly and colleagues (2010) found, for example, that a management information system and other related infrastruc-ture to collect and enable OST program staff to use data were critical supports for their efforts. A key lesson learned from this endeavor was that both big and small cities could effectively launch a systemic effort to support OST (Bodilly, et al., 2010), a finding that opens up the discussion of quality improvement to all pro-grams and systems involved in the provision of OST programming.

In 2012, the Wallace Foundation launched the "next generation" effort to bol-ster the initiatives of nine additional cities that had already begun system-building efforts of their own. This important investment fostered innovations in system-wide quality supports and bolstered existing commitments to afterschool quality. Four of these original Wallace grantees and other citywide intermediary organiza-tions forged together in 2006 to form Every Hour Counts (formerly known as the Collaborative for Building After-School Systems [CBASS]). Every Hour Counts now consists of nine city partners that work together to build capacity of the OST field to promote high-quality programs at the system and the program level. Every Hour Counts launched the National Learning Community in 2016 with 13 additional cities and regions around the country to provide additional supports and sharing among city systems (Every Hour Counts, n.d.). This is not an exhaus-tive inventory of national and citywide efforts—many multisite national youth serving organizations like the YMCAs and Boys and Girls Clubs of America also endeavor to support quality both at the system and program level—but it does il-lustrate the impact these coordinating systems can have.

Ideally, systemic supports for quality also include an infrastructure that pro-motes program-level quality. Program-level organizational policies and practices that support implementation of high-quality programs include those foundational aspects of a program such as having a shared vision, engaging a stakeholder advi-sory group, having policies for hiring and retaining staff, and the many aspects of program design and planning (McElvain et al., 2014). Point-of-service quality is a term used for the quality of the program that the participant experiences, or the place where youth and adults interact (Smith, Peck, Denault, Blazevski, & Akiva, 2010). Ultimately, system-wide supports for program quality are geared toward supporting continuous quality improvement, as opposed to static quality. Chapters 2 and 11 in this book discuss program-level quality in greater detail. In the follow-ing sections, we share the current state of the quality movement and methods at the system level to support quality at the program level.

## Methods to Support Quality

There are various components to quality, including national and statewide standards, quality assessment tools and systems, and structures to support staff. We explore those methods in the sections that follow and highlight findings from the 2016 Landscape of Quality as an illustrative example of the uptake and spread of quality efforts across a coordinated system-wide effort.

## Standards for OST Program Quality

Adopting shared standards provides systems, organizations, and agencies with a common language. It allows for organized communication, shared measurement goals, and a collective agenda for programmatic and policy endeavors (Dusenbury, Zadrazil, Mart, & Weissberg, 2011; Every Hour Counts, 2014; National Network of Statewide Afterschool Networks, 2013; Yohalem, Devaney, Smith, & Wilson-Ahlstrom, 2012). Standards clearly articulate what settings, structures, processes, and supports should be in place for quality programs. Ideally, standards are research-based and evidence-informed, presented in broad overarching categories with more specific and detailed indicators within. We know from implementation science that when program stakeholders (e.g., funders, staff, partnering organizations) speak the same language (i.e., based on the standards) and are intentional about program implementation, there are many potential benefits including but not limited to increased buy-in to these practices, higher quality

---

**System-Wide Efforts in Indiana**

The Indiana Afterschool Network started on their path to quality in 2009. The network used the NAA standards as a foundation for developing standards for Indiana's OST programs. The network formed a taskforce with a diverse group of close to 30 stakeholders including state agencies, citywide initiatives, intermediaries, providers, and universities. Once finalized by the taskforce, the network rolled the standards out to the field in a number of different ways, including their e-newsletter, at their annual statewide Summit on Out-of-School Learning, other statewide conferences, meet and greets, and anywhere afterschool programs came together. Over the next several years, the network collected feedback from the field, updated the standards, and eventually included observable evidence as part of the standards so that program staff knew what to look for in their own settings. The network also developed the Indiana Quality Program Self-Assessment (also known as the IN-QPSA) so that OST program staff could rate themselves on the standards and better plan for continuous program improvement. The network continues to market the standards by aligning every workshop at their annual Summit on Out-of-School Learning with the standards and ensuring that each one of the presenters understands how the standards are aligned with their presentations.

implementation, and sustainability. In the sections that follow, we describe the rise of OST program quality standards and detail their implementation across the country.

### National Standards for OST Program Quality

In 1998, NAA introduced the Standards for Quality School-Age Care, a set of program quality standards for the OST field. The NAA standards "describe the practices that lead to stimulating, safe, and supportive programs for young people ages 5 to 14 in out-of-school time" (National AfterSchool Association, n.d.b). The NAA standards include 36 "keys to quality" that cover a spectrum of topics that are relevant to OST programs: human relationships; indoor and outdoor environments; activities; safety, health, and nutrition; and administration. The NAA standards describe point-of-service practices as well as organizational processes that are essential for a high-quality program.

### State Standards for OST Program Quality

States also began developing and adopting statewide standards of OST program quality. Findings from the 2016 Landscape of Quality suggest that statewide afterschool networks—much like the field of OST—are continually evolving, revising their standards, and creating new resources to support implementation of those standards (American Institutes for Research, 2016). According to the Landscape of Quality, every statewide afterschool network[3] is making progress toward developing and supporting quality systems at the state level.

Detailed findings from the 2016 Landscape of Quality suggest that the majority of statewide afterschool networks are supporting quality through standards for their state. Findings from the most recent scan reveal that 60% of statewide afterschool networks have developed (or contributed to the development of) quality standards for their state, with another 16% currently in the development process (American Institutes for Research, 2016). A crosswalk of those standards against the NAA National Standards indicates that every statewide afterschool network has adapted the NAA standards (or another state's standards that were based on the NAA standards) to be specific to their state context. The standards development process for statewide afterschool networks often involves collaboration with other statewide afterschool networks that have standards in place. That being said, because states learn from each other and from the national model, it is hard, at this point, to identify where exactly the standards and indicators originated. What is clear is that there is significant consensus around the constructs that support quality.

As with the NAA standards, the statewide standards include standards and indicators for both the activity-level (e.g., human relationships, activities) and organization-level (e.g., administration, evaluation) quality. Many statewide afterschool networks have modified and/or expanded beyond the original NAA categories to include standards for other key areas, such as evaluation and sustainability. The full list of constructs covered across the existing statewide afterschool network standards includes:

1. Human Relationships—the interactions between and among youth participants and adults in the program
2. Indoor Environment and Outdoor Environment—the physical space in which the program operates
3. Activities—age-appropriate activities that are hands-on and engaging
4. Safety, Health, and Nutrition—physical safety of youth and staff, healthy environments, and food
5. Administration—well-documented policies and procedures
6. Staff Qualifications and Professional Development—recruitment and retention of high-quality staff and ongoing professional development
7. Evaluation—systems in place to collect and reflect on program data
8. Sustainability—planning to ensure fiscally sustainable programming
9. Youth Development and Engagement—youth voice and choice reflected in programming and opportunities for youth leadership
10. Diversity, Access, and Equity—policies and staff training focused on respecting and supporting diverse youth participants and families
11. Partnership—meaningful partnerships with schools, families, and communities

States often develop standards as a first step in a movement toward quality. The next step is to implement the standards, which often involves a process and/or tool for OST programs to rate how well they are adhering to the standards. In the next section, we explore various options for measuring program quality.

## PROGRAM-LEVEL ASSESSMENT TOOLS AND SYSTEMS

There are a number of ways OST staff members may approach measuring the quality of their programs. In the following sections, we first present information about tools to measure quality, including standards-aligned assessment tools and research-based tools grounded in a specific quality framework. We then turn attention to the growing prevalence of quality rating and improvement systems (QRIS) in the OST field as a comprehensive approach to improving quality.

### Tools to Measure Quality

Many statewide afterschool networks have developed standards-aligned assessment tools that are designed to provide a rubric-based rating system for assessing whether and how programs are meeting the standards. Akin to the spread of statewide standards, the majority of networks support program quality through the use of an aligned assessment tool. The 2016 Landscape of Quality indicated that 64% of statewide afterschool networks had developed their own assessment tool and 10% of statewide afterschool networks were in the development process

(American Institutes for Research, 2016). Additionally, some systems, organizations, and agencies used validated and/or evidence-based tools, which are described below.

While many statewide afterschool networks and other organizations (e.g., state departments of education, other government agencies) were developing standards and aligned resources, a number of research, evaluation, and practice organizations were in the process of understanding quality, with a focus on how to measure and continuously improve it. The results of these efforts include a decade of groundbreaking research in this area and a portfolio of evidence-based, reliable, and valid program quality assessment tools and aligned systems of support. The adoption of these tools and the development of support systems is widespread and growing. Systemic efforts to define, measure, and improve quality have become a priority.

There are multiple measures of program quality, each with an associated framework that specifies the quality-related mechanisms that are critical to programming. These tools and systems (e.g., Youth Program Quality Intervention from the Charles P. Weikart Center for Youth Program Quality, Afterschool Program Assessment System from the National Institute on Out-of-School Time at the Wellesley Center for Women, School-Age Care and Environmental Rating System from Environment Rating Scales Institute) are designed to measure quality at the point-of-service and/or at the organization level (e.g., physical environment, safety, and health; social and emotional environment/climate; interactions and relationships; program structure and activities; connections to the school day; program management, policies, and practices). Programs and systems may engage with the tools at different levels of rigor and for different purposes, from self-reflection for "low-stakes" program improvement purposes to external assessment for "high-stakes" research and evaluation purposes.

## Quality Rating and Improvement Systems

The purpose of a QRIS is to "assess, improve, and communicate the level of quality in early and school-age care and education programs" (QRIS Resource Guide, n.d., para. 3). These rating and improvement systems were born out of the early childhood education field in response to a need to organize the various quality systems (e.g., financial incentives, professional development, monitoring) into one coherent system. As described in the QRIS Resource Guide (National Center on Child Care Quality Improvement, 2015), QRIS is composed of five elements: program standards, supports for programs and practitioners, financial incentives, quality assurance and monitoring, and consumer education. While QRIS has been more prevalent in the early childhood field, OST programs are also participating in QRIS. According to the 2016 Landscape of Quality, 28% of statewide afterschool networks have developed or supported a QRIS and 16% were in process (American Institutes for Research, 2016).

While QRIS is designed to provide a coherent system for quality within a state, the OST field has engaged in these efforts at varying levels, often due to the connection between QRIS and state licensing bodies. The OST field generally serves youth up through grade 12, and sometimes beyond, while licensing bodies are most often meant for programs serving youth through age 12. As OST programs or systems at the state level work to align with QRIS intended for early childhood settings, many of these types of issues are being sorted out state by state; however, as with quality in general, there is no "one size fits all" approach to OST programs engaging in QRIS. This is a method of quality that is emerging for the OST field and one that researchers and practitioners should watch and engage in as more states include OST programs in QRIS. In the next section, we talk about the important role that the adults who work in OST programs play in the quality movement.

*Structures to Support Staff*

Standards were developed to clearly define what quality programming looks like so it follows that we, as a field, would need structures in place to support staff working in OST programs. This becomes especially important when one considers the nature of the OST workforce, which is comprised of both young professionals who are new to the field as well as those who switch careers later in life (Moroney, 2016). With a high rate of turnover among OST staff, many of whom are employed part-time, OST intermediaries and other organizations that support the field sought to implement sound systems and processes for supporting OST staff. Although it is beyond the purview of this chapter, core knowledge and competencies documents provide guidance around what OST program staff should know and be able to do to support high-quality OST programs (see Chapter 8 in this book for greater detail). Findings from the 2016 Landscape of Quality showed that 46% of statewide afterschool networks had developed a resource document that identified core knowledge and competencies at the state level (American Institutes for Research, 2016).

Staff also need professional development, including ongoing education and training, supports that are often a key component of aligned professional development and credentialing systems. The 2016 Landscape of Quality showed that 42% of statewide afterschool networks developed or supported the development of a credential system. Credential systems often consist of levels that require increasing levels of education and ongoing training and are generally tied to a financial incentive system. Currently, there is not a national credentialing body for the OST field. As such, there is variability in how credentials are developed and implemented in each state, which is beyond the scope of this chapter.

The 2016 Landscape of Quality revealed that a very small number of statewide afterschool networks are working on or starting to think about developing aligned professional development systems (American Institutes for Research, 2016). Program staff are a key component for building and sustaining quality programs yet

---

**System-Wide Efforts in Connecticut**

Since its inception in 1989 as the Connecticut School Age Child Care Alliance (now the Connecticut After School Network), a commitment to quality has been a driving focus of the work. The organization was formed in an effort to provide professional development to an emerging field and the network has offered an annual fall conference and continued to diversify professional development offerings ever since. The network has also focused on building and sustaining leadership in the field. This effort began with Director's Roundtable—a brown-bag lunch series that provided a space for program leaders to come together and share current issues, concerns, or questions—and expanded in 2010 when the network launched its Directors Seminar Series. These bimonthly trainings expanded upon key topics from the roundtable series while infusing current literature and best practices into the discussion. This was the first step to developing a community of practice that allowed practitioners to share their knowledge and experience with one another. In 2013, the Network launched the Coaching and Learning for Afterschool Professionals cohort. Developed to meet a growing need for professional learning, the pilot cohort was limited to 15 people receiving state funding through the Connecticut State Department of Education. It focused on intentional programming and planning. After a successful first year, the network expanded the program to all afterschool programs statewide, regardless of funding source. The model is designed to focus on a key topic of interest (the 2016 focus was social and emotional learning, for example) and includes reading assignments between sessions, a closed Facebook group page, and bimonthly in-person sessions over the course of an academic year.

---

the OST field has much work to do to build a professional pathway. We discuss this and other future directions later in this chapter.

*Focus on Continuous Improvement*

There is no "one size fits all" approach when it comes to OST quality; rather, we emphasize a focus on continuous improvement that involves many of the methods to support program quality referenced previously. Generally, this approach begins with a framework for quality followed by an assessment against that framework. The *continuous* part of continuous improvement comes from interacting with information that is collected to inform ongoing supports, such as professional development, which will help improve practice and promote quality. OST program staff and system leaders can and should engage in this continuous improvement process as the work of building quality programs is never truly done. By constantly collecting information to understand whether and how what we are doing is working, we are always engaged in a process of improvement.

## FUTURE DIRECTIONS

The last two decades have seen tremendous growth in what we know about structures that support quality OST programming. We know that there are components at both the system- and program-level that drive quality in OST programs. We know that having standards and aligned systems helps ensure consistency from program to program and state to state. This section outlines what we view as the ongoing needs for additional research to further our understanding of quality in the OST field, as well as the importance of supporting staff in practice that will ensure the effective implementation of what we learn from research.

### Research

Research on the OST field exists in different stages, depending on the topic of interest. We have witnessed significant contributions to the knowledge base on the relationship between program quality and youth outcomes (Durlak et al., 2010), and there is very good research on the levers for quality practice (Smith et al., 2010). Most recently, OST researchers have engaged in pivotal research on the relationship between staff professional learning (as a function of quality) and youth outcomes (Vandell, Simzar, O'Cadiz, & Hall, 2016). This body of research does well to compel programs to strive for high quality practices to meet the primary goal of OST—to support participants' personal and academic development. As we move forward, we have the opportunity to look more closely at two ends of the spectrum: the system level and the level of the individual experience.

At the system level, more research is needed to explore the value and function of broad-based supports (e.g., standards, QRIS) that are intended to convey a shared vision or create an infrastructure for high-quality practice. For example, the OST field may benefit from an exploration of standards and the uptake and spread of associated quality practices. The learning from this type of exploration may help system leaders determine resource allocations and inform the design and delivery of systemic supports.

There also remains a breadth of opportunities to explore the nuanced relationships between OST program quality, the many rich experiences and opportunities that OST programs offer, and the individual experience. For example, there is some evidence to suggest that OST programs have a positive influence on families, schools, and communities, but there is an opportunity to explore and describe the role of families and communities in promoting and contributing to quality (Durlak et al., 2007). There is also a need for additional research to provide deeper inquiry into the specific components of quality programming and whether and how those interact with activity content and programming. We know, for example, that the fields of education and OST are abuzz with endeavors to support participants' STEM learning and social and emotional learning (SEL), but how can we identify and describe what intentional STEM and SEL practices look like in high quality programs? We boldly assert that we need to know more about who (staff), where (situated in communities in partnership with families), and what (exactly does it look like, especially when it is combined with other initiatives like SEL and STEM).

Lastly, we recommend deeper inquiry and exploration of staff preparation (e.g., degrees, credentials, job experience), job retention, transition, professional pathways, and access to resources and professional learning. Staff members are critical actors in planning, providing, and sustaining high-quality programs (Moroney, 2016). Arguably, understanding the characteristics and pathways of staff who join the OST workforce, stay in the field, and implement quality programs matters for how we—as a field—decide to support the workforce and quality initiatives moving forward.

### Supporting Staff: Professional Pathways

We continue to see a need to support the career pathways for OST staff members in the policy and practice arena (in addition to the research endeavors recommended previously). While much of this is discussed in Section 3 of this book, we suggest three issues related specifically to quality. First, we have observed that the OST workforce is comprised of staff at two ends of a spectrum—those who entered the field and stay (often moving into site coordinator or program director roles, grants administrators, funders, intermediaries, or evaluators and trainers) and those who enter the field and use it as a stepping stone to their future careers or to their retirement. Both paths are valid, so there is a need to support both if we are to support quality OST programming.

Second, we know that the OST field has a high rate of turnover at the local level of programming (Smith et al., 2012; Yohalem, Pittman, & Edwards, 2010). To support staff who are new to the field, we must ensure they are prepared to implement quality programming and know the "basics" of quality. While intermediaries and funders may be looking at the horizon and pushing toward innovation, we must not lose sight of the fact that the adults who are interacting with the young people on a daily basis in OST programs are often new to the OST field and would benefit from ongoing professional development related to quality programing.

Finally, we need to find ways to support OST staff members in the implementation of quality components in their unique programs. One way to do this is through aligned professional development. As discussed previously, there are limited examples of these supports in practice; however, many systems builders and national youth-serving organizations are endeavoring in this area. There will be much to learn as the field moves forward and continues to push the envelope on quality programming.

### ACKNOWLEDGMENTS.

Special thanks to Debbie Zipes and Jamie Johnson at the Indiana Afterschool Network and Ken Anthony at the Connecticut After School Network for sharing their system-wide efforts for quality, to Gwynn Hughes at the Charles Stewart Mott Foundation for her insight and contribution, and to our AIR colleagues Zena Rudo and Marion Baldwin for contributing their thoughts to the Future Directions section of this chapter.

## NOTES

1.  Quality was established by the School-Age Care Environmental Rating Scale (SACERS), a measure of quality at the point-of-service.
2.  It is important to note that system-wide (national, state, local, or initiative) technical assistance and professional development also exist as freestanding outside of QRIS.
3.  The 2016 Landscape of Quality included a total of 46 statewide afterschool networks.

## REFERENCES

American Institutes for Research. (2016). *Landscape of quality among statewide afterschool networks* [Unpublished report]. Washington, DC: Author.

Bodilly, S. J., McCombs, J. S., Orr, N., Scherer, E., Constant, L., & Gershwin, D. (2010). *Hours of opportunity, volume 1: Lessons from five cities on building systems to improve after-school, summer school, and other out-of-school-time programs.* Santa Monica, CA: RAND.

Catalano, R. F., Berglund, M. L., Ryan, J. A. M., Lonczak, H. S., & Hawkins, J. D. (2002). Positive youth development in the United States: Research findings on evaluations of positive youth development programs. *Prevention and Treatment, 5,* 98–124.

Chung, A., Hughes, G., & Dunham, T. F. (2013). Making partnerships work for policies that expand learning opportunities: Statewide afterschool networks. In T. K. Peterson (Ed.), *Expanding minds and opportunities: Leveraging the power of afterschool and summer learning for student success* (pp. 364–370). Washington, DC: Collaborative Communications Group. Retrieved from http://www.expandinglearning.org/expandingminds/article/making-partnerships-work-policies-expand-learning-opportunities-statewide

Durlak, J. A., Mahoney, J. L., Bohnert, A. M., & Parente, M. E. (2010). Developing and improving after-school programs to enhance youth's personal growth and adjustment: A special issue of AJCP. *American Journal of Community Psychology, 45,* 285–293.

Durlak, J. A., Taylor, R. D., Kawashima, K., Pachan, M. K., DuPre, E. P., Celio, C. I., … Weissberg, R. P. (2007). Effects of positive youth development programs on school, family, and community systems. *American Journal of Community Psychology, 39*(3–4), 269–286.

Dusenbury, L., Zadrazil, J., Mart, A., & Weissberg, R. P. (2011). *State learning standards to advance social and emotional learning: The state scan of social and emotional learning standards, preschool through high school.* Chicago, IL: Collaborative for Academic, Social, and Emotional Learning.

Every Hour Counts. (n.d.). *Every Hour Counts: Expanding learning so every student can thrive.* Retrieved from http://www.afterschoolsystems.org/

Every Hour Counts. (2014). *Understanding key elements, processes, and outcomes of expanded learning systems: A review of the literature.* New York, NY: Author.

Halpern, R. (2002). A different kind of child development institution: The history of afterschool programs for low-income children. *Teachers College Record, 104*(2), 178.

Mahoney, J. L., & Cairns, R. B. (1997). Do extracurricular activities protect against early school dropout? *Developmental Psychology, 33*(2), 241.

McElvain, C. K., Moroney, D. A., Devaney, E. D., Singer, J. S., & Newman, J. Z. (2014). *Beyond the bell: A toolkit for creating effective afterschool and expanded learning programs* (4th ed.). Washington, DC: American Institutes for Research.

Moroney, D. A. (2016). *The readiness of the out-of-school time workforce to intentionally support participants' social and emotional development: A review of the literature and future directions.* Washington, DC: National Academies of Sciences.

National AfterSchool Association. (n.d.a). About us. Retrieved from http://naaweb.org/about-us

National AfterSchool Association. (n.d.b). The NAA standards for quality school-age care: Standards at a glance. Retrieved from http://naaweb.org/images/NAAStandards.pdf

National Center on Child Care Quality Improvement. (2015). *QRIS resource guide. Administration for Children & Families, Office of Child Care.* Retrieved from https://qrisguide.acf.hhs.gov/files/QRIS_Resource_Guide_2015.pdf

National Network of Statewide Afterschool Networks. (2013). *Quality standards: Afterschool and expanded learning.* Retrieved from www.statewideafterschoolnetworks.net/content/quality-standards

Peterson, T. K., Fowler, S., & Dunham, T. F. (2013). Creating the recent force field: A growing infrastructure for quality afterschool and summer learning opportunities. In T. K. Peterson (Ed.), *Expanding minds and opportunities: Leveraging the power of afterschool and summer learning for student success* (pp. 357–363). Washington, DC: Collaborative Communications Group, Inc. Retrieved from http://www.expandinglearning.org/expandingminds/article/creating-recent-force-field-growing-infrastructure-quality-afterschool-and

QRIS Resource Guide. (n.d.). About QRIS. Retrieved from https://qrisguide.acf.hhs.gov/index.cfm?do=qrisabout

Smith, C., Akiva, T., Sugar, S. A., Lo, Y. J., Frank, K. A., Peck, S. C., Cortina, K. S. & Devaney, T. (2012). *Continuous quality improvement in afterschool settings: Impact findings from the Youth Program Quality Intervention study.* Washington, DC: Forum for Youth Investment.

Smith, C., Peck, S., Denault, A., Blazevski, J., & Akiva, T. (2010). Quality at the point of service: Profiles of practice in after-school settings. *American Journal of Community Psychology, 45*(3), 358–369.

Statewide Afterschool Networks. (n.d.). About the Networks. Retrieved from http://www.statewideafterschoolnetworks.net/about-national-network/national-network

Vandell, D. L., Reisner, E. R., & Pierce, K. M. (2007). *Outcomes linked to high-quality afterschool programs: Longitudinal findings from the study of promising afterschool programs.* Washington, DC: Policy Studies Associates.

Vandell, D., Simzar, R., O'Cadiz, P., & Hall, V. (2016). Findings from an afterschool STEM learning initiative. *Journal of Expanded Learning Opportunities, 1*(3), 7–26.

Yohalem, N., Devaney, E., Smith, C., & Wilson-Ahlstrom, A. (2012). *Building citywide systems for quality: A guide and case studies for afterschool leaders*. Washington, DC: The Forum for Youth Investment and The Wallace Foundation.
Yohalem, N., Pittman, K., & Edwards, S. L. (2010). *Strengthening the youth development/ after-school workforce: Lessons learned and implications for funders*. Washington, DC: Forum for Youth Investment.

# SECTION V

OST ADVOCACY

CHAPTER 15

# MEETING THE GROWING DEMAND FOR AFTERSCHOOL AND SUMMER LEARNING PROGRAMS

## The Role of Federal Education Policy in Closing the Opportunity Gap

Jen Rinehart and Nikki Yamashiro

## WHY MIND THE OPPORTUNITY GAP?

In the five years since *New York Times* opinion columnist David Brooks first wrote a piece on Robert Putnam's research documenting the growing unequal access to enrichment opportunities between children living in higher-income families and those in lower-income families, what has been termed the "opportunity gap" has garnered nationwide attention, from national news outlets (PBS NewsHour, 2015; Reeves, 2015) to think tanks (American Enterprise Institute, 2015; Sawhill, 2013) to the White House (White House Council of Economic Advisers, 2015). Children spend close to 80% of their time outside of school (Peterson, 2013), and the opportunities that they are or are not afforded during this time over the course of their childhood can significantly affect their health and wellbeing, influence the paths they choose, and have an impact on their future economic mobility. Brooks (2012) stated, "Putnam's group looked at inequality of opportunities among children. They help us understand what the country will look like in the decades ahead. The quick answer? More divided than ever.... Equal opportunity, once the core to the nation's identity, is now a tertiary concern" (para. 2).

For more than a decade, closing the "achievement gap"—the disparity in educational performance measures between specific groups of students, most often looking at income and race and ethnicity—was the centerpiece to address educational and socioeconomic inequity among students. The disparities that impact students during the school day are critical to address; however, Putnam's research, rather than concentrating on the outcomes related to educational and socioeconomic differences, focuses on the underlying causes, highlighting the increasing divide between the opportunities afforded to children living in lower-income families compared to the opportunities available in higher-income families. For instance, in 1972 parents in the top $10^{th}$ income bracket spent just under $3,000 on their children's enrichment activities, compared to less than $1,000 by parents in the lowest income bracket (Putnam, 2015). By 2007, spending on enrichment activities increased to approximately $6,600 among parents in the top income bracket, while spending by parents in the lowest income bracket remained below $1,000. Over the course of 35 years, higher-income parents were now spending roughly nine times as much on their children's enrichment activities as poorer families. At the same time, Putnam found that a participation gap in school-based extracurricular activities was occurring between wealthy students and their less affluent peers. From 1972 and 2002, the participation gap in school-based extracurricular activities between these two groups of students not only almost doubled, but the percentage of wealthier high school students participating in extracurricular activities stayed relatively the same while participation among high school students in the lowest socioeconomic quartile dropped more than 10 percentage points (Putnam, 2015).

Clear differences between the opportunities afforded to children in low-income versus high-income families are also apparent when looking at the time spent with parents, relationships with informal mentors, and volunteering. Many studies have found that quality time between parents and their children is associated with positive outcomes for children (Moore, Kinghorn, & Bandy, 2011); however, an analysis of the Bureau of Labor Statistics' American Time Use Survey reported that higher-income married working men and women spent more time with their children compared to their lower-income peers (Guryan, Hurst, & Kearney, 2008). Connection to an informal mentor—an adult who is not their parent but who provides guidance and serves as a role model—is another area where low-income youth are at a disadvantage. Informal mentors have been associated with a positive impact on the educational success of youth, but low-income youth are less likely than their higher-income counterpart to have a relationship with a mentor (Erickson, McDonald, & Elder, 2009). Volunteerism is another notable indicator. Youth who volunteer are less likely to be disconnected from work and school, and volunteerism is linked to higher economic opportunity (Opportunity Nation, 2014). Examining parenting in America, a Pew Research Center study reported that close to two-thirds (64%) of parents with a household income greater than $75,000 said that their child had volunteered in the past year, 27 percentage points higher than parents with a household income below $30,000 (Pew Research Center, 2015).

Through the gaps that have emerged between families with greater financial means and those without, as a country we are moving further away from the ideal that all children, regardless of their zip code or family's economic status, are afforded the same opportunities to succeed. These opportunities—which include access to enriching activities outside of school, time with family, and having supportive mentors—provide students with additional academic supports, guidance, and encouragement to do well in school, as well as introducing them to new fields of interest, helping them develop essential communication and social skills, and illuminating the paths available to thrive in school and life.

We at the Afterschool Alliance believe that closing this opportunity gap is not only essential for the students and families who are most impacted; it is essential for our nation's future. All students, not only those who are fortunate enough to have access to opportunities that enrich and build upon their in-school learning, deserve to be and need to be well prepared for adulthood. The variety of opportunities available after school and in the summer helps students reach their maximum potential, giving them the supports, encouragement, and stability they need as they navigate through school and prepare to enter the workforce.

## WHAT CAN AFTERSCHOOL AND SUMMER LEARNING PROGRAMS DO TO HELP?

Fortunately, there are bright spots to point to that are helping close the opportunity gap, lifting up students and communities who are struggling to get ahead. Afterschool and summer learning programs are two such examples, providing a safe environment that inspires learning and offers academically enriching activities to 4.5 million students living in low-income families (Afterschool Alliance, 2014b). Together, the two types of programming take advantage of the hours when students are out of school, creating a year-round system of support. Afterschool programs run during the school year, generally operating between the hours of 3:00 p.m., when school lets out, and 6:00 p.m., when parents return from work, and summer learning programs, taking place during the summer months when school is out of session, are elaborated on in the following chapter.

Participation in afterschool and summer learning programs is also growing across rural, suburban, and urban communities—all of which are experiencing economic hardships. In rural communities, 1 in 4 children are poor (U.S. Department of Agriculture, 2015); in suburban communities, the number of people living in poverty areas has more than doubled between 2000 and 2010, from 9.9 million to 22.1 million (Bishaw, 2014); and urban communities continue to be where the largest percentage of people living in poverty areas reside, totaling 51.1%, or 39.5 million (Bishaw, 2014).

Access to affordable afterschool and summer learning programs turns time that children may have spent alone and unsupervised (Afterschool Alliance, 2014a) into an engaging and valuable learning opportunity led by caring adults and mentors in a safe environment. Afterschool programs are supporting students' academic growth, providing opportunities for reading or writing and science, technology, engineering, and math (STEM); setting aside time for arts and music; developing students' health and wellness, keeping students physically active and providing nutritious snacks and meals; and promoting students' social and emotional development, teaching them about teamwork, how to interact with their peers, and how to be a leader (Afterschool Alliance, 2014a). For older youth, afterschool programs can be a place where they have a choice in what they want to participate in, where they are confident that their opinions are heard and valued by adult mentors, and where they can develop leadership skills through practices such as providing input into programming (Deschenes, et al., 2010).

Increased engagement in school, improved academic performance, and better behavior are a few of the positive impacts associated with participation in high-quality afterschool programs. Students who regularly participate in such programs have demonstrated improved school day attendance levels (Devaney, Naftzger, Liu, & Sniegowski, 2016), gains in reading and math achievement (Lauer et al., 2006), and increased self-perceptions and positive social behaviors (Durlak, Weissberg, & Pachan, 2010).

## HOW DO AFTERSCHOOL PROGRAMS SUPPORT STUDENTS IMPACTED BY THE OPPORTUNITY GAP?

Increased access to quality, affordable afterschool and summer learning programs is combating the growing disparity between students in low-income and higher-income families. Students living in low-income families who participate in quality afterschool programs see significant benefits, demonstrating improved work habits and behavior in school (Vandell, Reisner, & Pierce, 2007). High levels of participation in afterschool programs have also been shown to eliminate the math achievement gap; as elementary students' participation in an afterschool program increases, the difference in math achievement between students from low-income and high-income families decreases (Pierce, Auger, & Vandell, 2013).

Among parents who have a child in an afterschool program, low-income parents and parents living in communities of concentrated poverty overwhelmingly report that their child's afterschool program offers a variety of academic supports and helps improve their child's social and emotional wellbeing (see Table 15.1). In *America After 3PM*, Afterschool Alliance's national household survey of more

TABLE 15.1.  Parents Who Agree That Their Child's Afterschool Program Provides the Following Supports and/or Benefits

|  | Low-Income Parents | Parents Living in Communities of Concentrated Poverty |
| --- | --- | --- |
| Homework assistance | 80% | 81% |
| Opportunities for reading and writing | 74% | 76% |
| Physical activity | 79% | 87% |
| Helps their child develop social skills | 79% | 86% |
| Reduces the likelihood that youth will engage in risky behaviors | 73% | 83% |
| Improves behavior in school | 67% | 77% |
| Improves school day attendance | 64% | 74% |

than 13,709 in-depth responses from parents of school-age children, parents with a child in an afterschool program report that the program provides homework assistance, opportunities for reading and writing, physical activity, as well as agree that the program helps their child develop social skills, reduces the likelihood that youth will engage in risky behaviors, and improves children's behavior in school and school day attendance (Afterschool Alliance, 2014b).

## THE CURRENT UNMET DEMAND FOR AFTERSCHOOL PROGRAMS HIGHEST FOR THOSE MOST IN NEED

Unfortunately, the demand for afterschool and summer learning programs far outweighs the availability of such programs. For every one student in an afterschool program, there are two students waiting to get into a program. This equates to close to 20 million students who are not currently in an afterschool program but would be enrolled if a program were available to them (Afterschool Alliance, 2014a). Similarly, although one-third of families reported that at least one child participated in a summer program, more than half of families reported that they would like their child to participate in a program the following summer (Afterschool Alliance, 2014a). Moreover, unmet demand for afterschool programs is higher among low-income students and students living in communities of concentrated poverty compared to the national average (50%, 56% and 41%, respectively).

Unmet demand for afterschool programs has consistently climbed higher over the span of 10 years, rising from 15.3 million students in 2004 to 18.5 million students in 2009 to 19.4 million students in 2014 (Afterschool Alliance, 2014a). Projections for the number of students who are likely participants in afterschool programs are based on the U.S. Census Bureau, Current Population Survey child-level data. (U.S. Census Bureau, 2012).

There are a variety of reasons for the high level of unmet demand, but a few reasons regularly rise to the top. Program cost and lack of access to afterschool programs are often among the top barriers to participation in afterschool programs (Afterschool Alliance, 2014a). Low-income families, including those living in communities of concentrated poverty, are especially likely to point to access and cost as barriers to enrollment (Afterschool Alliance, 2016). Among families fortunate enough to access afterschool and summer programs, the average cost per week is $114 and $250, respectively (Afterschool Alliance, 2014a). Single parents can spend up to 38% of their incomes for the school-age care of a single child, which includes afterschool and summer programs (Child Care Aware of America, 2015). Families without the financial means to afford quality afterschool programs often have no choice but to navigate a maze of afterschool arrangements that range from neighbor or adult relative care to kids home alone and unsupervised. Successfully ensuring access to quality afterschool and summer learning opportunities for all students requires coordination of resources among multiple partners.

## FEDERAL EDUCATION POLICY CAN HELP BRING OPPORTUNITY IN TO BALANCE

The charge of federal policy in education is to promote the academic success of all children and ensure equal access to a free, high-quality public education. Some of the best known examples of federal policy to promote equity in education include the Elementary and Secondary Education Act (ESEA), first enacted in 1965 to promote educational opportunity for all (U.S. Department of Education, n.d.); Title IX, which was established in 1972 to prohibit discrimination based on gender in schools (U.S. Department of Education, 2015b); and the Individuals with Disabilities Education Act, first passed in 1975 to ensure that students with disabilities are able to enroll in public schools and access special education services (Individuals with Disabilities Education Act, n.d.).

These landmark pieces of federal education legislation focus on helping to eliminate educational disparities during the school day. Under the 1994 reauthorization of ESEA, known as the Improving America's Schools Act, the vision of what constitutes a quality education began to expand to encompass the hours outside of the traditional school day as well.

Based on local models put forward by community and education leaders in small towns, rural areas, and cities to create a central hub of family and community supports both in and out of the school day, an amendment to fund an initiative named the 21st Century Community Learning Centers (21st CCLC) was introduced into the Improving America's Schools Act by Republican leaders in Congress and supported by Democratic leaders (Gayl, 2004). Two years later, that bipartisan support resulted in the first round of funding for 21st CCLC—$750,000 in 1996 (Phillips, 2010). Over a 5-year span, the 21st CCLC initiative—while maintaining its locally driven approach at its core—grew from a small, grant-funded project to a more than $1 billion investment spanning all 50 states, plus the District of Columbia providing before school afterschool, and summer learning opportunities to 1 million students living in low-income families who attend low-performing schools in 11,000 high poverty communities (U.S. Department of Education, 2015a).

Many factors contributed to the rapid success of the program, including high levels of demand among families across the nation, documented support for public funding of afterschool among voters, strong bipartisan support in the Congress, and a unique public–private partnership between the Department of Education and the Charles Stewart Mott Foundation. But despite strong ongoing support for afterschool from stakeholders at all levels and tremendous unmet requests for funding from communities across the nation, funding has remained roughly flat for more than a decade. The current investment in 21$^{st}$ CCLC stands at just over $1 billion ($1.167 billion), reaching 1.6 million students and 400,000 family members of those students (U.S. Department of Education, 2015a).

As one might expect when a federal funding stream grows to more than $1 billion, there have been challenges to 21$^{st}$ CCLC funding over the years. In 2004, facing pressures to reduce government spending, there was a massive proposed cut to 21$^{st}$ CCLC funding that would have deprived 400,000 children and families of their afterschool and summer programs. There have been efforts over the years to redirect funding for afterschool and summer programs to other priorities. Most recently, afterschool faced the threat of being included as just one of many possible uses of funds in a flexible block grant in the reauthorization of the Elementary and Secondary Education Act, which would have left our nation's students and families with no dedicated funding to support the valuable learning and enrichment that takes place outside the traditional school day. In all of these instances, strong grassroots and grass-tops engagement, clear evidence of parent demand and support for afterschool, and the legacy of bipartisan Congressional support helped overcome the challenges.

In the midst of these challenges, the evidence base for afterschool has continued to grow and the federal investment has served as a catalyst for engagement of and investment by other stakeholders. In recent years, governors and/or state legislatures have established task forces or councils to better understand the role of afterschool and summer learning in states like Arkansas, Texas, Nevada, Illinois, and more (National Conference of State Legislatures, 2012), while other states, such as California, Massachusetts, Nebraska, New York, Tennessee, Wyoming, and Vermont, have recognized the value of afterschool and summer programs and are now investing significantly in quality supports for such programs serving children and youth.

In California, a 2002 ballot initiative championed at the time by actor and now former Governor Arnold Schwarzenegger (Rivera, 2002) led to the state's $550 million annual investment in California's After School Education and Safety (ASES) program, a partnership between schools and local communities to provide kindergarten through 9th grade students with afterschool and summer learning programs (California Department of Education, 2015). The state funding is intentionally structured to complement federal 21$^{st}$ CCLC funding, resulting in nearly half of California's public schools (45%) now being home to an afterschool program, including 59% of California's low-income schools (California AfterSchool Network, 2016). Facing more challenging state budgets and political climates, other states have sought out creative funding solutions to help support youth in the afterschool and summer hours. For example, advocates in Tennessee and Nebraska looked to their state lottery systems, and in both states, a portion of the lottery revenue currently helps to support afterschool and summer learning opportunities for youth.

## THE MOST RECENT FEDERAL EDUCATION POLICY EFFORT TO PROMOTE EQUITY

On a national level, the preservation of 21$^{st}$ CCLC in the 2015 reauthorization of ESEA, known as the Every Student Succeeds Act (ESSA), proved to be a significant win for students and families. Under ESSA, 21$^{st}$ CCLC continues to be the only federal funding stream dedicated to providing out-of-school time programs that are locally designed to meet the students and families in rural, urban, and suburban high-poverty communities. With students spending only 20% of their waking hours each year in school (Peterson, 2013), the recognition of necessity for expanded opportunities and supports for students and families in high need was a major victory.

Afterschool advocates and allies worked for several years to identify potential changes to 21$^{st}$ CCLC to recommend for inclusion in ESEA reauthorization. In 2013, Senators Barbara Boxer and Lisa Murkowski worked in a bipartisan fashion to introduce the Afterschool for America's Children Act, which contained many of the improvements that the afterschool community wanted to see in the next federal education law. A companion bill, with just a few minor changes, was introduced in the House of Representatives in 2015.

Those bills set the stage for changes to 21$^{st}$ CCLC to be considered in the ESEA reauthorization process. Through a sustained campaign; champions in Congress; and the mobilization of programs, parents, and partners across the country, several of the afterschool community's proposed changes were incorporated in ESSA, including language that:

- Encourages sharing of data and resources to better support school–community partnerships and more intentional alignment between afterschool and summer programs and the regular school day.
- Promotes learning that complements, but looks different than the regular school day by emphasizing hands-on, experiential learning; STEM learning; physical activity and nutrition education; and opportunities to help

develop financial literacy, college and career readiness, and environmental literacy.

• Identifies performance measures that are connected to overall college and career readiness goals including school attendance, grades, and on-time grade level advancement.

• Provides increased emphasis on quality by offering flexibility to state education agencies to invest more resources in quality improvement efforts such as training and professional development.

• Allows funds to be used for "afterschool-like" activities as part of expanded learning programs. Requires school and community partnerships and at least 300 hours to be added during the year.

• Prohibits supplanting of other funding and prioritizing of any particular model of expanded learning.

The opportunities for afterschool and summer programs in ESSA implementation are not limited to 21st CCLC: ESSA includes mentions of afterschool and summer programs within Title I; a focus on STEM—including afterschool STEM—in Title IV, Part A, which is a formula grant program that supports "well-rounded" education, and the Community Support for School Success Program, which is designed to support grants to community schools that often include afterschool and summer programs as a key component (Peterson, 2015).

While ESSA presents numerous opportunities to close opportunity gaps and expand access to afterschool programs, at the time of writing this chapter, taking advantage of these opportunities will require dedicated effort by afterschool allies at the state and local levels. ESSA represents a significant shift away from what many saw as too much federal intervention in education under NCLB to strong state and local decision making with the federal government playing a supporting role (Klein, 2016). While ESSA state plans are in development, afterschool supporters are engaging with state education agencies to promote language that supports afterschool and summer programs. Similarly, as local districts move to implementing ESSA, afterschool advocates can play a key role in helping school and district leaders see where opportunity exists to better support students and families through evidence-based, high-quality afterschool and summer programs.

Afterschool advocates may find powerful allies in state and city elected officials, such as state legislators, governors, mayors, and city or county council members. In addition to the previously mentioned state-level support for afterschool, city leaders have embraced afterschool and summer programs as a strategy to help combat juvenile crime and safety while also providing learning opportunities that go beyond the traditional school day (National League of Cities, 2011). Leaders from cities as diverse as Fort Worth, TX; Nashville, TN; Providence, RI; New York, NY; South Salt Lake City, UT; and Brooklyn Park, MN have all turned to afterschool and summer programs as a strategy to help keep kids safe, healthy, and on the right track (Simonton, 2015).

## MAXIMIZING ASSETS TO MAKE THE CASE TO DECISION-MAKERS AT THE STATE AND LOCAL LEVEL

Afterschool advocates—and particularly statewide afterschool networks, networks that advance partnerships and policies to support and sustain quality afterschool and summer learning opportunities at the state level—are no strangers to speaking out on behalf of afterschool programs and the children and families who benefit from programs. While getting afterschool included in ESSA required an immense amount of advocacy at the federal level, the implementation of ESSA lies in the hands of the state and local education agencies.

Fortunately, many of the advocacy skills and strategies that state and local afterschool allies have been honing for years are being applied to shape the implementation of ESSA. For example, relying on the strength of diverse partnerships is essential in all advocacy efforts. The statewide afterschool networks are rooted in partnerships that engage both likely and unlikely allies in supporting afterschool. Given that the messenger is often as important as the message in advocacy work, having a strong network of partners who collectively can speak to a diverse set of stakeholders is essential for successful advocacy efforts. The networks also have a history of working across state lines to share successful strategies and materials. The Afterschool Alliance plays a supportive role in helping ensure that sharing across states happen. The statewide afterschool networks communicate with one another regularly to share strategies and tools via multiple platforms, including an online community and national conferences and meetings. One recent outcome of cross-state collaboration resulted in a set of resources available at essa.afterschoolalliance.org to help state afterschool networks make the case for afterschool and provide sample language for state ESSA plans to their allies in state departments of education.

The strong grassroots network that the afterschool community has worked for more than a decade to create is an important asset in ESSA implementation, as well as in other state and local advocacy efforts. Local leaders who work in communities and states have the capability to increase awareness of the need for afterschool and to act as a voice for the afterschool movement. Since 2001, it has been a goal of the Afterschool Alliance to lift up the voices of local champions of afterschool and in turn 21st CCLC, which is a locally shaped initiative at its core.

As is the case with any advocacy efforts, the key to ESSA related advocacy is connecting to issues that are top of mind for the state and local education leaders and helping them see how afterschool can support their overall education goals for students. Fortunately, the afterschool and summer learning community has a rich history of cultivating networks, training advocates, creating materials, and developing a field that can support afterschool in ESSA implementation and mobilize to address the next set of challenges and opportunities.

## WHAT'S AHEAD?

The topic of education was not a significant one throughout the 2016 election cycle, and there are few clear signals regarding the education priorities that the Trump administration will work to advance. Many education leaders see President Trump's selection and the U.S. Senate's confirmation of Betsy DeVos as U.S. Secretary of Education as a signal that school choice will be an education policy priority for the new administration (Emma & Stratford, 2016). Education policy scholars, including Gerard Robinson of the American Enterprise Institute (AEI), also point out that while education has not received much attention from President Trump, many of his priority issues—including safety, the economy, and the military—are education issues (Luchner, 2017).

Federal childcare policy also has implications for the afterschool and summer learning community. The Trump administration's childcare plan includes tax credits and a new dependent care savings account, with a federal match of $1,000 for low-income families, which could be used to pay for afterschool enrichment programs (Donald J. Trump for President, Inc., 2016). While there are concerns with the plan as proposed and the likelihood of enactment is uncertain, it is promising to see inclusion of afterschool as part of the childcare discussion right from the start.

Ultimately, it will be up to the 115th Congress to shepherd through legislation and funding that help advance the priorities of the Trump administration and Congress. Maintaining funding for current initiatives and securing funding for new priorities will be challenging given the spending caps, which limit the overall available federal funds. Beyond spending bills, many in Washington, DC expect a number of reauthorizations that were not wrapped up in 2016 to be tackled by the new Congress, including reauthorization of the Higher Education Act (HEA), the Perkins Career and Technical Education Act, Child Nutrition Act, and the Juvenile Justice and Delinquency Prevention Act.

As would be the case with any incoming president, new administration and Congress, it will be up to the afterschool and summer learning community to look for ways to connect afterschool and summer learning to the policies and priorities that our new leaders put forth. For instance, afterschool and summer learning programs have been, and will continue to be, in addition to a safe environment for children, the incubators for innovation and a setting where states and communities can focus on local priorities, including STEM, workforce development, physical fitness, and global learning. There is a window in the policy arena to draw connections for policymakers between their priorities and the world of possibility in the out-of-school hours.

While there is a great deal of uncertainty, it is important to remember that support for afterschool and summer programs has withstood several changes of administration and multiple sessions of Congress. As with previous changes in leadership, advocacy at the federal, state, and local levels will be critical to improve access to and the quality of afterschool and summer learning programs. The state of the afterschool field has flourished over the years, from the strength of community partnerships to the number of children and families who benefit from the resources and supports provided by programs, and it is essential to continue the forward momentum of this movement.

Together, we must promote the valuable work of afterschool and summer learning programs in rural, suburban, and urban communities, providing much-needed support to ensure that children across all zip codes are kept safe and given the opportunity to succeed. It remains the charge of those who understand the importance of these programs and have seen the positive impacts programs have on the students and families they serve, to continue to work together, develop new partnerships, and be champions for a cause that is helping more than 10 million students across the country.

## REFERENCES

Afterschool Alliance. (2014a). *America after 3PM: Afterschool programs in demand.* Washington, DC: Author. Retrieved from http://www.afterschoolalliance.org/documents/AA3PM-2014/AA3PM_National_Report.pdf

Afterschool Alliance. (2014b). [America after 3PM household survey]. Unpublished raw data.

Afterschool Alliance. (2016). *America after 3PM special report: Afterschool in communities of concentrated poverty.* Washington, DC: Author. Retrieved from http://www.afterschoolalliance.org/AA3PM/Concentrated_Poverty.pdf

American Enterprise Institute. (2015). *The American dream in crisis? A discussion with Robert Putnam, Charles Murray, and William Julius Wilson.* [Event]. Retrieved from https://www.aei.org/events/the-american-dream-in-crisis-a-discussion-with-robert-putnam-charles-murray-and-william-julius-wilson/

Bishaw, A. (2014). Changes in areas with concentrated poverty: 2000 to 2010. *American Community Survey Reports.* Washington, DC: U.S. Census Bureau. Retrieved from https://www.census.gov/content/dam/Census/library/publications/2014/acs/acs-27.pdf

Brooks, D. (2012, July 9). The opportunity gap. *The New York Times.* Retrieved from http://www.nytimes.com/2012/07/10/opinion/brooks-the-opportunity-gap.html

California AfterSchool Network. (2016). *State of the state of expanded learning in California 2015–2016.* Washington, DC: Author. Retrieved from http://www.afterschoolnetwork.org/post/state-state-expanded-learning-ca-2015-2016

California Department of Education. (2015). Program description: Background information, program objectives, and requirements for the After School Education and Safety Program. Retrieved from http://www.cde.ca.gov/ls/ba/as/pgmdescription.asp

Child Care Aware of America. (2015). *Parents and the high cost of child care: 2015 report.* Arlington, VA: Author.

Deschenes, S. N., Arbreton, A., Little, P. M., Herrera, C., Baldwin Grossman, J., Weiss, H. B., & Lee, D. (2010). *Engaging older youth: Program and city-level strategies to support sustained participation in out-of-school time.* Boston, MA: Harvard Family Research Project. Retrieved from http://www.wallacefoundation.org/knowledge-      center/Documents/Engaging-Older-Youth-City-Level-Strategies-Support-Sustained-Participation-Out-of-School-Time.pdf

Devaney, E., Naftzger, N., Liu, F., & Sniegowski, S. (2016). *Texas 21st century community learning centers: 2014–15 evaluation report.* Naperville, IL: American Institutes for Research.

Donald J. Trump for President, Inc. (2016). Fact Sheet: Donald J. Trump's New Child Care Plan. Retrieved from https://www.donaldjtrump.com/press-releases/fact-sheet-donald-j.-trumps-new-child-care-plan

Durlak, J. A., Weissberg, R. P., & Pachan, M. (2010). A meta-analysis of after-school programs that seek to promote personal and social skills in children and adolescents. *American Journal of Community Psychology, 45,* 294–309.

Emma ,C., & Stratford, M. (2016). Trump selects DeVos as education secretary. *Politico.* Retrieved from http://www.politico.com/story/2016/11/betsy-devos-education-secretary- trump-231804

Erickson L. D., McDonald, S., & Elder, G. H., Jr. (2009). Informal mentors and education: Complementary or compensatory resources. *Sociology of Education, 82,* 344–367. Retrieved from https://www.ncbi.nlm.nih.gov/pmc/articles/PMC3170563/

Gayl, C. L. (2004). *After-school programs: Expanding access and ensuring quality.* Washington, DC: Progressive Policy Institute. Retrieved from http://files.eric.ed.gov/fulltext/ED491206.pdf

Guryan, J., Hurst, E., & Kearney, M. (2008). Parental education and parental time with children. *Journal of Economic Perspectives, 22*(3), 23–46. doi: 10.1257/jep.22.3.23

Individuals with Disabilities Education Act (IDEA). (n.d.) Retrieved from https://www.disability.gov/individuals-disabilities-education-act-idea/

Klein, A. (2016). Inside the Every Student Succeeds Act. *Education Week.* Retrieved from      http://www.edweek.org/ew/issues/every-student-succeeds-act/index.html?intc=content-exlaineressa

Lauer, P. A., Akiba, M., Wilkerson, S. B., Apthorp, H. S., Snow, D., & Martin-Glenn, M. L. (2006). Out-of-school time programs: A meta-analysis of effects for at-risk students. *Review of Educational Research, 76,* 275–313.

Luchner, J. (2017). *Panel: When rethinking school governance, afterschool is a piece of the local puzzle.* Washington, DC: Afterschool Alliance. Retrieved from http://www.afterschoolalliance.org/afterschoolsnack/ASnack.cfm?idBlog=045A90A9-5056-A82E-7A436679B32D7AF9

Moore, K. A., Kinghorn, A., & Bandy, T. (2011). *Parental relationship quality and child outcomes across subgroups.* Washington, DC: Child Trends. Retrieved from http://www.childtrends.org/wp-content/uploads/2011/04/Child_Trends-2011_04_04_RB_MaritalHappiness.pdf.

National Conference of State Legislatures. (2012). *A legislative look at expanded learning opportunities: How state policies support learning outside the traditional school day.* Denver, CO: Author. Retrieved from http://www.ncsl.org/documents/educ/ExpandedLearning.pdf

National League of Cities. (2011). *Municipal leadership for afterschool: Citywide approaches spreading across the country.* Washington, DC: Author. Retrieved from http://www.nlc.org/sites/default/files/2016-12/municipal-leadership-afterschool-rpt-sept-2011.pdf

Opportunity Nation. (2014). *Connecting youth and strengthening communities: The data behind civic engagement and economic opportunity*. Boston, MA: Author. Retrieved from https://opportunitynation.org/wp-content/uploads/2014/09/Opportunity-Nation-Civic-Engagement-Report-2014.pdf

PBS NewsHour. (2015). *Wisdom from four decades of education reporting*. Retrieved from http://www.pbs.org/newshour/bb/wisdom-four-decades-education-reporting/

Peterson, E. (2015). Senate passes ESEA, 21st CCLC: sends to President for signature. Washington, DC: Afterschool Alliance. Retrieved from http://www.afterschoolalliance.org/afterschoolSnack/Senate-passes-ESEA-21stCCLC-sends-to-President-for_12-08-2015.cfm

Peterson, T. K. (2013). *Expanding minds and opportunities: Leveraging the power of afterschool and summer learning for student success*. Washington, DC: Collaborative Communications Group, Inc.

Pew Research Center. (2015). *Parenting in America: Outlook, worries, aspirations are strongly linked to financial situation*. Washington, DC: Author. Retrieved from http://www.pewsocialtrends.org/files/2015/12/2015-12-17_parenting-in-america_FINAL.pdf

Phillips, S. F. (2010). Honoring 15 years of the 21st Century Community Learning Centers program: A polity-centered analysis. *Afterschool Matters*. Retrieved from https://www.niost.org/2010-Fall/honoring-15-years-of-the-21st-century-community-learning-centers-program-a-polity-centered-analysis

Pierce, K. M., Auger, A., & Vandell, D. L. (2013). *Narrowing the achievement gap: Consistency and intensity of structured activities during elementary school*. Paper presented at the Society for Research in Child Development Biennial Meeting, Seattle, WA.

Putnam, R. (2015). *Our kids: The American dream in crisis*. New York, NY: Simon & Schuster.

Reeves, R. V. (2015). Four charts that show the opportunity gap isn't going away. *The Wall Street Journal*. Retrieved from http://blogs.wsj.com/washwire/2015/07/21/four-charts-that-show-the-opportunity-gap-isnt-going-away/

Rivera, C. (2002). Schwarzenegger's star power drives Prop. 49. *Los Angeles Times*. Retrieved from http://articles.latimes.com/2002/oct/22/local/me-prop4922

Sawhill, I. V. (2013). *Higher education and the opportunity gap*. Washington, DC: Brookings. Retrieved from https://www.brookings.edu/research/higher-education-and-the-opportunity-gap/

Simonton, S. (2015). Why should cities invest in after-school programs? Five mayors explain. *Youth Today*. Retrieved from https://youthtoday.org/2015/03/why-should-cities-invest-in- after-school-programs-five-mayors-explain/

U.S. Census Bureau. (2012). *Current Population Survey. Table 2: Single grade of enrollment and high school graduation status for people 3 years old and over, by sex, age (single years for 3 to 24 years), race, and Hispanic origin: October 2012. School enrollment in the United States: October 2012—Detailed Tables*. Retrieved from https://www.census.gov/data/tables/2012/demo/school-enrollment/2012-cps.html

U.S. Department of Agriculture (USDA). (2015). *Rural poverty & well-being*. Washington, DC: Author. Retrieved from http://www.ers.usda.gov/topics/rural-economy-population/rural-poverty-well-being/child-poverty.aspx

U.S. Department of Education. (2015a). *21st Century Community Learning Centers (21st CCLC) analytic support for evaluation and program monitoring: An overview of the 21st CCLC performance data: 2013–14* (10th report). Washington, DC: Author.

U.S. Department of Education. (2015b). *Title IX and Sex Discrimination*. Office for Civil Rights. Washington, DC: Author. Retrieved from http://www2.ed.gov/about/offices/list/ocr/docs/tix_dis.html

U.S. Department of Education. (n.d.). *Every Student Succeeds Act, ESSA*. Washington, DC: Author. Retrieved from http://www.ed.gov/essa?src=rn

Vandell, D. L., Reisner, E. R., & Pierce, K. M. (2007). *Outcomes linked to high-quality afterschool programs: Longitudinal findings from the study of promising afterschool programs*. Report to the Charles Stewart Mott Foundation.

White House Council of Economic Advisors. (2015). *Economic costs of youth disadvantage and high-return opportunities for change.* Retrieved from https://obamawhitehouse.archives.gov/sites/default/files/docs/mbk_report_final_update1.pdf

CHAPTER 16

# CLOSING THE SUMMER GAP

Sarah Pitcock

## INEQUITY IN THE SUMMER MONTHS

More than 100 years of research confirms that summer learning loss is real (White, 1906). More recent research confirms that it is cumulative and harmful (Alexander, Entwisle, & Olson, 2007) but also preventable (McCombs et al., 2012). The past decade has seen a proliferation of local, state, federal, and national efforts designed to stem the summer slide and increase access to a variety of summer programs promoting success in school, career, and life. This chapter brings together compelling data on the risks and challenges associated with the summer months with updates on how states and localities are addressing those challenges. The chapter begins with a discussion of the academic, health, and employment risks related to inequitable access to high-quality summer learning opportunities. Then I offer macro trends in summer learning, including a "new vision" for summer school in school districts and increased flexibility in when and where learning takes place in the summer, including at home, in libraries, online, and in the workplace. Next, this chapter highlights recent and forthcoming policy action that affects access to summer learning, including new state programs and opportunities for summer learning found in the Every Student Succeeds Act. Finally, I close

*The Growing Out-of-School Time Field: Past, Present, and Future,*
pages 229–242.
Copyright © 2018 by Information Age Publishing
**229**

with recommendations for researchers, policymakers, and practitioners to continue to expand access to high-quality summer learning opportunities.

Foundational research from Alexander, Entwisle, and Olson (2007) describes the relationship between summer learning loss and the achievement gap. Differences in spring and fall standardized test scores of rising first through fifth graders in Baltimore City Public Schools are used to estimate summer learning loss in reading and math. Whereas all young people, regardless of income level, lose skills in math over the summer without practice, reading growth varies by income level, with higher-income students continuing to gain skills in the summer and lower-income students losing skills when they are out of school, up to two or three months' worth on average. Losses can be attributed to a variety of factors, including fewer books in the home and lower educational attainment of parents and caregivers. Those losses accumulate and make a substantial contribution to the ninth-grade reading achievement gap. Studies show that the amount of summer learning loss may vary by age, with student skill levels more likely to grow or remain flat between kindergarten and first grade and more likely to decline between first and second grade (Augustine et al., 2016). More research is needed to understand whether and how the effects of summer learning loss change over the course of a young person's school career as well as the long-term benefits of participation in programs.

While research connecting summer experiences to the achievement gap has been critical for advocates to expand access to high-quality summer learning opportunities, it tells a narrow story of reading and math gains and losses during the summer months and often focuses on the elementary school years alone. The "faucet theory" (Entwisle, Alexander & Olson, 1997) captures a more expansive look at the inequities of the summer months, contrasting the more equitable flow of resources during the school year to all young people because of access to public schools with the sudden "shutting off" of the faucet of resources in the summer for low-income youth. Lower-income students not only lose access to instruction over the summer, but they may also lose access to books, meals, technology, structured enrichment, and a variety of other resources critical to their academic and social-emotional success.

The closing of school doors has a particularly acute impact on low-income families because of the widening gap in expenditures on extracurricular activities. Recent analysis of Consumer Expenditure Survey data (Putnam, 2015) and several national longitudinal youth survey data sets (Snellman, Silva, Frederick, & Putnam, 2015) from the 1970s to early 2000s reveal that class-based inequality in social and civic engagement has nearly quadrupled in three decades, driven by lower levels of public funding and increasing expenditures on activities and experiences like tutoring, camps, sports, and private schooling by higher income families.

As such, the cost of summer programs is likely a limiting factor in participation among low-income youth. The national average reported cost for summer programs of $288 per week is nearly 30% of household income for a family of four whose children qualify for reduced-price meals and nearly 40% of household income for a family of four whose children qualify for free meals under federal programs (Pitcock, 2016). State-to-state variance is substantial, with average per-week costs ranging from $115 (Idaho) to $639 per week (Nevada). Variations may be due to program intensity and length, local staffing and facilities costs, transportation, and other factors (Afterschool Alliance, 2015).

For older youth and youth of color, the summer months also present an unequal playing field when it comes to employment opportunities. There has been a nearly 40% decline in youth employment over the last 12 years and a gap of 3.6 million teen summer jobs (JP Morgan Chase & Co., 2015). This decline has affected low-income and minority youth the most. In 2013, White male teens in high-income families were five times more likely to be employed than Black male teens in low-income families (JP Morgan Chase & Co., 2015).

The effects of inequities in the summer months go beyond reading and math skills and employment trajectories. Additional research has confirmed the health risks inherent to the summer months. Nationally, there is a nearly 85% decline in the number of eligible students who receive federally subsidized meals in the summer as compared to the school year. After three years of significant growth, national participation in the Summer Nutrition Programs plateaued in summer 2015, serving just 0.3% more students (11,000) in July 2015 than in July 2014 (Hayes, Rosso, Anderson, & FitzSimons, 2016). Five states served at least 25% of their school-year totals in the summer of 2015: District of Columbia, New Mexico, New York, Connecticut, and Vermont. The same five states (exclusively) met this benchmark in 2014 as well.

A number of administrative barriers suppress the supply of summer nutrition programs, including eligibility thresholds that differ from federal education programs and disadvantage rural areas because of their low population densities. Additionally, schools and CBOs must apply separately for eligibility for afterschool and summer meals programs, with a high administrative burden creating a disincentive to apply again for the summer.

On the demand side, providers and families report that transportation, particularly in rural areas, is a significant barrier to participation. It is also likely that lack of awareness and perceived stigma associated with participation limits uptake in the summer. Particularly for older youth, the schedule and location of meal sites, as well as laws requiring meals to be consumed on site, can be barriers to participation. Advocates are working to eliminate these barriers in federal child nutrition legislation.

Likely related to the drop-in access to nutritious food during the summer, some young people gain weight twice as fast during the summer as the school year. Recent analysis of the Early Childhood Longitudinal Study, Kindergarten Class of 2010–2011 (von Hippel & Workman, 2016) shows a stark difference between school year and summer weight gain. The study analyzed measures of children's height and weight two times per year in kindergarten through second grade. Key findings include that among study children, the prevalence of obesity increased from 8.9% to 11.5%, and the prevalence of overweight children increased from 23.3% to 28.7% between the start of kindergarten and the end of second grade, with all of the increase occurring during summer vacations. During the school years, overweight prevalence did not change, and obesity prevalence slightly declined. Researchers suggest that because weight gain increases during the summer, it appears that major risk factors lie outside of schools.

## MACRO TRENDS IN SUMMER LEARNING

With the base of strong and compelling research related to summer risks and setbacks growing over the past decade, so has awareness of the inequities of the summer months and the solutions available to schools, communities, and families. The Hatcher Group tracked a substantial increase in the number of media stories mentioning the terms summer learning, summer slide, or summer learning loss from roughly 1,000 stories in 2007 to 30,000 in 2015. Notably, the term "summer slide" appeared considerably more often in reporting on the issue in 2015 (more than 9,000 stories), nearly catching up to the prevalence of the terms "summer learning" and "summer learning loss." This increase in awareness has led to an increased focus on summer learning, health, and employment in local, state, federal, and national efforts led by policymakers, practitioners, and advocates.

### Beyond Summer School

Since 2009, the National Summer Learning Association (NSLA) has convened a national network of school districts called the New Vision for Summer School Network (NVSS). NVSS districts share a common commitment to a set of five principles:

1. Increase and enhance the scope of traditional summer school
2. Target participation by students who would benefit the most
3. Strengthen systems-level supports through community-wide partnerships and coordination
4. Provide innovative professional development for staff
5. Embed summer learning into the district's school-year operations

Initially spurred by American Recovery and Reinvestment Act funding and sustained at lower service levels by Title I, district general funds, and private funding, many NVSS member districts have adopted several common components of summer programming. The NVSS model goes beyond traditional summer school to offer full-day programming that includes high-quality enrichment, typically through partnerships with local community-based organizations. Programs are jointly staffed and planned by certified teachers and youth workers and typically run five to six weeks. Students who are mandated to summer school may be integrated into a common program with students whose participation is voluntary. Centralized supports create opportunities for common measurement frameworks and professional development across sites. NVSS districts in Boston, Pittsburgh, Dallas, and Rochester have been awarded the New York Life Excellence in Summer Learning Award for innovative and effective programming.

Boston Public Schools and Boston Afterschool and Beyond have created a year-round learning community for schools and their more than 70 community-based partners through the Boston Summer Learning Project (SLP). The SLP places a strong emphasis on continuous quality improvement, using a common measurement framework for both student outcomes and program quality. The SLP is also noteworthy for its strong support from both school and city leadership, with Mayor Marty Walsh leading a citywide challenge to serve 10,000 youth in summer 2017, a goal the city met a year early in 2016.

The Pittsburgh Public School's Summer Dreamers Academy is known for fostering a summer camp culture in its school-based programs. The culture is defined by morning greetings at the bus ramp, common program chants, morning spirit rallies, strong program branding, and celebration of youth-produced work. Summer Dreamers Academy also offers highly specialized enrichment offerings that young people likely would otherwise not have access to, such as kayaking and cycling.

The Dallas Independent School District and Big Thought have partnered to connect schools with more than 200 community-based organizations for a rich array of summer programming. Robust data-sharing agreements enable all providers to understand and track improvements in academic and nonacademic indicators. Dallas is also noteworthy for its use of Title II funding to offer training for summer school teachers and a unique learning lab model that pairs mentor and mentee teachers for a summer of joint professional development and teaching.

Bucking the trend of summer program siloes in districts, Rochester City School District has taken a project management approach to summer learning, combining more than 20 programs under one unified structure to enable cost sharing for facilities, transportation, and food and centralized staff supports for curriculum, evaluation, and professional development across many programs.

### Anytime, Anywhere Learning

In unpublished data from the New Vision for Summer School Network, districts report operating an average of 15 programs in the summer and typically serve no more than 10% of their students in school-based programs. Even cities with the most robust summer systems (such as Boston) do not reach more than 25% to 33% of students with programs. These city-level data collected by NSLA align with national data collected by the Afterschool Alliance in its *America After 3PM* (AA3PM) national survey, conducted every five years to document participation in and perceptions of afterschool and summer programs among a representative sample of households. AA3PM data in 2013 showed that nationally, one-third of households reported having at least one child enrolled in a summer program, with higher than average participation among minority students.

Given the increased awareness of summer learning loss and the fact that the majority (two-thirds) of young people are not in an enrollment-based program in the summer, we are seeing an increase in "anytime, anywhere" programs that take advantage of books, technology, and easy-to-access community settings such as homes, libraries, and public housing authorities to infuse learning into the summer months.

One common model is to focus on distributing books for young people to read at home during the summer. More than a decade of rigorous studies of summer reading programs in grades K–5, including formal, informal, and at-home models, have shown that these programs can prevent and reverse summer learning loss and promote multiyear advantages in reading for participants. Kim and White (2008) establish key components of this approach: matching low-income students in elementary grades with books based on their interest and ability, and including teacher-led oral reading scaffolding and checks for comprehension by an adult. Several studies confirm that access to books alone during the summer does not improve reading comprehension and that this model may not be effective for English language learners (Allington & McGill-Franzen, 2013).

Organizations like Reading is Fundamental (RIF) and myON have used this research to create summer reading programs for districts. RIF focuses its Read for Success model in rural schools, providing classroom and take-home book collections, research-based training, and activities for students and teachers. As a digital literacy platform, myON takes the approach online, using Lexile assessments and interest-based surveys to connect young people with thousands of digital books matched to their abilities and interests. Schools can monitor how much their students are reading over the summer and track their progress. Education agencies in Indiana and Arizona have adopted myON statewide in the past to offer summer learning at scale.

In a similar approach to scaling access through technology, many cities have joined Cities of LRNG, which helps them build summer learning "playlists" for young people across sectors and settings throughout their city. The "connected learning" approach of LRNG is designed to promote interest-based and often self-paced learning that bridges online resources with experiences in local institutions such as schools, museums, libraries, and businesses. Participating students can earn digital badges that credential their learning. In addition to city-specific playlists, LRNG offers a number of national playlists developed by their partners that can be accessed and completed anywhere there is connectivity.

Libraries nationally are enhancing their traditional incentive-based summer reading programs by offering skill-building opportunities and even enrollment in more formal learning experiences. The Urban Libraries Council (ULC) and NSLA conducted research as part of the Accelerate Summer initiative to create a better understanding of the summer learning strategies used by libraries, as well as the challenges they face in implementing those strategies. The study included a survey completed by 90 libraries, site visits to eight library systems, and interviews with additional libraries during the summer of 2015. In an online toolkit, NSLA and ULC (2016) summarize the findings of common library summer learning strategies into three categories:

- Summer Reading PLUS adds hands-on and inquiry-based learning activities to traditional summer reading programs.
- Skill-based, drop-in learning activities include flexible, active learning designed for participants to gain academic or 21st-century skills such as experimentation and problem solving, collaboration and teamwork, and so on, while accommodating families' needs for flexible summer opportunities that don't require enrollment in a 5- or 6-week camp.
- Focused enrollment programs are offered on a week-by-week basis, address specific learning outcomes, and are targeted to youth and families who do not have access to other summer learning and educational opportunities.

The Chicago Public Libraries Rahm's Readers Summer Learning Challenge is an example of a program that has incorporated skill-based, drop-in learning activities. Through partnerships with the Museum of Science and Industry and Boeing, the library summer reading program has been infused with STEM activities and experiences that can be completed at home or in libraries with the support of trained facilitators and experts.

### Summer Jobs

It is important to note a growing focus on summer jobs nationally. A steep decline in federal funding for youth employment programs combined with a growing gap in skilled workers has precipitated an increased focus on summer jobs programs by city and business leaders. Since the elimination of the federal funding stream for summer youth employment in 2008, summer jobs programs have become the domain of mayors and cities. Mayors in Boston, Washington, DC, and Baltimore expanded their programs in 2015, reflecting an overall trend toward growth in recent years seen in Chicago, Seattle, New York City, Los Angeles, and Detroit as well. Washington, DC serves the most young people per capita in summer jobs and is entirely publicly funded at just over $19 million (Office of the District of Columbia Auditor, 2016). Other cities have tapped into private investment, with Detroit reportedly raising $7 million in private investment in 2015. Philanthropic divisions at JP Morgan Chase, Citi, Wells Fargo, and Bank of America have all made recent investments in summer youth employment efforts either through local or national grant making.

The Obama Administration made significant investments in summer jobs programs in 2016 through the Summer Opportunity Project, providing funding and technical assistance in 16 high-need cities as well as brokering partnerships with national partners like LinkedIn. President Obama's 2016 budget called for an additional $2 billion for summer jobs programs, and Rep. Bobby Scott (D-VA) introduced the Opening Doors for Youth Act in 2016, authorizing $1.5 billion in formula grants for subsidized summer jobs for youth in- and out-of-school ages 14–24 and $2 billion in formula grants for partially subsidized year-round jobs for youth ages 16–24 who have been out of school and work for more than four months.

## POLICY TRENDS

While there are important federal bills in play addressing summer meals and summer jobs, there is currently tremendous opportunity and action for summer learning at the state level, both as part of the implementation of the Every Student Succeeds Act (ESSA) and in unique state programs and initiatives. As such, this section focuses primarily on state policy advancements.

### State-Level Action

States have taken a more active role in expanding access to high-quality summer learning opportunities in recent years. In 2016, governors in seven states (AL, FL, IA, NC, NJ, NM, and RI) included summer learning in their priorities. State legislatures also introduced more than 230 bills relating to summer learning. NSLA (2016b) summarizes recent themes from state bills related to summer learning as follows:

- Integrating summer learning in related education efforts such as after-school, community schools, community investment initiatives, and expanded learning time
- Supporting summer learning in public libraries
- Expanding programs that focus on specific demographic groups, such as middle school, high school, girls, low-income students, and gifted students
- Engaging students in career exploration and skill development
- Improving staffing and safety standards for summer programs
- Promoting summer as a time for students to explore designated disciplines such as STEM, STEAM, digital learning, arts, and recreational activities
- Establishing and expanding commissions and councils to study, develop, and implement strategic plans for learning outside of the traditional school day
- Proclamations and resolutions recognizing National Summer Learning Day and other out-of-school time educational activities

As noted in the 2015 themes, many state legislatures begin a more intentional focus on summer or expanded learning opportunities by establishing a special legislative task force or commission to study the issue. Early adopters of this strategy included legislatures in California, Washington, and Texas, where task force recommendations have led to additional research, new programs and quality improvement efforts. In 2015 and 2016, additional state legislatures including Indiana, Oregon, Vermont, Hawaii, and Louisiana introduced advisory boards, commissions, and task forces to study summer issues like learning and hunger and to develop recommendations for moving these issues forward.

Other states are making new investments in OST grant programs. Massachusetts legislators are exploring expansion of the successful Boston Summer Learning Project model into other parts of the state. The proposed grant program would require programs to:

- include at least 150 hours of programming with a focus on academic and college and career readiness skills, including critical thinking, collaboration, and perseverance
- implement a research-based summer program model
- engage a variety of organizations and leverage a cost-sharing partnership with local districts, private funders, and nonprofit institutions

The Nebraska legislature is considering a new statewide expanded learning grant program that would build on and expand successful federally funded 21st Century Community Learning Center programs by providing additional funds to school–community partnerships in high-needs districts, defined as having 40% or more students who quality for free and reduced-price meals.

States are also taking a strong focus on literacy in the summer. In an effort to improve third-grade reading proficiency in the state, by May 2018 every Iowa school district must offer a summer reading program for students who are not proficient in reading at the end of third grade. The requirement is part of an early literacy law that also requires schools to identify and intervene with students in kindergarten through third grade who are struggling to read. The Iowa Reading Research Center conducted a study to test which among three different curriculum approaches was related to strongest gains in reading during the summer. Participating schools were randomly assigned to either a designated computer-based, designated print-based, or "business as usual" (in which they determined their own) curriculum. On average, all strategies were equally effective at preventing summer learning loss, but none produced statistically significant reading gains. Other findings from the study include that schools struggled to find enough qualified teachers and to get kids to show up and attend regularly throughout the entire program (Reed, Schmitz, Aloe, & Folsom, 2016).

The New Mexico legislature passed a bill in 2016 to pilot a successful K–3 statewide summer math and literacy program in the fourth and fifth grades. The New Mexico K–5 Plus programs adds at least 25 instructional days to the school year for students in schools with at least 80% eligibility for free or reduced-price meals or with a D or F grade in the state accountability system the previous year. A 2013 cost-benefit analysis of the K–3 program found the benefits from reduced grade retention and remediation services offset all program costs (Goetze & Hughes, 2013).

## The Every Student Succeeds Act and Summer Learning

Implementation of the Every Student Succeeds Act (ESSA) offers many additional opportunities for states to increase access to high-quality summer learning programs, whether the law explicitly mentions "summer" as an allowable use of funds or uses more general terms such as "out-of-school time," "periods when school is not in session," or "nonschool hours."

In an ESSA guide for stakeholders NSLA (2016a) recommends states include summer in their ESSA implementation plans through a focus on four broad themes:

- Promoting flexibility of funding and allowing program delivery during the summer months
- Fostering collaboration and coordination among partners, programs, and schools to ensure maximum impact of out-of-school time efforts and seamless year-round integration of services
- Engaging a wide range of stakeholders who support students with education services during the summer months, including schools, teachers, libraries, community-based and faith-based program providers, public housing partners, and others
- Acknowledging professional development opportunities in summer programs for preservice and inservice teachers.

NSLA's recommendations for specific parts of the law include, in part:

### Title I

- Clarify summer as an allowable use of direct student services for named activities such as credit recovery, career and technical education, and advanced coursework that are primed for summer implementation.
- Engage community partners in their process of selecting the fifth "nonacademic" indicator in state accountability systems.

### Title II

- Encourage schools to combine Title I with Title II funding to offer summer school programs that build skills for both teachers and students.
- Go beyond traditional summer school models when considering what summer support looks like as part of Title II, Part B, Subpart 2: Literacy Education for All, Results for the Nation (LEARN). This may include summer reading programs in public libraries, particularly when school libraries are closed during the summer.

### Title III

- Leverage two critical funding streams into one program by integrating English language learner summer schooling with other mandated summer school activities.

### Title IV

- Clarify that summer is an allowable time to use Title IV Part A, student support and academic enrichment grants and encourage true collaboration between in-school and out-of-school educators to prevent duplication of effort or underserving certain populations.
- Require or prioritize that applicants include summer learning in their 21st Century Community Learning Center subgrant proposals and be clear about how schools and community-based organizations should be sharing data about the students they serve.

## FUTURE DIRECTIONS FOR SUMMER LEARNING

### Recommendations for Researchers

It is clear from an abundance of research across academic, health, and workforce disciplines that summer is a time of risk and setback for low-income students and students of color who are not engaged in a meaningful program or learning opportunity. Still, there is more to understand about those risks and possible interventions to help strengthen practice and policy. To date, rigorous research on the impact of summer learning programs has not looked at more than two years of participation in a program and has not tracked outcomes beyond two years postparticipation. We don't know very much about *how much* summer learning, *of what kind*, and *for whom* is most effective. Future research should extend what we know generally to examine what works for different subgroups, like English language learners, students in rural schools, and students with disabilities. Research should also examine the impact of year-round participation in expanded learning programs; states are looking at expanded learning as a year-round endeavor, and research should follow suit. NSLA's Research Advisory Council is developing a research agenda for the field that includes many more detailed recommendations and should be an important resource for the field.

### Recommendations for Policymakers and Practitioners

There are currently disconnects among summer learning research, policy, and practice that states like Iowa are taking meaningful steps to eliminate through previously mentioned connected research-to-policy efforts. Still, there is much work to be done at the federal, state, and local levels to expand access to a variety of proven and promising summer learning opportunities. While additional research is needed, policymakers and practitioners could do more with the available rigorous research and data on summer learning, health, and employment.

### *Know Where You Stand*

Providers and policymakers can do more to understand current levels of supply and demand for summer learning in their communities and their states. Major questions around where young people are in the summer, what kinds of programs are being offered and by what entities, how much programs cost, how much families can afford to pay, and how programs are funded go largely unanswered in any systematic way at the state and local levels.

- Use summer supply and demand data to make sure there is coverage across schools, neighborhoods, and rural areas and that programs in all settings are of high quality.
- Conduct family and community surveys to shed light on fee structures that are viable and equitable for working families.

### *Meet Basic Needs*

In many communities, struggles to fund school-year programming create a perception that summer services are a "nice to have" when times are good. But national and state-level data tell us that young people are hungry during the summer, and few, if any, public officials will stand by and do nothing when faced with these facts. If resources are tight, begin with basic needs of health and wellness in the summer months.

- Bring together community feeding resources and get creative about food delivery systems, such as take-home backpacks or mobile vans or food trucks.
- Engage medical system and health care companies in two- and three-generation approaches to summer wellness.

### *Invest in What Works*

Currently, state summer school policies generally include little to no research-based components around things like staffing, dosage and intensity, and class sizes (Borman, Schmidt & Hosp, 2016). It is likely that we could see far greater impact from these investments and many others if attention was paid to what research has demonstrated to be effective.

- Ensure state summer school policies reflect research-based best practices, such as hiring well-qualified teachers, building in enough instructional time, and making sure attendance is consistent (Augustine et al., 2016).

### Make Summer Count

Low-income youth need opportunities to advance academically and earn a wage to support their families or themselves. Whether through credit recovery, advanced coursework, or dual enrollment, summer is an important time to catch up and get ahead academically. It is also an important time to gain paid work experience that will support future employability.

### Start Braiding

Breaking through barriers of scale will require innovation in how we fund summer programs. Many state policies and bills, including many new state child care plans, require programs to secure funding across several public and private sources, a move directly tied to their sustainability. With little dedicated public funding and the temporary nature of private funding, summer programs will only be sustainable and reliable for families through true cross-sector collaboration and funding, or braiding of resources.

- Require other public and private matching funds for publicly funded summer learning programs.

### REFERENCES

Afterschool Alliance. (2015). *America after 3pm*. Washington, DC: Author. Retrieved from http://afterschoolalliance.org/AA3PM/

Alexander, K. L., Entwisle, D. R., & Olson, L. S. (2007). Lasting consequences of the summer learning gap. *American Sociological Review, 72*(2), 167–180.

Allington, R. L., & McGill-Franzen, A. (2013). Summer reading loss. In R. Allington & A. McGill-Franzen (Eds.), *Summer reading: Closing the rich/poor achievement gap* (pp. 1–19). New York, NY: Teachers College Press.

Augustine, C. H., McCombs, J. S., Pane, J. F., Schwartz, H. L., Schweig, J., McEachin, A. & Siler-Evans, K. (2016). *Learning from summer: Online technical appendices*. Santa Monica, CA: RAND. Retrieved from http://www.rand.org/content/dam/rand/pubs/research_reports/RR1500/RR1557/RAND_RR1557.appendixes.pdf

Borman, G., Schmidt, A., & Hosp, M. (2016). A national review of summer school policies and the evidence supporting them. In K. Alexander, S. Pitcock, & M. Boulay (Eds.) *The summer slide: What we know and can do about summer learning loss* (pp. 90–107). New York, NY: Teachers College Press.

Entwisle, D. R., Alexander, K. L., & Olson, L. S. (1997). *Children, schools and inequality*. Boulder, CO: Westview Press.

Goetze, L. D., & Hughes, S. (2013, March). *Innovations in education: financing a voluntary extended school year program*. Paper presented at the American Educational Finance Association Meeting, New Orleans, LA.

Hayes, C., Rosso, R., Anderson, S., & FitzSimons, C. (2016). Hunger doesn't take a vacation. Washington, DC: Food Research & Action Center. Retrieved from http://frac.org/pdf/2016_summer_nutrition_report.pdf

JP Morgan Chase & Co. (2015). *Building skills through summer jobs: Lessons from the field*. New York, NY: Author.

Kim, J. S., & White, T. G. (2008). Scaffolding voluntary summer reading for children in grades 3 to 5: An experimental study. *Scientific Studies of Reading, 12*(1), 1–23.

McCombs, J. S., Augustine, C., Schwartz, H., Bodilly, S., McInnis, B., Lichter, D., & Cross, A. B. (2012). Making summer count: How summer programs can boost children's learning. *Education Digest: Essential Readings Condensed for Quick Review, 77*(6), 47–52.

National Summer Learning Association and Urban Libraries Council. (2016). Libraries at the center of summer learning and fun: An online toolkit to expand from summer reading to summer learning. Baltimore, MD: Author. Retrieved from http://www.summerlearning.org/wp-content/uploads/2016/09/ULC_NSLA_SummerLearningOnlineToolkit.pdf

National Summer Learning Association (2016a). *Inclusion of summer opportunities within state plans for the Every Student Succeeds Act: A guide for stakeholders.* Baltimore, MD: Author. Retrieved from http://www.summerlearning.org/wp-content/uploads/2016/10/NSLA-ESSA-guide-for-state-level-stakeholders.pdf

National Summer Learning Association (2016b). *State of summer learning, 2015 State policy snapshot.* Baltimore, MD: Author. Retrieved from http://summerlearning.org/wp-content/uploads/2016/06/NSLA_2015_State_Policy_Snapshot.pdf

Office of the District of Columbia Auditor. (2016). *Review of summer youth employment programs in eight major cities and the District of Columbia.* Washington, DC: Author. Retrieved from http://www.dcauditor.org/sites/default/files/DCA142016.pdf

Pitcock, S. (2016). Summer learning and the opportunity gap. In K. Alexander, S. Pitcock, & M. Boulay (Eds.), *The summer slide: What we know and can do about summer learning loss* (pp. 70–79). New York, NY: Teachers College Press.

Putnam, R. D. (2015). *Our kids: The American dream in crisis.* New York, NY: Simon and Schuster.

Reed, D. K., Schmitz, S., Aloe, A. M., & Folsom, J. S. (2016). *Report of the 2016 intensive summer reading program (ISRP) study.* Iowa City, IA: Iowa Reading Research Center, University of Iowa.

Snellman, K., Silva, J. M., Frederick, C. B., & Putnam, R. D. (2015). The engagement gap: Social mobility and extracurricular participation among American youth. *The ANNALS of the American Academy of Political and Social Science, 657*(1), 194–207.

von Hippel, P. T., & Workman, J. (2016). From kindergarten through second grade, U.S. children's obesity prevalence grows only during summer vacations. *Obesity, 24,* 2296–2300. doi:10.1002/oby.21613

White, W. (1906). Reviews before and after vacation. *American Education,* 185–188.

# SECTION VI

## FUTURE DIRECTIONS FOR THE OST FIELD

CHAPTER 17

# OUT-OF-SCHOOL TIME LEARNING AND 21ST-CENTURY SKILLS

## Building on the Past to Shape the Future

### Elizabeth Devaney and Deborah Moroney

We are at a pivotal moment in the history of the out-of-school time (OST) field. Multiple sectors, previously siloed, have begun to collaborate under the common notion that 21st-century skills and social and emotional competencies are critical to success in school, in work, and in life. For OST, we have an unprecedented opportunity to lead—to be experts, build on our best practice, collaborate and provide systemic support, and have a voice in this movement. Social and emotional skill building is something the OST field has historically done well and has an ideal setting to provide. Together, with the fields of education, workforce development, and mental health, we can provide the platform for youth to create their positive futures. Without a doubt, this coming together will be messy. We have to sort through language, rectify differing strategies and practice approaches, and determine how best to leverage and build upon past work rather than creating a new task. But if we can sort through those challenges, the opportunity to create systemic supports for social and emotional development is huge. This chap-

*The Growing Out-of-School Time Field: Past, Present, and Future,*
pages 245–265.
Copyright © 2018 by Information Age Publishing

**245**

ter proposes a way to think about that process—it offers a proposal for how to sort through the not-so-complicated-but-seemingly-so tango that OST has danced with skill building over the years. We begin with some history, including a definition of 21st-century skills and how they have historically been supported in OST programs. We then talk about current policy and practice movements that have influenced the discussion of 21st-century skill development. Finally, we end with some new directions for the field and a charge for how OST can take a leadership role in this work in the years to come. Our aim is to elevate the rich history of the OST field and highlight the ideal opportunity we have to support 21st-century skill building in partnership with our allies in other sectors.

## WHAT ARE 21ST-CENTURY SKILLS AND WHY DO THEY MATTER?

The term 21st-century skills has been used for at least 15 years to define a set of skills that all children and youth need to be successful. The movement began as a way to rally schools, businesses, communities, and the government to focus on what young people need to succeed in an increasingly digital and global economy and to be equipped for the jobs of tomorrow. Several frameworks (i.e., the National Education Association's 4 C's, 2010; National Research Council, 2012; Partnership for 21st Century Learning's Framework, 2007) define and elaborate on these skills. For the sake of ease and clarity, and recognizing that most frameworks are consistent about which skills fall under the moniker 21st-century skills, we define 21$^{st}$-century skills as the following (see Wan & Gut, 2011):

### Knowledge
- Information literacy
- Technical/digital literacy
- Environmental literacy
- Financial literacy

### Internal Processes
- Flexibility and adaptability
- Initiative and self-direction

### Learning Processes
- Critical thinking and problem-solving
- Learning to learn/metacognition
- Creativity and innovation

### Interacting With Others
- Communication
- Collaboration/teamwork
- Citizenship/global awareness/cross-cultural competence

• Decision making and leadership

### *Ways of Working*
• Personal and social responsibility
• Productivity and accountability

Over time, as globalization and technology have become realities rather than future trends, the conversation about 21st-century skills has shifted slightly to emphasize not only digital and cultural literacy but also social and emotional skills, as well as attributes that help young people to manage their emotions, build and maintain relationships, and interact with those around them in positive ways. This new emphasis emerged as a result of the growing recognition that in order to use 21st-century skills successfully, one must know him- or herself and be able to build relationships with others. The shift has led to some confusion as 21st-century skills frameworks have been placed side-by-side and sometimes combined with other frameworks that aim to define the skills and competencies that young people need to be successful. These frameworks, such as the Collaborative for Academic, Social, and Emotional Learning's (CASEL) five core social and emotional competencies (Weissberg, Durlak, Domitrovich, & Gullotta, 2015), the Wallace Foundation and Consortium on Chicago School Research's Foundations for Young Adult Success (Nagaoka, Farrington, Ehrlich, & Heath, 2015), and the Asia Society's Rosetta Stone for Noncognitive Skills (Roberts, Martin, & Olaru, 2015), to name a few, include some 21st-century skills (e.g., communication, decision making, problem solving, appreciating diversity); eliminate others (e.g., financial, environmental, and technical literacy); and, finally, add new skills that are not included in the 21st-century skill lexicon, such as impulse control, stress management, self-confidence, and the ability to identify and manage emotions. It is confusing, at best, for OST programs to sort through the terms and frameworks being used and decide where to focus attention, how to allocate resources, and when to measure success. In Table 17.1, we present an attempt to clarify some of this confusion by summarizing the key frameworks and highlighting points of overlap and difference.

The reality is, whatever you call them, research points to the fact that all of these skills and competencies are critical to lifelong success (Durlak, Weissberg, Dymnicki, Taylor, & Schellinger, 2011; Farrington et al., 2012; Hawkins, Kosterman, Catalano, Hill, & Abbott, 2008; Weissberg et al., 2015). More specifically, research has shown that youth who participate in high-quality OST programs with intentional opportunities for social and emotional learning (SEL) are better able to manage their emotions, build essential skills, and ultimately, do better in school (Durlak & Weissberg, 2007; Durlak, Weissberg, & Pachan, 2010; Kataoka & Vandell, 2013). In addition, improvement in skills and competencies in children and youth leads to more positive relationships between and among peers and adults and reduced behavioral problems and risky behaviors (Weissberg et al., 2015).

TABLE 17.1. Crosswalk of 21st Century and Social and Emotional Skills Frameworks

| Framework | Knowledge | Internal Processes | Learning Processes | Interacting with Others | Ways of Working | Contextual Factors |
|---|---|---|---|---|---|---|
| National Research Council | • Knowledge | • Positive core self-evaluation | • Cognitive processes and strategies<br>• Creativity<br>• Intellectual openness | • Teamwork<br>• Collaboration and leadership | • Work ethic and conscientiousness | • Standards and assessment<br>• Curriculum and instruction<br>• Professional development<br>• Learning environments |
| Partnership for 21st Century Skills | • Content knowledge, information/media literacy<br>• Financial literacy<br>• Environmental literacy | • Initiative and self-direction<br>• Flexibility and adaptability | • Critical thinking and problem solving<br>• Creativity and innovation | • Communication<br>• Collaboration<br>• Leadership and responsibility<br>• Social and cross-cultural skills<br>• Global awareness | • Productivity and accountability | |
| CASEL | | • Self-awareness (Identify emotions, accurate self-perception)<br>• Self-management (impulse control, self-discipline, stress management) | • Responsible decision making (solving problems, identify solutions) | • Relationship skills (teamwork, communication)<br>• Social awareness (perspective taking, appreciating diversity) | • Self-management (goal setting, motivation, organization skills) | • Classrooms<br>• Schools<br>• Home<br>• Communities |

| | | | | | |
|---|---|---|---|---|---|
| Wallace Foundation/ CCSR | • Knowledge and skills (set of facts, information, understanding about world) • Skills (academic, technical) | • Self-regulation (awareness of self, managing emotions) • Mind-sets (beliefs and attitudes about oneself and the world) | • Values (ideas or beliefs about good and bad) | • Knowledge (set of facts, information, understanding about oneself) • Skills (professional, institutional) | • Work • Health • Education • Family • Friends • Civic Engagement |
| Asia Society | • Emotional stability (Confidence, self-regulation, self-esteem) | • Openness (Creativity, curiosity, imagination, innovation) | • Agreeableness (collaboration, collegiality) • Extraversion (communication, leadership) | • Conscientiousness (dependability, planning, punctuality, etc.) | |

The importance of these skills extends beyond school. Studies have shown that adults with social and emotional competencies (often referred to as *emotional intelligence*) do better in the workforce (Brackett, Rivers, & Salovey, 2011). Furthermore, studies have found that employers value 21$^{st}$-century skills; they rank lack of problem solving, leadership, and managerial skills as the biggest deficiencies among current employees today and cite these deficiencies as a reason they cannot fill vacancies in their companies (American Management Association, 2012; Committee for Children & CASEL, 2016; Fischer, 2013; Morrison et al., 2011). Finally, researchers have found that 21$^{st}$-century skills and competencies matter for a variety of outcomes later in life. One study found a significant relationship between children's social and emotional skills in kindergarten, as assessed by teachers, and their outcomes 13–19 years later. Those with early prosocial skills were more likely to graduate from high school on time, complete a college degree, and get and keep full-time employment (Jones, Greenberg & Crowley, 2015). They were also less likely to receive public assistance, be involved with the police, abuse alcohol, and be on medication for emotional or behavioral issues through high school (Jones, Greenberg & Crowley, 2015). Taken together, the wealth of frameworks and research behind them point to the importance of supporting 21$^{st}$-century and social and emotional skill development.

## OUT-OF-SCHOOL TIME AND 21ST-CENTURY SKILLS: PAST

The OST field always has played a key role in contributing to the development of 21st-century skills in young people. Although schools historically have had the pressure and primary mission to improve academic achievement, OST programs have had more flexibility to focus on other kinds of skills. Although there is a growing recognition today that learning focused on both content knowledge and skills is essential and should be intertwined, that has not always been the case (Elias, Parker, Kash, Weissberg, & O'Brien, 2008).

### Positive Youth Development as the Foundation for High-Quality Out-of-School Time Programs

To begin with, it is important to understand the foundations of OST programming and its roots in a positive youth development framework. Although prior chapters in this volume (see Section I of this book) have ably covered youth development and its impact on key outcomes, it is worth touching here on how a youth development approach, as a foundation for OST programming, directly supports the development of 21$^{st}$-century skills.

The core features of the positive youth development approach are centered on creating positive environments in which youth can be active participants in their own growth and development. Thus, the primary job of OST staff, whether it be in summer camp, at a school-based before- or afterschool program, or in a community-based center, has been to provide opportunities to foster young people's positive development. This has been framed in a variety of ways over the past three decades: providing skills and knowledge to help young people make good choices and avoid "risk" (Catalano & Hawkins, 1996), helping youth build upon their assets (Benson, 2003) or character (Berkowitz & Bier, 2005), and using a holistic and strengths-based approach to positive youth development (Hamilton, Hamilton, & Pittman, 2004). Early research found that these strategies had an impact on positive outcomes. For example, providing age-appropriate and intentional activities to support skill building was found to be a factor in promoting skills and competencies such as self-efficacy, self-management, and positive relationships, and it reduced engagement in risky behavior (Fredricks & Eccles, 2006; Jagers, 2001; Morrisey & Werner-Wilson, 2005; Riggs, Jahromi, Razza, Dillworth, & Mueller, 2006). More recent research suggests that giving youth opportunities to lead, problem solve, and have autonomy in decision making may also be associated with positive youth outcomes and skill building, including increased self-awareness and respect for other cultures (Ettekal, Callina, & Lerner, 2015; Larson & Walker, 2010).

With the lens of positive youth development as a foundation, the OST field then turned to improving program quality as a catalyst for creating positive experiences, engagement, and ultimately improved youth outcomes (Durlak et al., 2011). These quality improvement efforts have been guided by positive youth development principles and focus on adult/youth interactions, creating positive and supportive environments, and building in opportunities for reflection and engagement. Research has shown that these intentional quality improvement and staff preparation efforts have, indeed, improved the quality of programming and that higher quality programming contributes to greater youth engagement (Devaney et al., 2016; Miller, 2005; Naftzger et al., 2013; Smith et al., 2012; Vandell, Simzar, O'Cadiz, & Hall, 2016). And youth engagement in quality programming matters for outcomes. Youth who report high levels of engagement in their OST programs have better 21st-century skills, such as prosocial skills, task persistence, and work habits (Kataoka & Vandell, 2013). Research has also found that creating a supportive environment and positive relationships between youth and staff has an influence on positive youth outcomes and skills including character, confidence, persistence, and teamwork (Hall, Yohalem, Toleman & Wilson, 2003; Lerner et al., 2005; Vandell, Larson, Mahoney, & Watts, 2015). Thus, research and practice efforts over the past several decades have found that intentionally applying a positive youth development approach to offer high-quality programming that engages youth contributes directly to improved 21st-century skills.

Although positive youth development is the foundation for high-quality OST programming that contributes in a broad way to improved 21st-century skills, OST programs have taken two key strategies or approaches that directly target those types of skills: project-based learning and college and career readiness.

*Strategies to Promote 21st-Century Skills*

### Project-Based Learning

According to the Buck Institute for Education (2016), project-based learning is an instructional approach wherein youth gain knowledge and skills by exploring a complex question or problem over time. Again, unlike formal education, OST programs have had the flexibility to "go deep" and can use project-based learning to focus on specific content, such as science, technology, engineering, and mathematics (STEM). Because the approach specifically provides young people an opportunity to engage in projects over a long period of time, think in complex ways about a topic, and persist when they encounter challenges, project-based learning is an excellent way to foster 21st-century skills. For example, in Providence, Rhode Island, middle school youth spend the summer engaged in STEM programs in which they study marine life on Narragansett Bay and build solar-powered go-carts. In Oakland, California, girls in the Techbridge program design prosthetic hands for the disabled, take apart machines and put them back together, design and mix new lip balm recipes, and build machines. In both cases, youth learn to work in teams, make important decisions, build their sense of confidence and competence, and learn time management, and they are required to think critically. In addition, through STEM content, youth may learn additional 21st-century skills such as digital and information literacy.

Project-based learning can be applied in non-STEM disciplines too, such as the arts. For example, youth can participate in scaffolded opportunities to plan, design, create, and install a piece of public art. The planning process requires teamwork, active listening, and creativity. The process to identify a space and secure a permit requires problem-solving, initiative, and patience (i.e., self-management). In general, the focus on identifying a problem or challenge and working through possible solutions over time builds key 21st-century skills regardless of content.

### College and Career Readiness

Another approach that OST programs take to promote 21st-century skills is a focus on college and career readiness. Although most common at the high school level, college and career readiness approaches can take place across the age spectrum. Service learning and apprenticeships are two specific examples of this type of programming that directly help young people to develop 21st-century skills. For example, the Afterschool Matters program in Chicago provides high school students with paid apprenticeships in which they are paired with industry professionals to learn specific skills (e.g., culinary arts) while at the same time building key 21st-century skills such as communication, time management, problem solving, social awareness, and initiative. Citizen Schools, founded in Boston, MA, has a similar model in which they pair middle school students with experts who teach them a specific skill during a 10-week intensive class with a culminating project. In addition to developing content skills, participants gain skills in communication, collaboration, data analysis, advanced literacy, global awareness, effective reasoning, problem solving, innovation, and technology (Edutopia, n.d.).

In a service learning approach, OST programs go beyond community service to engage young people in projects that combine meaningful service in their own communities with instruction and reflection outside the service experience. That instruction and reflection helps to bridge learning so young people not only build a sense of self-worth from engaging in service but also build an understanding of cultural competence and civic responsibility, all key 21st-century skills.

## Social and Emotional Learning as a Process to Promote 21st-Century Skills

In the previous section, we identified two approaches that OST programs historically have used to foster the development of 21st-century skills. Although not a comprehensive picture of all that OST programs do to promote 21st-century skills, these two examples point to what providers know intuitively, and increasingly through data collection and evaluation: that OST participants build key 21st-century skills in their programs. However, we have an opportunity to be clearer in our language and more intentional in our practice as to how that process happens. Collectively, the fields of OST, workforce, and K–12 education are in need of a common process and shared language that help to connect opportunities and supports for young people in an intentional way. SEL has emerged as that common framework linking schools with OST *and* OST with workforce efforts. In a way, SEL has become the thread between previously disparate efforts to support children in achieving their best possible future and as the foundation for skill building and academic success.

Social and emotional learning is the intentional process of building social and emotional competencies or skills (most of which are also 21st-century skills, as highlighted in Table 17.1). There are two strong connections between SEL and 21st-century skills. First, as noted, 21st-century skills include many social and emotional competencies (e.g., communication, collaboration). Therefore, SEL is a process that is already designed to support 21st-century skill building although the frameworks are slightly different. Second, the 21st-century skills that are not precisely the same as social and emotional competencies are still supported by social and emotional competencies. For example, creativity and innovation are 21st-century skills that generally are not included in social and emotional competency frameworks. However, for youth to be creative and innovative, they must have a sense of self-confidence, know their own abilities, and, if their innovation is designed to serve others, be able to understand others' perspectives. Thus, SEL may be a good process for supporting the development of 21st-century skills.

Conversely, some 21st-century skills, such as the ability to process and use information, or to have global and digital literacy, stand alone. They are neither social and emotional competencies, nor do they logically build on social and emotional competencies. Some may argue, then, that SEL is not a perfect process for building 21st-century skills. In reality, however, all young people are complicated puzzles of competencies, skills, and traits who learn, live, and play in a variety of settings using a variety of approaches. SEL happens both intentionally (through focused instruction and/or instructional practices) and as a part of natural personal development and in our daily lives. Until now, SEL in OST programs primarily has been of the latter variety. Increasingly, using a foundation of positive youth development to undergird their efforts, OST programs are employing more intentional SEL strategies to build 21st-century skills that are critical for youth success. We discuss this further in the next section.

## OUT-OF-SCHOOL TIME AND 21ST-CENTURY SKILLS: PRESENT

In the previous sections, we defined 21st-century skills and how they historically have been supported in OST through a foundation of positive youth development and strategies such as project-based learning and college and career readiness. Furthermore, we have noted that 21st-century skills today are recognized as critical for life success and that there is growing realization that SEL may be a process through which those skills get developed. Figure 17.1 highlights how the various components described in this chapter align to contribute to 21st-century skill development.

To support learning, OST programs must have two important preconditions. The first is high-quality youth development practice. The previous section and other sections in this book discuss how positive youth development fosters 21st-century skills. In addition to high-quality youth development practice, all OST programs must recognize the context in which youth participants live, learn, and play. A high-quality OST program functions in the context (family, school, com-

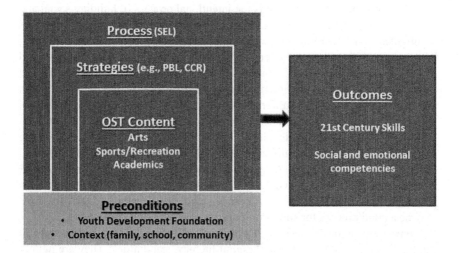

FIGURE 17.1.  A conceptual model for supporting 21st century skills in out-of-school time

munity) of the lives of its participants (Durlak et al., 2011). In fact, many of the newer skills frameworks explicitly note the contextual factors that are central to skill building, as highlighted in Table 17.1.

Once these preconditions are in place, OST programs must consider which of the many possible strategies or approaches they will use to promote learning and skill building. In this chapter, we focus on the two strategies that most closely align with promoting 21st-century skills: project-based learning (STEM, experiential learning, summer learning) and college and career readiness (apprenticeships, service learning, internships, workforce development).

Finally, with preconditions and strategies in place, there is still one essential component missing: the process that all people go through to build skills and competencies. As noted earlier, SEL is an ideal process for developing 21st-century skills because it builds upon the practices and strategies inherent in youth development, project-based learning, and college and career readiness activities. SEL does not stand alone but, rather, infuses the other activities and strategies that OST providers use to contribute to the development of 21st-century skills and social and emotional competencies. Collectively, this continuum of approaches and strategies address the 21st-century skills that are also social and emotional competencies (e.g., teamwork, communication, perspective taking), those 21st-century skills that are supported by social and emotional competencies (e.g., creativity, initiative, accountability), and, finally, the 21st-century skills that stand alone (e.g., information and media literacy).

In the following section, we describe the current context for 21st-century skill promotion, including the growth of the SEL movement; policy shifts that are playing a role in how K–12 education, workforce development, and OST are thinking about the promotion of 21st-century skills; and opportunities to bridge the three fields to better support youth success.

## The SEL Movement: Why Now?

The movement to incorporate SEL and related frameworks in K–12 education has created a modest rumble over the last two decades. So why is SEL now at the forefront of education? Likely, there are many contributing factors. First, there has been popular backlash against the stringent accountability of the No Child Left Behind Act and, thus, the instructional focus on academic content (Zakrzewski, 2015). Second, a growing body of research has shown definitively that social and emotional competencies contribute to students' positive academic and personal outcomes (Durlak et al., 2011; Jones et al., 2015). Third, the workforce has been clear (and for a while now) that social and emotional competencies and 21st-century skills are important to career attainment and success (Lippman, Ryberg, Carney, & Moore, 2015; National Research Council, 2012). In addition to these overarching influences, there are specific policy changes and systems-level supports that exemplify the focus on social and emotional competencies and skill building, and these are worthy of mention here.

*Policy Change in Support of 21st-Century Skills*

The Every Student Succeeds Act (ESSA), signed into law in 2015, includes language that aligns with 21st-century skill building and SEL. One section requires states to focus on educating the whole child. Another encourages states to identify additional, nonacademic measures for accountability purposes to demonstrate that schools are supporting school quality and student engagement. The popular press and education circles have focused on social and emotional competencies, school climate, and college and career readiness, in addition to existing administrative data, such as attendance, as possibilities for this "fifth measure" of accountability. As part of that work, the U.S. Department of Education now offers a free survey of school climate (ED School Climate Surveys, or ED SCLS), which provides school-level reports to use for both continuous improvement and reporting. Many states have agreed to pilot that survey in 2016–2017. In addition, states are increasingly adopting SEL standards and enacting supports for systemic implementation of SEL (Blad, 2016; CASEL, 2016). All of this activity signals a growing state and federal commitment to SEL as the chosen process for promoting the 21st-century skills described at the outset of this chapter.

The second recent movement that has influenced the focus on social and emotional competence is the convergence between the fields of education and the workforce. As we noted earlier, the recognition among employers that 21st-century skills are essential is not new. Dan Goleman (1995) wrote his popular press book on emotional intelligence as an essential tool for workplace success fairly early in the history of 21st-century skills and SEL. But those conversations focused more heavily on how employers might make changes within their companies to promote and support emotional intelligence. More recently, policy and practice shifts have occurred at the national and local levels, bringing this research to conversations about workforce preparation and readiness—and, thus, linking conversations about emotional intelligence in the workplace to conversations about primary, secondary, and postsecondary education. More specifically, the Office of Career, Technical, and Adult Education (OCTAE) released a framework of essential skills for workforce readiness and success in 2014 (U.S. Department of Education, Office of Career, Technical, and Adult Education, n.d.). These skills look strikingly similar to social and emotional competencies and 21st-century skills. As we have posited elsewhere (Devaney & Moroney, 2015), there is a deep connection among key 21st-century skills, social and emotional competencies, and the employability skills promoted by the OCTAE framework. For example, in order to develop the personal qualities that the OCTAE framework promotes, a person must have the ability to recognize his or her own emotions and have a sense of self-confidence. Similarly, in order to have good communication skills, as suggested by OCTAE, one needs the 21st-century skills to be able to listen well and to resolve conflicts.

Just as ESSA provides a logical link for the OST field to begin working with schools and formal educators, the employability skills framework provides an avenue and common language to help OST form strategic connections with local places of employment and workforce development programs to prepare young people for the jobs of tomorrow.

## Systems Change in Support of 21st-Century Skills

Although the SEL movement in OST has also been influenced by the authorization of ESSA, the adoption of SEL standards across states, and the convergence of education and workforce, it is important to note that adopting SEL as a process was simply the next logical step in the path that OST has been forging for the past two decades. SEL articulates the *how* in our equation of high-quality implementation toward the OST goals of learning and positive development. That is to say, OST programs have not necessarily changed their outcome goals; rather, the formal education community has recognized that the OST processes we have been using for many years are a legitimate means to an end. Given this recognition and the policy implications, OST systems builders and intermediary organizations are becoming more intentional about incorporating SEL and support for building 21st-century skills into our work. For example, Boston After School and Beyond developed its ACT (*Achieving, Connecting,* and *Thriving*) framework several years ago, before the SEL movement kicked into high gear, as a way to identify the 21st-century skills that OST programs in Boston promote. Today, that framework provides a foundation for the social and emotional skill building that takes place and is measured as part of the organization's summer learning and other programs. Boston After School and Beyond is part of the larger network, Every Hour Counts, whose members have partnered for more than 10 years to promote system-wide practices that support a variety of youth outcomes, including growth mindset, communication, collaboration, self-regulation, and critical thinking (Every Hour Counts, 2014). At the local level, the Silicon Valley Out-of-School Time collaborative recently brought together funders and program leaders to collectively define, build capacity for, implement, and evaluate SEL programs for teens in a place-based initiative in seven diverse youth programs in Northern California.

Out-of-school time intermediaries are not alone in their endeavor to support 21st-century skill building in OST. As noted in their chapter earlier in this volume, the National Afterschool Association (NAA) has been exploring ways to equip OST professionals as the field moves toward a more intentional approach to skill building. To inform those efforts, NAA conducted a survey of its members to ascertain what they know about SEL, what they are already doing, and what supports they need to further their work in SEL and skill building. They found that staff value SEL and are implementing SEL practices to some extent, but they want clarification and more resources on what SEL is and how to do it well. As a result of that survey, NAA is aligning their Core Knowledge and Competencies for Afterschool and Youth Development Professionals with the competencies that adults need to support and implement SEL.

This is merely a snapshot of existing systemic work that builds on the policy momentum related to social and emotional skill building. Moving ahead, part of the practice and research agenda is to elevate these systems to support a greater understanding of what they involve, and also to surface other assets that may not lie at the forefront. A compelling question for future research and practice is as follows: How do we prepare staff to implement SEL practices in the context of existing high-quality youth development programs that employ project-based learning and college and career readiness strategies and activities?

## OUT-OF-SCHOOL TIME AND 21ST-CENTURY SKILLS: FUTURE

The OST field has come a long way over the past three decades: Programs are goal-oriented and structured, activities are content-driven and intentional, staff have gained new skills to offer higher quality experiences, and research is showing that participants are gaining important skills when they participate for substantial periods of time (Durlak et al., 2011; Smith et al., 2012; Vandell, Reisner & Pierce, 2007). With that maturity comes greater responsibility—a responsibility to provide not only safe, caring spaces where young people can build skills but also structured, intentional learning opportunities grounded in evidence-based practice. Thus, there are some concrete next steps that practitioners and researchers alike can take to bring OST programming and its support for 21st-century skill building to the next level of sophistication.

### Agree on a Common Language, Strategies, and Practices

#### In Practice

We recognize, given considerations of history and turf, that it is not realistic to expect every sector across the country to agree on a common language or framework to describe 21st-century skill building. We *do*, however, recommend that local or regional sectors and networks engaging in joint planning and practice across settings, establish a shared language. It is difficult to engage in systemic work without a common language to promote discussion. It is also important to recognize the value and utility of using evidence-based frameworks. Most established, research-based frameworks include skills that are malleable and teachable. Finally, we recommend that OST programs ensure that their strategies and practices (e.g., project-based learning) are aligned with their intended outcomes (e.g., 21st-century skills).

#### In Research

Researchers should explore—through implementation studies, observation, and rigorous qualitative methods—which high-quality practices result in the greatest growth in social and emotional competencies and 21st-century skills. Durlak and Weissberg (2007) began this work, and more recently, the Susan Crown Exchange and the David P. Weikart Center have taken up the challenge (Smith et al., 2016), but more needs to be done to help practitioners understand which specific practices are best suited to promoting 21st-century skills. Once collected, this information needs to be shared with practitioners in a user-friendly way (i.e., not only published in scholarly journals but also described in practice briefs or developed into trainings).

## Be Intentional

### *In Practice*

High-quality OST programs have many benefits. They can be fun and engaging, and they can promote opportunities for learning and building 21st-century skills. The key word here is *can*. Studies and decades of good practice across multiple disciplines have shown that intentional or purposeful activities are more likely to yield the outcome of interest than those in which skill building is an unintended benefit, perhaps the result of one savvy staff member's natural ability to connect. OST programs should plan for and support staff in the design and implementation of intentional practices, grounded in practice-driven research, that support 21st-century skill building.

### *In Research*

Although the research is clear that high-quality programs with intentional opportunities for SEL support skill building, we need to better define what it means to be intentional and how to implement evidence-based practices. Researchers need to examine programs that are successful in accomplishing these goals and share that learning with practitioners.

## Invest in Staff

### *In Practice*

We know that staff preparation, retention, and ongoing professional learning are all essential for high-quality programs and positive youth outcomes, including skill building (Moroney & Devaney, in press). We propose a threefold approach to investing in staff. First, create professional pathways that honor the expertise in promoting skill building that staff already bring to the table. Second, support staff in reflecting on and building their own social and emotional competencies and 21st-century skills. As with children and youth, these skills can be taught and developed in adults. Finally, create opportunities for staff to learn strategies and skills to intentionally support 21st-century skill building. In addition to professional learning opportunities, staff need time to plan for learning how to incorporate skill-building into their activities, reflecting on their own practice, and sharing strategies with colleagues. Professional learning communities across or within role-alike groups can be a powerful tool to help staff reflect, share ideas, understand new concepts, make plans, and learn from each other. For example, the Partnership for Children and Youth in California facilitates professional learning communities composed of in-school and OST professionals focused on SEL. The goal of these professional learning communities is to foster collaboration and share knowledge in this emerging field in education and OST.

### In Research

We need to better understand the characteristics of today's OST workforce (who they are, what they know, how they learn best) to effectively provide the supports described above. We also need to confirm the value of professional learning methods that we know, from adult learning science, work well in other fields to ensure they are most appropriate for our unique workforce. Finally, studies should explore whether preparing staff to provide opportunities for skill building, reflecting on their own social and emotional competencies and practices, and acknowledging their increased capacity to deliver intentional programs impact factors such as staff retention and longevity in the field.

## Pay Attention to Context

### In Practice

Twenty-first-century skill building happens in context. Therefore, families, schools, and communities need to have a meaningful role in determining the skills frameworks and associated practices that support skill building. This work is still very new in OST. For example, the Asia Society has been working across the globe with communities to identify 21st-century competencies that are valued by and reflective of community members (Russell, 2016). In the popular media, there has been some backlash against specific constructs associated with 21st-century skills—for example, grit—based on the idea that they are reflective of or benefit only particular groups of people (Herold, 2015). Others challenge frameworks related to 21st-century skills based upon their monocultural origin (Jagers, 2001). These issues must be at the forefront as OST works to support 21st-century skill building.

### In Research

As a start, we need to further research the influence of context on social and emotional competency and how to best reflect context in skill-building strategies. Perhaps even more important, we need to engage in ethnographies to learn from community-based initiatives that are reflective of local community assets and driven by the values of youth, families, staff, and community members.

## Partner

### In Practice

Partnerships are essential for the OST field as we endeavor to support young people's 21st-century skill building. Kindergarten through grade 12 education, workforce development, juvenile justice, mental health services, and other sectors are starting to have conversations about how to collectively support social and emotional development and 21st-century skill building. Out-of-school time can be a foundational partner in these efforts by providing high-quality staff with expertise in SEL practices, offering professional development on evidence-based strategies, and contributing to conversations about how to promote cross-sector learning opportunities.

### In Research

Researchers and OST professionals can partner to promote better and more useful knowledge building. True researcher–practitioner partnerships (see Ken Anthony's chapter, this volume) should guide the aforementioned research inquiries to ensure that research does not drive practice but, rather, serves it.

## CONCLUSION AND CHARGE FOR THE FIELD

In closing, the OST field is at an important turning point as the expertise we have built and the goals we have promoted for decades are gaining prominence across sectors. It is time for OST to take ownership and lead the charge in helping to prepare young people for the future. We know for certain that tomorrow's livelihoods will be different from our own and that we cannot imagine the creations and innovations that today's young people will contribute to our future society. OST programs have the opportunity and the substance not only to provide opportunities for SEL, project-based learning, and college and career readiness but also to create places in which young people can dream up and lead projects, make proposals for a better world, and be the visionaries of the future. Passion, inspiration, aspiration—these are the real 21st-century skills.

## REFERENCES

American Management Association. (2012). *AMA 2012 critical skills survey.* New York, NY: Author. Retrieved from http://www.amanet.org/uploaded/2012-CriticalSkills-Survey.pdf

Benson, P. L. (2003). Developmental assets and asset-building community: Conceptual and empirical foundations. In R. M. Lerner & P. L. Benson (Eds.), *Developmental assets and asset building communities: Implications for research, policy, and practice* (pp. 19–43). New York, NY: Kluwer Academic/Plenum Publishers.

Berkowitz, M., & Bier, M. (2005). *What works in character education: A research-driven guide for educators.* St. Louis, MO: The Character Education Partnership.

Blad, E. (2016, August 1). Social-emotional learning: States collaborate to craft standards, policies. *Education Week.* Retrieved from http://blogs.edweek.org/edweek/rules-forengagement/2016/08/social-emotional_learning_states_collaborate_to_craft_standards_policies.html

Brackett, M. A., Rivers, S. E., & Salovey, P. (2011). Emotional intelligence: Implications for personal, social, academic, and workplace success. *Social and Personality Psychology Compass, 5*(1), 88–103. https://doi.org/10.1111/j.1751-9004.2010.00334.x

Buck Institute for Education. (2016). *What is project based learning (PBL)?* Retrieved from http://www.bie.org/about/what_pbl

Catalano, R. F., & Hawkins, J. D. (1996). The social development model: A theory of anti-social behavior. In J. D. Hawkins (Ed.), *Delinquency and Crime: Current Theories* (pp. 149–197). New York, NY: Cambridge University Press.

Collaborative for Academic, Social, and Emotional Learning. (2016). *State scan scorecard project.* Retrieved from http://www.casel.org/state-scan-scorecard-project/

Committee for Children & Collaborative for Academic, Social, and Emotional Learning (CASEL). (2016). *CASEL and Committee for Children host congressional briefing on SEL and employability skills.* Retrieved from http://www.casel.org/wp-content/uploads/2016/09/Sept.-14-2016-Congressional-Briefing-on-SEL-and-Employability-Skills.pdf

Devaney, E., & Moroney, D. (2015). *Ready for work? How afterschool programs can support employability through social and emotional learning.* Washington, DC: American Institutes for Research.

Devaney, E., Naftzger, N., Liu, F., Sniegowski, S., Shields, J., & Booth, E. (2016). *Texas 21st Century Community Learning Centers: 2014–15 evaluation report.* Washington, DC: American Institutes for Research.

Durlak, J. A., & Weissberg, R. P. (2007). *The impact of after-school programs that promote personal and social skills.* Chicago, IL: Collaborative for Academic, Social, and Emotional Learning.

Durlak, J. A., Weissberg, R. P., Dymnicki, A. B., Taylor, R. D., & Schellinger, K. B. (2011). The impact of enhancing students' social and emotional learning: A meta-analysis of school-based universal interventions. *Child Development, 82*(1), 405–432. doi:10.1111/j.1467-8624.2010.01564.x

Durlak, J. A., Weissberg, R. P., & Pachan, M. (2010). A meta-analysis of after-school programs that seek to promote personal and social skills in children and adolescents. *American Journal of Community Psychology, 45*, 294–309. https://doi.org/10.1007/s10464-010- 9300-6

Edutopia. (n.d.). Engaging students by expanding learning time. Retrieved from http://www.edutopia.org/stw-expanded-learning-time-research

Elias, M. J., Parker, S. J., Kash, V. M., Weissberg, R. P., & O'Brien, M. U. (2008). Social and emotional learning, moral education, and character education: A comparative analysis and a view toward convergence. In L. P. Nucci & D. Narvaez (Eds.), *Handbook of moral and character education* (pp. 248–266). New York, NY: Routledge.

Ettekal, A. V., Callina, K. S., & Lerner, R. M. (2015). The promotion of character through youth development programs: A view of the issues. *Journal of Youth Development, 10*(3), 6–13. doi:10.5195/JYD.2015.4

Every Hour Counts. (2014). *Measurement framework: How to measure success in expanded learning systems.* New York, NY: Author.

Farrington, C. A., Roderick, M., Allensworth, E., Nagaoka, J., Keyes, T.S., Johnson, D.W., & Beechum, N. O. (2012). *Teaching adolescents to become learners. The role of noncognitive factors in shaping school performance: A critical literature review.* Chicago, IL: University of Chicago Consortium on Chicago School Research.

Fischer, K. (2013, March 4). The employment mismatch. *Chronicle of Higher Education.* Retrieved from http://www.chronicle.com

Fredricks, J. A., & Eccles, J. S. (2006). Extracurricular involvement and adolescent adjustment: Impact of duration, number of activities, and breadth of participation. *Applied Developmental Science, 10*(3), 132–146. https://doi.org/10.1207/s1532480xads1003_3

Goleman, D. (1995). *Emotional intelligence: Why it can matter more than IQ.* New York, NY: Bantam.

Hall, G., Yohalem, N., Toleman, J., & Wilson, A. (2003). *How afterschool programs can most effectively promote positive youth development as a support to academic achievement.* Wellesley, MA: National Institute on Out-of-School Time. Retrieved from www.niost.org/WCW3.pdf

Hamilton, S. F., Hamilton, M. A., & Pittman, K. (2004). Principles for youth development. In S. F. Hamilton, & M. A. Hamilton (Eds.), *The youth development handbook: Coming of age in American communities* (pp. 3–23). Thousand Oaks, CA: SAGE.

Hawkins, J. D., Kosterman, R., Catalano, R. F., Hill, K. G., & Abbott, R. D. (2008). Effects of social development intervention in childhood 15 years later. *Archives of Pediatric Adolescent Medicine, 162*(12), 1133–1141. https://doi.org/10.1001/arch-pedi.162.12.1133

Herold, B. (2015, January 24). Is "grit" racist? *Education Week.* Retrieved from http://blogs.edweek.org/edweek/DigitalEducation/2015/01/is_grit_racist.html

Jagers, R. J. (2001). Cultural integrity and social and emotional competence promotion: Work notes on moral competence. *The Journal of Negro Education, 70*(1/2), 59–71.

Jones, D. E., Greenberg, M., & Crowley, M. (2015). Early social-emotional functioning and public health: The relationship between kindergarten social competence and future wellness. *American Journal of Public Health, 105*(11), 2283–2290. doi:10.2105/AJPH.2015.302630

Kataoka, S., & Vandell, D. L. (2013). Quality of afterschool activities and relative change in adolescent functioning over two years. *Applied Developmental Science, 17*(3), 123–134. doi: 10.1080/10888691.2013.804375

Larson, R., & Walker, K. (2010). Dilemmas of practice: Challenges to program quality encountered by youth program leaders. *American Journal of Community Psychology, 45*(3), 338–349. doi:org/10.1007/s10464-010-9307-z

Lerner, R. M., Lerner, J. V., Almerigi, J. B., Theokas, C., Phelps, E., Gestsdottir, S., …von Eye, A. (2005). Positive youth development, participation in community youth development programs, and community contributions of fifth-grade adolescents: Findings from the first wave of the 4-H study of positive youth development. *Journal of Early Adolescence, 25*(1), 17–71. doi:10.1177/0272431604272461

Lippman, L., Ryberg, R., Carney, R., & Moore, K. (2015). *Key "soft skills" that foster youth workforce success: Toward a consensus across fields.* Washington, DC: Child Trends.

Miller, B. M. (2005). *Pathways to success for youth: What counts in after-school.* Wellesley, MA: National Institute on Out-of-School Time.

Moroney, D., & Devaney, E. (in press). Ready to implement? How the out-of-school time workforce can support character development through social and emotional learning: A review of the literature and future directions. *The Journal of Character Education.*

Morrison, T., Maciejewski, B., Giffi, C., DeRocco, E., McNelly, J., & Gardner, C. (2011). *Boiling point? The skills gap in U.S. manufacturing.* New York, NY: Deloitte and Washington, DC: The Manufacturing Institute. Retrieved from http://www.themanufacturinginstitute.org/~/media/A07730B2A798437D98501E798 C2E13AA.ashx

Morrissey, K. M., & Werner-Wilson, R. J. (2005). The relationship between out-of-school activities and positive youth development: An investigation of the influences of communities and family. *Adolescence, 40*(157), 67–85.

Naftzger, N., Manzeske, D. Nistler, M., Swanlund, A., Rapaport, A., Shields, J.,…Sugar, S. (2013). *Texas 21st Century Community Learning Centers: Year 2 evaluation report.* Naperville, IL: American Institutes for Research.

Nagaoka, J., Farrington, C., Ehrlich, S., & Heath, R. (2015). *Foundations for young adult success: A developmental framework.* Chicago, IL: University of Chicago Consortium on Chicago School Research.

National Education Association. (2010). *Preparing 21st century students for a global society: An educator's guide to the "Four Cs."* Retrieved from http://www.nea.org/assets/docs/A-Guide-to-Four-Cs.pdf

National Research Council. (2012). *Education for life and work: Developing transferable knowledge and skills in the 21st century.* Committee on Defining Deeper Learning and 21st Century Skills, J.W. Pellegrino and M.L. Hilton, Editors. Board on Testing and Assessment and Board on Science Education, Division of Behavioral and Social Sciences and Education. Washington, DC: National Academies Press.

Partnership for 21st Century Learning. (2007). *Framework for 21st century learning.* Retrieved from http://www.p21.org/storage/documents/docs/P21_framework_0816.pdf

Riggs, N. R., Jahromi, L. B., Razza, R. P., Dillworth, J. E., & Mueller, U. (2006). Executive function and the promotion of social-emotional competence. *Journal of Applied Developmental Psychology, 27,* 300–309. https://doi.org/10.1016/j.appdev.2006.04.002

Roberts, R., Martin, J., & Olaru, G. (2015). *A Rosetta stone for noncognitive skills: Understanding, assessing, and enhancing noncognitive skills in primary and secondary education.* New York, NY: Asia Society.

Russell, C. (2016). *System supports for 21st century competencies.* New York, NY: Asia Society for Global Education and Policy Studies Associates.

Smith, C., Akiva, T., Sugar, S., Lo, Y. J., Frank, K. A., Peck, S. C., . . . Devaney, T. (2012). *Continuous quality improvement in afterschool settings: Impact findings from the Youth Program Quality Intervention study.* Washington, DC: Forum for Youth Investment.

Smith, C., McGovern, G., Peck., S. C., Larson, R., Hillaker, B., & Roy, L. (2016). *Preparing youth to thrive: Methodology and findings from the social and emotional learning challenge.* Washington, DC: Forum for Youth Investment.

U.S. Department of Education, Office of Career, Technical, and Adult Education. (n.d.). *Employability skills framework.* Washington, DC: Author. Retrieved from http://cte.ed.gov/employabilityskills/

Vandell, D. L., Larson, R., Mahoney, J., & Watts, T. (2015). Children's organized activities. In M. H. Bornstein & T. Leventhal (Eds.), *Handbook of child psychology and developmental science, Volume 4. Ecological settings and processes in developmental systems* (7th ed., pp. 305–344). New York, NY: Wiley Interscience.

Vandell, D. L., Reisner, E. R., & Pierce, K. M. (2007). *Outcomes linked to high-quality afterschool programs: Longitudinal findings from the study of promising afterschool programs.* Washington, DC: Policy Studies Associates.

Vandell, D., Simzar, R., O'Cadiz, P., & Hall, V. (2016). Findings from an afterschool STEM learning initiative. *Journal of Expanded Learning Opportunities, 1*(3), 7–26.

Wan, G., & Gut, D. M. (Eds.) (2011). *Bringing schools into the 21ˢᵗ century.* New York, NY: Springer.

Weissberg, R., Durlak, J., Domitrovich, C., & Gullotta, T. (2015). Social and emotional learning: Past, present, and future. In J. Durlak, C. Domitrovich, R. Weissberg, & T. Gullotta (Eds.), *Handbook of social and emotional learning: Research and practice* (pp. 3–19). New York, NY: Guilford Press.

Zakrzewski, V. (2015, January 7). *Social-emotional learning: Why now?* Berkeley, CA: Greater Good Science Center. Retrieved from http://greatergood.berkeley.edu/article/item/social_emotional_learning_why_now

CHAPTER 18

# KNOWING BETTER, DOING BETTER

## Three Gaps to Fill in the Next Decade of Research on Out-of-School Time

Joseph L. Mahoney and Shannon Haley-Mize

The scientific knowledge base on out-of-school time (OST) has grown markedly over the past three decades (e.g., Mahoney, Vandell, Simpkins, & Zarrett, 2009; Vandell, Larson, Mahoney, & Watts, 2015). Great strides have been made in understanding the significance of a variety of out-of-school contexts in the lives of young people and their families. Nonetheless, important gaps in the knowledge base exist where little research is available. In this chapter, we discuss three areas that our field needs to understand better: (a) the role of OST in supporting developmental transitions, (b) the inclusion of students with disabilities in OST research, and (c) the need for an international perspective to OST research, practice, and policy. In doing so, we describe their significance, briefly overview the state of knowledge, and then suggest avenues for future research to begin narrowing the gaps. Consistent with a bioecological perspective to development (Bronfenbrenner & Morris, 2006), we note that these gaps range across several levels of organization, beginning with developmental and person-context differences and

*The Growing Out-of-School Time Field: Past, Present, and Future,*
pages 267–292.

ending with macro-level differences across nations and cultures. Accordingly, we begin by discussing the need for theory and research on the role of OST in developmental transitions, then move to person-context gaps in OST research that pertain to young people with disabilities, and conclude by pointing to a macro-level gap in OST research at the international level.

## TRANSITIONS

Although educational settings can be, and often are, disaggregated into discrete time periods (e.g., early childhood, elementary school, secondary school, postsecondary school), modern views of education recognize the experience as a continuous one for the individual (e.g., PK–20 education). Because educational experiences at one point are foundational for future points of learning and development, there has been significant work linking traditional educational settings over time and understanding the transitional processes therein (Eccles, 2004). However, similar attention to the role of OST in developmental transitions has not occurred.

### What Are Transitions?

There is general agreement that individuals go through developmental periods characterized by significant change and that age alone provides no explanation for such change. Following seminal work by Simmons and Blyth (1987), an upsurge of conceptual and empirical publications on the topic of developmental transitions occurred in the 1990s (e.g., Graber & Brooks-Gunn, 1996; Rutter, 1996). We use the term *transition* to refer to biological, psychosocial, and/or ecological changes that result in structural or functional reorganization of the individual in relation to the environment (Graber & Brooks-Gunn, 1996). Transitions involve altered patterns of behavioral adaptation that emerge over time in response to these changes. Behavioral adaption might involve the emergence of new behaviors, the cessation of established behaviors, or the maintenance of ascertained behaviors that persist in the light of significant individual, social, and/or ecological change (Rogoff, 1996).

Some transitions lead to mere perturbations in behavior whereas others result in fundamental changes that endure (Rutter, 1996). Transitions that involve enduring or lifelong change to the established developmental trajectory of individual behavior patterns (e.g., a change in lifestyle) may be thought of as transitionally linked *turning points* (Graber & Brooks-Gunn, 1996). It is important to note that transitions may accentuate either positive or negative adjustment patterns (or both) and that there are individual differences in response to the same transitional experience (Rutter, 1996). Individual differences can be understood in terms of pre-existing differences, accumulation of new and ongoing stressors, and person and environmental resources to cope with adversity across the transition (Graber & Brooks-Gunn, 1996), as well as the individual's own active role engaging with the social ecology in an effort to adapt. Thus, person and environment are insepa-rable during transitions (Rogoff, 1996).

But what is a "successful" transition? Masten and Coatsworth (1998) proposed that competence may be understood with respect to the attainment of salient, age-graded developmental milestones that indicate positive adaption with the envi-ronment appropriate to one's culture. In this view, a successful transition would culminate in competence in the present that increases the likelihood of adapting positively to new developmental milestones in the future (see also Mahoney & Bergman, 2002). Examples of such milestones include the attainment of self-control and compliance during early childhood that would set the stage for rule-governed, moral, and prosocial behavior during middle childhood.

With this discussion as a backdrop, we note that prior work on transitions has emphasized studying different contexts (e.g., family, school, peers) during the pe-riod from late childhood to adolescence. However, these efforts generally ignore the role of OST settings. OST contexts play an important role in how effectively transitions are navigated. To illustrate this point, we consider three types of transi-tions receiving limited attention in the OST literature: namely, (a) the transition from early childhood to middle childhood education, (b) the transition from sec-ondary school to college, and (c) participation-related transitions.

## The Early-to-Middle Childhood Education Transition

In many countries around the world, a large financial investment is made in ed-ucational programming and childcare for low-income families (Ecarius, Klieme, Stecher, & Woods, 2013). In the U.S., billions of dollars are spent annually to pro-vide early childcare education and afterschool programming through initiatives such as Head Start, Early Head Start, and the 21st-Century Community Learning Centers. These programs provide support to economically disadvantaged children and their families to foster educational success, social competence, and healthy development. However, despite having common goals, research has seldom stud-ied connections between early childhood education and afterschool programming. Thus, we know little about whether and how the early-to-middle childhood transi-tion may be affected by participation in OST activities.

When compared to children who do not attend early childhood education pro-grams, those who do show varied outcomes following the transition to formal schooling. Specifically, some children maintain the competence gained through their involvement in early childhood education programs and others do not (e.g., Barnett, 2011; Ramey & Ramey, 1996). Thus, an important question is: What helps some individuals make successful transitions from early to middle child-hood education settings? Which person–environment factors might assist chil-dren who continue to be disadvantaged economically and in other, related ways, such as school resources, climate, curriculum, language, and parent involvement? Again, the answer likely depends on pre-existing differences, accumulation of new and ongoing stressors, and person and environmental resources to cope with adversity across the transition (Graber & Brooks-Gunn, 1996). But we suggest that participation in organized OST programs may be one such person–environment resource that facilitates positive adaptation during this transition.

Specifically, research shows that OST activities can build multiple competencies that contribute to the salient developmental tasks of middle childhood. Examples include academic achievement (e.g., Mahoney, Lord, & Carryl, 2005a), positive peer relations (e.g., Fredricks & Simpkins, 2013), health (e.g., Mahoney, Lord, & Carryl, 2005b), and appropriate conduct (e.g., Durlak, Weissberg, & Pachan, 2010). In fact, one important function of organized OST activities during middle childhood may be to facilitate mastery of newly acquired capacities attained during early childhood through the interpersonal interactions with peers and adults that occur in these settings (e.g., Reisner, White, Birmingham, & Welsh, 2001; Rogoff, 1996).

But without an intentional effort to connect these developmental experiences in a coherent manner, the role of afterschool programs for low-income children may ordinarily be one of remedial education rather than a continuation of services that provide social-educational support. To help make the early opportunities become opportunities for lifetime, educational programming should be integrated before, during, and following the transition from early to middle childhood. To do so, we need to understand much better the role that early childhood education plays in facilitating adaptation to organized OST activities during middle childhood and, at the same time, how OST activities may contribute to the ongoing development of skills initiated during early childhood. Efforts to integrate early childhood education and traditional schooling have revealed a variety of modifiable barriers (e.g., Early, Pianta, Taylor, & Cox, 2001), and such obstacles also need to be studied in the transition to OST activities. Fortunately, because many researchers who now study afterschool programs initially focused their research on early childhood programs (Halpern, 1999), the expertise to study the role of afterschool programming in the transitional processes from early to middle childhood exists.

## The Secondary School to College Transition

As noted earlier, successful transitions depend, in part, on the extent to which stressful life events characterize the process and whether adequate coping resources are available to manage the stress. In particular, when many stressors occur together and/or accumulate rapidly over time, the risk for poor adaption increases (Graber & Brooks-Gunn, 1996). This circumstance characterizes the transition to college for many young people. Although the changes in residence, autonomy and time management, reorganization of social supports, heightened academic challenge, identity exploration, and changing social roles that typically accompany the transition to college often result in some level of psychological distress, most individuals adapt to college successfully. However, some do not adjust well and experience significant psychological disturbance (e.g., Hunt &

Eisenberg, 2010). Campus counseling can be a source of support once problems develop, but many students with psychological distress do not seek the help they need (e.g., Ziven, Eisenberg, Gollust, & Golberstein, 2009).

Participation in OST activities may help students transition to college successfully. On the one hand, activity participation encourages the development of social and emotional competencies (e.g., Hirsh, 2016) that may make students both more competitive for college entry and better prepared for the demands of higher learning. On the other hand, prior experience in OST activities may facilitate continued participation in extracurricular activities across the transition into college. Participation in college-based extracurricular activities can, in turn, provide positive developmental experiences that include belonging and social support that foster positive adaptation without undermining time devoted to academics (e.g., Bohnert, Wargo Aikins, & Edidin, 2007; Greene & Maggs, 2015). They may also help to prepare young people for the transition to adulthood and work (e.g., Csikszentmihalyi & Schneider, 2000).

Interestingly, although some of the earliest studies of adolescent participation in extracurricular activities in the U.S. were concerned with the transition to adulthood (e.g., Clem & Dodge, 1933; Shannon, 1929), only a handful of investigations have examined this connection in recent decades. There is evidence that participation in organized OST activities positively predicts educational attainment (e.g., Mahoney, 2000; Mahoney & Vest, 2012), but few studies have assessed the antecedent processes by which youth participation translates to college attendance (e.g., Mahoney, Cairns, & Farmer, 2003; Morris, 2016) or explored the role of leisure in the transitional process itself (e.g., Bohnert et al., 2007; Raymore, Barber, & Eccles, 2001). What this work does suggest is that the social and emotional skills (e.g., interpersonal competence, identity development, organizational skills, teamwork, leadership, and time management) developed through OST activities are important for understanding the transition to college and work (e.g., Hirsh, 2016; Morris, 2016).

Longitudinal research that tracks youth through the transition to adulthood with a focus on studying continuity and change in activity patterns as they relate to the salient developmental tasks of emerging adults is needed (Busseri et al., 2010). To accomplish this, we follow Rogoff (1996) in advocating for a sociocultural perspective to understanding this transition. In this view, the task is to assess how young people's participation in organized OST activities changes over time as new social-contextual opportunities, responsibilities, and roles are introduced. These new developmental experiences should, in turn, affect each individual's contribution to the activity setting, change the activity context as a whole, and influence the type and degree of competencies that result.

### Participation-Related Transitions

Research on the construct of participation has grown exponentially over the past 15 years. Beyond the simplistic, dichotomous measure of whether or not a child enrolls in OST activities, studying facets of participation such as intensity (e.g., amount of time) and duration of involvement, breadth or diversity of activities, and level of engagement is becoming commonplace (e.g., Bohnert, Fredricks, & Randall, 2010; Fredricks & Eccles, 2006). Scholars have begun to examine patterns of participation (e.g., Peck, Roeser, Zarrett, & Eccles, 2008; Zarrett et al., 2009) and what leads youth to participate in these ways (e.g., Akiva & Galletta Horner, 2016; Larson, Walker, & Pearce, 2005). What we know is that each facet of participation may be important for developing competencies and/or reducing problem behaviors and that they appear to interact in complex ways (e.g., Busseri & Rose-Krasnor, 2010).

However, transitions in the facets of participation themselves are not well understood. For instance, we know little about why some youth drop out (or burn out) of OST activities, what it means to "stop out" of participation (i.e., suspend participation for a period of time), the extent to which individual engagement varies across activities or time, or why youth transition into and out of different activities. In other words, the developmental dynamics of participation (i.e., the chronosystem) is a gap in the knowledge base (e.g., Denault & Poulin, 2009).

For example, in terms of activity dropouts, most of our knowledge comes from cross-sectional studies of male adolescents who have ceased participation in one particular sport (e.g., Crane & Temple, 2015). Intrapersonal factors (e.g., lack of enjoyment, low perceived competence, self-imposed stress), interpersonal factors (e.g., pressure from coaches, peers, and families), and structural constraints (e.g., insufficient time, injuries, and cost) relate to dropping out of organized youth sports. But whether these factors operate similarly in other types of OST activities is largely unknown. To understand the transition out of activities, this work requires that theoretical models be developed to explain activity dropout and that prospective, longitudinal studies be designed to assess them (e.g., Guzman & Kingston, 2012; Persson, Kerr, & Stattin, 2007). A similar need exists to understand activity "stopouts." For instance, Darling's (2005) three-year analysis of participation durability shows that activity participation may be most beneficial when it is continuous and, for those with variable participation over time, benefits are most apparent during times of active participation. But we have limited work—theoretical or empirical—on the factors that affect variability in patterns of participation over time. This includes a lack of accounting for seasonal transitions in OST participation between the school year and summer months.

Finally, we note the need to employ analytic approaches able to assess change in multiple facets of activity participation over time. As Busseri and Rose-Krasnor (2010) have discussed, the interdependence and nonlinear relations between the facets of participation poses a challenge for convention analytic approaches. In cross-sectional work, they have shown the effectiveness of a *variable-based method*—latent composite variable (LCV)—that allows for different types activities and multiple facets of participation (e.g., enrollment, breadth, intensity) for each activity type to be measured simultaneously in one analytic model. A complementary *pattern-based method*—Linking of Clusters after Removal of Residue (LICUR)—has been developed by Bergman (1998). This method permits person-oriented profiles of participation to be identified at several time points. The individual profiles identified at different ages can then be linked together to examine stability and change in patterns of participation across time. Both approaches allow for nonlinear relations between facets of participation. However, these and other methods will ultimately need to address the fact that transitions in OST activities are also nested in larger contexts (e.g., schools, communities) that may impact the transitions. Ideally, these interrelated contexts will be studied in tandem with OST activities to understand the interdependence between developmental contexts during participation-related transitions (i.e., changes in person-mesosystem relations).

## Toward a Solution

In order to better integrate OST programming with traditional educational initiatives over time and place, we suggest that family–school–community partnerships and community schools, whereby the school serves as a multipurpose resource center, are promising. For example, the Schools of the 21st Century (21C) programming follows a developmental model with integrated components to serve the whole child (Finn-Stevenson, 2014). 21C components include home visitation beginning at birth to age 3; all-day, year-around early childhood education from ages 3–5; and before- and afterschool programming through the end of middle school. Because the school serves as the basis for all components, a long-standing relationship is established with each family, and services can be provided in an integrated and seamless fashion across transitions. Indeed, an integrated planning team that involves educators from early childhood, afterschool, and the school day codevelop curricula, learning goals, and activities. Adding the 21C components to an existing high-quality statewide early childhood education program shows that the addition of these integrated components relates both to better quality early education and superior developmental outcomes for children (e.g., Ginicola, Finn-Stevenson, & Zigler, 2013).

A second example is the community schools approach, a strategy supported by the Coalition for Community Schools at the Institute for Educational Leadership (Geiser, Rollins, Gerstein, & Blank, 2013). These schools facilitate a smooth transition from early childhood care to elementary education by taking a whole child approach to ensure that schools, families, and community partners work together to provide conditions for learning and successful transition (Jacobson, Jacobson, & Blank, 2012). Continuity across the transition is created through a shared understanding among the multiple key stakeholders who emphasize an intentional focus on educational linkages over time and place. Community schools have been shown to support a variety of positive developmental outcomes with extracurricular activities serving to reduce risky behavior and facilitate educational attainment (Heers, Klaveren, Groot, & van den Brink, 2016).

## INCLUDE YOUNG PEOPLE WITH
## DISABILITIES IN OST RESEARCH

Youth with disabilities comprise about 13% of the school-age population (Kena et al., 2016), and the challenges inherent to transitions across developmental periods are often more pronounced for these students. These struggles are especially evident in the transition to adulthood as indicated by statistics on outcomes for individuals with disabilities in young adulthood (see Sanford et al., 2011). There is a way forward, however. Synthesis of research provides insight into how we might improve outcomes for this population and OST has a promising role.

Inclusion of youth with disabilities has been prioritized in the broader field of education since the passage of the Education of all Handicapped Children Act (PL 97-142) in 1975 (McLeskey, Waldron, & Redd, 2014). This push for inclusion in schools has resulted in a significant increase in the number of students included with their peers in the general education classroom. In 2014, 61% of students with disabilities were included for 80% or more of the school day, compared to 33% in 1990 (Kena et al., 2016). This trend has generated a wealth of research and resources on the topic of inclusion that we believe could support efforts to improve accessibility in OST programming.

To examine current issues related to youth with disabilities and OST, we have included studies that cut across disability categories, but the focus is on youth with developmental disabilities. Developmental disability is a widely used umbrella term defined by the American Association of Intellectual and Developmental Disabilities (AAIDD) as including intellectual disability and other disabilities that are evident before the age of 22 (AAIDD, 2013). Developmental disabilities are usually lifelong conditions and often include physical limitations. Examples of developmental disabilities include Down syndrome, autism spectrum disorder, and spina bifida.

### Who Is (Dis)Engaged?

While limited, existing research on the topic of students with disabilities and OST gives some indication of the rate and potential benefits of participation. There is evidence that students with identified disabilities do not participate at a comparable rate in OST opportunities relative to their peers. Data from a 2004 longitudinal study indicated that 49% of students with learning disabilities, 60% of students with speech/language impairments, and only 35% of students with emotional and behavioral disorders participated in any organized school activities outside of class time (Wagner, Cadwallader, Garza, & Cameto, 2004). More recent work does not demonstrate much change in rates of participation in OST activities for students with disabilities despite increasing rates of inclusion in PK–12 general education classrooms over the last decade. One study reported that 62% of parents of students with disabilities indicated that their child *never* participated in extracurricular activities at their school or in the community (Coster et al.,

2012). An early examination of participation found a rate of 56% for students with Down syndrome (Sloper, Knussen, & Cunningham, 1990). Likewise, Taheri, Perry, and Minnes (2016) found that students with intellectual disabilities and autism spectrum disorder (ASD) reported low rates of activity participation and infrequent participation in social and physical activities. These students also reported having relatively few friends and poor-quality friendships.

A review of individualized education plans (IEPs) written for adolescents, another way to examine the capacity for participation, found that only 11.3% included any information regarding participation in extracurricular activities (Powers et al., 2005). This low percentage is in spite of the language included in the IDEA directing IEP teams to outline extracurricular activities in which the student will participate in the educational plan. This mandate reflects the law's emphasis on least restrictive environment (LRE) and is motivated in part by a demonstrated range of social skill deficits in students receiving services under IDEA that can significantly impact their functioning across contexts and result in poorer outcomes (Gresham, Sugai, & Horner, 2001). We also know that few social activities, the absence of friends, and loneliness are some of the most common issues facing individuals with disabilities across age ranges (Newton & Horner, 1993). These deficits and the impact across the lifespan serve as impetus for teams to identify and implement services that allow for the development of these skills, and existing work has demonstrated that there are prospective benefits directly related to social functioning for students with special needs who participate in structured OST recreation programs such as sports (Solish, Perry, & Minnes, 2010). These benefits include forming positive relationships and gaining social acceptance (Ghosh & Datta, 2012; Siperstein, Glick, & Parker, 2009), reducing rates of school dropout for students with behavioral challenges (Kortering & Braziel, 2005; Sinclair, Christenson, & Thurlow, 2005), increased social competence (Brooks, Floyd, Robins, & Chan, 2015), and adaptive skills (Cummins & Lau, 2003; Kraemer, McIntyre, & Blacher, 2003).

*Defining Participation*

Mahoney and Stattin (2000) defined structured OST activities as those comprised of "regular participation schedules, rule-guided engagement, direction by one or more adult activity leaders, an emphasis on skill development that is continually increasing in complexity and challenge, activity performance that requires sustained active attention, and clear feedback on performance" (pp. 114–115). However, when considering profiles of time spent participating in structured and unstructured extracurricular activities, Brooks et al. (2015) reported that more time involved in unstructured social activities predicted greater social competence for children with intellectual and learning disabilities. This association was not significant for time spent participating in structured activities. The finding that participation in unstructured activities relates to relatively high social competence is inconsistent with earlier studies (Gilman, 2001; Siperstein et al., 2009). The authors speculate that the discrepancy may result from the nature of the activities in that structured activities tended to involve large number of participants and rigid rules. In such situations, it may be that the interactions with typically developing peers are more likely to be negative and thus have limited benefit on social competence. Given previous work demonstrating that involvement of students with disabilities may be especially low in unstructured activities (Bedell et al., 2013), this raises further concern. As Brooks et al. (2015) state, "children with intellectual disability seem to be participating in relatively few of the social activities that might be most beneficial for them" (p. 685).

Several barriers are known to contribute to reduced rates of OST activity participation by students with disabilities. Identified barriers include lower family education and income and increasing age of the student (Imms, 2008; Shikako-Thomas, Majnemer, Law, & Lach, 2008). Another contributing factor is the finding that parents reported that their children had less environmental support in the community than children without disabilities, which, for some, may translate into lower rates of participation or diminished quality of participation (Bedell et al., 2013). Carter, Swedeen, Moss, and Pesko (2010) also identified lack of experience with choice making and possible "difficulty articulating their strengths, interests, preferences, and future plans" (p. 278) as potential obstacles to participation in OST activities. Opportunities to make decisions and the freedom to pursue those goals are prerequisites to self-determination. Self-determination includes actions that individuals take to control their own life and pursue self-identified goals (Blank & Martinis, 2015). There also appears to be a negative relationship between level of functioning and participation in OST (King, Petrenchick et al., 2010), and this translates into a decrease in participation for students who have more complex needs and require more extensive support. Acknowledging the critical role that the staff have in shaping quality programming, Mahoney, Levine, and Hinga (2010) also advocate for training and education for individuals who work in OST programs. The competencies of the OST staff have significant implications for the involvement of students with disabilities, and lack of sufficient training for staff serves as yet another barrier to successful engagement for these students.

## Moving Forward

We propose that students with disabilities must become a priority for OST research and related efforts to improve practice. To do so, we should begin by making better use of the existing knowledge base, including what is known about the barriers to full inclusion in OST spaces and programs as well as the rich literature on successes and concerns in the quest for inclusion in traditional educational spaces (e.g., Katz & Mirenda, 2002; Sauer & Jorgensen, 2016) and by espousing a strength-based approach to planning and support. To this end, the goals should foreground increasing the rate of participation of students with disabilities in OST activities, examining disparate levels and quality of involvement, designing effective professional development for OST practitioners, and exploring the types of activities that are the most efficacious in achieving sustainable positive outcomes.

### Increasing Rates of Participation

The discrepancy between rates of participation of students with disabilities when compared to peers without identified disability should be understood better. Some of the contributing factors to lower rates of participation for this population of students have been identified, but these barriers could be further articulated to inform efforts to increase access. Specifically, methods to increase self-determination and choice making skills are critical. These areas have an established relation to participation in OST opportunities that, in turn, relate to significant impact across the lifespan. The President's Committee for People with Intellectual Disabilities (2016) recently issued a report that stressed the importance of these skills. In this report, several areas were identified as imperative to ensuring that individuals with intellectual disabilities, a subset of those with developmental disabilities, realize full access to "follow a truly inclusive trajectory that will create opportunities to be included, to be full participants, to live independently, and to be economically self-sufficient" (p. 2). Self-determination and supported decision-making were considered essential to an engaged life.

The IEP team has a potentially potent role in determining and supporting OST opportunities and facilitating more robust participation. As evidenced by IEP review (Powers et al., 2005), few teams are prioritizing extracurricular activities in IEP design. At the very least, these discussions are not documented and guided by the IEP. The IEP team could function to identify possible environmental supports and adaptations to activities and expectations that encourage more meaningful and active participation in OST. IEP teams and other professionals who routinely provide educational services to students with special needs should also form partnerships with OST programs to make collaborative decisions about the types of training and education that would most benefit the OST staff facilitating the activities and ensuring that students with special needs are included and adequately supported.

In addition to forming partnerships to provide training and support to OST program staff, IEP teams should guarantee that students have opportunities for meaningful participation in the IEP process. Student involvement in the IEP planning and design process is a promising practice that empowers young people to self-advocate, articulate their special interests, and work with the team to identify needed supports for access—all of which serves to facilitate self-determination skills.

Future work should also aim to assess rates of participation in OST activities for students with disabilities more precisely and consistently and identify practical ways to increase participation across the full range of developmental levels. At present, methodological challenges make it difficult to draw conclusions about participation rates for students with disabilities owing to variation in the definitions of activities, degree of social inclusion, amount of participation, and types of leisure activities considered (i.e., for some studies this includes activities that are passive or solitary). Indeed, the measurement of participation itself has varied from simple enrollment via self-reports to meaningful, social inclusion (Solish, Minnes, & Kupferschmidt, 2003). In addition, some investigations have considered enjoyment and autonomy in choosing activities as a means to assess successful participation. Although there is potential value in all of these facets, assessing both actual participation and social inclusion is needed to understand and develop OST activities that foster friendships and contribute to social competence for students with disabilities.

### Facilitating Social Inclusion

We need to know more about how to ensure social inclusion rather than just physical inclusion. There is some consensus that level of functioning is a more useful determinant of participation than type of disability (King, Law, Hurley, Petrenchik, & Schwellnus, 2010). This finding should parlay into a focus on research that examines the level of support required for students with various profiles of functioning. This also shifts the conversation from deficit-based thinking (i.e. focus on disability labels and associated symptoms) to an emphasis on individual strengths and support needed to maximize authentic involvement.

There is also indication that students with disabilities show higher rates of participation in passive and solitary activities such as watching television, playing video games, and going for walks (Buttimer & Tierney, 2005; Orsmond, Krauss, & Seltzer, 2004). Additionally, previous research indicates that students with disabilities are more likely to engage in activities with family or alone than with peers (Abells, Burbidge, & Minnes, 2008; Pretty, Rapley, & Bramston, 2002). These findings support the notion that students with disabilities are not involved in the activities that are most likely to result in development of friendships with peers. It is probable that this social vacuum during childhood and adolescence contributes to the wish for more opportunities to make new friends articulated by many young adults with disabilities (Kampert & Goreczny, 2007). Professionals and researchers should examine how to alter these profiles of participation before adulthood and shift them from passive pursuits done in solitude or with a family member to active engagement in OST activities with same age peers.

### Determining Quality Indicators of Impactful Programming

Another area that warrants further investigation includes the programmatic nature of OST activities and the desired outcomes for students with disabilities. One aspect of programming is the amount of structure. The findings from the Brooks et al. (2015) study problematize unilateral application of the conclusion that structured activities are more impactful for students with disabilities and lead to more favorable outcomes. More work is needed in this area both to describe better the characteristics of the activities in which students participate and to examine the best fit between the amounts of structure in the activity context and individual differences in level of functioning. We also need to know the level of support required for students with disabilities to reap the benefits of participation in high-quality, structured OST activities that is characteristic of students without disabilities.

There are several groups that have synthesized existing research to aid in development of high-quality, inclusive programs. These groups include the National Collaborative on Workforce and Disability for Youth (NCWD/Youth) at the Institute for Educational Leadership, The PACER Center, and The Institute on Community Integration (ICI) at the University of Minnesota. Each of these organizations espouse a mission aligned with inclusion of youth with disabilities in community programming and provide guidance to professionals on evidence-based practice. The NCWD/Youth, for example, created the "Guideposts for Success" (2005; see also NCWD, n.d.). This series of documents, some of which are disability-specific, provides guidance to policymakers, youth service professionals, and youth and families on research-based practices that support successful transitions to adulthood for adolescents with disabilities. The PACER Center, dedicated to positively impacting the quality of life and extending the opportunities available to children with disabilities, is another organization at the forefront of translating research into accessible guides for families and professionals. Founded and led by parents of children with disabilities, the PACER Center offers a wide variety of programs, publications, web-based resources, webinars, videos, and public policy action information. Many of these are accessible via their website (www.pacer.org). The ICI is a University Center for Excellence in Developmental Disabilities (UCEDD) that houses numerous projects and centers that deal with disability issues across the lifespan, and we direct the reader to publications on their website (www.ici.umn.edu) for further information.

### *Professional Development*

As noted, professional development is a critical piece in meaningful and successful inclusion of youth with disabilities in OST programming. There is evidence that targeted professional development effectively improves practices that directly relate to the inclusion of youth with disabilities such as modification of program activities or environment in order to accommodate individual needs (Smith, 2011), but we also know that OST staff often do not have the type of formal educational experience that would enable them to shape high-quality programming (Mahoney et al., 2010). This is especially true when the demands of making modifications and accommodations to facilitate access for students with disabilities is beyond the purview of their work. To exacerbate this challenge, professional development opportunities incorporating topics on including students with disabilities are uncommon in OST settings and, when available, staff may not take advantage of them (Huang & Dietel, 2011).

Program evaluation is a necessary first step to designing and implementing data-driven, powerful professional development opportunities that parlay into improved outcomes for all youth, including those with disabilities. Use of established evaluation tools could prove valuable in design of targeted professional development for OST providers. These instruments, all of which represent the literature on characteristics of high-quality programs to some degree, can serve as evaluation and fodder for programmatic self-reflection to create dialogue around existing program strengths and weaknesses. These tools can then be incorporated into ongoing evaluation to gauge the effectiveness of the professional development provided.

One example of a tool that may prove helpful is the Youth Program Quality Assessment (YPQA). The YPQA was developed by the High Scope Foundation to assess best practices in OST programs (Smith & Hohmann, 2005). While this tool is not focused specifically on assessing program quality in relation to youth with disabilities, it probes program areas that are essential for successful inclusion. For example, the instrument incorporates sections on supportive environment and access. Within those sections, there are items that delve into the program's capacity to support active engagement of all participants and actively addressing barriers to participation.

In addition to integrating ongoing evaluation to positively impact professional development for OST staff, researchers and practitioners should consider existing professional development models. The Certificate in After-School Education (CASE) program is one notable example of a professional development program to inform future endeavors. CASE is a university–community partnership that was designed to provide supervised, ongoing learning opportunities for individuals working in a variety of OST settings (Mahoney et al., 2010). CASE evolved to include coursework and fieldwork for OST professionals on best practices in working with students with special needs.

### Exemplar Programs

Existing programs that embrace practices to support access and meaningful participation in OST activities provide promise for increasing participation rates and realizing the potential of students with disabilities. One example is the Partnership for Success (PFS), funded by the Georgia Council on Developmental Disabilities and implemented in 20 schools throughout the state (Vinoski, Graybill, & Roach, 2016). This OST program is fully inclusive and student-directed, provides opportunities for students with and without disabilities to engage in OST activities, and integrates self-determination instruction. Two additional examples of intentional inclusive programming in OST are the Easterseals Child Development Center Network and the Ready to Achieve Mentoring Program (RAMP). Easterseals is a national network of high-quality, inclusive centers that prioritizes supportive environments that incorporate "individualized learning plans, highly-qualified teachers, low child-adult ratios and high staff retention, and close partnerships with caregivers" (Easterseals, 2017). RAMP is a "career-focused mentoring program for at-risk youth, including those with disabilities," (RAMP, n.d., para 1.) designed to promote successful transitions to learning, employment, and independent living.

## BUILDING A FIELD WITHOUT (INTERNATIONAL) BORDERS

In recent decades, a widespread expansion of OST programming has taken place throughout the world (Mahoney, 2016). The expansion often reflects educational reforms to provide services that supplement traditional schooling. As illustrations of this expansion, Ecarius and colleagues (2013) describe the evolution of "all-day schools" in Germany and Switzerland, Dutch all-day "Brede schools," Korean school-based afterschool programs, Japanese afterschool classes and clubs, and the growth of afterschool programs in the United States.

Nonetheless, research on OST programming has tended to be ethnocentric. Most often, the research is done within one's own nation and, far less often, in other countries and cultures through the lens of one's own culture. What we do know is that OST proceeds quite differently around the world (e.g., Ecarius et al., 2013; Larson & Verma, 1999; Vest, Mahoney, & Simpkins, 2013). For a complete understanding of this field, it is essential to begin studying, appreciating, and learning from these differences. By comparing and understanding different international practices as they occur in their social, cultural, and historical contexts, researchers and practitioners may reach a broader point of view of OST that refines their existing perspective of their society's practices and policies (Bae, Mahoney, Stecher, & Sabine, 2017).

Nevertheless, there have been limited efforts to develop an international field of OST. In our experience, OST researchers or practitioners from different nations do not necessarily communicate with one another. Indeed, efforts to develop the first international volume on OST (Bae et al., 2017) suggest that OST scholars may know very little about the OST work occurring in other nations. Therefore, we devote the remainder of this chapter to outlining some of the basic challenges to, and progress made in, developing an international field to the study of OST.

There are several reasons for the international disconnect. First, aside from the very real barrier of international differences in language, OST programming does not have a set of terms and concepts that share a common meaning across cultures. This is especially true when one contrasts Anglophone and non-Anglophone nations. Even familiar sounding terms such as "all-day schools," "expanded learning time," and "extracurricular" are, to some extent, culture-specific, as are the origins, policies, and practices that support them. Thus, developing a shared knowledge of terms, theories, and methods used in OST work around the world seems a necessary first step toward cross-national understanding and collaboration. This will, in turn, allow us to define the scope of the international field of OST research and practice.

Second, we need dedicated venues for OST researchers and practitioners from around the world to connect and share their knowledge. These venues might take several forms. For example, face-to-face meetings that bring together international scholars to discuss perspectives to OST research and practice should occur regularly. For instance, in the U.S., one could envision support for such meetings over the next decade from the American Educational Research Association's Out-of-School Time Special Interest Group or the Society for Research in Child Development's preconference and special topics series. Another example would be the development of publication outlets that are specific to international issues in OST research and practice. A final example would be the use of the Internet to foster international connection through blogs, webinars, publication listings, database sharing, training videos, and so on.

Some significant international OST collaborations have emerged in recent years. For instance, in 2010 the Network on Extracurricular and Out-of-School Time Educational Research (NEO ER) was formed. The NEO ER is comprised of approximately 20 scholars from across the world conducting research on OST programming and meets annually to discuss the field. This group has begun to clarify terminology and create a shared language by situating OST research within the field of extended education (Ecarius et al., 2013). Extended education includes a broad range of structured, pedagogical learning experiences that occur outside of the traditional school day. Led by Ludwig Stecher in Gemany, NEO ER has also launched the *International Journal of Extended Education*, which publishes peer-reviewed articles focused on OST programming. Finally, members of NEO RE are currently developing the first volume devoted to international perspectives on extended education (Bae et al., 2017). This volume aims to provide a common framework that can serve to connect international work on extended education including theoretical, methodological, and empirical perspectives on OST across the world. Over the next decade, we hope to see continued growth in NEO ER participants as well as the emergence of other international OST collaborations. In particular, OST research and practice from South America, the Middle East, India, and Eastern Europe needs greater representation.

Finally, we concur with many conclusions offered by Hargreaves and Shirley (2012) concerning the value of international comparisons of policies and practices around the world in education. The field of PK–20 education has benefited from studying the practices of nations where students perform very well on international benchmarks. The goal is not to replace one nation's educational system with that of another. Rather, this process allows for the identification and incorporation of effective international strategies that make sense for any given culture and education system. For example, successful models of traditional school day education from nations such as Finland and Singapore underscore the importance of beginning with highly qualified individuals who are then supported by opportunities for lifelong professional development in an environment that both respects the education profession and emphasizes collaborative planning and innovation to encourage high quality instruction. Although a parallel effort to understand highly effective models of OST programming has not been undertaken, we note that the National AfterSchool Association (NAA) initiated the International Learning Exchange (ILE) in 2015. The ILE convenes annually in different locations around the world to compare international similarities and differences in practice and professional development for NAA members. Such efforts should be expanded over the next decade. The greatest potential for learning will occur if international models of both in-school and out-of-school education can be studied in tandem and as an interdependent system.

## CONCLUSION AND RECOMMENDATIONS

For the coming decade, we have called for a broader and more inclusive framework for the OST field that targets all young people from early childhood through emerging adulthood. This includes understanding and attending to the needs of young people undergoing developmental transitions, intentional inclusion of students with disabilities, and learning from diverse perspectives that transcend international borders. This will involve a greater integration of OST programming across time and place that is guided by evidence-based practices and policies designed to promote positive development. Reaching this goal will necessitate that funding prioritize the bridging of research and practice through the provision of ongoing professional development for the OST workforce that is anchored by a strong scientific knowledge base.

On this score, we note that a considerable financial investment has been made through social policies supporting the development of OST programs and in funding initiatives to generate scientific knowledge concerning their effectiveness (e.g., Tseng, 2012). However, the extent to which OST program practitioners have used the existing research to inform their decision making is unclear. One recent study of OST practitioners shows that a wide science-to-practice gap exists (Mahoney, 2016). Because scientific knowledge can be used to support high-quality OST program practice and promote positive youth development, the economic and social capital loss resulting from this gap is potentially enormous. To make the scientific knowledge on OST useful and used, a closer collaboration is needed between the science and practice communities in the planning, conduct, and dissemination of OST research than has characterized this field to date (e.g., Gould, 2016; Larson, Walker, Rusk, & Diaz, 2015). Therefore, we conclude with following three recommendations:

1. Collaborative efforts between OST programs, intermediaries, and school districts have emerged in recent years (e.g., American Institutes for Research, 2015; Russell, Hildreth, & Stevens, 2016). These collaborations have the potential to integrate education over time and place. However, both the processes of partnership development and outcomes resulting from these collaborative efforts require careful study. Therefore, we rec-

ommend funding to support both the development and continuous improvement of such collaborations and longitudinal research to evaluate them.

2.   Funding should be provided to support OST researcher–practitioner partnerships that emphasize collaborative training approaches, knowledge dissemination, and professional development (e.g., Mahoney, 2016). Institutions of higher education can play a vital role in this process through the provision of both preservice and inservice professional development that includes the knowledge and skills to serve students with disabilities in OST settings.

3.   Expand the knowledge base and increase innovation by developing international partnerships focused on OST research, practice, and policy. Although there may be some reluctance and uncertainty about forging such relations, we identified venues and organizations that can begin leading the way toward a global understanding OST programming. With funding to support these initiatives, our knowledge of evidence-based best practices and policies should increase and help to augment positive developmental outcome for all young people.

## REFERENCES

Abells, D., Burbidge, J., & Minnes, P. (2008). Involvement of adolescents with intellectual disabilities in social and recreational activities. *Journal on Developmental Disabilities, 14,* 88–94. Retrieved from http://oadd.org/publications/journal-on-developmental-disabilities/

Akiva, T., & Galletta Horner, C. (2016). Adolescent motivation to attend youth programs: A mixed-methods investigation. *Applied Developmental Science, 20,* 278–293. doi: 10.1080/10888691.2015.1127162

American Association on Intellectual and Developmental Disabilities. (2013). *Frequently asked questions on intellectual disability.* Retrieved from https://aaidd.org/intellectual-disability/definition/faqs-on-intellectual-disability#.WHbJpneZOi4

American Institutes for Research. (2016). *Beyond the bell: Supporting social and emotional development through quality after-school programs.* Chicago, IL: Author.

Bae, S. H., Mahoney, J. L., Maschke, S., & Stecher, L. (Eds.). (2017). *International developments in research on extended education: Perspectives on extracurricular activities, after-school programs, and all-day schools* [manuscript in preparation]. Berlin, Germany: Barbara Budrich.

Barnett, S. (2011). Effectiveness of early educational intervention. *Science, 333,* 975–978. doi:10.1126/science.1204534

Bedell, G., Coster, W., Law, M., Liljenquist, K., Kao, Y., Teplicky, R., ... Khetani, M. A. (2013). Community participation, supports, and barriers of school-age children with and without disabilities. *Archives of Physical Medicine and Rehabilitation, 94,* 315–323. doi:10.1016/j.apmr.2012.09.024

Bergman, L. R. (1998). A pattern-oriented approach to studying individual development: Snapshots and processes. In R. B. Cairns, L. R. Bergman, & J. Kagan (Eds.), *Meth-*

ods and models for studying the individual (pp. 83–121). Thousand Oaks, CA: SAGE.

Blank, P., & Martinis, J. (2015). The right to make choices: The National Resource Center for Supported Decision-Making. *Inclusion, 3*, 24–33. Retrieved from http://aaid-djournals.org/loi/incl

Bohnert, A. M., Wargo Aikins, J., & Edidin, J. (2007). The role of organized activities in facilitating social adaptation across the transition to college. *Journal of Adolescent Research, 22*, 189–208. doi:10.1352/2326-6988-3.1.24

Bohnert, A., Fredricks, J., & Randall, E. (2010). Capturing unique dimensions of youth organized activity involvement. *Review of Educational Research, 80*, 576–610. doi:10.3102/0034654310364533

Bronfenbrenner, U., & Morris, P. (2006). The bioecological model of human development. In W. Damon & R. M. Lerner (Eds.), *Handbook of child psychology: Vol 1. Theoretical models of human development* (6th ed., pp. 793–828). New York, NY: Wiley.

Brooks, B. A., Floyd, F., Robins, D. L., & Chan, W. Y. (2015). Extracurricular activities and the development of social skills in children with intellectual and specific learning disabilities. *Journal of Intellectual Disability Research, 59*, 678–687. doi:10.1111/jir.12171

Busseri, M. A., & Rose-Krasnor, L. (2010). Addressing three common issues in research on youth activities: An integrative approach for operationalizing and analyzing involvement. *Journal of Research on Adolescence, 20*, 583–615. doi:10.1111/j.1532-7795.2010.00652.x

Busseri, M. A., Rose-Krasnor, L., Adams, G. R., Polivy, J., Pancer. S. M. Pratt, M. W., ... Wintre, M. G. (2010). A longitudinal study of breadth and intensity of activity involvement and the transition to university. *Journal of Research on Adolescence, 21*, 512–518. doi:10.1111/j.1532-7795.2010.00691.x

Buttimer, J., & Tierney, E. (2005). Patterns of leisure participation among adolescents with a mild intellectual disability. *Journal of Intellectual Disabilities, 9*, 25–42. doi:10.1177%2F1744629505049728

Carter, E. W., Swedeen, B., Moss, C. K., & Pesko, M. J. (2010). "What are you doing after school?" Promoting extracurricular involvement for transition-age youth with disabilities. *Intervention in School and Clinic, 45*, 275–283. doi:10.1177/1053451209359077

Clem, O. M., & Dodge, S. B. (1933). The relation of high-school leadership and scholarship to post-school success. *Peabody Journal of Education, 10*, 321–329. doi:10.1080/01619563309535159

Coster, W., Law, M., Bedell, G., Liljenquist, K., Kao, Y.-C., Khetani, M., & Teplicky, R. (2012). School participation, supports and barriers of students with and without disabilities. *Child: Care, Health, and Development, 39*, 535–543. doi:10.1111/cch.12046

Crane, J., & Temple, V. (2015). A systematic review of dropout from organized sport among children and youth. *European Physical Education Review, 21*, 114–131. doi:10.1177/1356336X14555294

Csikszentmihalyi. M., & Schneider, B. (2000). *Becoming adult: How teenagers prepare for the world of work.* New York, NY: Basic Books.

Cummins, R. A., & Lau, L. D. (2003). Community integration or community exposure? A review and discussion in relation to people with an intellectual disability. *Journal of Applied Research in Intellectual Disabilities, 16*, 145–157. doi:10.1046/j.1468-3148.2003.00157.x

Darling, N. (2005). Participation in extracurricular activities and adolescent adjustment: Cross-sectional and longitudinal findings. *Journal of Youth and Adolescence, 34*, 493–505. doi:10.1007/s10964-005-7266-8

Denault, A. S., & Poulin, F. (2009). Intensity and breadth of participation in organized activities during the adolescent years: Multiple associations with youth outcomes. *Journal of Youth and Adolescence, 38*, 1199–1213. doi:10.1007/s10964-009-9437-5

Durlak, J. A., Weissberg, R. P., & Pachan, M. (2010). A meta-analysis of after-school programs that seek to promote personal and social skills in children and adolescents. *American Journal of Community Psychology, 45*, 294–309. doi:10.1007/s10464-010-9300-6

Early, D. M., Pianta, R. C., Taylor, L. C., & Cox, M. J. (2001). Transition practices: Findings from a national survey of kindergarten teachers. *Early Childhood Education Journal, 28*, 199–206. doi:10.1023/A:1026503520593

Easterseals (2017). *High quality child care.* Retrieved from http://www.easterseals.com/our-programs/childrens-services/high-quality-child-care.html

Ecarius, J., Klieme, E., Stecher, L., & Woods, J. (Eds.). (2013). *Extended education—an international perspective: Proceedings of the international conference on extracurricular and out-of-school time educational research.* Berlin, German: Barbara Budrich.

Eccles, J. S. (2004). Schools, academic motivation, and stage-environment fit. In R. M. Lerner & R. Steinberg (Eds.), *Handbook of adolescent psychology* (2nd ed.) (pp. 125–153). Hoboken, NJ: Wiley.

Finn-Stevenson, M. (2014). Family, school, and community partnerships: Practical strategies for afterschool programs. *New Directions for Youth Development, 144*, 89–100. doi:10.1002/yd.20115

Fredricks, J. A., & Eccles, J. S. (2006). Extracurricular involvement and adolescent adjustment: Impact of duration, numbers of activities, and breadth of participation. *Applied Developmental Science, 10*, 132–146. doi:10.1207/s1532480xads1003_3

Fredricks, J. A., & Simpkins, S. D. (2013). Organized out-of-school activities and peer relationships: Theoretical perspectives and previous research. *New Directions for Child and Adolescent Development, 140*, 1–17. doi:10.1002/cad.20034

Geiser, K. E., Rollins, S. K., Gerstein, A., & Blank, M. J. (2013). *Early childhood community school linkages: Advancing a theory of change.* Retrieved from http://www.communityschools.org/about/current_early_childhood_projects.aspx

Ghosh, D., & Datta, T. (2012). Functional improvement and social participation through sports activity for children with mental retardation: A field study from a developing nation. *Prosthetics & Orthotics International, 36*, 339–347. doi:10.1177/0309364612451206

Gilman, R. (2001). The relationship between life satisfaction, social interest, and frequency of extracurricular activities among adolescent students. *Journal of Youth and Adolescence, 20*, 749–769. doi:10.1023/A:1012285729701

Ginicola, M., Finn-Stevenson, M., & Zigler, E. (2013). The added value of the school of the 21st century when combined with a statewide preschool program. *American Journal of Orthopsychiatry, 83*, 89–93. doi:10.1111/ajop.12004

Graber, J. A., & Brooks-Gunn, J. (1996). Transitions and turning points: Navigating the passage from childhood through adolescence. *Developmental Psychology, 32,* 768–776. doi:10.1037/0012-1649.32.4.768

Greene, K. M., & Maggs, J. L. (2015). Revisiting the time trade-off hypothesis: Work, organized activities, and academics during college. *Journal of Youth and Adolescence, 44,* 1623–1637. doi:10.1007/s10964-014-0215-7

Gresham, F. M., Sugai, G., & Horner, R. H. (2001). Interpreting outcomes of social skills training for students with high-incidence disabilities. *Exceptional Children, 67,* 331–344. Retrieved from http://journals.sagepub.com/doi/pdf/10.1177/001440290106700303

Gould, D. (2016). Conducting coaching science that counts: The forgotten role of knowledge integration and dissemination. *International Coaching Science Journal, 3,* 197–203. doi:10.1123/iscj.2015-0113

Guzman, J. F., & Kingston, K. (2012). Prospective study of sport dropout: A motivational analysis as function of age and gender. *European Journal of Sport Science, 12,* 431–442. doi:10.1080/17461391.2011.573002

Halpern, R. (1999). After-school programs for low-income children: Promise and challenge. *The Future of Children, 9,* 81–95. doi:10.2307/1602708

Hargreaves, A., & Shirley, D. (2012). *The global fourth way: The quest for educational excellence.* Thousand Oaks, CA: SAGE.

Heers, M., Klaveren, C. V., Groot, W., & van den Brink, H. (2016). Community schools: What we know and what we need to know. *Review of Educational Research, 86,* 1016–1051. doi:10.3102/0034654315627365

Hirsh, B. (2016). *Job skills and minority youth: New program directions.* New York, NY: Cambridge University Press.

Huang, D., & Dietel, R. (2011). *Making afterschool programs better* (CRESST Policy Brief). Los Angeles, CA: University of California.

Hunt, J., & Eisenberg, D. (2010). Mental health problems and help-seeking behavior among college students. *Journal of Adolescent Health, 46,* 3–10. doi:10.1016/j.jadohealth.2009.08.008

Individuals with Disabilities Education Act, 20 U.S.C. § 1400 (2004). Retrieved from http://idea.ed.gov/download/statute.html

Imms, C. (2008) Review of the children's assessment of participation and enjoyment and the preferences for activity of children. *Physical and Occupational Therapy in Pediatrics, 28,* 389–404. Retrieved from https://www.ncbi.nlm.nih.gov/pubmed/19042479

Jacobson, R., Jacobson, L., & Blank, M. J. (2012). *Building blocks: An examination of the collaborative approach community schools are using to bolster early childhood development.* Washington, DC: Coalition for Community Schools, Institute for Educational Leadership. Retrieved from http://www.communityschools.org/assets/1/AssetManager/REVISED%20BB%20DOC-1-7-13.pdf

Kampert, A. L., & Goreczny, A. J. (2007). Community involvement and socialization among individuals with mental retardation. Research in Developmental Disabilities, 28, 278–286. doi:10.1016/j.ridd.2005.09.004

Katz, J., & Mirenda, P. (2002). Including students with developmental disabilities in general education classrooms: Educational benefits. International Journal of Special Education, 17, 14–24. Retrieved from http://www.internationaljournalofspecialed.com/docs/Educ._Benefits(2).doc

Kena, G., Hussar, W., McFarland, J., de Brey, C., Musu-Gillette, L., Wang, X., ... Dunlop Velez, E. (2016). *The condition of education 2016* (NCES 2016-144). Washington, DC: U.S. Department of Education, National Center for Education Statistics. Retrieved from https://nces.ed.gov/pubsearch/pubsinfo.asp?pubid=2016144

King, G., Law, M., Hurley, P., Petrenchik, T., & Schwellnus, H. (2010). A developmental comparison of the out-of-school recreation and leisure activity participation of boys and girls with and without physical disabilities. International Journal of Disability, Development and Education, 57, 77–107. doi:10.1080/10349120903537988

King, G., Petrenchick, T., DeWit, D., McDougall, J., Hurley, P., & Law, M. (2010). Out-of-school time activity participation profiles of children with physical disabilities: A cluster analysis. *Child: Care, Health, and Development, 36*(5), 726–741. doi:10.1080/J006v23n01_05

Kortering, L., & Braziel, P. (2005). Fostering student success: Five strategies you can (and should) do, starting next week. *Impact, 18*, 6–7. Retrieved from https://ici.umn.edu/products/impact/182/over3.html

Kraemer, B. R., McIntyre, L. L., & Blacher, J. (2003). Quality of life for young adults with mental retardation during transition. *Mental Retardation, 41*(4), 250–262. doi:10.1352/0047-6765(2003)41<250:QOLFYA>2.0.CO;2

Larson, R. W., & Verma, S. (1999). How children and adolescents spend time across the world: Work, play, and developmental opportunities. Psychology Bulletin, 125, 701–736. doi:10.1037/0033-2909.125.6.701

Larson, R. W., Walker, K., & Pearce, N. (2005). A comparison of youth-driven and adult-driven youth programs: Balancing inputs from youth and adults. *Journal of Community Psychology, 33*, 57–74. doi:10.1002/jcop.20035

Larson, R. W., Walker, K. C., Rusk, N., & Diaz, L. B. (2015). Understanding youth development from the practitioners' point of view. A call for research on effective practice. *Applied Developmental Science, 19*, 74–86. doi:10.1080/10888691.2014.972558

Mahoney, J. L. (2000). Participation in school extracurricular activities as a moderator in the development of antisocial patterns. *Child Development, 71*, 502–516. doi:10.1111/1467-8624.00160

Mahoney, J. L. (2016). Practitioners' use of research in decision making about organized out-of-school time programs serving adolescents. *International Journal of Research on Extended Education, 4*, 65–84. Retrieved from http://budrich-journals.de/index.php/IJREE/article/view/25780

Mahoney, J. L., & Bergman, L. R. (2002). Conceptual and methodological issues in a developmental approach to positive adaptation. *Journal of Applied Developmental Psychology, 23*, 195–217. doi:10.1016/S0193-3973(02)00104-1

Mahoney, J. L., Cairns, B. D., & Farmer, T. (2003). Promoting interpersonal competence and educational success through extracurricular activity participation. *Journal of Educational Psychology, 95*, 409–418. doi:10.1037/0022-0663.95.2.409

Mahoney, J. L., Levine, M. D., Hinga, B. (2010). The development of after-school program educators through university–community partnerships. *Applied Developmental Science, 14*, 89–105. doi:10.1080/10888691003704717

Mahoney, J. L., Lord, H., & Carryl, E. (2005a). An ecological analysis of after-school program participation and the development of academic performance and motivational attributes for disadvantaged children. *Child Development, 76*, 811–825. doi:10.1111/j.1467-8624.2005.00879.x

Mahoney, J. L., Lord, H., & Carryl, E. (2005b). Afterschool program participation and the development of child obesity and peer acceptance. *Applied Developmental Science, 9*, 202–215. doi:10.1207/s1532480xads0904_3

Mahoney, J. L., & Stattin, H. (2000). Leisure activities and adolescent antisocial behavior: The role of structure and social context. *Journal of Adolescence, 23*, 113–127. doi:10.1006/jado.2000.0302

Mahoney, J. L., Vandell, D. L., Simpkins, S. D., & Zarrett, N. R. (2009). Adolescent out-of- school activities. In R. M. Lerner & L. Steinberg (Eds.), *Handbook of adolescent psychology* (3rd ed.). Vol. 2: *Contextual influences on adolescent development* (pp. 228–267). Hoboken, NJ: Wiley & Sons.

Mahoney, J. L., & Vest, A. E. (2012). The over-scheduling hypothesis revisited: Intensity of organized activity participation during adolescence and young adult outcomes. *Journal of Research on Adolescence, 22*, 409–418. doi:10.1111/j.1532-7795.2012.00808.x

Masten, A. S., & Coatsworth, J. D. (1998). The development of competence in favorable and unfavorable environments: Lessons from research on successful children. *American Psychologist, 53*, 205–220. doi:10.1037/0003-066X.53.2.205

McLeskey, J., Waldron, N. L., & Redd, L. (2014). A case study of a highly effective, inclusive elementary school. *Journal of Special Education, 48*, 59–70. doi:10.1177/0022466912440455

Morris, D. S. (2016). Extracurricular activity participation in high school: Mechanisms linking participation to math achievement and 4-year college attendance. *American Educational Research Journal, 53*, 1376–1410. doi:10.3102/0002831216667579

National Collaborative on Workforce and Disability/Youth. (2005). *Guideposts for success*. Washington, DC: Institute on Educational Leadership. Retrieved from http://www.ncwd-youth.info/guideposts

National Collaborative on Workforce and Disability/Youth. (n.d.). Retrieved from http://www.ncwd-youth.info

Newton, S., & Horner, R. (1993). Using a social guide to improve social relationships of people with severe disabilities. *Journal of the Association for Persons with Severe Handicaps, 18*, 36–45. doi:10.1177/154079699301800106

Orsmond, G. I., Krauss, M. W., & Seltzer, M. M. (2004). Peer relationships and social and recreational activities among adolescents and adults with autism. *Journal of Autism and Developmental Disorders, 34*, 245–256. doi:10.1023/B:JADD.0000029547.96610.df

Peck, S. C., Roeser, R. W., Zarrett, N., & Eccles, J. S. (2008). Exploring the roles of extracurricular quantity and quality in the educational resilience of vulnerable adolescents: Variable- and pattern-centered approaches. *Journal of Social Issues, 64*, 135–155. doi:10.1111/j.1540-4560.2008.00552.x

Persson, A., Kerr, M., & Stattin, H. (2007). Staying in or moving away from structured activities: Explanations involving parents and peers. *Developmental Psychology, 43*, 197–207. doi:10.1037/0012-1649.43.1.197

Powers, K. M., Gil-Kashiwabara, E., Geenan, S. J., Powers, L., Balandran, J., & Palmer, C. (2005). Mandates and effective transition planning practices reflected in IEPs.

*Career Development for Exceptional Individuals, 28,* 47–59. doi:10.1177/0885 7288050280010701

Pretty, G., Rapley, M., & Bramston, P. (2002). Neighbourhood and community experience and the quality of life of rural adolescents with and without intellectual disability. *Journal of Intellectual and Developmental Disability, 27,* 106–116. doi:10.1080/13668250220135079-5

Ramey, C. T., & Ramey, S. L. (1996). Early learning and school readiness: Can early intervention make a difference? In N. F. Watt, C. Ayoub, R. H. Bradley, J. E. Puma, & W. A. LeBouef (Eds.), *The crisis in youth mental health: Critical issues and effective programs* (pp. 291–317). Westport, CT: Praeger Publishers.

Raymore, L. A., Barber, B. L., & Eccles, J. S. (2001). Leaving home, attending college, partnership and parenthood: The role of life transition events in leisure pattern stability from adolescence to young adulthood. *Journal of Youth and Adolescence, 30,* 197–223. doi:10.1023/A:1010345825065

Ready to Achieve Mentoring Program (RAMP). (n.d.). Retrieved from http://ramp.iel.org/

Reisner, E. R., White, R. N., Birmingham, J., & Welsh, M. (2001). Building quality and supporting expansion of after-school projects: Evaluation results from the TASC after-school program's second year. Washington, DC: Policy Studies Associates.

Rogoff, B. (1996). Developmental transitions in children's participation in sociocultural activities. In A. J. Sameroff & M. M. Haith (Eds.), *The five to seven shift: The age of reason and responsibility* (pp. 273–294). Chicago, IL: University of Chicago Press.

Russell, C. A., Hildreth, J. L., & Stevens, P. (2016). *ExpandED schools national demonstration: Lessons for scale and sustainability.* Washington, DC: Policy Studies Associates.

Rutter, M. (1996). Transitions and turning points in developmental psychopathology: As applied to the age span between childhood and mid-adulthood. *International Journal of Behavioral Development, 19,* 603–626. doi:10.1177/016502549601900309

Sanford, C., Newman, L., Wagner, M., Cameto, R., Knokey, A.-M., & Shaver, D. (2011). *The post-high school outcomes of young adults with disabilities up to 6 years after high school. Key findings from the National Longitudinal Transition Study-2* (NLTS2) (NCSER 2011-3004). Menlo Park, CA: SRI International. Retrieved from https://ies.ed.gov/ncser/pubs/20113004/pdf/20113004.pdf

Sauer, J. M., & Jorgensen, C. M. (2016). Still caught in the continuum: A critical analysis of least restrictive environment and its effect on placement of students with intellectual disability. *Inclusion, 4,* 56–74. doi:10.1352/2326-6988-4.2.56

Shannon, J. R. (1929). The post-school careers of high-school leaders and high-school scholars. *The School Review, 37,* 656–665. doi:10.1086/438921

Shikako-Thomas, K., Majnemer, A., Law, M., & Lach, L. (2008). Determinants of participation in leisure activities in children and youth with cerebral palsy: Systematic review. *Physical & Occupational Therapy in Pediatrics, 28,* 155–169. doi:10.1080/01942630802031834

Simmons, R. G., & Blyth, D. A. (1987). *Moving into adolescence: The impact of pubertal change and school context.* Hawthorne, NY: Aldine de Gruyter.

Sinclair, M. F., Christenson, S. L., & Thurlow, M. L. (2005). Promoting school completion of urban secondary youth with emotional or behavioral disabilities. *Exceptional Children, 71,* 465–482. Retrieved from http://eric.ed.gov/?id=EJ697215

Siperstein G., Glick, G., & Parker, R. (2009). Social inclusion of children with intellectual disabilities in a recreational setting. *Intellectual & Developmental Disabilities, 47*, 97–107. doi:10.1352/1934-9556-47.2.97

Sloper, P., Turner, S., Knussen, C. & Cunninghan, C. (1990). Social life of school children with Down's syndrome. *Child Care Health and Development, 16*, 235–251. doi:10.1111/j.1365-2214.1990.tb00658.x

Smith, C., & Hohmann, C. (2005). *Full findings from the Youth PQA validation study.* Ypsilanti, MI: High/Scope Educational Research Foundation.

Smith, K. (2011). *The need for skilled inclusion in out-of-school time programs: Kids Included Together responds.* San Diego, CA: Kids Included Together. Retrieved from http://docplayer.net/17336593-The-need-for-skilled-inclusion-in-out-of-school-time-programs-kids-included-together-responds.html

Solish, A., Minnes, P. M., & Kupferschmidt, A. (2003). Integration of children with developmental disabilities in social activities. *Journal on Developmental Disabilities, 10*, 115–121.Retrieved from: http://citeseerx.ist.psu.edu/viewdoc/download?doi=10.1.1.582.34&rep=rep1&type=pdf

Solish A., Perry, A., & Minnes, P. (2010). Participation of children with and without disabilities in social, recreational and leisure activities. *Journal of Applied Research in Intellectual Disabilities, 23*, 226–236. doi:10.1111/j.1468- 3148.2009.00525.x

Taheri, A., Perry, A., & Minnes, P. (2016). Examining the social participation of children and adolescents with intellectual disabilities and autism spectrum disorder in relation to peers. *Journal of Intellectual Disability Research, 60*, 435–443. doi:10.1111/jir.12289

Tseng, V. (2012). The uses of research in policy and practice. *Social Policy Report, 26*, 1–24. Retrieved from http://files.eric.ed.gov/fulltext/ED536954.pdf

The President's Committee for People with Intellectual Disabilities. (2016). *Report to the president: Strengthening an inclusive pathway for people with intellectual disabilities and their families.* Retrieved from http://www.acl.gov/Programs/AIDD/Program_Resource_Search/docs/PCPID-Report-2016.pdf

Vandell, D. L., Larson, R. W., Mahoney, J. L., & Watts, T. R. (2015). Children's activities. In M. H. Bornstein and T. Leventhal (Eds.), *Handbook of child psychology and developmental science (7ʰ edition). Volume 4: Ecological settings and processes in developmental systems* (pp. 305–344). New York, NY: Wiley.

Vest, A. E., Mahoney, J. L., & Simpkins, S. D. (2013). Patterns of out-of-school time use around the world: Do they help to explain international differences in mathematics and science achievement. *International Journal for Research on Extended Education, 1*, 69–83. Retrieved from http://budrich-journals.de/index.php/IJREE/article/view/19836

Vinoski, E., Graybill, E., & Roach, A. (2016). Building self-determination through inclusive extracurricular programs. *Teaching Exceptional Children, 48*, 258–265. doi:10.1177/004005991562612

Wagner, M., Cadwallader, T. W., Garza, N., & Cameto, R. (2004, March). *Social activities of youth with disabilities* (NLTS2 Data Brief No. 3). Minneapolis, MN: SRI International. Retrieved from http://www.ncset.org/publications/viewdesc.asp?id=1470

Zarrett, N., Fay, K., Li, Y., Carrano, J., Phelps, E., & Lerner, R. M. (2009). More than child's play: Variable- and pattern-centered approaches for examining effects of sports participation on youth development. *Developmental Psychology, 45,* 368–382. doi:10.1037/a0014577

Zivin, K., Eisenberg, D., Gollust, S. E., & Golberstein, E. (2009). Persistence of mental health problems and needs in a college student population. *Journal of Affective Disorders, 117,* 180–185. doi:10.1016/j.jad.2009.01.001

CHAPTER 19

# SECURING THE FUTURE

## Pivoting OST From Where and
## When to What and How

### Karen Pittman

Supplemental learning opportunities that support the development of well-round-ed children and teens have always been in abundance for those who can afford them. The quality, quantity, and variety of structured nonschool opportunities are much more limited for low-income families, particularly those who live in disad-vantaged neighborhoods. As Halpern (2002) and others have documented, these opportunities, when available, were traditionally offered by nonprofit, civic, and religious organizations with strong social missions, supplemented by public li-braries and recreation departments. Funding for these services over the decades—both public and private—has come from sources interested in safety, socializa-tion, nutrition, enrichment, and prevention.

It was the creation of a dedicated funding stream to address education achieve-ment gaps (between racial and income groups and between overall performance and governmentally set standards); however, that sparked perhaps the greatest growth and changes in the field, including galvanization of the use of the terms *out-of-school time* (OST) and *afterschool*.

*The Growing Out-of-School Time Field: Past, Present, and Future,*
pages 293–306.
Copyright © 2018 by Information Age Publishing
**293**

The original intent of the federal 21st Century Community Learning Centers Program (CCLC), established in 1994, was broad. Funding for the program, however, only grew once administration of the program was shifted from the Department of Health and Human Services to the Department of Education and outcomes and delivery systems were tied to school-day schedules and school achievement goals. This federal funding was matched by significant philanthropic funds to develop the state and local infrastructure needed to knit together the diverse set of local organizations, programs, and staff that share a common commitment to complementing, supplementing, or compensating for the academic instruction offered during the school day.

The good news is that value of creating this infrastructure has been established. Most large and mid-sized school districts *and* governments not only recognize but have responded to the need to increase, if not guarantee, the availability of afterschool programs usually targeted at students who are academically or socio-economically at risk, supplementing CCLC funds with a variety of other funding sources such as Supplemental Educational Services, the Child Care Block Grant and Nutrition, and prevention funding.

The bad news is that public funding for these services was and, to some extent, still is tethered to a commitment to expand the *when and where* of structured "educational" services, such as homework help and supplemental instruction offered before or after school and during the summer by community-based nonprofits, faith organizations, libraries, and recreation departments. Performance standards, established at the federal level, include GPRA (Government Performance and Results Act) results such as improvement in math, English/reading, homework completion, class participation, and student behavior (U.S. Department of Education, 2015). Having the prioritized list of OST outcomes so closely tethered academic outcomes has, in this author's opinion, reduced the push to further define the distinguishing characteristics of OST programs that are broadly spelled out in the federal government's definition of the characteristics of CCLC:

- Participants in 21st Century Community Learning Centers programs will demonstrate educational and social benefits and exhibit positive behavioral changes.
- 21st Century Community Learning Centers will develop afterschool activities and educational opportunities that consider the best practices identified through research findings and other data that lead to high-quality enrichment opportunities that positively affect student outcomes.

While vague, the language in the CCLC regulations that references "social benefits," "positive behavioral changes," and "high-quality enrichment opportunities" opens a door through which the OST field could harness its knowledge to bring new, practice-relevant research on the science of learning and the art of improving contexts for social-emotional learning into the mainstream of education reform (Durlak, Weisberg, & Pachan, 2010).

The terms *afterschool* and *out-of-school time* were strategically chosen to help enrichment programs, especially those focused on elementary school students, secure a place in the politics of school reform as played out in the recent past. These terms, in the author's opinion, not only hamstring the field's capacity to contribute to current reform efforts to improve schools' accountability for social and emotional learning, but they threaten the field's future relevance. As schools expand their time and place boundaries, OST programs may find it useful to reference the type of learning experiences they provide (e.g., active learning, experiential learning, community learning) or the social, emotional, civic, and career preparation outcomes they are better positioned to achieve.

To prepare for the future, the OST field should begin to deliberately shift its research and advocacy priorities from blunt (but effective) efforts to describe advantages or differences that can be associated with programs defined primarily by *where and when* they operate. There is now ample research evidence and practice muscle that the field could use to pivot to embrace sharper, cleaner criteria that describe and differentiate these programs not only based *where and when* they operate, but also on *what* skills, behaviors, and capacities they hold themselves accountable for developing, *which* groups of students they best support, *how* they create environments that support predictable growth for these populations, and *how well* they monitor and manage their performance. This chapter offers arguments for each of these proposed shifts.

## WHERE AND WHEN

### Descriptions of OST Programs Will Become Increasingly Constraining

There are at least five trends within K–12 education that explain why a defensive shift from defining the field by where and when programming is offered needs to be signaled and started within the next few years:

- The community schools movement, which combines academic, social, health, and family supports, is becoming an increasingly popular vehicle for delivering afterschool opportunities as a part of a comprehensive package of services (Coalition for Community Schools, 2014).
- The charter schools movement, whose members often commit to both an expanded school day and a more explicit set of behavioral goals, continues to grow in popularity and serves a significant minority of the student population in several major cities (Mead, Mitchel, & Rotherham, 2015).
- The expanded day movement is growing as mayors and school administrators make explicit commitments to expand the length of the school day and school year, blurring the traditional time boundary between school and out-of-school. The number of expanded day schools has almost doubled in three years, with over 2,000 schools now in existence (Farbman, 2015).

- The STEM education movement has turned a spotlight on the need to revamp learning environments to support active, project-based, inquiry-driven, mastery-focused learning. STEM funders have recognized the contribution OST providers can make to STEM learning because of their readiness and willingness to marry their general commitment to active, project-based learning to more rigorous, STEM content but remain committed to improved STEM education within the K–12 education system (American Institutes for Research, 2016).
- The SEL movement is rapidly building the capacity to advocate for K–12 policy changes not only within school systems, but at the federal and national levels. These efforts gain legitimacy from, but are not limited to the recent provisions in the Every Student Succeeds Act (ESSA) to expand the use of "nonacademic indicators" of student engagement and success (S. D. Bechtel, Jr. Foundation, 2016).

Combined, these movements push the traditional boundaries of K–12 education after 3:00 p.m. and into the summer hours while simultaneously stretching the goals of K–12 education to include nonacademic or noncognitive outcomes. Official commitments to extend the school day could potentially shift the provision of off-site or separately staffed OST programs from an advantage to an inconvenience. Official commitments to support noncognitive skill growth could potentially lessen the value-add of OST programs that promise focused attention on character, confidence, and social competencies.

OST programs have been a valuable learning lab for observing and testing the value of providing structured opportunities for learning and engagement that operate outside of the bureaucratic constraints of K–12 education, allowing them to be nimble, more child- and family-centered, choice focused, and better able to build contexts that support social and emotional development, especially for youth who don't get these supports elsewhere. These are the lasting advantages of being "nonschool." K–12 systems will and should work to expand learning time and support broader learning outcomes but will, for the foreseeable future, do so under the constraints of current accountability structures. The OST field can and should pivot to position itself as an able, nimble partner.

## DEFINITIONS OF WHAT SKILLS AND CAPACITIES
## YOUTH NEED TO BE READY ARE CONVERGING

The development of social and emotional skills, once considered secondary to the development of academic content proficiency, is now considered a necessary correlate, if not a prerequisite of academic development. SEL skills transfer across learning settings and improve skill learning in other content areas (Durlak, Domitrovich, Weissberg, & Gullotta, 2015). SEL skills, in short, are also learning skills. Both SEL interventions (adult practices aimed at teaching skills) and SEL skills (the skills young people bring in) are associated with successful learning outcomes (Smith, McGovern, Peck, Larson, & Roy, 2016).

This recognition of the centrality of social and emotional skills has been accompanied by a shift away from an à la carte approach to the teaching of specific skillsets and mindsets to a more integrated approach that posits young people as active builders of an inventory of skills they can draw on in different contexts.

Several recent studies that have taken on the task of making order of the rapidly growing body of research and reports on nonacademic outcomes by creating practical theories and frameworks that organize and prioritize the myriad lists of social and emotional skills, link them to academic skills, and explain how they relate to supportive practices (Krauss, Pittman, & Johnson, 2015; Nagaoka, Farrington, Ehrlich, & Heath, 2015; Smith, McGovern, Larson, Hillaker, & Peck, 2016). Each of these starts by backing up from the specifics to define what a ready youth looks like:

> We define a person who is ready to make a successful transition into young adulthood as having three key factors: the agency to take an active role in shaping one's path, the ability to incorporate different aspects of oneself into an integrated identity, and the competencies needed to effectively navigate a range of social contexts. (Nagaoka et al., 2015, p. 14, emphasis in original)

This reverse design approach has also been taken by economists and policy researchers who have been looking for better ways to quantify the skills linked to college and workforce readiness and success (Heckman, Kautz, Diris, Weel, & Borghans, 2014; Schanzenbach, Nunn, Bauer, Mumford, & Breitwieser, 2016). These studies have amplified calls to integrate the teaching of social, emotional, and academic skills.

The OST field prioritized nonacademic outcomes long before they were fashionable. To stay relevant in future, however, the field will need to move towards a common language and framework that reflects the research, has relevance for practitioners, and tracks well against those being used by schools and other public systems. Educators and policymakers are already moving beyond definitions to look for measures. The OST field is well suited to set the pace for this measurement development work because it has much more ability to experiment than school systems.

## THE SCIENCE OF HOW CONTEXT SHAPES THE DEVELOPMENT AND USE OF SEL SKILLS IS COMPELLING

OST programs understand the importance of context. Attendance is not mandatory. Young people and their families "vote with their feet." Statements such as "they came for the basketball but stayed for the relationships" have been included in countless funder proposals, case studies, and brochures. Rather than starting with specified content that has been parsed into curriculum segments designed to achieve academic outcomes, OST programs typically start with a focus on context.

The science behind what many youth workers would describe as a common-sense approach to creating SEL-supportive contexts are not new (Epstein, 1985), but the arguments for this approach are now being made more strongly and clearly than before (Berg, Osher, Cantor, Steyer, & Rose, 2016; Krauss et al., 2015; Nagaoka et al., 2015; Rose, 2015; Smith, McGovern, Peck, et al., 2016).

> The fundamental biological principle that biological, emotional, behavioral, and cognitive factors interact with environmental factors throughout development implies that our genetic make-up is more malleable than previously thought.... There is a critical need to understand how developmentally positive environments for children and for the adults who support them activate genetic instructions that drive [development]. Similarly, there is a need to understand how developmentally harmful environments disrupt these same developmental processes. (Berg et al., 2016, p. 2)

This basic statement kicks off a review of the new knowledge about how children develop and how and why context matters that draws from the diverse fields of neuroscience, epigenetics, adversity science, psychology, and the social sciences. The authors note, "This powerful scientific knowledge is largely under-utilized in new education models and approaches, and this deficiency is a major factor in the persistent problems of excellence and equity from cradle to career" (Berg et al., 2016, p. 1).

The counterpart to the argument that youth are active builders of their own skills is the argument that youth respond to contexts in ways that give them increased or decreased sense of agency. Smith, McGovern, Peck, et al. (2016) have assembled a theory that emphasizes youth agency as the primary purpose for building contexts that focus on social and emotional learning. They build on co-author Peck's research (2007) that distinguishes between two types of agency:

- Type 1 agency corresponds to the concept of primary appraisal. It is the more or less automatic activation of skills (often outside of the immediate focus of awareness) in response to an appraisal of whether the environment is safe, supportive, and interesting. If the environment is perceived as positive, the self-regulatory process will be more likely to activate mental processes that create engagement rather than avoidance.
- Type 2 agency corresponds to the concept of secondary appraisal often referred to as executive function or executive control. If the context is appraised as safe and supportive, youth will focus "their attention and awareness on specific aspects of (a) the context, (b) their own mental engagement within the context, (c) their own behavior in relation to the context, and (d) the wide array of meanings that accompany each of these parts of youth experience in an OST setting" (Smith, McGovern, Peck, et al., 2016, p. 13).

The most important context is the point of service, the place where youth and adults come together and where SEL practices are implemented. Context includes the physical, social, and informational features of the setting that are most proximal to participants. The opportunity for youth to have the desired skill-building experience is dependent upon the power of the context to activate prior knowledge and skills and present content-specific challenges for their use and growth. This power is in the hands of the adults who co-create context with youth by observing their engagement levels, creating opportunities to get to know them, tailoring the scaffolding of the official content (e.g. art, algebra, advocacy) to support high levels of agency among the majority of participants, and being prepared to respond, as needed, when opportunities to reward and reflect on the use of social and emotional skills arise. The relevance of these lessons to K–12 can be summed up in one phrase: personalized learning.

## RESEARCH ON WHICH YOUTH BENEFIT THE MOST FROM WHICH TYPES OF PROGRAMS IS GROWING

As noted, one of the primary reasons the partnership between OST providers and schools was forged was to try to close the achievement gaps between racial, ethnic, and income groups. The simplest arguments for the partnership on extending learning time for disadvantaged students is that these students are caught in a cycle of widening achievement gaps and widening opportunity gaps (Putnam, 2015).

There is mounting evidence, however, that *hour for hour*, out-of-school-time, extracurricular, enrichment activities may have a disproportionately positive impact on the social, emotional, and academic development of low-income, minority, and immigrant youth. Ryan Heath and colleagues (Heath, Anderson, Turner, & Payne, 2017) from the University of Chicago review research on a broad range of extracurricular programs (e.g., sports, arts, or academic enrichment) offered in both school and community settings. A few of their very specific findings are paraphrased here:

- Disadvantaged youth participate less but show equal, stronger, or different gains.
- Lower-SES youth may gain more from program participation than their higher SES peers.
- When lower-SES youth do benefit more, it is not limited to one type of outcome but appears across a range of outcomes: educational, psychological, social, and behavioral.
- White youth who participate often report greater academic outcomes, while youth of color report greater psychosocial or noncognitive outcomes.
- Youth of color report greater academic achievement and psychological adjustment with increased dosages.

- Youth of color may have academic gains from high-dosage participation in school-based versus community-based programs.
- Latino immigrant youth who participate report higher social and academic skills.
- There are benefits for students doing things that are not typical for their identity or status (e.g., White students learning African dance, Black students golfing). Both boys and girls may benefit from nonsports and gender atypical activities.

The authors are careful to cluster their reviews by demographic group (gender, race/ethnicity, low SES) and by program type (sports, nonsports, with further specifications of each). Two common threads link their findings about different gains for different groups: context and agency. Not all youth experience a program in the same way because of the skills and prior experiences they bring with them (Type 1 agency). Youth who are able to engage with the program, however, coregulate their experience with the adults in the program to focus their attention on challenges that resonate with them. Skill growth, therefore, occurs in different outcome areas for different youth.

Smith, McGovern, Larson, et al. (2016) press the need to adjust contexts to youths' sense of agency and presenting capacities for self-regulation further.

> Young people who have been exposed to traumatic or chronically-stressful experiences may require more intensive supports for successful skill-building in either the more passive or active senses of agency... These concerns with regulation skills, and the corresponding experiences of agency that result, are particularly germane to OST contexts that are intentionally designed to help youth feel safe and interested so that attention can focus on the task at hand, motivation can emerge around task success, and skill learning and mastery can occur through repeated practice. (Smith, McGovern, Larson, et al., 2016, pp. 13–14)

There is clearly a push for schools to integrate academic, social, and emotional skill building into general instruction. Schools, however, are likely to never have the flexibility to adjust context that OST programs have, especially at the price points at which even high-quality OST programs currently operate. The importance of investing in integrated strategies to support social, emotional, and cognitive skill development (including but not limited to academic subjects) will only become clearer moving forward. The OST field should begin now to ensure that all branches have the capacity and commitment to disaggregate student data, tracking social, emotional, and cognitive growth so that they can begin to document the cost-effectiveness of these investments.

## PRACTICAL MEASUREMENT OF HOW WELL PRACTITIONERS ARE CREATING CONTEXTS THAT INCREASE AGENCY IS WELL WITHIN OUR REACH

Developmentally supportive settings start with an emphasis on creating safe, welcoming, relationship-rich environments in which children and youth have some choice over the learning activities and teams they participate in. Settings that demonstrate growth in participants' social, emotional, and academic skills, however, push beyond safety and structure to emphasize skill building, challenge, and task engagement (Durlak & Weissberg, 2010; Eccles & Gootman, 2002; Smith, 2013).

This more robust definition of program quality is reflected in the Program Quality Pyramid (Figure 19.1) developed by the Weikart Center for Youth Program Quality. The YPQA quality standards are similar to those used in other OST quality assessment tools (Yohalem, Wilson-Ahlstrom, Fischer, & Shinn, 2009) and consistent with those identified by the Eccles and Gootman (2002). The YPQ intervention includes quality standards, observational assessments, and improve-

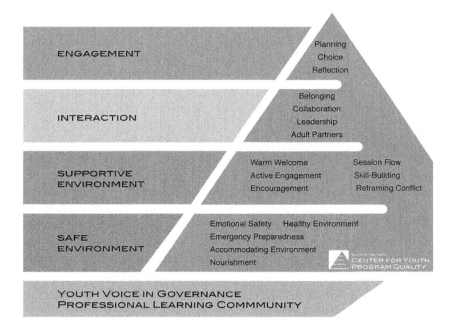

FIGURE 19.1.   Youth program quality assessment pyramid
*Note:* Adopted from Smith, C., Akiva, T., Sugar, S., Lo, Y. J., Frank, K. A., Peck, S. C., Cortina, K. S., & Devaney, T. (2012). *Continuous quality improvement in after-school settings: Impact findings from the Youth Program Quality Intervention study.* Retrieved from http://www.cypq.org/sites/cypq.org/files/publications/YPQI%20 Study%20Executive%20Summary.pdf

ment modules built around the pyramid and was specifically designed to be content-neutral. As of 2015, the intervention is currently used by 115 state and local afterschool intermediaries that support over 4,200 program sites and over 27,000 staff that vary widely in content focus (from sports to arts to pregnancy prevention) but share a common philosophy (positive youth development).

These kinds of scale-up numbers are important. They demonstrate the existence of a sizeable appetite among OST staff, directors, and programs who want to speak the same context language, use the same context assessment tools, and collect and review performance data that (a) transcends the variation in their explicit programmatic foci (the what) and (b) is independent of the time and location of their operations (the where and the when). This capacity, while impressive, does not fully position the OST field for the future.

Multiple research studies have confirmed that OST quality matters. The decade of continuous improvement supports interventions the Weikart center has managed with OST partners across the country (moving the needle) has confirmed that, when this research can be translated into replicable improvement interventions that demonstrate that quality is *measurable* in ways that have meaning for practitioners, *malleable* in degrees that encourage practitioners to lean into rather than resist coaching and training, and *marketable* to OST systems that are strapped for cash but committed to improvement.

To be credible standard bearers of what OST systems and researchers have learned about the art and science of designing contexts that accelerate youths' readiness into discussions with leaders outside of OST (including but not limited to those in K–12 education), the OST field has to demonstrate that the specific suite of practices common to very high-quality OST programs are measurable, malleable, and marketable to some of the new types of formal learning settings that blur the "where/when" lines that have traditionally demarked school and OST.

The SEL Challenge, a partnership among the Susan Crown Exchange, which created a learning group comprised of staff teams from eight exemplary OST programs, staff from the Weikart Center for Youth Program Quality, and technical consultants, was designed to achieve two ambitious goals: to identify promising practices for building SEL skills with vulnerable adolescents, and to develop technical supports to scale these practices in OST settings (Smith, McGovern, Larson, et al., 2016). The Challenge's contribution is in its granularity. The research focuses on creating proximal descriptions and measures of youth SEL skills that are demonstrated and observed in the OST context and of the specific staff practices and curriculum features that help structure the context for skill learning. The research demonstrated all four Ms described above. The measures were valid and feasible to use. The practices matter—skill growth was observed in all of the six broad skill domains, and growth happened at an equal or greater rate among youth who started the programs with low SEL skills. The measures and the intervention process are marketable, even to high-quality programs. And the contexts are malleable. Program staff identified areas for improvement and made changes based on the assessments and the data.

The key to getting program staff, managers, and system leaders to buy into this type of continuous improvement intervention is trust. Staff have to trust the standards and assessments—they have to be relevant to their work. Resources (coaching, information, training, release time) have to sufficient enough that staff believe they will have the support they need to improve. Stakes have to be set correctly: low enough that all actors are willing to engage, but high enough that staff are challenged to improve. The voluntary adoption of quality improvement interventions such as those offered by the Weikart Center for Youth Program quality is evidence that striking this balance is possible (Smith, 2013). Public and private funders can promote the adoption of continuous improvement interventions by (a) funding the development of intermediary organizations that support service improvement but do not provide services and (b) giving these entities time to build trust and demonstrate value and create a culture that emphasizes the internal benefits of standards and assessments before introducing external carrots and sticks.

The OST field has demonstrated that it is possible to produce these conditions for success in dozens of local and state systems with strong results. Helping education leaders translate these lessons into the high-stakes school environment is a task we should prepare for and a service we should offer when we are ready. We have rigorous proof that quality learning environments have the same characteristics in school and out (Durlak, Weissberg, Dymnicki, Taylor, & Schellinger, 2011; Durlak et al., 2010). We have, but have not adequately packaged and shared, consistently reported *performance data* from a critical mass of local and state networks that used quality improvement strategies. We need better community *positioning*—ways to consistently communicate intended outputs and outcomes with educators and other key stakeholders.

## CONCLUSION

The vision of the future of OST painted in this chapter, starting with a proposed name change for the field, may generate considerable resistance. Practitioners and advocates who have grown comfortable with where/when funding criteria may not want to relinquish this lower threshold definition if it remains associated with dedicated funding. Researchers who have used where/when definitions as a rough proxy for program philosophy, program services, and/or program practices may have to adopt tougher (and more labor-intensive) selection criteria.

In the near future, all of these groups may have to adjust to the fact that the when and what attributes formerly associated with OST field by default may be not only owned but advertised by schools that embrace an expanded, extended vision of learning. As this future becomes a reality, the OST field, broadly defined, has two options: (a) stay the course and become a dependable "second shift" delivery system, or (b) pivot to become a desirable "first shift" applied research system that uses its experience and flexibility to accelerate change in larger public systems. The first does not require the second. The second, however, enhances the first.

## REFERENCES

American Institutes for Research. (2016). STEM 2026: A Vision for Innovation in STEM Education. Retrieved from http://www.air.org/system/files/downloads/report/STEM-2026-Vision-for-Innovation-September-2016.pdf

Berg, J., Osher, D., Cantor, P., Steyer, L., & Rose, T. (2016). *Science of learning and development* (Unpublished). Washington, DC: American Institutes for Research & Education Counsel.

Coalition for Community Schools. (2014). *The growth and impact of community schools: 2014.* Washington, DC: Institute for Educational Leadership. Retrieved from http://www.communityschools.org/assets/1/AssetManager/Top%20Ten%20List%202014.pdf

Durlak, J. A., Domitrovich, C. E., Weissberg, R. P., & Gullotta, T. P. (2015). *Handbook of social and emotional learning: Research and practice.* New York, NY: Guilford Press.

Durlak, J. A., & Weissberg, R. P. (2010). Afterschool programs that follow evidence-based practices to promote social and emotional development are effective. In T. K. Peterson (Ed.), *Expanding minds and opportunities: The power of afterschool and summer learning for student success* (pp. 194–198). Washington, DC: Collaborative Communications Group, Inc.

Durlak, J. A., Weissberg, R. P., Dymnicki, A. B., Taylor, R. D., & Schellinger, K. B. (2011). The impact of enhancing students' social and emotional learning: A meta-analysis of school-based universal interventions. *Child Development, 82,* 405–432.

Durlak, J. A., Weisberg, R. P., & Pachan, M. (2010). A meta-analysis of after-school programs that seek to promote personal and social skills in children and adolescents. *American Journal of Community Psychology, 45,* 294–309.

Eccles, J., & Gootman, J. A. (2002). *Community programs to promote youth development.* Washington, DC: The National Academies Press, Institute of Medicine and National Research Council. doi:10.17226/10022

Epstein, S. (1985). The implications of cognitive-experiential self-theory for research in social psychology and personality. *Journal for the Theory of Social Behavior, 15*(3), 283–310.

Farbman, D. (2015). *Learning time in America: Trends to reform the American school calendar.* Boston, MA: National Council on Time and Learning. Retrieved from http//www.timeandlearning.org/publications/lta

Halpern, R. (2002). A different kind of child development institution: The history of after-school programs for low-income children. *Teachers College Record, 11,* 178–211.

Heath, R. D., Anderson, C. Turner, A. C., & Payne, C. M. (2016). *Extracurricular activities and disadvantaged youth: A complicated—but promising—story* (Unpublished). Chicago, IL: University of Chicago School of Social Service Administration.

Heckman, J. J., Kautz, T., Diris, R., Weel, B., & Borghans, L. (2014). *Fostering and measuring skills: Improving cognitive and non-cognitive skills to promote lifetime success.* Paris, France: OECD. Retrieved from https://www.oecd.org/edu/ceri/Fostering-and-Measuring-Skills-Improving-Cognitive-and-Non-Cognitive-Skills-to-Promote-Lifetime-Success.pdf

Krauss, S. M., Pittman, K. J., & Johnson, C. (2016). *Ready by design: The science (and art) of youth readiness.* Washington, DC: The Forum for Youth Investment. Retrieved from http://sparkaction.org/sites/sparkaction.org/files/readybydesign.pdf

Mead, S., Mitchel, A. L., & Rotherham, A. J. (2015). *The state of the charter school movement.* Washington, DC: Bellwether Education Partners. Retrieved from http://bellwethereducation.org/sites/default/files/Charter%20Research%200908%20FINAL.pdf

Nagaoka, J., Farrington, C. A., Ehrlich, S. B., & Heath, R. D. (2015). *Foundations for young adult success: A developmental framework.* Chicago, IL: University of Chicago Consortium on School Research. Retrieved from https://consortium.uchicago.edu/sites/default/files/publications/Wallace%20Report.pdf

Peck, S. C. (2007). Tempest in gallimaufry: Applying multilevel systems theory to person-in-context research. *Journal of Personality, 75*(6), 1127–1156.

Putnam, R. (2015). *Our kids: The American dream in crisis.* New York, NY: Simon & Schuster.

Rose, T. (2015). *The end of average: How we succeed in a word that values sameness.* New York, NY: HarperOne.

S. D. Bechtel, Jr. Foundation. (2016). *Character initiative snapshot.* Retrieved from http://sdbjrfoundation.org/wp-content/uploads/2016/06/Bechtel-EDU-Character_2016Jun27.pdf

Schanzenbach, D. W., Nunn, R., Bauer, L., Mumford, M., & Breitwieser, A. (2016). *Seven facts on noncognitive skills from education to the labor market.* Washington, DC: The Hamilton Project. Retrieved from http://www.hamiltonproject.org/assets/files/seven_facts_noncognitive_skills_education_labor_market.pdf

Smith, C. (2013). *Moving the needle on "moving the needle": Next stage technical guidance for performance based accountability systems in the expanded learning field with a focus on performance levels for the quality of instructional services.* Ypsilanti, MI: David P. Weikart Center for Youth Program Quality. Retrieved from http://cypq.org/content/moving-needle-moving-needle/

Smith, C., Akiva, T., Sugar, S., Lo, Y. J., Frank, K. A., Peck, S. C., Cortina, K. S., & Devaney, T. (2012). *Continuous quality improvement in afterschool settings: Impact findings from the Youth Program Quality Intervention study.* Ypsilanti, MI: David P. Weikart Center for Youth Program Quality. Retrieved from http://www.cypq.org/sites/cypq.org/files/publications/YPQI%20Study%20Executive%20Summary.pdf

Smith, C., McGovern, G., Larson, R., Hillaker, B., & Peck, S. (2016). *Preparing youth to thrive: Promising practices for social & emotional learning.* Washington, DC: The Forum for Youth Investment. Retrieved from https://www.selpractices.org/resources

Smith, C., McGovern, G., Peck, S. C., Larson, R., & Roy, L. (2016). *Preparing youth to thrive: Methodology and findings from the social and emotional learning challenge.* Ypsilanti, MI: David P. Weikart Center for Youth Program Quality. Retrieved from https://www.selpractices.org/resources

U.S. Department of Education. (2015). *21ˢᵗ Century Community Learning Centers (21ˢᵗ CCLC) analytic support for evaluation and program monitoring: An overview of the 21ˢᵗ CCLC performance data: 2013-14* (10ᵗʰ Report). Retrieved from http://www2.ed.gov/programs/21stcclc/performance.html

Yohalem, N., Wilson-Ahlstrom, A., Fischer, S., & Shinn, M. (2009). *Measuring youth program quality: A guide to assessment tools* (2nd ed.). Washington, DC: The Forum for Youth Investment. Retrieved from http://forumfyi.org/files/MeasuringYouthProgramQuality_2ndEd.pdf

# CONCLUSION

# CHAPTER 20

# CONCLUSION

## Tara Donahue

The Current Issues in Out-of-School Time book series is designed to emphasize the most pressing questions relevant to the OST field today, intentionally bridging research and practice. The chapters in this volume take stock of our field, while offering emerging theories, promising practices, and systems thinking needed to chart the future. What follows is a summary of key considerations for the field as expressed in this anthology.

### LESSONS LEARNED AND QUESTIONS TO BE ADDRESSED

A common theme across the chapters is the unique position of OST as vital links for youth, school, family, and community contexts and environments. OST programs may take place in a variety of places—schools, faith-based organizations, community organizations, museums—and represent "anywhere, anytime learning" (Lopez & Caspe, 2014). OST may build or expand upon what youth experience during the school day by providing additional learning opportunities or giving youth access to opportunities that do not exist during within their schooling experiences.

Family members become involved in that learning process by encouraging their children, and when the opportunity presents itself, participating with their children and youth. By their nature, OST programs typically encourage family

*The Growing Out-of-School Time Field: Past, Present, and Future,*
pages 309–314.
Copyright © 2018 by Information Age Publishing
All rights of reproduction in any form reserved.

involvement by providing family programming or offering services specifically to adults (e.g., computer or financial literacy classes). However, OST stands to benefit by expanding beyond involvement and moving toward family engagement, whereby families have voice, choice, and shared responsibility in OST programs supporting their children. There is limited research on the impact of family engagement in OST settings. This is an area that the OST community can continue to promote and study.

OST programs are critical in providing links for youth, school, family, and community; however, more intentional and strategic efforts need to be made to promote connections and to share strategies of the impact that these linkages have on youth, both academically and socially. Programs that have successfully integrated linkages with youth's schools, families, and/or the community need to share their stories on how they have been able to create these linkages. Programs should also be able to articulate how they know these relationships are effective. What are their measures of success? How do they know that these measures are reliably assessing measures of success? Developing research–practice partnerships (RPPs) (see Chapter 13) can help programs determine how to address these questions and others as RPPs allow researchers to test the "why" and "how" these practices work, which builds the field's knowledge and capacity to develop ways to establish linkages and test their effectiveness.

Although there are countless ways in which OST programs can form linkages to the community, one example is through linking OST with workforce development, especially for older youth, as a critical postsecondary pathway. For example, youth may participate in credentialing or apprenticeship programs. After School Matters, based in Chicago, is one such program that provides adolescents with an opportunity to participate in apprenticeships, assistantships, or internships (see www.afterschoolmatters.org for more information). An impact study of the program showed that participants had more positive outcomes on measures such as attendance, course failures, and graduation rates (Goerge, Cusick, Wasserman, & Gladden, 2007). Beyond work experience, OST programs can provide opportunities for connections between OST programs and local technical schools, community colleges, or four-year universities. Giving students the opportunity to become involved in work and experiences at institutions of higher education could help them develop interests and realize their passions. OST programs could serve as a vehicle for transitions—to help prepare students for their postsecondary paths.

Furthermore, as noted throughout the volume, OST programs need to increase their efforts to ensure access and equity for all children and youth. This means that programs need to be offered in all geographic areas, including urban and rural, as well as in high- and low-socioeconomic neighborhoods. Programs also need to be equitable to all youth. By focusing programming on areas that meet the academic and social-emotional needs of all youth—regardless of their race/ethnicity, gender, identity, or sexual orientation, disability, language, socioeconomic status, and other demographic variables—OST programs have the opportunity to be considered safe environments by all youth who want to participate (see Dawes, Chapter 4). This is especially important for underserved youth.

Understanding the shifting demographics and the challenges that a more culturally diverse society continues to face is critical for the success of all youth. The OST field has an opportunity to promote conditions that allow the OST programs to meet the needs of increasingly diverse young people by providing programming that provides children and youth with a sense of voice, agency, engagement, and developmentally appropriate and learning-oriented exploration. As the authors suggest, recruiting and hiring staff who reflect these cultural aspects may be one way for programs to support and promote diversity while providing youth a place that gives them a sense of belonging.

When young people feel welcome in a place, they are more likely to engage with staff and with the offered activities. For example, children and youth who develop relationships with OST staff and believe that the OST program offers them a safe environment in which to participate, particularly individuals who may not have a sense of belonging at school or in other places in their life may be more inspired to work harder for increased academic achievement or develop an interest that will spur their future academic or career development. However, we need to learn more about engagement: What activities interest special populations? What will bring them to the programs? What will retain them in the programs? And, as Simpkins, Liu, and Dawes posed in the first chapter, "How do we create activities that are responsive to youth?"

The Scales Chapter 3 provides one answer to this question by proposing the RISE (relationships, interests and sparks, empowerment) method of youth development. This chapter emphasizes that young people involved in OST programming have opportunities for positive experiences as well as opportunities to discover their passions can guide their future career paths and interests. Yet work remains to be done on how both programs and activities can continue to help children and youth build and apply these opportunities to authentic life experiences, particularly as they become older and start focusing on potential careers and postsecondary experiences.

Quality OST programs are not possible without quality staff, as emphasized in Section 3. The challenges of staffing OST programs were highlighted in the Starr and Gannett chapter (Chapter 7) and include issues such as fragmentation of the workforce, low compensation, high turnover rates, stress, and a lack of professionalization in the field. Often, these challenges exist because OST staff members see this work as a stepping stone to other career pathways, such as teaching. Efforts to professionalize the OST field have been underway and include strategies such as providing quality professional development.

One way the OST field is coming together is through the development of core competencies. For example, the National AfterSchool Association (NAA) has created the Core Knowledge and Competencies (CKCs) for Afterschool and Youth

Development Professionals (see Warner, Ham, and Pearman Fenton, Chapter 8) to provide consistency across all OST professionals. Uniting the field through shared competencies sets a standard for quality OST programming. Although it takes time to be disseminated and implemented across the entire field, developing such system-wide approaches is the leverage needed to continue to increase OST quality. Similarly, quality standards have evolved across states to influence state policy, practice, and research (see Singer, Newman, and Moroney, Chapter 14). Understanding the influence of these system-level standards is an area that still needs to be researched to address questions such as how does system-level approaches impact quality at the state level? How do those standards drill down to the local level? What types of changes have programs made to meet the quality standards? Answering these questions could change the way that OST professionals regard standards and system-wide approaches.

A call also has been made to increase the availability and quality of professional development for all working with children and youth in OST programs. Nancy Peter (2007) argues that professional development can benefit all OST staff, including "volunteers, teenagers, parents, or other non-staff members, provided that the [professional development] experience transfers to and culminates in supporting OST youth participants" (p. 1). By providing professional development and training to *everyone* involved in OST, consistency can be provided within and across programs.

Another approach raised for OST professional development is inquiry-based professional development (see Hill, Connolly, Akiva, and McNamara, Chapter 9). Highlighting the National After School Matters Practitioner Fellowship model, the authors discuss how inquiry-based professional development can build the capacity of OST professionals. Beyond inquiry-based professional development, challenges with providing professional development within OST programs include a lack of sufficient resources. Often, programs have limited funds for quality professional development or staff members are unable to participate because they may only work part-time or may not be available to complete a comprehensive professional development program due to limited working hours or other obligations. OST leaders need to understand the professional needs of their staff and work to provide them with professional development opportunities that will meet those needs. By sharing different models of professional development that OST programs have implemented, the field can come together to discuss what approaches have the most impact on staff (and consequently youth) and how to solve potential challenges, such as financial issues.

Similarly, comprehensive leadership training was raised in this volume as a potential way to increase capacity of OST staff (see Fowlkes & McWhorter, Chapter 10). OST staff serve as role models and mentors and have a responsibility to provide guidance for youth. To do this effectively, OST staff need to fully understand what it takes to be a successful leader of a program and how to lead other OST staff members to be able to work with youth, provide positive youth development services, and engage youth through programmatic activities. When leaders understand the all aspects of the field, they can ensure that their staff are receiving the training they need and working effectively with the youth they serve. The goal is to ensure that all OST leaders can effectively lead and encourage their staff to deliver services that meet the highest standards in the field.

This anthology has not only reflected to where the field is at present, but has also proposed new directions in research and practice. There is a need to continue to develop, implement, and apply data collection systems, including agile instruments and evaluation tools (see Noam, Allen, Mathur Shah, and Triggs, Chapter 12). The field also needs to increase the use and usefulness of the tools and systems that are already available. By developing a system-wide data collection approach, the programs will have a much more comprehensive set of data points to examine. By sharing these results in a user-friendly way, the entire field will be able to glean insights into what works and what does not work. When OST professionals come together to have these discussions, the knowledge they share and the collaborations they form can continue to move the OST field further ahead.

Over the past 20 years, the field has come a long way in understanding what constitutes program quality, how to measure program quality, and how to measure outcomes (see Russell, Chapter 10), but many studies have shown minimal impact. We know that OST positively impacts young people; however, we need to demonstrate how they have been impacted across multiple dimensions.

The final section of this volume presents several ideas on future directions for OST programming. With a focus on 21$^{st}$-century skills, Devaney and Mahoney (Chapter 17) discuss how these skills can be integrated with social-emotional learning (SEL) needs. This builds upon the positive youth development work that the OST field has focused on but relates it to the growing field of SEL. This is an appropriate avenue for OST because programs could provide enrichment activities and programs that can help youth increase their SEL. Integrating 21$^{st}$-century skills into this approach also helps the youth gain skills for future career development and prepare them for citizenship.

The final two chapters push the field even further. Mahoney and Haley-Mize, (Chapter 18) as one of their three core recommendations, argue for expansion of OST inquiry to global perspectives: What is working in other nations? What have they tried that we have not tried? Having these conversations with those outside of the United States can also create and foster relationships that will greatly benefit OST leaders, staff, and the students they serve.

The final chapter offers a provocative charge for OST field. Pittman (Chapter 19) asks the field to move beyond the "where and when" to the "how and why." With the rise of, for example, community schools, the time has come to create new areas of focus—system-wide competency and quality standards, ensuring access and equity for all young people, high-quality programming, positive youth development strategies, system-wide data collection measures and strategies, rigorous research and evaluation, and effective professional development—to ensure that the future of OST continues on the path of a highly regarded field that impacts youth, families, and communities in positive ways.

## FUTURE VOLUMES IN THE CURRENT ISSUES IN OUT-OF-SCHOOL TIME SERIES

The field of OST has come a long way in a relatively short time. The authors in this book pose questions that move the field forward. The Current Issues in Out-of-School Time series is designed to facilitate the conversation between OST researchers and practitioners and to begin a discourse on how best to integrate research, practice, and policy. Focused on research, the goal of the series is to encourage discussion about how research can better support practice and how both research and practice can inform policy.

This inaugural volume only touches upon the diverse and vast work OST researchers and practitioners have completed over the past two decades. We encourage practitioners and researchers to bring to this book series their own lessons and experiences. By better integrating research and practice, the OST field will continue to grow and prepare all children and youth for successful futures as they become global citizens.

## REFERENCES

Goerge, R., Cusick, G. R., Wasserman, M., & Gladden, R. M. (2007). After-school programs and academic impact: A study of Chicago's After School Matters. Chapin Hall Center for Children at the University of Chicago. Retrieved from www.chapinhall.org/sites/default/files/publications/ChapinHallDocument(2)_0.pdf

Lopez, M. E., & Caspe, M. (2014, June). Family engagement in anywhere, anytime learning. *Harvard Family Research Project*. Retrieved from http://www.hfrp.org/var/storage/fckeditor/File/Family%20Engagement%20in%20Anywhere%20Anytime%20Learning_HarvardFamilyresProj.pdf

Peter, N. (2007). *Promising practices in out-of-school time professional development.* Philadelphia, PA: Out-of-School Time Resource Center. Retrieved from http://repository.upenn.edu/cgi/viewcontent.cgi?article=1098&context-spp_papers

# BIOGRAPHIES

## EDITORS

**Helen Jane Malone**, EdD, is director of education policy and institutional advancement and is national director of the Education Policy Fellowship Program at the Institute for Educational Leadership. She is also an adjunct professorial lecturer at the American University. She is the editor-in-chief of the Current Issues in Out-of-School Time book series (Information Age Publishing), serves on the editorial board of a peer-reviewed *Journal of Expanded Learning Opportunities*, is the chair of the American Educational Research Association (AERA) Educational Change Special Interest Group (and a former chair of the Out-of-School Time SIG), and a board member of the International Congress for School Effectiveness and Improvement. She is a peer reviewer for academic journals focused on educational change, youth development, and school–community partnerships. Her most recent books include: Future Directions of Educational Change (co-editor, Routledge, 2018), "Empowering Teachers: The Role of School-Community Partnerships" (co-authored chapter in *Flip the System: Changing Education from the Ground Up*, 2015), and *Leading Educational Change: Global Issues, Challenges, and Lessons on Whole-System Reform* (Teachers College Press, 2013; available

*The Growing Out-of-School Time Field: Past, Present, and Future,*
pages 317–329.

in Spanish through Fondo de Cultura Económica). She holds EdD in education policy, leadership, and instructional practice from Harvard University.

**Tara Donahue**, PhD, is a managing evaluator at McREL International. She received her doctorate in educational policy from Michigan State University, where she wrote her dissertation about connections between afterschool programs and the school day. She then spent the next five years providing research, evaluation, professional development, and technical assistance services to out-of-school time programs at the national, state, and local level. At McREL, she works on a variety of projects including college and career readiness; community college policy; science, technology, engineering, and mathematics; teacher preparation, specifically in relation to English learners; and policies impacting state education agencies.

## CONTRIBUTING AUTHORS

**Thomas Akiva**, PhD, is an assistant professor in the Department of Psychology in education at the University of Pittsburgh. He received his PhD in education and psychology at the University of Michigan. Prior to this, Akiva spent nearly two decades working as a practitioner and consultant in the youth development field, with most of that time at the Weikart Center for Youth Program Quality. His research focuses on understanding and improving OST programs for children and youth. Current research projects include ongoing examination of the Simple Interactions (www.simpleinteractions.org) professional development approach and studies of youth employment, youth activism, and educational maker spaces. He is the winner of the 2016 Out-of-School Time Scholar Award from the American Educational Research Association.

**Patricia J. Allen**, PhD, is the research manager at The PEAR Institute: Partnerships in Education and Resilience and an instructor in psychiatry at Harvard Medical School. She was awarded a PhD in experimental psychology from Tufts University in 2013 after gaining expertise in psychology and behavioral neuroscience research. Today, she manages the implementation and development of The PEAR's quantitative assessments that measure student outcomes in science, technology, engineering and math (STEM; using the Common Instrument Suite) and socioemotional learning (using the Holistic Student Assessment). She is currently leading two national evaluation efforts to collect evidence of STEM learning to help ensure that children across the country have positive, high-quality experiences when they participate in informal/out-of-school time STEM activities.

**Ken Anthony**, EdD, is director of professional development and research, Connecticut After School Network. For over 20 years, Anthony has worked as a front-line staff, site supervisor, program director, district coordinator, and currently at the Network for the past 9 years. His roles include overseeing training, professional and leadership development, program consultation, quality advising, and research. His areas of expertise include school–community partnerships and leadership development. Recent publications include articles in the spring 2016 issue of the Journal of Expanded Learning Opportunities (Filling in the Gaps) and Fall 2016 Afterschool Matters Journal (Creating Holistic Partnerships Between School and Afterschool). He holds a bachelor's degree in psychology from Southern Connecticut State University; a master's degree in human services from Springfield College; and a doctorate in educational leadership from the University of Hartford in 2015. He was also part of the inaugural class of White-Riley-Peterson Policy Fellows at Furman University.

**Dale A. Blyth,** PhD, is a strategic consultant and professor emeritus and former endowed chair in the College of Education and Human Development at the University of Minnesota, where he remains a senior research fellow with the Center for Applied Research and Educational Improvement. He led efforts to bridge research and practice in out-of-school time as associate dean and director of the university's Center for Youth Development. Prior to this, he directed research and evaluation at Search Institute, co-created the department of adolescent health at the AMA, served on the faculty at Cornell and Ohio State universities, and was a research fellow at the Boys Town Center for Youth Development. He has published extensively with over 40 book chapters and peer-reviewed article as well as editing multiple special issues. He helped found the Society for Research on Adolescence and has started four journals and served on many editorial boards.

**Keshara Cochrane** was born and raised in Baltimore, MD. She is a recent graduate from the University of Maryland, Baltimore County (UMBC) with a Bachelor of Arts degree in sociology and is currently pursuing a Bachelor of Science in nursing. During the summer of 2016, Cochrane served as a servant leader intern for the Children's Defense Fund (CDF) Freedom Schools. She spent the summer teaching rising 4th graders at Lakeland Elementary/Middle School in South Baltimore. Although committed to a career in nursing, Cochrane's experience with CDF Freedom Schools has influenced her to dedicate a portion of her life to educating African American children and youth.

**Joy Connolly** is director of education program services at Child Care Council of Nassau, Inc. She holds an MA in educational policy studies from University of Wisconsin-Madison. Her research interests include critical policy analysis; OST and early learning programs; and equity, diversity, and inclusion. Connolly holds an MPA from New York University in public policy/non-profit management, and earned her BA from Wesleyan University. She has been an adjunct lecturer for the teacher education department at York College, City University of New York. In 2016, she co-authored "Democratizing Urban Spaces: A Social Justice Approach to Youth Work" in an edited volume: *Youth and Inequality in Education: Global*

*Actions in Youth Work* (Routledge). She served as co-chair for the NYS Early Care and Learning Council 2016 Leadership Summit. Prior to her graduate studies, Connolly ran an arts and literacy afterschool program in three elementary schools and one middle school in Brooklyn, NY.

**Judith Cruzado-Guerrero**, PhD, is an associate professor of early childhood education, serves as a professional development school liaison, and supervises student interns in early childhood settings at Towson University. Her research interests have focused on culturally and linguistically diverse children and families as well as the preparation of student teachers in diverse and inclusive early childhood settings. Her publications include articles in journals such as the *School University Partnerships Journal* and the *Social Studies Journal for the Young Learner.* She has made numerous presentations at local, national, and international professional conferences such as the National Association for the Education of Young Children.

**Nickki Pearce Dawes**, PhD, is an assistant professor at the University of Massachusetts Boston. She graduated from the University of Illinois–Urbana Champaign, with a PhD in clinical/community psychology. After completing her internship at the APA accredited Institute for Juvenile Research in the department of psychiatry at the University of Illinois–Chicago, she was a postdoctoral fellow at the Prevention Research Center within the psychology department at Arizona State University. Her research interests include how experiences in afterschool or out-of-school programs promote positive outcomes for adolescent participants. She is particularly interested in the topic of motivation and engagement in this context.

**Elizabeth Devaney** is the inaugural director of the Center for Social and Emotional Learning at the Children's Institute in Rochester, NY. Prior to being at the Children's Institute, she was a researcher at the American Institutes for Research (AIR), where she studied the implementation and impact of high-quality afterschool programs with an emphasis on social and emotional learning (SEL) and the intersection between research and practice. Devaney has co-authored a series of research to practice briefs on SEL and afterschool as well as several resource guides, including Beyond the Bell®: A Toolkit for Creating Effective Afterschool and Expanded Learning Programs and Sustainable Schoolwide Social and Emotional Learning (SEL): Implementation Guide and Toolkit. Previously, she was deputy director of the Providence After School Alliance and a project director at the Collaborative for Academic, Social, and Emotional Learning (CASEL). Devaney received a master's degree from the Heller School at Brandeis University.

**Melissa S. Pearman Fenton** is the extension educator and project manager for Click2SciencePD, developed by the University of Nebraska–Lincoln in partnership with the Noyce Foundation. She holds a Master of Applied Science degree from the University of Nebraska–Lincoln with a specialization in leadership education and a Bachelor of Science degree from the University of Nebraska–Lincoln majoring in child, youth, and family studies. She is committed to improving the quality of afterschool programs through STEM professional development. She manages project development, collaborates with out-of-school time (OST) partners, develops and delivers professional development, and provides technical assistance for Click2SciencePD. She also has experience writing and developing curricula designed for youth audiences in both formal and informal educational environments. She collaborated with faculty members, subject matter experts, and youth to develop 4-H curricular resources used by national audiences. Fenton previously served as the Nebraska 4-H curriculum graduate assistant and Nebraska 4-H youth curriculum committee coordinator at the University of Nebraska-Lincoln.

**Elizabeth M. Fowlkes** is the senior vice president of planning and measurement for Boys & Girls Clubs of America (BGCA), where she is responsible for leading the organization's operational planning, measurement and evaluation strategies, and coordinating cross-functional implementation efforts. She led the design and development of BGCA's National Youth Outcomes Initiative, an unparalleled system built to measure youth perceptions and behaviors in a consistent, credible way across the national network of Boys & Girls Clubs. Prior to joining BGCA, Fowlkes served as the associate director of school evaluation services at Standard & Poor's, where she led the development of analytical platforms to support school improvement. Her experience also includes developing and leading youth programs and community and school partnerships. She holds a master's degree in education leadership, policy and politics from Teacher's College at Columbia University and an undergraduate degree in performance studies from Northwestern University.

**Ellen S. Gannett** is director of the National Institute on Out-of-School Time, a research and action project at the Wellesley Centers for Women at Wellesley College. She ensures that research bridges childcare, education, and youth development to promote programming that supports whole child development and the professional advancement of the field. Currently, she serves as a senior advisor for the National Center on Afterschool and Summer Enrichment, launched by the Administration for Children and Families, Office of Child Care. Gannett's honors include the National AfterSchool Association's Top 25 Most Influential People in Afterschool and the American Camp Association's 2015 Hedley S. Dimock Award. With more than three decades at NIOST, she has served as training director, associate director, co-director and now has been the director since 2006. Gannett received her MEd from the Graduate School of Education at Lesley College.

**Shannon Haley-Mize**, PhD, is an assistant professor of education at Elizabeth-town College. Haley-Mize completed doctoral study in special education at the University of Southern Mississippi in Hattiesburg. Previous work includes experience in a psychiatric setting, federal grant administration, and service-learning program development. She also completed a graduate degree in early childhood and served as an educator, early interventionist, and administrator in an inclusive early childhood education program. Haley-Mize's areas of expertise include: technology in teacher education, inclusion, and universal design for learning. Her research has appeared in Technological Pedagogical Content Knowledge and The International Journal for Learning in Higher Education.

**Heidi Ham** is the vice president of the National AfterSchool Association (NAA). As a product of afterschool programs, a long-time NAA member, and leader in national youth work, she holds a historical and national perspective. Her expertise mirrors her experience in producing quality programs and professional development. She currently works to increase professional development opportunities, affiliate and member engagement, and strategic relations. Her work drives many of NAA's offerings, including the Leading with Emotional Intelligence Fellowship, the Core Knowledge and Competencies Self-Assessment Tools, virtual conventions, and the STEM Credential Badges. Prior to NAA, she was a senior quality advisor for an organization with afterschool programs nationwide. Now she is fulfilling a commitment to professionals who meet the critical need of providing quality experiences for young people. She has earned K–12 teaching certification and bachelor's degrees in social science and education. She is currently exploring graduate options in training and development.

**Sara L. Hill**, EdD is currently an editor of the Youth Today OST Hub, a senior consultant to the National Institute on Out-of-School Time, and has worked on a research project documenting innovative strategies in 21st Century Community Learning Centers funded by the U.S. Department of Education. She has written many articles about critical issues in OST, and edited a book published by Corwin Press: Afterschool Matters: Creative Programs that Connect Youth Development and Student Achievement. She is also currently an educational specialist at a large afterschool program in Brooklyn, NY, SCO Family Services, Family Dynamics, where she provides professional development for frontline staff at four school-based afterschool programs. She earned her MEd at Harvard University School of Education, and her EdD at Vanderbilt University, Peabody College.

**Yangyang Liu** is second-year PhD student in the School of Education in University of California, Irvine. Yangyang's research examines the development of diverse children and youth across contexts. She is particularly interested in the roles of family and out-of-school activities in children and youth's development across time. Yangyang Liu is a graduate student researcher in Dr. Sandra Simpkins' lab working on multiple research projects, including a William T. Grant funded project on Latino adolescents' organized activities, and an NSF-funded project on Latino high school students' STEM learning. Yangyang graduated with a MA degree in developmental psychology from Teachers College, Columbia University.

**Joseph L. Mahoney**, PhD, is director of translational science at the Collaborative for Academic, Social, and Emotional Learning. He was a professor in the department of psychology at Elizabethtown College for a portion of the time during which this chapter was written. His areas of expertise include positive youth development; out-of-school time; and applied developmental science, practice, and policy. Mahoney previously served as a professor in the School of Education at University of California, Irvine and was an associate professor in the department of psychology at Yale University. He earned his PhD in psychology through the Center for Developmental Science at the University of North Carolina at Chapel Hill. His research has most recently appeared in the International Journal of Research on Extended Education, New Directions for Youth Development, and Handbook of Child Psychology and Developmental Science.

**Gilda Martinez-Alba**, EdD, is the chair for the department of educational technology and literacy and the director of the graduate reading program at Towson University. She has been at Towson University (TU) for 10 years. Prior to working at TU, she worked at Loyola University and Johns Hopkins University. Her areas of expertise include working with English language learners, reading motivation, technology for motivation, and adolescent literacy. She recently wrote a chapter entitled "Language Teaching Strategies: Five Countries Compared Through Study Abroads" (*Advancing Teacher Education and Curriculum Development through Study Abroad Programs*, IGI Global) and also edited the book *Wordless Books: So Much to Say* (TESOL Press), which is intended for teachers working with English language learners. She received her EdD in teacher development and leadership, a graduate certificate in school administration and supervision, and a M.S. in Education-Reading from the Johns Hopkins University. Her B.S. in Elementary Education-Science is from the University of Maryland.

**Anne McNamara** is a doctoral student in applied developmental psychology at the University of Pittsburgh studying out-of-school time contexts. She earned both her bachelors in elementary education and human development and masters in developmental and educational psychology from Boston College. She previously worked in several afterschool and summer programs and she was the lead coordinator of an extended day program for children ages 3–9. She was also involved with the boOST program in Pittsburgh and has led other professional development workshops with out-of-school time staff.

**Tony McWhorter** is the national vice president of strategic leadership development for Boys & Girls Clubs of America (BGCA), where he is responsible for developing and delivering the learning strategy for leaders throughout the national network of Boys & Girls Clubs. Previously, he was the senior regional service director for BGCA's Southeast Region, where he provided leadership on the delivery of organizational development services to Boys & Girls Clubs in the southeast United States, including its more than 1,000 Clubs serving some 775,000 children and teens. His tenure with Boys and Girls Clubs began in the role of executive director for the Boys & Girls Clubs of Blount County in Maryville, Tennessee. He joined the National Staff in 2000. He received a bachelor's degree from Tennessee Technological University and a master's degree from the University of Tennessee.

**Deborah Moroney**, PhD, is managing director at American Institutes for Research (AIR) and director of the youth development and supportive learning environments. Moroney's research and practice experience is in youth development and social and emotional learning (SEL) in out-of-school time settings. Moroney has co-authored a series of research to practice briefs on SEL and afterschool as well as several practice guides, including *Beyond the Bell*®: *A Toolkit for Creating Effective Afterschool and Expanded Learning Programs and Ready to Assess* (Social and Emotional Learning). Prior to joining AIR, she was a clinical faculty member in educational psychology at the University of Illinois at Chicago in the youth development graduate program and worked as an organizational development consultant to agencies and youth-serving organizations. Moroney has a PhD from the College of Education at the University of Illinois–Chicago.

**Jessica Newman** is a researcher at American Institutes for Research (AIR) where she focuses on a variety of national, state, and local initiatives to promote high-quality out-of-school time programs for youth. Her research and practice expertise is in social and emotional learning and positive youth development, both in and out of school. She is particularly interested in the structures and settings that support whole child growth and development. Through ongoing research, evaluation, and practice work, she endeavors to connect the dots in the field by conducting rigorous research and evaluations to create meaningful resources that ultimately promote high-quality programming for youth. Newman's goal is to ensure that practice work is grounded in evidence and that work in the field informs science.

**Gil G. Noam**, EdD, PhD habil., is the founder and director of The PEAR Institute: Partnerships in Education and Resilience at McLean Hospital, a Harvard Medical School affiliate. He is an associate professor at Harvard Medical School focusing on prevention and resilience. He served as the director of the Risk and Prevention Program and is the founder of the RALLY Prevention Program, a Boston-based intervention that bridges social and academic support in school, afterschool, and community settings. He has published over 200 papers, articles, and books in the areas of child and adolescent development as well as risk and resiliency in clinical, school, and afterschool settings. He also served as the editor-in-chief of the journal *New Directions in Youth Development: Theory, Practice and Research* with a strong focus on out-of-school time. He is trained as a clinical and developmental psychologist and psychoanalyst in both Europe and the United States.

**Sarah Pitcock** is a freelance writer and consultant for nonprofits and foundations. She held progressive leadership positions in a 10-year career at the National Summer Learning Association, culminating as its chief executive officer from 2013 to 2016. Sarah is a leading national expert on summer learning, authoring numerous white papers and practitioner guides, making regular presentations to state policymaking bodies and overseeing implementation of multiple state and federal initiatives. She has served as an expert source for NPR, *Education Week*, *Essence Magazine*, and the *Baltimore Sun*, among other media outlets. She is coeditor and coauthor of the research anthology, *The Summer Slide: What We Know and Can Do About Summer Learning Loss* (Teachers College Press, 2016). She holds a master's degree in public policy from Johns Hopkins University and bachelor's degrees in public relations and political science from the University of Florida.

**Karen Pittman** is the president and CEO of the Forum for Youth Investment, which she co-founded in 1998. Before starting the Forum, she joined the Clinton administration as director of the President's Crime Prevention Council, where she worked with 13 cabinet secretaries to create a coordinated prevention agenda. She then worked with the International Youth Foundation to strengthen its program content and develop an evaluation strategy before supporting ret. Gen. Colin Powell's creation of America's Promise. She has written three books and dozens of articles on youth issues throughout her career. She is also a respected public speaker and has served on numerous boards. She currently sits on the board of YouthBuild USA and has recently been asked to serve on the Aspen Institute's National Commission on Social, Emotional, and Academic Development. Pittman holds degrees in sociology from Oberlin College and the University of Chicago.

**Jen Rinehart** is the senior vice president for policy & research at the Afterschool Alliance, a national nonprofit public awareness and advocacy organization dedicated to ensuring that all children and youth have access to quality, affordable afterschool programs. She joined the Afterschool Alliance in September 2002 and takes a primary role in the Afterschool Alliance's coalition building, policy, and research efforts, and she serves as a spokesperson for the organization. She oversees research and policy initiatives, including the *Afterschool for All Challenge,* an annual afterschool advocacy day, and works closely with the statewide afterschool networks to help them use research to advance their state policy goals and to engage them in federal advocacy efforts. Prior to joining the Afterschool Alliance, she served for more than 5 years on the staff of the Department of Education, primarily as a project officer for the 21st Century Community Learning Centers program. She has a BA in psychology with a minor in elementary education from Gettysburg College and a master's degree in human development from the University of Maryland at College Park. She works closely with a number of national organizations and initiatives that share the Afterschool Alliance's vision of afterschool for all.

**Christina A. Russell** is a managing director at Policy Studies Associates, where she directs evaluations that assess and inform efforts to improve the operations and effectiveness of out-of-school time and other education initiatives for government agencies, foundations, and nonprofit organizations. Russell also leads projects to increase the evaluation capacity and improvement efforts of education systems and partner organizations serving youth, their families, and communities. She specializes in designing evaluation approaches and generating findings that are relevant to both a practitioner and a policy audience. Since 2000, Ms. Russell has evaluated national and local out-of-school time program initiatives and system-building efforts, including for ExpandED Schools, Higher Achievement, the New York City Department of Youth and Community Development, After-School All-Stars, Asia Society, the YMCA of the USA, The Wallace Foundation, and the U.S. Department of Education. She received her AB from Stanford University and EdM from the Harvard Graduate School of Education.

**Mavis Sanders**, PhD in education from Stanford University, is professor of education and affiliate professor for the doctoral program in language, literacy, and culture at the University of Maryland–Baltimore County (UMBC). Her research and teaching focus on the processes and outcomes of school, family, and community collaboration. She has authored over 60 publications, including four books, on how schools and districts develop and scale up their partnership programs; the effects of home, school, and community collaboration on African American adolescents' school success; and how community engagement can improve educational experiences and outcomes for students in U.S. public schools and out-of-school time programs. Sanders also serves as senior adviser to the National Network of Partnership Schools at Johns Hopkins University. Her current research, funded by the Spencer Foundation, examines the role of principal and teacher leadership in restructuring learning opportunities for low-income students through full-service community schools.

**Peter C. Scales**, PhD, USPTA, is an internationally recognized developmental psychologist, author, and senior positive youth development research consultant. Among other collaborations, he has worked with Search Institute (most recently as senior fellow), Child Trends, America's Promise Alliance, American Institutes for Research, and World Vision International. Certified as a tennis teaching pro by the United States Professional Tennis Association, he works with youth as a high school tennis coach. His special expertise is child and adolescent development, the reduction of inequities in developmental opportunities, and the development of healthy families, schools, and communities where all children and youth can thrive. Recent publications include: "The Crucial Coaching Relationship" in *Phi Delta Kappan*, 2016; "Aligning Youth Development Theory, Measurement, and Practice Across Cultures and Contexts: Lessons From Use of the Developmental Assets Profile" in *Child Indicators Research*, 2016; "The Dimensions of Successful Young Adult Development: A Conceptual and Measurement Framework" in *Applied Developmental Science*, 2016. He earned his AB in psychology and MS and PhD (1976) in child and family studies from Syracuse University.

**Ashima Mathur Shah**, PhD, is the manager of STEM quality, research, and training at The PEAR Institute: Partnerships in Education and Resilience. She has designed and helped to implement inquiry-based science curricula in urban elementary and middle school settings as well as studying new approaches to elementary science teacher education. Currently, she manages the nationwide effort of training observers in the Dimensions of Success (DoS) observation tool that measures the quality of STEM learning experiences for youth in out-of- school and school settings. She has led the National Science Foundation-funded study of the psychometric properties of DoS and is currently studying the links between program quality and student outcomes. She earned her BS in child development and biology from Tufts University and her doctoral degree in science education from the University of Michigan.

**Sandra Simpkins**, PhD in psychology, joined the University of California, Irvine School of Education in summer 2015. She was formerly a professor at Arizona State University. Through her research, she examines how youth development unfolds over time and how the contexts in which youth are embedded influence their development. Generally, her work has focused on how families, friendships, and social position factors (such as ethnicity and culture) shape adolescents' organized afterschool activities and motivation. Funded by two career awards, she addresses these issues for Latino adolescents. Her work strives to understand the unique role of SES, immigration, ethnicity, and culture in family functioning and youth development.

**Jaime Singer** is a senior consultant at American Institutes for Research, where she works on projects for out-of-school time (OST) programs. She designs and implements state and national learning opportunities for the field of OST, provides technical assistance to OST practitioners on systemic support, and participates in OST policy meetings. Singer has expertise in developing, implementing, and managing projects related to continuous quality improvement. She believes that bringing evidence-based tools, briefs, and professional development opportunities to practitioners in the field is the key to professionalizing the field and enhancing quality in OST. Singer is co-author of the fourth edition of the seminal OST resource, *Beyond the Bell®: A Toolkit for Creating Effective Afterschool and Expanded Learning Programs*, a resource for afterschool program leaders and staff. Singer earned a master's degree in industrial/organizational psychology from the University of Tulsa.

**Elizabeth Starr** is a research associate at the National Institute on Out-of-School Time, a research and action project at the Wellesley Centers for Women at Wellesley College. Her work has focused on professional development, quality improvement, and system-building for the afterschool and youth development field. She, with her colleagues, conducted the research and made the recommendations for the Core Knowledge and Competencies for Afterschool and Youth Development Professionals, which were adopted by the National Afterschool Association in 2011. She also co-authored the chapter "Credentialing for Youth Work: Expanding Our Thinking" in *The Changing Landscape of Youth Work* published in 2016 by Information Age Publishing. Before joining NIOST, Starr enjoyed her work with children, teens, and families in schools, clinics, and residential programs. Starr holds a MEd from the Harvard Graduate School of Education and an AB from Bowdoin College.

**Bailey Triggs** is the project manager of product design and development at The PEAR Institute: Partnerships in Education and Resilience at McLean Hospital. At The PEAR Institute, she oversees the design of data dashboards and reporting tools and manages communications. Prior to her work at the PEAR Institute, Bailey served as the communications director of the Children's Safety Network, a national injury and violence prevention resource center funded by the Health Resources and Services Administration of the U.S. Department of Health and Human Services, centered at the Education Development Center. She earned her MS in public relations from Boston University.

**Gina Hilton Warner**, JD, is the president and CEO of the National AfterSchool Association. She has a bachelor's degree in special education, gifted and talented, from the University of South Alabama, a juris doctor from Loyola University School of Law, and a certification in executive coaching for organizational well-being from George Mason University. In her role with NAA, Warner focuses on meeting the needs of both emerging and experienced afterschool professionals through enhanced training and development, as well as increased communication, outreach, and membership engagement. She has a particular interest in developing and encouraging strong afterschool leaders and was instrumental in the creation of the Afterschool Leadership Lab. Prior to her time at NAA, Warner served as the executive director of the Partnership for Youth Development in New Orleans, Louisiana. She is also a former public school teacher and U.S. Senate staffer.

**Karen Watkins-Lewis**, PhD, is a university lecturer and research affiliate at the University of Maryland–Baltimore County (UMBC), where she teaches and engages in research on bio-ecological factors that place underrepresented youth and emerging adults at promise for academic success. Her most recent publications include: "The Non-Traditional Student: Challenges to Academic Success and Degree Completion" (2016), "Enhancing the Number of African Americans Pursuing the PhD in Engineering" (2015) and "African-American Parenting Characteristics and Their Association with Children's Cognitive and Academic School Readiness" (2012). Her areas of expertise are in sociocultural development, academic achievement, and psychology of the STEM experience. Lewis was a research fellow at the University of Maryland's Institute for Child Study and the National Center for Research on Early Childhood Education at the University of Virginia. She holds Master of Science and doctorate degrees in developmental psychology and a Bachelor of Science in mechanical engineering.

**Nikki Yamashiro** is the director of research at the Afterschool Alliance, a national nonprofit public awareness and advocacy organization dedicated to ensuring that all children and youth have access to quality, affordable afterschool programs. The most recent initiative is work on America After 3PM, a comprehensive national household survey examining how children and youth spend the hours after school. Her work has covered a range of topics, including K–12 education, juvenile justice, and women's issues. Prior to joining the Afterschool Alliance, she served in a variety of research capacities, including as policy advisor at Third Way and as legislative assistant to former Rep. Hilda L. Solis. She holds a BA in political science and sociology from the University of California, San Diego, and a master's in public policy from University of Southern California's Sol Price School of Public Policy.

CPSIA information can be obtained
at www.ICGtesting.com
Printed in the USA
LVOW03s2136071217
558796LV00003B/45/P